Family Therapy Specialists
1011 Holtz Lane
Chaska, MN 55318
Office: (66~) 646-3879

D1071483

The Family's Construction of Reality

The Family's Construction of Reality

David Reiss

Harvard University Press
Cambridge, Massachusetts
London, England
1981

Library of Congress Cataloging in Publication Data

Reiss, David, 1937-
  The family's construction of reality.

  Bibliography: p.
  Includes index.
  1. Family—Attitudes. 2. Reality. 3. Model theory.
4. Social interaction—Psychological aspects. I. Title.
HQ728.R383   306.8   81-2703
ISBN 0-674-29415-7   AACR2

For Jo Ann

Collaborating Investigators

Ronald Costell was co-investigator in the studies of families' perceptions of the psychiatric ward and their perceptions of other families. These investigations are described in Chapter 2. In addition, he was co-investigator on studies of the organizational objective and the short-term links between the family and the multiple family group described in Chapter 8.

Mary Ellen Oliveri collaborated in studies of intelligence and perceptual style in families described in Chapter 2 and the investigation of the family's long-term links to its kin described in Chapter 8. She also revised the card sort procedure, as described in Chapter 8, and collaborated in theory construction.

In addition, Richard Almond was co-investigator in the study of the organizational objective described in Chapter 8, Jo Ann Reiss collaborated on the historical analyses in Chapter 3, and Carl Salzman was co-investigator in the secobarbital experiment described in Chapter 2.

Acknowledgments

This book reports empirical and theoretical work extending over a seventeen-year period. During that time many people have joined me in completing various phases of the work.

Three teachers played a central role. George Miller introduced me to the psychology laboratory and its use as a subtle probe of sophisticated human thought. Elliot Mishler taught me about rigorous research on family process and helped in many ways to get me started as a family researcher. Through many years he has given me crucial intellectual stimulation and has provided a challenging and incisive critique of this manuscript at several points in its development. Lyman Wynne was a consummate teacher of clinical research; he showed me how to integrate my direct knowledge of patients and their families with my formal research observations.

Several professional colleagues have helped me at times when I needed it most. Nancy Waxler helped with the design of my first studies. John Zinner provided invaluable critiques of many manuscripts, including this one. He also made clinical diagnoses of patients used in the earlier studies. Robert Cohen provided important administrative support at NIMH, as did John Naughton, Thomas Webster, and Jerry Wiener at the George Washington University. Jack Durell generously supported our work at the Psychiatric Institute in Washington, D.C.

Throughout my work I have been blessed with an intelligent, sensitive, and energetic research staff. In the early days Patricia Foley and Elaine Faunce provided meticulous data analysis. While I was at NIMH, Loann Drake, with great originality, helped design apparatus, developed coding manuals, analyzed data, and made many clinical observations that I still use. Minerva Wright handled all the administrative work of our research section with fastidious care and sober judgment. Also during the NIMH years, William Sheriff helped me design our computer-automated procedures—the first in the family field.

During my years at the George Washington University many talented people helped in the work. Janet Moyer added to many other duties to help move our interaction laboratory from NIMH into its new quarters. In the first years at George Washington, Paula Sendroff sensitively and conscientiously tested many families. For most of the years at George Washington, Carole Jones has been an indispensable part of the work. She administrated all phases of our study at the Psychiatric Institute: testing families, coding their performance, supervising data analysis, and assisting us with keen interpretation. During the same period Sharon Cooper did a splendid job of administering our first studies of nonclinical families. She recruited and supervised the testing of over two hundred families and helped improve our work in countless ways; she administered the largest data set we ever assembled, and not a jot was lost or mislaid along the way. Helen Berkman collected all the data obtained at the Psychiatric Institute; her keen personal observations of the families and the ward community were invaluable in helping us design procedures and interpret their results. She also ably assisted in our studies of nonclinical families. Nancy Moran provided steady, careful, and invariably cheerful assistance in our work with nonclinical families. For several years at NIMH, and for all the years at George Washington University, Mary Lee has designed many highly original programs, supervised endlessly complex data analysis, and helped us systematize our data collection. She remains invaluable to almost every component of our work.

This book itself is a product of five years of labor, and its completion is due to the help of several colleagues. Peter Steinglass has helped me recognize the importance of family development and change; his work has illuminated for me the importance of directly observing the family in its own home. Steven Wolin has immeasurably enriched my understanding of the relationship between generations in the same family and of the central symbolic importance of family rituals and family identity. Linda Bennett has sensitized me to the role of the family in transmitting the symbols and experiences of culture from one generation to the next; she has introduced me to an anthropological literature which will be of enduring value to me. Major sections of this book—particularly Chapters 4, 5, 6, and 7—were greatly strengthened by insights and critiques from Peter, Steve, and Linda.

This book would still be a pile of unintelligible notes were it not for the tireless investment of Judy Piemme. She not only has typed every word you will read but has meticulously supervised every phase of the book's construction, from the preparation of figures and tables to the proofreading of the galleys.

I am indebted to two learned and perceptive colleagues for invaluable critiques of early drafts of this manuscript, Pauline Boss and Eric Bermann.

Writing this book has required long periods of solitude as well as considerable encouragement and emotional support. For both I gratefully thank my family — Jo Ann, Sharon, and Benjamin. They have each recognized the importance to me of this task. They have allowed me to be alone when I needed it, often filling in for me in countless ways. I have treasured the moments when I have simultaneously been writing about families and have felt so supported by my own.

The first phases of this work, at the Massachusetts Mental Health Center, were supported by grants from the Milton Fund of Harvard University and the Medical Foundation. For the next eight years the work was supported by the Intramural Research Program of the National Institute of Mental Health, of which I was a full-time member. Subesequently the work was supported by a grant from the Psychiatric Institute Foundation, an allotment from the Rehabilitation Research and Training Center at the George Washington University (DHEW, RSA, 6-P-56803-3-10), and a grant from the National Institute of Mental Health (DHEW MH 26711).

Several journals and publishers graciously permitted me to reproduce tables and figures and to adapt text material originally published by them:

Archives of General Psychiatry: parts of Chapter 2, including Table 2.5, are from Costell, R., Reiss, D., Berkman, H., and Jones, C., "The Family Meets the Hospital: Predicting the Family's Perception of the Treatment Program from its Problem Solving Style," 38: 569-577, 1981; parts of Chapter 1, including Tables 1.1 and 1.2 and Figures 1.3, 1.5, 1.6, and 1.8, are from Reiss, D., "Individual Thinking and Family Interaction. I. An Introduction to an Experimental Study of Problem Solving in Families of Normals, Character Disorders and Schizophrenics," 16: 80-93, 1967; parts of Chapter 2 are from Reiss, D., "Intimacy and Problem Solving: An Automated Procedure for Testing a Theory of Consensual Experience in Families," 25: 442-445, 1971; parts of Chapter 2, including Figures 2.19, 2.20, and 2.21, and parts of Chapter 8, including Tables 8.1, 8.2, 8.3, 8.4, 8.5, 8.6, 8.7, and 8.8, are from Reiss, D.,

Costell, R., and Almond, R., "Personal Needs, Values and Technical Preferences in the Psychiatric Hospital: A Replicated Study," 23: 795-804, 1976; parts of Chapter 8, including Tables 8.9, 8.13, 8.14, 8.16, and 8.17 and Figures 8.1 and 8.2, are from Reiss, D., Costell, R., Jones, C., and Berkman, H., "The Family Meets the Hospital: A Laboratory Forecast of the Encounter," 37: 141-154, 1980; parts of Chapter 2, including Figures 2.1, 2.4, 2.15, 2.17, and 2.18, are from Reiss, D., and Salzman, C., "The Resilience of Family Process: Effects of Secobarbital," 28: 425-433, 1973.

Brunner/Mazel Publishers: parts of Chapter 2, including Figures 2.2, 2.3, and 2.6, are from Reiss, D., "Pathways to Assessing the Family: Some Choice Points and a Sample Route," in *The Family: Evaluation and Treatment,* C. K. Hofling and J. M. Lewis, eds., New York, 1980.

Family Process: parts of Chapter 1 are from Reiss, D., "Varieties of Consensual Experience. I. A Theory for Relating Family Interaction to Individual Thinking," 10: 1-28, 1971; parts of Chapter 2, including Tables 2.7, 2.9, and 2.10 and Figures 2.12, 2.13, and 2.14, are from Reiss, D., Costell, R., Berkman, H., and Jones, C., "How One Family Perceives Another: The Relationship between Social Constructions and Problem Solving Competence," 19: 239-256, 1980.

John Wiley and Sons, Inc.: Figure 1.1 is from Bruner, J.S., Goodnow, J. J., and Austin, G. A., *A Study of Thinking,* New York, 1956.

Journal of Marriage and the Family (copyrighted by the National Council on Family Relations): parts of Chapter 8 are from Oliveri, M. E., and Reiss, D., "The Structure of Families' Ties to their Kin: The Shaping Role of Social Constructions," 391-407, May 1981.

Journal of Nervous and Mental Disease (© The Williams and Wilkins Co., Baltimore): parts of Chapter 1, including Figure 1.7, are from Reiss, D., "Individual Thinking and Family Interaction. IV. A Study of Information Exchange in Families of Normals, Those with Character Disorders and Schizophrenia," 149: 473-490, 1969; parts of Chapter 1, including Table 1.11, are from Reiss, D., "Individual Thinking and Family Interaction. V. Proposals for the Contrasting Character of Experiential Sensitivity and Expressive Form in Families." 151: 187-202, 1970; parts of Chapter 2, including Table 2.1 and Figures 2.8, 2.9, and 2.10, are from Reiss, D., "Varieties of Consensual Experience III. Contrast between Families of Normals, Delinquents and Schizophrenics," 152: 73-95, 1971.

Contents

Introduction
Charting Our Course

This book presents a new model of the family. The model explores how relationships between the family and its social environment are related to the ways the family regulates and orders its own inner life. The central idea around which our model is built is that the family, through the course of its own development, fashions fundamental and enduring assumptions about the world in which it lives. The assumptions are shared by all family members, despite the disagreements, conflicts, and differences that exist in the family. Indeed, the core of an individual's membership in his own family is his acceptance of, belief in, and creative elaboration of these abiding assumptions. When a member distances himself from these assumptions, when he can see no further possibility for creatively elaborating them, he is diluting his own membership and begins a process of alienation from his family.

These shared assumptions of family life are rarely explicit or conscious in the experience of any family. Only rarely can we, as observers, know of these assumptions directly. They are manifest, more typically, in a mixture of fleeting experiences of the family and in its enduring patterns of action—action within its own boundaries, and between the family and the outside world. We first encountered evidence of these assumptions in a curious place: a social interaction laboratory. Initially, we came to the laboratory to measure the problem-solving skills of the family group. We thought we might discover some specific deficits in families of schizophrenic patients, and we hoped for precise comparisons between these families and several control groups. Our aims, however, were thwarted. We found that many of our families regularly misunderstood or misinterpreted our experimental instructions. This was the first clue that each family—those with patients and those without—came to our laboratory with its own version of what we were, in actuality, investigating. The explanations we had given them beforehand seemed much less important to them than to us. Some families, for example, thought we were trying to determine who in the family was most intelligent. Other families thought we were trying to disrupt the relationships between the members; they felt we were out to test the loyalty each member felt toward the others.

As we looked more closely, the families' fleeting but vivid perceptions of us, the research team, seemed to reflect more general, though less accessible, conceptions the families held about the nature of their social world. Thus, the family that saw us as menacing and intrusive had, in many instances, an abiding conception of its world as unstable, unpredictable, and potentially dangerous. A family that viewed us as trustworthy and as offering it solvable and intriguing puzzles took a similar stance toward broad reaches of its social world: like the laboratory, that world was perceived as ordered, predictable, and masterable.

After our initial experiences in the laboratory we began to look elsewhere for evidence of these underlying assumptions in family life. We examined both the conscious experiences of the family and the actions presumably guided by those experiences. For example, we were interested in how one family perceives other families it knows. Does the family's underlying assumptions about the social world — for example, the extent to which that world is perceived as unpredictable and dangerous — become manifest in its perceptions of other families with which it interacts? In terms of action, does the behavior of a family toward other families also reflect the underlying assumptions which come to light in the problem-solving laboratory?

The evidence we have collected so far seems to confirm that our first observations in the laboratory did indeed uncover some underlying shared experiences of family life and, further, that these experiences play a significant role in shaping the family's perception of and transaction with its external world. These experiences can be thought of as assumptions, constructs, fantasies, sets, or expectations; each word captures only a portion of the critical features. The metaphorical use of Kuhn's concept of paradigm is helpful in aggregating these meanings. We now speak of the *family paradigm* as a central organizer of its shared constructs, sets, expectations, and fantasies about its social world. Further, each family's transactions with its social world is guided by its own paradigm, and families can be distinguished — one from another — by the differences in their paradigms.

Three characteristics are particularly helpful in making distinctions among families. First, families differ in their experience of the world as ordered, and the belief that its mysteries are discoverable through reasoned search. Second, families differ in the extent to which they believe the world is equally open, accessible, accomodating, or malleable for each member and, conversely, how much the world perceives them as a single family or, in contrast, as a group of unrelated individuals. Some families, whether or not they believe the world is masterable, think of themselves as a unitary group. What happens to one family member automatically has implications for what happens to the others. Other families feel the world treats them as individuals; what one individual can know, achieve, experience, or endure suggests little for the potential experience and action of others. Third, and finally, families differ in their experience of novelty in their world. For some families all experience is reminiscent. Family members apprehend each event with some reference to their family history. In contrast, for other families each experience is new. The past is forgotten or is not perceived as relevant.

This book is an effort to take these threads — our observations of families interacting with their social world and our ideas about fundamental experiences which shape these interactions — and weave them into a more coherent theoretical fabric. In doing so, we have become engaged in constructing a more general model of family process. We hope, on the one hand, that the model remains faithful to our empirical work, that it serves to explain our own findings and shape meaningful hypotheses for our own future work. On the other hand, we hope that a more general model evolving from our work may be applicable to other areas of inquiry. Later in this book, for example, we have applied our ideas to three problems of family life which have been of great interest to scholars. First, we have considered family development and change, and the relationship between crisis and change has become central to our evolving model. Second, we have considered the remarkable stability of basic patterns in family life, particularly as they are carried forward across generations within the same family. Finally, we have considered the family's relationship to specific aspects of its social world: the extended family, the neighborhood, and formal organizations such as schools, hospitals, and places of employment. Our hope is that our general model — although still in rudimentary form — may make some contribution to these areas of inquiry as well as to the more parochial concerns of our own laboratory research.

We claim no intrinsic superiority for our evolving model of family process. On empirical grounds, the evidence is far from sufficient to claim it as convincing support. We have used many methods—from laboratory procedures to naturalistic observations and clinical interviews—to study over four hundred families. The data constitute an intriguing rationale for the model but fall far short of strong empirical support. Likewise, on logical grounds, we can make no forceful claim. Indeed, we refer to our model as preliminary primarily because we know there are many unsolved logical problems in our basic argument. We have tried to bracket these in the course of exposition.

Despite its empirical and logical shortcomings, our model deserves attention in the rapidly growing field of family studies. First, it is an attempt at a general theory of family process that is built—from the ground up—on observation of families. Although it owes a great deal to thinking outside the family field, it is one of the few attempts at *intrinsic* family theorizing—that is, beginning with observations and interpretations of family life and extending the theory outward to other social collectivities. Most current theorizing about the family works in reverse. Some of it comes upward from the psychology of the individual: psychoanalysis, stimulus-response theory, and symbolic interactionism. Some of it—for example, exchange theory and role theory—comes laterally from social psychology. And still more comes downward from anthropology, sociology, economics, and political theory.

The second important feature of our model is that it offers a new perspective or emphasis on the transactions between the family and its social environment. The study of these transactions is, of course, as old as sociology. However, the traditional perspective accords primacy to the social environment. The family is seen as a passive receptacle of influence from the wider social context in which it lives. Our approach accords considerable adaptability and creativity to the family itself, at the same time recognizing the enormous influences and strong forces in its social world.

Third, the development of our model—a development spanning fifteen years—has been intertwined with the development of methods untried by others in the family field. These methods include a large variety of laboratory-based methods for assessing family interaction, the use of multiple family groups for the precise measurement of family-environment transactions, new methods for directly assessing shared family experiences of the environment, and the use of psychopharmacologic tools for exploring family process. For the most part, these new methods have been directed at exploring the resilience and resourcefulness of families in their transactions with the social world. At a minimum, our model serves as a rationale for the use of these methods, by clarifying the questions about family life to which they can be addressed. Wider use of these methods will help investigators see the considerable amount of initiative families take in dealing with their social world, even if the wider use does not confirm the specific lines of our theoretical argument.

As already indicated, our model is first an attempt to make sense out of a compelling set of experiences — ours and our families' — in the family interaction laboratory. Second, it is an effort to account for equally compelling correlations between the family's experience and performance in the laboratory and in everyday settings. Finally, it is an attempt to apply ideas drawn from these observations to more general problems of family change and crisis, family stability, and family-environment transactions. It is our intent that this application serve to broaden and deepen the model itself. The form and exposition of our model follows from its aims and origins. It is more precise and concrete when it treats laboratory observations and the more recent field observations; it becomes more speculative and intuitive when our actual observations are applied to crisis, change, and stability within and across generations. For the latter, we rely on our own clinical observations (more informal than our systematic research) and on the ideas and observations of others.

This book is organized into three parts to reflect the nature of the model. In Part I, "Family Problem Solving and Family Interpreting," we clarify our reasons for studying family problem solving in the laboratory, we report the first evidence about the influence of the family's shared assumptions on their problem-solving performance, we elaborate some initial concepts to explain the relationship of assumptions to performance, and we describe a number of laboratory-based studies to substantiate this explanation. Part II, "Family Crisis and Family Paradigm," attempts to extend our ideas about shared family assumptions to broader reaches of family life. We introduce the concept of family paradigm and explain how it can be shaped through family initiative during periods of crisis and maintained for long periods of time thereafter. In Part III, "The Family's Bond to Its Social World," our basic model is further explicated and a small portion of it is transformed into hypotheses sufficiently specific and concrete for empirical testing. We are concerned here with the reciprocal relationship between the family and its social world. The family's paradigm determines its choice of a social environment from among the available options, and determines the kinds of links it fashions with that environment; reciprocally, those links — and the environment itself — play an important role in stabilizing the family paradigm.

Part I, Family Problem Solving and Family Interpreting.
Chapter 1 clarifies how the problem-solving laboratory can be used
as a gauge for assessing interpretative processes in family life. We
begin by clarifying the assumptions and empirical traditions which
led us to construct a set of laboratory problem-solving procedures
for studying family process. We describe our first experiences with
these procedures and the findings that suggested the role in family
performance of shared fantasies, constructions, and assumptions.
Our first attempts to account systematically for the role of these
shared experiences in family problem solving are described, and the
possible connections between shared assumptions in the laboratory
and those in the family's everyday life are explored briefly.

Chapter 2 describes a strategy for examining our notions about
shared assumptions and family problem solving. Three approaches
are used. In the first, an indirect approach, we compare the performance of three groups of families who are likely to differ in their
shared assumptions about a novel social setting. If, as we have
argued, shared assumptions determine the family's performance in
the laboratory, then, using our knowledge of the shared assumptions of each of the three groups of families we should be able to
make precise and detailed predictions of the problem-solving
behavior of each group. Based on previous clinical research of ours
and of others, we selected three groups of families, each containing
adolescents, for this comparison. In the first group the adolescents
were schizophrenic, in the second group the adolescents had impulsive character disorders, and in the third group the adolescents
had no significant psychiatric disorders. A second approach to
testing the relationship of shared assumptions and problem solving,
a direct approach, utilized two new methods: assessing the family's
perception of other families, and measuring the family's perception
of the psychiatric ward to which its adolescent was admitted. A
third approach to testing our core hypothesis examined the
plausibility of an important alternative hypothesis, which focused
on the information-processing and problem-solving skills of individual members. The alternative hypothesis stated that the
differences in group function we observed might have been due to
differences in the individual members, rather than to differences in
the shared assumptions of the group.

Part II, Family Crisis and Family Paradigm. This section relates
the phenomena observed in the laboratory to broad processes of
family life. Chapter 3 centers on the importance of personal explanatory systems to each individual. These systems are the crucial
guides for action in both the animate and inanimate world. The
chapter postulates that each person must develop his personal ex-

planatory systems in concert with others. Indeed, it is likely that groups, rather than individuals, are the primary focus for elaborating such systems. The chapter concludes with a brief historical analysis suggesting that the family has become the most important group for shaping personal explanatory systems and for reconciling any differences which develop between individuals.

After the general introduction to the family as an interpreting group presented in Chapter 3, Chapter 4 begins to outline the specifics of our own model of shared interpreting and construing in family life. We suggest that shared family assumptions develop or are altered in times of intense and disorganizing family crises. Disorganizing crises are periods when family members seek to disown their membership in the family and even the family itself. At a time when the family comes close to dissolution, its reorganization is shaped by hidden potentials within individual family members or strong influence from the surrounding social environment. The first step in this reorganization is an emerging concept — shared by the whole family — of the nature of the crisis itself, which then forms a nucleus of the family's pattern of recovery.

Chapter 5 shows how the shared construct of the crisis becomes elaborated and refined into a new system of assumptions, expectations, and fantasies which we call the family paradigm. The central attributes of the family's pathway to recovery from crisis and disorganization are highlighted through a specific reshaping of family routines. We refer to this recovery process as "social abstraction" because it is the emotionally rich processes of social interaction (rather than cognitive or logical processes) which lead to a final refined or abstracted concept of the social world. When recovery is complete the family will have developed — through a creative group process — a broad and coherent set of assumptions about its social world and its own place in that world.

Chapter 6 proposes a mechanism within the family which maintains its paradigm over long stretches of time. Our model gives primary emphasis to an idea about the organization of family behavior in everyday life. This concept pictures family behavior as a sphere. At the center are a set of family ceremonials which organize and shape a set of routine pattern regulators at the periphery. Family ceremonials are episodic, highly prescribed sequences engaged in by the whole family; they are rich in affect and symbolic meaning. Pattern regulators are the daily, highly routinized sequences of family life which ordinarily have little affective charge or symbolic meaning. We propose that ceremonials conserve the family's conception of the outer world. Pattern regulators reinforce, often subliminally, the role of ceremonials.

Part III, The Family's Bond to Its Social World. This section extends our model to explain the relationship of the family to specific components of its social world. We focus specifically on the extended family, the neighborhood, and organizations. The major idea here is the cycle hypothesis. We posit that the family's paradigm determines its experience of any specific social environment. These experiences in turn determine which social environments the family selects from among the available alternatives and the nature of the links it fashions with those environments. The nature of the environments selected by the family, and the nature of the links themselves, reinforce the central attributes of the family's paradigm. The steps in this sequence complete a full circle.

Chapter 7 outlines the cycle hypothesis. It focuses, in particular, on two components of the hypothesis not previously considered in the exposition of the model: family-environment links and the notion of a social organizer in extended families, neighborhoods, and organizations. The family's link to its environment is analyzed from three perspectives. First, the medium of the link focuses on the specific individuals and the specific interaction processes which are the concrete or observable "carriers" of the familys' ties to its community. Second, the architectural perspective considers the form of those links: the conspicuousness of the family in the community, the openness of its boundaries to relationships and experience in the community, and the depth of the family's engagement in the community. Third, we examine the links from a motivational perspective. Here we distinguish links which the family forges with its environment as an expression of its own values and objectives in contrast to those which it is forced to make.

The concept of the social organizer provides a nidus for conceptualizing how differences in various social environments may relate to family process and the character of family-environment transactions. We posit that, within the extended family, transactions between members are organized by a social organizer we call the "kinship code." This code epitomizes a shared sense of mutual obligations between members and a shared conception of how these obligations may be honored. We argue that transactions between neighborhoods are organized by a shared "map," a joint conception of the social space of the neighborhood which serves to regulate social interaction as well as conserve significant aspects of the community's history. Finally, we propose that formal organizations are shaped by an "organizational objective," a shared conception of the primary objective or task of the organization and the methods fundamental to achieving that objective.

Chapter 8 returns to empirical analysis; three aspects of the cycle hypothesis are explored. The first study examines the concept of organizational objective. In a study of two psychiatric hospitals we delineate two dimensions by which organizational objectives may be distinguished. A hospital's organizational objective may influence its structure and the interaction processes among its staff; in turn, the organizational and interactional processes in the hospital can shape family-hospital transactions. A second study focuses directly on the types of links a family fashions with the social community of a psychiatric hospital. If we know major attributes of a family's paradigm—by observing the family in the problem-solving laboratory—we can predict, with considerable precision, the character of its links with the psychiatric hospital. However, the family's links with the hospital are relatively short-term—they begin on admission of one of its members and end on that member's discharge. A third study, therefore, explores the role of the family paradigm in shaping more enduring links, in this case links between the nuclear family and its extended family. Here, too, a knowledge of the family's paradigm can predict the type of links between the family and its extended family.

Part I
Family Problem Solving
and Family Interpreting

1 | The Family's Construction of the Laboratory

Our studies of the family's construction of its social environment use a broad range of methods: perceptual and intelligence tests, projective tests, questionnaires, inventories of the family's network of social relationships, psychoactive drugs,and direct observations of families interacting with one another. The keystone in our array of methods, and a foundation of our theoretical work, is a set of closely related laboratory assessments of the skills and style with which families solve abstract puzzles. Procedures of this kind have for decades been quite commonplace in laboratories studying individual thinking and perception; they have also been used in many social psychology laboratories. To our knowledge, our laboratory had been the only one to use such procedures for studying family process.

When we first designed our problem-solving procedures we were most interested in how a family — functioning as an integrated group — explored its environment for information, how members of a family distributed this information among themselves, and how they interpreted its significance. At first, our major interest was in schizophrenia. We believed that measuring a family's skill in information processing might help explain why children in some families became schizophrenic whereas children in others did not. The procedures we designed to measure family information processing were a natural outgrowth of several lines of investigation: the experimental psychology of thinking, studies of psychological deficits in schizophrenia, studies of communication and information measurement, and clinical studies of aberrant family functioning associated with schizophrenia.

The first results of our laboratory studies confirmed our hope that we could measure a number of aspects of how families process and utilize information; further, interesting parallels between family process and schizophrenic syndromes were revealed. Now, over a decade after our initial studies of families of schizophrenics, we think our laboratory procedures measure something much more interesting and important than family information processing. They are excellent tools for delineating how the family—as a group—experiences or views the laboratory. They clearly reflect the fantasies and feelings the family members have while they are in the laboratory and, more important, the group's implicit and unspoken assumptions about the objectives, the trustworthiness, and the power of the laboratory staff and the institution in which they work. Moreover, the feelings and assumptions about the laboratory revealed by our procedures are not unique to the laboratory. They pervade the life of each family and are manifest whenever the family is in a strange setting. We believe that these shared family experiences—we call them *constructs*—guide and shape the way families approach specific problems, including the logical puzzles we gave them.

The processes of shared construing have never before been systematically studied, perhaps because there were no good methods for bringing them out of the shadows of family life. Since we are claiming for our procedures the power to examine these otherwise obscure processes, it is important to review the basis for these claims.

Family Information Processing and Schizophrenia

Our laboratory procedures ask families to do a number of things they rarely do in real life: sort cards, press signal buttons, examine sequential patterns of numbers and letters, pass notes through slots, and fill in lattices. All these activities are intended to model processes which we believe are of central importance in everyday family life: how families explore and interpret their stimulus world. In the mid-1960s we believed that a careful study of these processes might help explain the etiology and pathogenesis of schizophrenia. The schizophrenia question is no longer important in our work, although it played an important role in the development and initial validation of our methods. Four separate intellectual traditions suggested to us the methods we developed. A very schematic and brief review of these traditions will help explain the basic logic of our procedures.

Experimental Psychology of Thinking

At several key points in its history, the experimental psychology of thinking formulated its problem and methods in ways that had a major impact on our work. At its earliest, in the late nineteenth

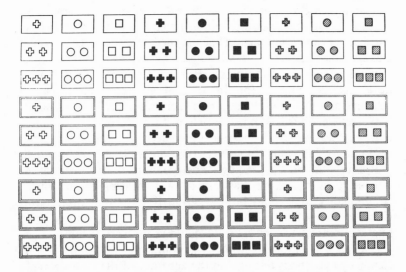

Figure 1.1. *Bruner, Goodnow, and Austin presented their subjects with an array of cards like these. The plain figures were green, the striped figures were red, and the solid figures were black. The subject's task was to infer the proper concept by selecting a series of cards from this array; for each card the experimenter would indicate whether or not the card was an instance of the underlying concept. "Green crosses," "red figures," "squares and three borders," and "circles or squares" are all examples of the concepts to be discovered.*

century, psychologists in the so-called Würzburg school were fascinated with the notion that an experimental subject's behavior depended on his understanding and organization of the experimental task.[1] The methods of those days explored these understandings—they were called "sets"—through the use of introspection. The subject was trained to report his own experiences. A half-century later, psychologists resumed these studies in a more complex form that no longer depended on introspection. Psychologists then studied how individuals developed complex schema of their. immediate stimulus world and focused particularly on the concepts and category systems which people developed and by which they recognized underlying equivalence between superficially dissimilar stimuli. A sample task is shown in Figure 1.1. Here the subject is asked to recognize what these superficially dissimilar cards have in common. Workers in this area felt they were studying a very simplified version of a critical everyday function of the human mind. The simple task of classifying cards was thought to represent the much more complex process of selective organization by which we make sense of our stimulus world. Bruner, Goodnow, and Austin (1956) added another major dimension to this trend in the psychology of thinking. They argued that people formed classificatory schemes of this kind step by step as they systematically tested various hypotheses. Bruner, Goodnow, and Austin developed techniques for inferring both these classificatory schemes and the subjects' strategies for testing hypotheses about those schemes. This yielded a rich picture of conceptual thinking — exploration and classification — derived from nonverbal responses of individual subjects to the standardized test situations.

Bruner, and most psychologists before him, studied a certain restricted form of concept. Basically it was a principle or underlying commonality that could be logically deduced from information given to the subject. Thus, hypothesis testing and the concept finally attained — for any subject — could be measured against a logical ideal. The emphasis in analysis could always be on the efficiency of hypothesis testing and the accuracy of the final concept. George Miller, as a consequence of his work with Noam Chomsky, introduced methods for studying a different kind of concept: those with infinitely many instances.[2] This represented a considerable departure because such concepts could never be logically derived from the information given. The subject could never collect enough data to be certain he had the right idea. Concepts of this kind are illustrated in Figure 1.2. The shift in emphasis induced by these new approaches was to investigate the qualitative nature of how the subject structured or came to understand the experimental stimulus materials.

The impact of this line of work on our investigation was to give emphasis to three points: (1) the objective of the study was to discover how individuals organized their experience of their immediate stimulus world (a tradition begun with the Würzburg school); (2) this organization could be thought of as divided into an exploratory phase with a special emphasis on hypothesis testing and a concept elaboration phase where a categorization or pattern generating system became established; (3) most important for our methods, these subtle, complex, experiential phenomena could be assessed by precise measures of subjects' responses to standard test situations.

PSYCHOLOGICAL DEFICIT STUDIES

The concept of schizophrenia is first, and foremost a clinical one. The nucleus of present-day concepts was elaborated by Kraepelin, who made a fundamental distinction between manic depressive psychosis and *dementia praecox*.[3] They were to be distinguished

Figure 1.2.   *The use of finite state grammars in concept formation tasks*

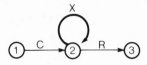

Illustrated above is a very simple finite state grammar. It is a simple set of rules specifying how a set of symbols — C, X, and R — can be ordered in a sequence. The rules govern the passage from one state to another. In order to pass from state 1 to state 2, a C must be produced. One can then go from state 2 to state 3 by producing an R, or one may stay at state 2 and produce any number of Xs. Thus, the following sequences or "sentences" are correct according to this grammar:

C R
C X R
C X X R
C X X X R
etc.

The following is not correct:

R C
C X
C X X X X X X X C R
etc.

The concept formation task involves presenting the subject with a large number of sequence of this kind and asking him to infer the underlying rules by which they were produced. For example, consider the following set of sequences:

A B V
A B Q V
A B Q Q V
A B Q Q Q Q V
A B Q Q Q Q Q Q V

A reasonable inference is that the following rules were used to produce this set:

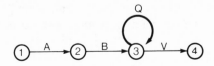

18   *Family Problem Solving and Family Interpreting*

Figure 1.2.   (continued)
However, the relationship between the instances and the concept is not as airtight as in the procedures used by Bruner, Goodnow, and Austin (Figure 1.1). First of all, other rules could also have produced these sequences. For example:

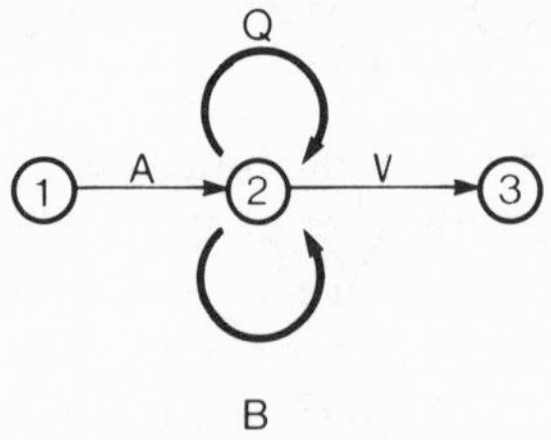

Q

①—A→②—V→③

B

Secondly, neither the first set of rules, inferable from these examples, nor the second set can be derived from the examples by pure logic. In order to do so we would have to consider an infinite array of instances. In other words, the recursive loop in the finite-state grammar cannot be logically inferred from a finite set of instances. It is a plausible but not logical inference.

---

primarily by their clinical course: manic-depressive patients recovered; schizophrenic patients deteriorated. The second major conceptualization of schizophrenia by Eugen Bleuler (1950) was perhaps more psychological but still clinical in the sense that it organized observations that could be made by a clinician in an ordinary clinical setting. Bleuler described the concept of splitting of psychic processes and their clinical manifestations in disturbed associations of thought, inappropriate affect, immobilizing ambivalence, and inability to integrate reality and fantasy, leading to autism. Even in the last decade, research in the diagnosis of schizophrenia has focused almost exclusively on clinically observable symptoms and good history taking. Nonetheless, another, less dominant trend has been experimental or laboratory studies of psychopathology, which have sought to characterize the psychological processes underlying clinically observable psychopathologic manifestations and to explain the diversity of clinical manifestations by locating a core deficit among the simpler psychological functions. Most pertinent for our studies was the voluminous evidence pointing to a substantial deficit—in most schizophrenic patients—of a capacity to selectively utilize information for the elaboration of accurate, stable, and comprehensive concepts.[4] This inability could explain, investigators argued, many of the clinical phenomena of schizophrenia. If schizophrenia could be understood, at least in part, as a disorder of concept-forming abilities, then it seemed relevant to the problem of schizophrenia to study those factors that might impair concept formation. When it came to the family, it made sense to study how family interaction might influence concept formation.

STUDIES OF COMMUNICATION

The concept of communication—now a term that has been abused through overuse—had by the early 1950s demarcated a special area in studies of human exchange and interaction. It referred to the transmission of information, cognitive and affective, between two or more individuals. Within this very broad field two developments were particularly pertinent to our work. Both of them tended to illustrate the analytic power inherent in simplifying and abstracting the complexities of human communication. The first development was "information theory."[5] This approach—misnamed because it is not a theory but a system of measurement—viewed communication very generally. It was concerned with quantifying the information inherent in any set of signals, including human speech. Information theory helped set the stage for a large number of studies in human interaction. It defined methods by which the inordinate complexities of human speech and ordinary nonverbal communication could be simplified.[6] For example, information theory permitted the measurement of the communicative significance of a signal without the complexities of interpreting its meaning. Information was measured instead by reference to the size, and probability of use, of all the signals in the set from which the actual signal was drawn. Thus, one could assess the capacities of individuals and groups to transmit and receive information using formal mathematical techniques. A second development, running parallel to information theory, was experimental studies of communication processes in small ad hoc groups such as those of Bavelas (1950), Heise and Miller (1951), and Leavitt (1951). This line of work demonstrated that one could study communication in highly restricted settings: it complemented information theory which demonstrated one could study communication with extremely limited signals. To be sure, much of the subtle innuendo and poetic expressiveness of ordinary speech was filtered out by these procedures; however, a rich range of communicative processes were retained and the simplification of setting and symbol greatly enhanced the power of systematic analysis. These restrictions—in the service of analysis—have been retained in almost all of our work.

THE STUDY OF ABERRANT FAMILY PROCESS

By the mid 1960s a significant amount of theoretical work and some empirical studies were under way in the field of the family and schizophrenia. We were attracted to a relatively circumscribed subset of this work. Lidz, Rosman, and Wild, working as a group, tried to define the relationship between cognitive deficits in parents and the character of the parents' interaction with their families — particularly the schizophrenic offspring.[7] Likewise, Wynne and Singer focused on attentional processes in parents and on how deficits in parents of schizophrenics might influence parents' interaction with their children.[8]

These studies helped us to formulate our own work by pointing to the dual function of information. Information is, first of all, a critical medium of exchange between the individual and his animate and inanimate environment. Cognition — studied in its simplest forms by the Lidz group — led to the grouping or segregation of those signals according to certain of its properties. Information is also a critical medium of exchange between one individual and another. Beyond that, it has a critical impact as a factor in the organization and internal control of groups such as families.

Both the Lidz group and the Wynne and Singer team recognized that disordered attention and thinking in parents had a profound influence on how they organized their families. Both groups analyzed the impact of the parents on the family by considering them as transmitters of environmental information. If parents cannot sustain a focus of attention on a selected or demarcated set of environmental signals, they will transmit impressions which are confusing and difficult to follow. For example, consider several responses from parents in Wynne and Singer's test situation. These parents are viewing Rorschach cards and comment as follows:

"Some sort of species for a special occasion" (Card VI).
"Well, it looks like a blended color species" (Card VIII).
"That looks like a bat. The more I look at it, the less it seems like that, I guess. I'm not sure about that bat anymore" (Card I).

Each parent's attention is blurred, shifting, and evanescent. In the last example, the percept offered at the beginning is disqualified by the end. A child listening to a parent's speech in a setting similar to the test situation will be unable to visualize what the parent is observing. The parent, who functions as a transmitter of information (or, in this case, as a transmitter of confusion), effectively seals the child off from access to the original source of signals (we will assume, for simplicity, that the child has no independent access to that stimulus or for some reason does not seek it). Equally important, the parent's relationship with the child is blurred. A child hearing observations of the kind illustrated above will be confused about what responses to make. Is the parent the perceiver and perhaps the instructor in this situation? Or is the parent helpless and confused, requiring some form of support and structuring from the child?

A Theoretical Sketch of Family Information Processing

We began our investigations with a simple model that owed a great deal to all four of these traditions: studies of cognition, communication studies, investigations of core psychological deficits in schizophrenia, and studies of family process. Aspects of this initial model are illustrated by the following case example.[9]

The Brady family was seen in treatment for over a year as part of a comprehensive treatment program for the son, Fred, age twenty-seven who had become depressed, socially withdrawn, and—finally—immobilized by frightening somatic delusions. He felt his body was empty, falling apart, decaying; he became suicidal. Fred was the only child of a father, a successful surgeon, who had died twenty years previously, and a mother who was in her late sixties. Shortly after father's death, father's younger brother came to live with Fred and mother. Uncle was a timid clerk in the local branch of a national retail chain. The trio continued to live in the apartment that Fred, mother, and father had lived in. Father's medical books, photographs, and many others possessions were left in place. The trio felt themselves to be a doctor's family and occasionaly referred to the dead father in the present tense. Clearly, they were preserving an important shared illusion about themselves.

Mother was the specialist in obtaining information from the outside world. She was the only one in the family who watched television news and read the papers; she also answered all incoming phone calls when she was at home. In virtually every aspect of the family's life it was mother who selected the relevant outside data and provided the interpretations. For example, after many months in the hospital, Fred received a partial discharge, which enabled him to begin his first job as a technician's helper in a hospital laboratory. He never did well in the job, but mother focused exclusively on the medical aspects and presented the job to the family and therapist as evidence that Fred might soon return to college, go to medical school, and become a doctor. Fred and his uncle acquiesced, quite willingly, to mother's highly filtered selection and interpretation of signals. It provided them both with a sense of the family's vigor, prestige, and permanence.

The family—working as an integrated group—can be viewed as an information-processing unit. In the case of the Bradys, although mother's role is most conspicuous, all three members have an investment in preserving the illusion of family prominence and permanence. In order to accomplish this, the Bradys must be highly selective in sampling and interpreting data; they have to weed out or fail to attend to information that denies or undercuts their treasured self-concepts. One member is assigned the role of informational gatekeeper. This reduces the risk that the family group might be loaded with too much information—particularly information discordant with the family's self-conception. The Bradys illustrate how a whole family can be thought of as an information-processing unit—a deficient one, in their case. From this perspective we began to sketch out our initial theory.

Our comments about the Brady family are schematic and oversimplified; one simplification in particular must be highlighted. Our interpretative comments all assume certain characteristics of the informational world in which the family lives. For example, when we say that the family attends to a very narrown or circumscribed set of information, we are assuming that a much wider range of information is available to them. Assumptions of this kind are always easier to examine when a pertinent event arises in the context of therapy. Mother's view of Fred's menial laboratory job seems particularly convincing because we are confident that mother, if she wanted to, might have attended to more data about the job itself. A similar example is our assumption about mother as information transmitter. We say that once she has selected and interpreted certain data, as she did for Fred's job, she effectively transmits that to the rest of the family—maintaining this cherished sense of strength and perpetuity. We again assume what it is that the mother knows and thinks. In other words, we assume there is not a vast storehouse of additional facts and interpretations in mother's head which she is, in this instance, withholding from the rest of the family.

Our aim in constructing observational settings for our very first studies was to make these assumptions about the family's informational world as certain and justifiable as possible. To do this we created an artificial informational environment and asked the family members to explore, organize, and interpret this environment for themselves, and to transmit their observations and interpretations to others in the family. Two of the problem-solving situations required the family to recognize patterns underlying complex stimulus arrays; a third required the family to learn and use a simple artificial language in order to exchange, among themselves, a clearly specified set of information. Within this type of setting we conceived the family's information processing to consist of three interpenetrating phases.

First, the family obtains a subset of information from the environment. Roughly speaking, this corresponds to the selective aspects of attention in the individual. Selection in the Brady family was narrow and restricted. Second, the individual categorizes or interprets signals. We have already described how Bruner, Goodnow, and Austin linked the concepts of categorization and interpretation. Third, information which has been selectively obtained and interpreted is transmitted within the family. We posited that, like the Bradys, many families would have one specialist, or perhaps two, who would be the most active in selecting and interpreting environmental signals. In a related case, all individuals might work on their own to obtain and interpret signals, and then—after some work—they might compare notes. Whether the family had just one information specialist or whether all individuals worked on their own, a process of intrafamily transmission would be required if the family as a whole were to acquire a shared set of signals and interpretations. Families would, presumably, vary in this third phase as well; some would share information effectively, others would not.

Information gathering. In individual psychology, attention is seen as an active process of selecting stimuli for further internal processing by the perceiver. When we transpose this concept to the family group we can conceive of it as an even more active process. Groups organize themselves to seek out information actively. In particular, information can be generated by the active construction of hypotheses or test situations. For illustrative purposes, consider a second family.

The Whitesides believed in the importance of a cohesive family. In fact, they shared the view that each member was strengthened and supported, as the father put it, by staying close to "the bosom of the family." Signs of disagreement within the family or moves away from the family regularly produced anxiety. If a person attempted to assert his own independence it threatened the family's shared view of the family as an essential source of life. The father, aged forty-six, had at first had a successful career as an accountant. However, at the point of greatest success he resigned from a major post, and after some years in a much less significant position he accepted a position in a bank. Mother, after two years of college, had worked as a housewife. There were three children: a nineteen-year-old daughter was entering college but planned to remain living at home; a fifteen-year-old son, Elliot, had dropped out of school and ultimately ran away from home; a thirteen-year-old son remained closer to the family but had grades that were slipping.

Interviews with the family revealed that all members felt bound into the family and were intensely curious about what it would be like to leave. In fact, some months after his older son's escapades, father arranged a business trip in a way that permitted him to visit several of the stops on Elliot's adventure. Because of his overwhelming anxiety and disorganization, Elliot was hospitalized, and the entire family was seen together for treatment. During this period Elliot planned and occasionally carried out several impulsive departures from the hospital. These rather desperate escapes became a primary focus of family discussion. Often the family looked carefully for any sign that the hospital had in some way permitted these escapes. At first, this highly restricted focus of the family's attention was perplexing. Further discussion revealed, however, that the family was trying to see these trips as signs of Elliot's improvement, perhaps covertly arranged by the staff. The escapes could then be viewed as a sign of his improvement and that he would soon return to "the bosom of the family."

For the Whiteside family, Elliot's runaway attempts were test situations which provided them with a highly selected set of data. In fact, the case illustrates a special complexity. Elliot's trips provided two sorts of data. The first set was the observations and experiences Elliot gathered on his travels, which the family learned about in snatches and by innuendo from Elliot. The family never openly discussed what they learned. This information seemed to be disavowed because it related to a hidden or disavowed feeling in the family: the wish all members felt to break loose from the entanglements of mutual dependency. A second set of data was more openly sought: data that would confirm the family's view that the trips were not a rebellion but rather a prelude to the reconstruction of a fully cohesive family group. Here the family saw a very restricted set of data: a few fragmentary signs that the hospital staff might have supported or failed to prevent the escapes.

Interpretation of information. The Whiteside family also illustrates another phase in processing information: interpretation. In effect, family members thought they could discern a pattern of events for which they had an explanation. The pattern was simple: Elliot expressed a wish to leave the family; hospital staff gave minimal evidence of not opposing this; Elliot ran away. The family understood this sequence to mean that Elliot was improving. They interpreted the hospital's actions as indicating that running away was in some way curative, and they assumed cure meant Elliot's return to the family. It should be emphasized that this interpretation was not arrived at in a straightforward way. However, it became apparent that all members of the family — except Elliot — shared this view and expressed it in a fragmentary and indirect way. In our experimental setting we tried to make this interpretative process more overt. In our artificial puzzle situation the families search for patterns, once they have selected a certain set of information.

Communication of information. Gathering and interpreting information are processes in which individuals engage. What is it that makes such processes pertinent to the family? The Brady and Whiteside families suggest one distinctive pattern: it looks as if the family builds up a collective view or schema of its informational world. Thus, the Brady family saw Fred's menial job as a first step on his way to becoming a doctor; Elliot's family saw his runaway attempts as the first sign of cure and the restoration of the cohesive family. It must be assumed that information and interpretation are shared or exchaned between members. It is, of course, true that if family members share interpretations they will not necessarily believe them. Thus, Fred's mother might have shared her views about Fred's job with Fred and his uncle, and they, in turn, might have disbelieved either the evidence or the interpretation. Nonetheless, insofar as a family does construct a shared schema of the informational world, its members must share at least some of their individual observations and interpretations. To further illustrate our point, we might imagine a family where such sharing or exchange does not occur. In that case each member would develop its own schema and, in effect, inhabit his own sector of the informational world; overlap between members would occur only by chance. If that world were sufficiently complex and variegated, however, chance alone would rarely produce any overlap. Indeed, we have encountered such families in our clinical work.

The Ramos-Anthony-Cooper family needs three names to describe it, a fact which reflects the deep division within it. It is a family of three women living together — daughters aged twenty-four and twenty-six and a twice-divorced mother aged fifty-one. Maureen Ramos, the younger daughter, has the last name of her biological father whom her mother divorced when Maureen was five. Mary Anthony is the older daughter; her last name is that of her estranged husband. The last name of the mother, Molly Cooper, is that of her second husband, from whom she was divorced ten years previously. The family does not feel itself a connected, integral unit, in sharp contrast to the Brady and Whiteside families. Maureen is constantly preoccupied with her fantasies and is given to wandering; the content of her fantasies or wanderings is unknown to the other two. Mary is sexually promiscuous, has been illegitimately pregnant at least twice, and has been involved in petty crimes. The other two know of her bad reputation, but her feelings, the specifics of her impulsive behavior, and indeed much of her life are entirely her own. Mother deals with her two daughters as if they are external burdens. She longs to put them in a psychiatric treatment program; yet, constantly lonely, she is comforted by their presence. In fact, all three women feel that their home is barren, lonely, ungiving. They rarely bring friends there. Among themselves the roles are clear: mother the stoic, Maureen the withdrawn introvert becoming periodically psychotic, and Mary the irresponsible floozie. Although their roles are clear, their alliances are constantly shifting, with two—any two—often teaming up against the third.

As one might expect, this family threesome had not consistently stuck together, as had the Bradys and the Whitesides. Maureen had been frequently hospitalized and Mary had left the family for extended periods. Their bond, such as it was, was an unacknowledged dependency on one another. However, they stand in clearest contrast to the Bradys and the Whitesides in having no clear shared conception about themselves and no distinctive shared view of a significant aspect of their informational enviornment. Their lack of shared information cannot be attributed to any deficiencies of each individual's selection or interpretation of information. Mary, for example, was a highly intellegent and perceptive young woman and, in her own way, vastly experienced. However, her "research" in the outer informational world was not reported to her family, unlike Elliot's research, and her family did not draw any conclusions from her experiences. In this family, information—however selectively it was obtained by its individuals—was never shared.

Three Measures of Family Information Processing

For our first study we gave each family three puzzles. The procedures were designed so that for each puzzle a different one of the three hypothesized phases of information processing was especially required for success. The "phasic" portion of the overall hypothesis was not directly tested; that is, we did not examine how families integrated the successive, though interpenetrating, phases in information processing in one problem-solving effort.

THE HYPOTHESIS-TESTING TASK: GATHERING INFORMATION

In this procedure, the basic task was to recognize underlying patterns in sequences of circles (C), triangles (T), and squares (S). These underlying patterns were, in fact, very simple finite state grammars of the kind we described in the previous section.

Consider this simple sequence of symbols:

C C C T T T

What is the underlying pattern? We are immediately tempted to say, "Any uninterrupted sequence of circles followed by an uninterrupted sequence of triangles." How could we find out? One way is to make up more sequences and test them out with someone who knows what the underlying pattern is. Suppose we test the following sequences and get the results indicated alongside them:

C T   Right
C C T T T T   Right
C T C   Wrong
T T T T C C C C   Wrong
C C C C   Wrong
C T T T T T   Right
C C T T T T   Right

This set would seem to confirm our initial hunch. We might, of course, be wrong. For example, we might then test the following:

C C C T T T T T T T T T T C   Right

This would suggest that the underlying pattern rule is more complicated than we had guessed. At this point, a plausible revision of our hypothesis would be, "An uninterrupted run of Cs followed by an uninterrupted run of Ts except if there are ten or more Ts in which case the sequence must end with a C."

As proposed in the previous sections, hypothesis testing is a systematic form of information gathering. If we require a family to engage in puzzles of the kind we have just illustrated, we will, presumably, be testing that capacity to gather information in this way. If we also tell the family to find the underlying pattern, then we are, in effect, also requiring them to interpret the information they receive. Finally, if we permit family members to observe one another testing hypotheses we will also get some data on information exchange. However, we reasoned that the primary skill required in this type of puzzle is information gathering. In order to clarify this procedure further we will describe the performance of one of our families. This case description also conveys, more generally, the absorbing and significant emotional events in the family's interaction which leave their mark on the objective record of our laboratory procedures. Thus the case serves a second function: to show, in a direct way, something of the connection between significant emotional issues in the life of a family and their performance in our laboratory puzzles.

In the Friedkin family the father, fifty-three, is president of a small newspaper and also a rubber goods company. Mother, forty-six, is a housewife. There are five children aged twelve to twenty. Father is an ambitious, aggressive, and highly successful business-man. At home he is deeply involved with his children, and fills the role of both mother and father. Mother is obese and chronically depressed. Her clothing is disorganized. Talks with the family revealed that everyone in the family feels a sense of despair and disappointment in one another. We included both parents and the two oldest children (both female) in the testing. The oldest, Frieda, had been very shy, withdrawn, and occasionally depressed since early childhood. The younger of these two, Betty, was able to leave home and remain in college for a year. She was more outgoing, academically successful, and, superficially at least, more social.

As with other families, when the Friedkins entered the laboratory each member was placed in a booth as shown in Figure 1.3.[10] They were instructed in how the puzzle worked. Each was given an example sequence and then told to make up his or her own by writing out a sequence on a slip of paper when he or she received a signal to do so. They were to pass their hypotheses to the experimenter through open slots in the booth walls. The experimenter would rate it right or wrong; then the slip would be passed around, through other slots, for the rest of the family to see. When each member thought he had discovered the underlying pattern he turned on a "finish" light which all could see. He was still required to make up se-quences when it was his turn. However, once he pressed the "finish" light he would get no response (right or wrong) from the ex-perimenter.

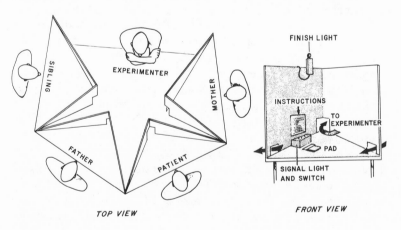

Figure 1.3. *Top and front views of the booths for the hypothesis-testing task*

Following a sample puzzle, the Friedkin family was given the first of two experimental puzzles. We wanted to make the problem somewhat harder in order to elicit more performance from each family member before he decided to discontinue testing, so we distributed only one example sequence to each person. We also wanted to know whether family members worked in isolation or whether they were responsive to what the others were doing. To this end, we gave examples with one pattern to the parents:

Mother: C T T T T T T T C
Father: C T C

and another pattern to the children:

Frieda: T C T
Betty: T C C C C C C C T

Thus, the parents got sequences of the C T$_n$C type, and the children received the T C$_n$T type. From pre-experimental trials we knew that when family members working alone are given only one example they are likely to be quite dependent on it; they construct hypotheses very much like it and their final pattern concept is very closely related to it. However, if individual members are responsive to what others are doing when the family is working together, they are likely to test hypotheses if either the C T$_n$ C or T C$_n$ T type are confirmed by the experimenter. In other words, each generation has the chance to learn from the hypothesis testing of the other that two different patterns are correct. We assumed, then, that individuals who tested hypotheses of both kinds, and learned that two patterns are correct, are responsive to the performance and ideas of others.

In order to measure carefully the pattern concept formed by each individual at the start and conclusion of each puzzle, we constructed a multiple choice test called the private inventory. Figure 1.4 shows the initial private inventory given to each family member in the first experimental problem. It consists of twenty sequences; each individual is asked to place a check next to those sequences he believes are correct based on the single example he has received, and an X next to the others. We inferred, using a formal algebraic system for scoring, the pattern he recognized in his example sequence from sequences next to which he placed a check. For instance, Frieda checked the sequences listed below (she was given the example T C T):

T C C T
T C C C C C T
T C C C C C C C C C T

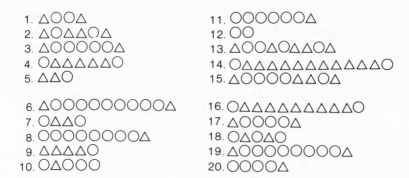

Figure 1.4. *The initial inventory given to the Friedkin family, and the others in our sample, on the first test problem in the hypothesis-testing task*

T C C C T
T C C C C C C C T

She rejected, by marking an X, all the remaining fifteen sequences on the inventory. We may infer that she formed a concept of the pattern which could be stated: "A correct sequence must begin with a triangle, to be followed by any number of circles, and must end with a triangle."[11] After completing the private inventory, all families were told to make up their own sequences until they thought they had the right answer. If, on the private inventory at the end of the task, Frieda accepted these sequences and all five sequences of the C T_n C as well, this would be evidence that she had learned that two patterns were correct, and we would infer she had been responsive to what others — particularly her parents — had been doing in the hypothesis-testing part of the task. The private inventory is one of knowing what the individual is thinking at the beginning and at the end of the task. The subject was never told whether his choices on this inventory were right or wrong. He received feedback only in the public, exploratory phase of hypothesis testing. Further, other family members never knew what sequences he checked on the private inventory.

We will not further describe the performance of the Friedkin family in problem 1, but will skip to what they did in problem 2. The overall design of this experiment is summarized in Table 1.1. Note that there were three problems: one sample and two test problems. Each test problem began with distribution of the examples followed by the initial private inventory and hypothesis testing, and concluded with the final inventory.

In the second test problem a third symbol, a square, was introduced into some of the examples in order to heighten the con-

TABLE I.I   DESIGN OF HYPOTHESIS-TESTING TASK

Problem	Phase	Summary of method
Sample problem	1. Examples given	The same four examples are given to each family member.
	2. Hypothesis testing	Family members construct their own sequences.
Test problem 1 (no squares)	1. Examples given	One example sequence is given to each member; parents and children receive different patterns.
	2. Initial private inventory	Each family member is given the same multiple choice test consisting of twenty sequences.
	3. Hypothesis testing	Family members construct their own sequences.
	4. Final private inventory	Each family member is given another multiple choice test.
Test problem 2 (squares)	1. Examples given	
	2. Initial private inventory	
	3. Hypothesis testing	Procedure the same as in problem 1.
	4. Final private inventory	

trast between the examples given to the parents and those given to the children.

Mother: C S T S   Frieda: C T T T T T T C
Father: C S T T T T T T S   Betty: C T C

The examples given to the children in the second test problem were the same as those given to the parents in the first test — that is, sequences of the C T„ C type. We made the same kind of inferences as in the first test. If, for instance, children tested hypotheses with squares and accepted hypotheses with squares on the final inventory, we assumed they were responsive to their parents. If they never seemed to consider squares — despite the fact that both parents were testing a number of hypotheses with squares — we assumed they worked in considerable isolation from their parents.

In the Friedkin family, mother accepted fifteen of the twenty sequences on the initial private inventory (she had received the example C S T S):

```
C T T T T T T T C          C T T
C S T T S                  C S T T T T T S
C C T C C S                C T C T T C
C T C C C C C T            C S S S S C
C C                        S S C T C C
C S S S S S S S S C        C T T T T T T C
C T T T T T T T T T T C    C T C T T
C T T C
```

There seems to be no pattern common to all these sequences, and our inference was that mother was thinking in a confused or scattered way. Frieda's selection performance was more orderly (she had received the example C T T T T T T T C):

```
C T T T T T T T C          C T T T T T T C
C C                        C S S C
C T T T T T T T T T T T C  C S S S C
C T T C                    C S S S S S S S S C
```

We inferred that Frieda made a reasonable guess about how to use squares: she was using them in the same way as triangles. Her concept might be stated: "An acceptable sequence must begin with a circle, to be followed by any number of triangles or any number of squares, and must end with a circle."

Father accepted the following sequences (he had received the example C S T T T T T T T S):

```
C S T T S                  C S T T T T T T T T S
C S T T T T T T T T T S    C S T T T T T S
C S T T S
```

We inferred that his concept might be stated: "An acceptable sequence must begin with a circle, to be followed by a square, to be followed by any number of triangles, and must end with a square." Betty accepted these (she had the example C T C):

```
C T T T T T T T C          C C
C T T T T T T T T T T C    C T T C
C T T T T T T C
```

We inferred her concept as: "An acceptable sequence must begin with a circle, to be followed by any number of triangles, and must end with a circle." Thus, each member of the Friedkin family began the task with a different concept; the differences could be ascribed in part to the different examples but also to differences in their interpretations.

The family then was instructed to make up their own hypothesis sequences, as in previous problems. Although they were never told this, any hypothesis sequence of the C S T_n S type or the C T_n C type was confirmed. We will skip this phase of the task for a moment and consider what the Friedkin family did on the final inventory. This inventory was similar but not identical to the initial private inventory.

Mother performed very much as she had on the initial inventory. She accepted twelve of the twenty sequences, and these seemed to have no common pattern. Frieda and Betty accepted these:

C T T T T C   C T T T T T T T T T C
C T T T T T T T T C   C T T C
C T T T T T C   C S S S S S S S S S S C

For Frieda, this selection was an improvement over her initial performance in the sense that she accepted only one incorrect sequence, but she appeared to be flirting still with the notion of the interchangeability of squares and triangles. But she did not learn the correct use of squares, as demonstrated by her failure to accept any of the C S T_n S type of sequence. Neither did Betty; her performance deteriorated in the sense that she accepted an incorrect sequence where she had not on the initial inventory. Father, who had received the C S T T T T T T T S sequence, accepted these:

C T T T T C   C T T T T T T T T T C
C T T T T T T T T C   C T T T C
C T T T T T C

He rejected all five of the sequences of the C S T_n S type on the final inventory, despite the fact that this was the only type of sequence he accepted on the initial inventory, and that his initial example lay directly in front of him.

In sum, mother showed no change in her scattered, chaotic performance from initial to final inventory. Frieda and Betty shared half-views of the correct patterns, neither learning the correct use of squares; Frieda showed some improvement, but Betty deteriorated. Father completely reversed his original concept, ending up with a concept that was consistent with his two children's. He was the only one who had, at any point in the puzzle, ever learned the proper use of squares. Apparently he could not teach it to others, but instead gave it up in favor of the concepts held by his children. To repeat, he did so despite the fact that the example with squares was before him throughout the task. Consequently, his reversal of concept required him to surrender his initial—and appropriate—concept, as well as to ignore a major piece of evidence at hand.

Figure 1.5 shows the hypothesis sequences constructed by the Friedkin family. They are arranged in the order in which they were constructed. The stop line indicates that father and sibling stopped after each had tested three hypotheses. The instructions required each individual to continue making up sequences each time it was his turn, until everyone had stopped; these sequences are listed below the stop line. Frieda stopped at the end of four turns and mother had to be stopped by the experimenter (as was the usual procedure) at the end of ten. Confirmed hypotheses are checked, the remainder marked X. We used this array of hypotheses to detect family influence and interaction during the public hypothesis-testing phase of the experiment. The set of hypotheses produced by the Friedkins shows a significant discrepancy between their work together in the public hypothesis-testing phase and their work as individuals on the private inventory. In the public phase, father, Betty, and Frieda made a great effort at unanimity, copying each other's hypotheses; their behavior looks as if they have made a pseudo-agreement in the last two-thirds of this phase not to consider the use of squares. This is a pseudo-agreement because at the conclusion of the task, mother, Frieda, and Betty still accepted sequences with squares. In public, they acted as if they thought squares were unimportant; in private, they still entertained erroneous notions about their use. The press for unanimity in the public phase seemed to take precedence over family members' personal interest in the use of squares. The press for unanimity had its greatest effect on father, who was induced to surrender his accurate conception of the use of squares; in fact, he joined the no-square ethos most completely, rejecting the use of squares on both the public and the private level. But this family process took its toll on the children too: they never learned the use of squares.

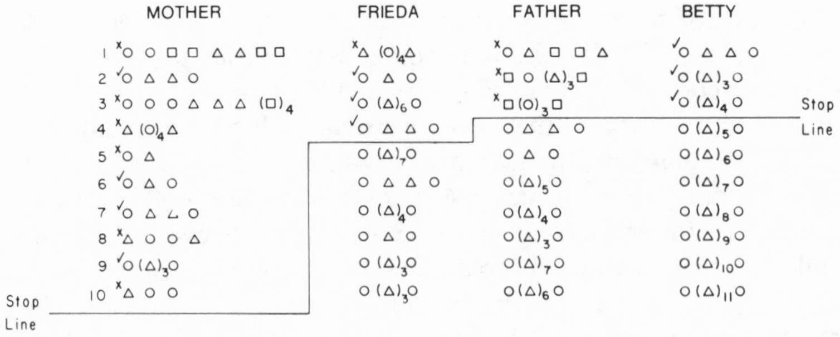

Figure 1.5. *The hypotheses tested by the Friedkin family*

This vignette, many years later, is still poignant. Although some of our responses to this family's work depend on interpolation, we are struck with a profoundly significant little drama. The family is somehow split. They present themselves in the laboratory in that way. Father and daughters exchange glances and words that convey their bond and mother seems alone—disheveled, disorganized, and worn. Their split shows up again in their performance; father and daughters stop early; only mother goes on, trial after trial. To an observer in the room her loneliness and desperation can be clearly felt; even the objective record of the family performance (Figure 1.5) shows how isolated she is. We cannot, from the record, understand why this split has occurred. Are father and daughters protecting themselves from the influence of a disturbed and disturbing mother? Have they actively excluded her from the family as a kind of scapegoat to conceal other, more invidious processes in themselves? Or, more intricately, is this split arranged—in some way— for the benefit of the observer in order to conceal deeper and more painful splits and alliances in the family? We cannot answer these questions, but we can see the toll such intrafamily splitting takes on each member. Clinically, we could have recognized the family split and perhaps guessed at its cost. Our procedure not only captures this in the objective record but shows how this family process is interwoven with a severe poverty of individual concept. To phrase the matter more generally, we can see the interweaving between the restricted grasp each member has of underlying patterns, on the one hand, and the splits and alliances within the family, on the other.

THE CARD SORTING TASK: INTERPRETING INFORMATION

Earlier in this chapter we summarized Bruner, Goodnow, and Austin's attempts to simplify the concept of meaning and interpretation. A partial approach to this simplification is to study how people sort varied experiences into categories. The kinds of categories a person uses tells us something about how he organizes his world. In this task we asked the family to work as a group to sort some cards into groups or categories. We encouraged them to develop their own categories for sorting and to assign whichever cards they wished to the categories they had developed.

Suppose we are given cards with a sequence of letters on each, as shown below:

P M S V K   P M F K
V S S P F M K   P M S M S M S V K

```
V S P F K                    V S S P F M M K
P M S S F K                  P M S F K
V S P F M K                  P M S M S V K
P M S S S S F K              P M S S S F K
P M S M S M S M S V K        V P F K
P V K
```

We are told simply to sort these cards into piles. We may use as many piles as we wish, up to seven, and put as many cards in each pile as we wish. If we were very casual or superficial we might say to ourselves, "Well, these cards have a different number of letters. Let's put the cards with three letters in one pile, those with four letters in the next, all the way up to nine letters. When we get to that point we'll exhaust the maximum number of permissible piles — seven. So let's just put everything with nine or more in this last pile." The sort would look like this.

```
P V K        P M F K        P M S V K        P M S S F K
             V P F K        V S P F K        V S P F M K
                            P M S F K

V S S P F M K        P M S S S S F K
P M S M S V K        V S S P F M M K
P M S S S F K

P M S M S M S M S V K
P M S M S M S V K
```

When we looked over this arrangement we might not be satisfied. Something more subtle might strike us. "How about alphabetizing them? You know, they all begin with either P or V." So we'd try the following:

```
P V K                        V P F K
P M F K                      V S P F K
P M S V K                    V S P F M K
P M S S F K                  V S S P F M K
P M S M S V K                V S S P F M M K
P M S S S F K
P M S S S S F K
P M S M S M S M S V K
P M S M S M S V K
```

Once we have them arranged that way, we might notice that the P pile has two different sorts of cards. One kind has repeating M S pairs, the other repeating Ss. This observation might also help us see too that most of the V cards have repeating Ss and Ms. So we might rearrange twelve of the fifteen cards like this:

P M S V K	P M S F K	V S P F K
P M S M S V K	P M S S F K	V S P F M K
P M S M S M S V K	P M S S S F K	V S S P F M K
P M S M S M S M S V K	P M S S S S F K	V S S P F M M K

We'd hold our V P F K, P M F K, and P V K. They don't have any letters that can be repeated. But then we might suddenly notice that they have *zero* repeating elements. That's exactly the point; they can justifiably be placed at the top of the related piles to produce the following:

P V K	P M F K	V P F K
P M S V K	P M S F K	V S P F K
P M S M S V K	P M S S F K	V S P F M K
P M S M S M S V K	P M S S S F K	V S S P F M K
P M S M S M S M S V K	P M S S S S F K	V S S P F M M K

We have come through several stages, each one more sophisticated and elegant than the next, because each subsequent stage recognizes more subtle sequential relationships within and among the cards. We can regard each sort as if it were some kind of interpretative conclusion. The first is very simple; it is drawn from a very limited observation about the length of sequences and, in comparison to the final sort above, seems very superficial or insubstantial. This limited and premature conclusion resembles the one reached by the Whiteside family. They paid attention to a very limited sequence of data. Elliot said he wanted to leave the hospital — the hospital staff gave limited evidence it was not actively preventing this — Elliot left: from this sequence the family drew the conclusion that Elliot was getting better. The conclusion failed to take account of other information available to the family (evidence that the staff did oppose Elliot's leaving, Elliot's continuing turmoil, and so on).

In the card sorting procedure we gave the family two tasks. In each we asked them to sort a deck of fifteen cards into as many piles as they wished, up to and including seven. We did not give them any feedback. All the information was in the deck of cards we gave them; their main task was to organize or interpret the information given. In contrast to the hypothesis-testing task, the card sorting procedure gave family members no opportunity to seek out additional information. Since this was a very simple task we permitted family members to talk with one another. This was the only one of our original tasks where talking was permitted. We hoped the family's discussion might give us some additional clues about how they organized their interaction patterns to deal with the interpretative task in the puzzle.

The family sat around a semi-octagonal table. When a deck of cards was placed in the middle of the long edge of the table, each member was—by virtue of the table's shape—the same distance from the cards as the others. When the family felt it had the best sort possible one member was to raise his hand. The family's card sort was recorded; the discussion was recorded on tape. A typist transcribed the tape as exactly as possible, and coders divided the discussion into very small units called acts. An act contained a single idea and usually was three to five words long. A typescript divided into acts, sequentially numbered in order of occurrence, is shown in Table 1.2.

THE LATTICE TASK: INFORMATION EXCHANGE

The card sorting task required the family to organize and interpret information already given to them. But it also required them to

TABLE 1.2   A TYPESCRIPT FROM THE DISCUSSION OF A FAMILY OF A
SCHIZOPHRENIC IN THE CATEGORIZATION TASK

Sibling:	(01) Did they leave that tape recorder going?/
Father:	(02) Oh be quiet./ (03) You better not sign up for any more of these/ (05) you're coming alone, kid./ (06) Yeah./
Mother:	(04) Move over/
Sibling:	(07) (L)/
Mother:	(08) (L) What are you doing?/
Patient:	(09) Putting all the TRs together/
Mother:	(10) (L) Didn't get a chance to look at them yet./
Father:	(11) They're all TRs/
Mother:	(12) They're all TRs/
Patient:	(13) No/ (14) they aren't/ (15) they beginning we're beginning with TR/
Father:	(16) Oh come on./
Sibling:	(17) No/ (18) look it./ (19) You get the longest one first or the shortest one/ (21) take your choice./
Patient:	(20) Then take this one/ (22) hah not that's another well you don't/
Mother:	(23) Shh/
Sibling:	(24) Will you let us look at them?/
Mother:	(25) (L) I didn't get chance to look at them yet./
Patient:	(26) I know how to do it already./
Mother:	(27) Gee you're smart./

Note: Slash marks divide the statements into acts. The acts are consecutively numbered as they occurred in time during the discussion. (L) refers to laughter.

talk. At first glance one might say, then, that the sorting task measured information exchange as well. But often family members talk in order to conceal, rather than reveal, information to one another. (Consider the husband who, on his return home from work, regales his wife with a dramatic account of his workday in order to conceal the fact that he has just smashed up the front of the family car.) Family discussion may give us an insight into certain interaction patterns in the family, but it will not always tell us how *information* is exchanged. In order to study the latter we developed a puzzle for directly measuring information exchange rather than verbal discussion. Each individual was given a unique set of information and was required to share it with the rest of the family as a crucial component of solving the laboratory puzzle. The booth arrangement here, shown in Figure 1.6, was a little different from that in the hypothesis-testing task. Each member received a lattice of circles (Figure 1.7); each circle contained a letter. The lattices of each were identical except for three missing letters. The locations of the missing three were different for each member.

Each member should have been able to fill in his empty circles with information obtained from the others. However, we provided only a very limited means for the necessary exchange of information. Each subject was given pads with two circles joined by a line imprinted on each page. The pads were used by subjects to send messages which could contain only adjoining letters in the sender's matrix. For example, mother could send J-A or Z-T but not J-B. If the letters were in a right-left spatial relationship, the sender indicated that relationship by orienting his pad horizontally. Up-down spatial relationships were conveyed by orienting the pad vertically before writing the message. Members went in turn; mother (A), patient (B), father (C), and sibling (D). Each member could

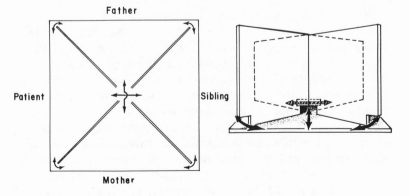

Figure 1.6. *Top and front views of the booths for the lattice task*

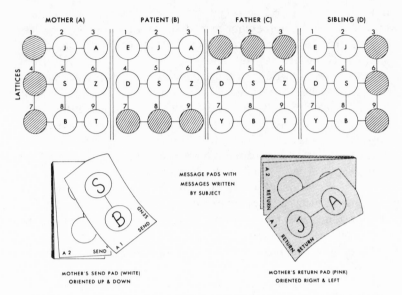

Figure 1.7. *Lattice for the example task used to teach the family the details of the procedure. Also shown are the white and pink pads each family used to send or return messages.*

choose his recipient by sending his message through the appropriate booth slot. The recipient then had to return a message of his own. As soon as an individual filled his empty circles he turned on a finish light. The task was over when all four members had filled their lattices.

We used the lattices in Figure 1.7 to teach families the basic procedures. The actual tasks used more complicated lattices such as those shown in Figure 1.8. These lattices were hard to fill, particularly if family members made up messages randomly. In order to avoid spending the entire night in the laboratory, every family had to devise a strategy for sending messages. Suppose I'm mother and decide to send all of my messages to father. I might choose the following: D-K; H-Z; O-I; Z-B; I-Q; H-Z; K-P. After a while, father, if he's at all attentive to such things, ought to recognize that this is a very restricted set of messages. Both letters in each message come from the edge of the lattice. In later discussion families referred to these simply as "edges." Father might ask himself, "I wonder what she is getting at?" In other words, an additional message is being conveyed by a particular selection and sequencing of messages; this additional message is a form of metacommunication. Many family members in our hypothetical father's position seemed to conclude, "She's sending me all these edge messages to tell me her empty

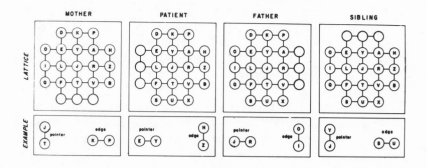

Figure 1.8.   *The twenty-one circle lattice from the second test problem in the lattice task*

circles are on the edge. If I look over what she *hasn't* sent me I'll know where her empties are and be able to fill her up right away." This strategic approach to shortening the task was spontaneously invented by many families; many of them actually referred to this approach as "the edge strategy" when we talked to them at the conclusion of the study. Another way of shortening the task is illustrated by the following hypothetical sibling. Let's say he sends the following set of messages to mother (a (v) indicates that the pad was held vertically for this letter pair): (v) E-L; (v) Y-J; (v) A-R; (v) A-R; (v) E-L; (v) Y-J. This is an even more restricted set of messages; many members receiving a set like this concluded, "He's using his message to point to his empties." The strategic response to a "pointer" is a "joiner." (V) E-L should get a (v) D-E; (v) Y-J should get a (v) K-Y; and (v) A-R a (v) P-A.

In the course of each task every member accumulated a pile of messages. The sender and the page number were indicated on each message, and the color (pink or white) specified whether it was a first initiative (white) or a response (pink). Thus, it was possible at the end of the task to reconstruct exactly who sent which message to whom, in what order.

Schizophrenia and Family Information Processing

Earlier in this chapter we reformulated and extended the concept of the Lidz and Wynne group. We emphasized a missing link in their ideas: they had not explained how family process converted parental abnormalities into deficiency in offspring. Our notion of interpenetrating phases of information processing, on the family level, was a first attempt to supply part of that missing link. We expected families of schizophrenics to show clear-cut deficits in all three phases when compared to families where members had no major psychopathology. In beginning our empirical work it might have been sufficient to compare a small number of families of both kinds in a pilot study. However, even if the two groups could be matched on such important variables as age, intelligence, and social class, families of schizophrenics differ from families of normals in one major respect relevant to our study. Families of schizophrenics have suffered all the traumata associated with having one of their members hospitalized. Even if we studied the families of schizophrenics during periods when the schizophrenic member was not in the hospital, we could expect major residue of the traumata. The shame and stigma would persist; so would the effects of prolonged separation and of continuing treatment (including medications). In order to control this set of extraneous variables we added a third subsample, families containing at least one offspring who had been psychiatrically hospitalized for a major, nonschizophrenic illness: severe character disturbance usually of the impulsive type.[12]

Our entire sample of families — except for one family, as explained in Table 1.3 — was tested with all three puzzles. As shown in the table, the three groups of families were comparable on seven of nine dimensions. The groups differed in only two ways. The first difference was the number of subjects who had attended at least some college. The character disorder group had the smallest number. The influence of the difference on the results is difficult to measure. All three groups were in fact quite well educated: every parent had graduated from high school. The other difference, raw verbal ability scores, is unlikely to have influenced our findings, since this variable had near-zero correlations with virtually every dependent variable in all three studies.

Our laboratory puzzles yielded two types of variables, summarized in Table 1.4. First, there are variables which reflect the quality of the family's solution to the puzzle. We will call this set of variables the *product*. In the hypothesis-testing task we could measure, at the end of the puzzle, changes in the concepts which the members had developed early in the puzzle. Recall that each member received a test before and after hypothesis testing. Did he improve his performance after testing his own hypotheses and seeing the results of testing by others in his family? In the card sorting task we can assess the logical sophistication and consistency of the card sorting scheme. In the example with the P and V letter sequences, using the length of sequences to group the cards is clearly less sophisticated than using the sequential pattern of the letters. On the lattice task, the assessment of the family's solution is simply how many turns it takes them for all members to fill their lattices. The three puzzles also yielded variables assessing the strategies and

TABLE 1.3   CHARACTERISTICS OF FAMILIES IN OUR FIRST SAMPLE

	Normal	Character disorder	Schizophrenic	Probability level
Number of families	5	5	5[a]	
Sex of index	2M, 3F	2M, 3F	2M, 3F	
Number of same-sex sibs	5	3	3	
Age				
Parents	51.6	46.4	51.6	n.s.[b]
Children	20.3	19.0	21.9	n.s.[b]
Number of college-matriculated	15	8	18	$p < .05$[c]
Intelligence (family mean)				
Shipley-Hartford full (max = 80)	62.2	56.8	60.8	n.s.[b]
Verbal (max = 40)	33.5	30.1	34.4	$p < .10$[d]
Abstract (max = 40)	28.7	26.4	26.4	n.s.[b]
WAIS block design (max = 40)	38.0	33.8	36.2	n.s.[b]

a. One family who was given the hypothesis-testing and card sorting tests dropped out of the study before taking the lattice test. They were replaced by a family who had taken the first tests in a pilot phase of the study. The data given here are for the fifteen families who took the first two tests. The replacement family was almost identical to the family who dropped out; thus, between-group comparisons are not significantly affected by the family replacement.

b. $p > .25$ by one-way ANOVA.

c. Chi square.

d. One-way ANOVA.

styles each family used to develop their final product; we call this set the *process* variables. These various measures, which will be described in further detail later, assess the styles, strategies, and interaction patterns that each family used to arrive at the puzzle's solution. Logical connections can be shown between the family's process and its product.

TABLE 1.4   DEPENDENT VARIABLES DERIVED FROM THE THREE PUZZLES

	Hypothesis testing	Card sorting	Lattice
Major focus of puzzle	Information gathering	Information interpretation	Information exchange
Product variable	Concept change	Category elegance	Lattice completion
Process variables	Mutual influence 1. Simply copying 2. Exchange of ideas	Verbal information 1. Clarity 2. Abstraction	Strategies for information exchange
	Risk taking 1. Risking being wrong 2. Risking change from safe course	Responsiveness Control Flexibility	Network of communication

PRODUCT MEASURES: THE QUALITY OF THE SOLUTION

Table 1.5 shows a somewhat more detailed account of the product scores and how our three groups of families fared on these measures. Concept change, in the hypothesis-testing task, was measured in two ways. We'll focus on just one here. Recall that in the hypothesis-testing task we gave each individual a clue sequence. For example, on one puzzle we gave each parent a clue sequence of the type $C\ S\ T_n\ S$ and each child a sequence of the type $C\ T_n\ C$. Most people can get some idea of the type of sequences that are correct from just one example. Thus, parents may think of a principle something like, "One C, one S, then any number of Ts, then another S." Children may think something like, "C, any number of Ts, C." In the course of testing either type is rewarded; thus, parents and children have a chance to learn an entirely new concept. Usually they get the first clue to its existence by watching each other test. Thus, if we assess each member's concept of what is a correct sequence before and after hypothesis testing, the following changes are possible:

1. The concept a family member learned originally is retained and he learns the other generation's concept. We call this *penetration*.
2. He clarifies and makes more precise the concept he held initially — *sharpening*. Frieda Friedkin showed this kind of change.
3. No change. Mother in the Friedkin family showed this.
4. The concept he held initially seems more fuzzy or is lost entirely — *dulling*. Betty Friedkin showed this.

5. The initial concept is given up in favor of the other generation's concept; we call this *reversal*. The father in the Friedkin family showed this.

As Table 1.5 shows, families without serious psychopathology
did well, those with character disorders showed a very modest improvement overall, but families of schizophrenics did poorly. In
particular, almost every case of reversal was in the schizophrenic
group. It is important to emphasize that these families performed

TABLE 1.5   PATTERNS OF FINDINGS FOR THE PRODUCT OR SOLUTION VARIABLES

Major Focus	Variable	Normal	Character disorder	Schizophrenic
Information gathering	Concept change	Good: mostly penetration and sharpening	Fair: penetration sharpening but also some dulling	Poor: frequent no change, dulling and reversal
Interpretation	Card sorts	Good: logical, consistent categories	Fair: some pattern groups unnecessarily split	Poor: frequent illogical categories
Information exchange	Turns to completion	Good: few turns ($\overline{X} = 20$)	Poor: many turns required ($\overline{X} = 38$)	Good: few turns required ($\overline{X} = 25$)

Note: In the original publications the data for the concept change and card sort
variables were displayed graphically. In the hypothesis-testing task, the three groups of
families were equal in their performance on the initial inventories of test problems 1
and 2 and also for the concept changes scores in problem 1. However, the differences in
change scores for problem 2, as indicated in this table, were very large and obvious by
inspection. In the categorization task, the major differences among the three groups
were on the second of two problems, and these too were obvious by inspection. In the
information-exchange task, differences in the three groups were noted primarily on the
second test problem. Here a Kruskal-Wallis analysis of variance yielded a $p < .05$. For
the hypothesis-testing and information-exchange tasks, within-role, across-group
analyses were also done for all four roles (for example, a comparison of fathers of normals with those of character disorders and schizophrenics) to be sure that the overall
group differences were not attributable to differences in just one or two roles. For the
hypothesis-testing task, differences in all four roles replicated the differences found at
the family level; for the information-exchange task the roles showed a nonsignificant
trend in the same direction as the family findings for fathers, patients, and sibs but not
for mothers. Within-role analyses were not possible for the card sort variable in the
categorization task, because this was derived from the performance of the family as a
group.

quite comparably on the initial test, when they had only a single clue. This provides some assurance that as individuals all subjects were equally skilled in working with the puzzles. The major differences occurred after they had worked as a family group testing hypotheses.

Our assessment of the family's solution of the card sorting task rested on a comparison of their sort with an ideal sort which was one that used the pattern system with perfect consistency (the last sort in the sequence illustrated earlier in the chapter). Overall, two deviations from this ideal were noted. First, some sorts used a pattern method but did not fit all the cards belonging in one group together. The usual problem was that sequences with zero repeated elements, such as V P F K and P V K, were placed separately. The second and greater deviation from the ideal was for family members to use a much simpler system or a manifestly illogical system for grouping. In that case the groupings bore no resemblance to our ideal sort. As Table 1.5 shows, the performance here tended to parallel that for the hypothesis-testing task—the families of normals did best, those with schizophrenics did worst, and those with character disorders fell in between.

On the lattice task we can see a very different pattern of findings. The families of the schizophrenics do about as well as families of normals; families of character disorders—on this measure—are clearly the worst. Already we can draw a clear conclusion: families may be deficient in some but not all phases of information processing. Selective deficits are possible. Later we will explore the ramifications of this finding.

PROCESS MEASURES: STYLE, STRATEGY AND INTERACTION

In the hypothesis-testing task, process measures could be derived directly from the set of hypotheses which the family tested. Recall how clearly these data revealed significant process events in the Friedkin family. In deriving variables we concentrated on two aspects of the hypotheses. The first was *mutual influence*; this is a measure of the similarity between hypotheses constructed by different members of the same family. We distinguished two different mutual influence measures. The simple copying score measures the similarity of any hypothesis to any tested in the immediately preceding turn.[13] (For example, for father, we compared father's sequence with those tested by mother and the two children in the immediately preceding turn.) The score is the proportion of an individual's total set of hypotheses (before he indicates he's solved the problem) that are similar or identical to any of the preceding three. Presumably, this variable measures the family's tendency to simply copy or imitate one another's hypotheses. With the second mutual influence measure, exchange of ideas, we were interested in assessing evidence that the family responds to one another's ideas, rather than more slavishly and superficially copying the details of one another's behavior. We measured this by determining the number of hypotheses tested by each individual that were similar[14] to the example given the other generation. For example, consider a case where we gave father an example of the C S T$_n$-S and a child the C T$_n$ C type. The following sequences by a child would be rated as exemplars of the mutual influence idea: C S S S-C; C S T S; C S S S S. The reasoning here is that father, almost invariably, can be counted on to be exploring how to use Ss in a sequence in his first few trials (given the nature of his clue); experience with many families confirms this. If a child (whose clue sequence did not contain an S) constructs sequences of the same kind, he too seems to be exploring the idea that one can use Ss (an idea unlikely to have occurred to him based on his own clue alone).

A second aspect of the hypotheses was what they conveyed about *risk taking* in the family. Here we distinguished two types of risk. Risking being wrong is simply the proportion of tested hypotheses which were incorrect. Since all subjects are equal in intelligence and, more important, were equal in their performance on the initial test (before hypothesis testing), we assume they have comparable grasps of the problem. Thus, a subject who constructs an incorrect hypothesis may not be indicating his confusion or inability to solve the problem; more likely he is showing a willingness to risk an incorrect hypothesis as part of his efforts to gather information. Risking change measures the subject's willingness to construct an hypothesis different from the member who immediately preceded him, even if that hypothesis was correct. This would be changing a good hypothesis in mid-stream.

Table 1.6 summarizes the results. Every finding shows the families of normals and those with schizophrenics at the extremes, with families containing character disorders in the middle. Simple copying and the two risk measures precisely parallel the product findings (concept change, for this puzzle): families of normals highest, families of schizophrenics lowest. Simple copying measures are exactly opposite.

In the card sorting task we used the family's discussion as the sole source of all process variables. The variables and illustrative examples are shown in Table 1.7 and the results in Table 1.8. Recall that the family discussion was tape-recorded, typed, and divided into very brief units—usually three to five words long—called "acts." Each act was then coded along each of the dimensions il-

TABLE 1.6 PROCESS VARIABLES FOR THE HYPOTHESIS-TESTING TASK

Variable	Process	Family type		
		Normal	Character disorders	Schizophrenics
Influence				
Simple copying	Blind copy of other's hypothesis	Low	Medium	High
Exchange of ideas	Recognizing other's ideas	High	Medium	Low
Risk				
Being wrong	Risk of exploration	High	Medium	Low
Change	Differing from another's successful hypothesis	High	Medium	Low

Note: All data shown are for problems 1 and 2 combined. Kruskal-Wallis analysis of variance did not show a significant difference among the three groups on any of the four variables, at the family level of analysis. However, Mann-Whitney tests did show a trend, $p < .22$, in the differences between the lowest and highest groups. Within-role analysis replicated family-level analysis precisely or nearly so as follows: idea exchange measures were replicated by mothers, patients, and sibs; simple copying measures were replicated by patients and sibs; risking wrong hypothesis by mothers, patients, and sibs; and risking change by all four roles. Five of these replications were significant by Kruskal-Wallis at or beyond the .20 level.

lustrated in Table 1.7. The first three dimensions assess the *information processing pool*. Here we test our assumption that an examination of what people say does not reveal how they exchange task-relevant information. If it did, we would expect certain reasonable relationships between what family members said to one another and how they actually performed in the task. In fact, as shown in Table 1.8, there is no parallel between discussion and performance. All families show a high frequency of task talk (over 70 percent of every case). The families all talked about the task—noting the cards, suggesting comparisons, declaring groupings—and little else. From their discussion it would have been impossible to tell that some families were doing a careful and elegant job and others were not. Nor was there any difference between the family groups in their level of abstraction. We might expect a family who solved the puzzle effectively to have a balance between simple observations (alerts), expressed observations of similarities between cards (comparisons), and expressed principles for grouping them (organizations). No differences on any of these measures emerged. Finally, one might expect the best problem solvers to speak most explicitly about the task and their ideas. In fact, the most explicit speakers were the families of schizophrenics and normals, the worst and the best problem solvers on this task; most implicit acts were uttered by the character disorder group, whose solutions were intermediate between those of the normal and the schizophrenic groups.

The next set of variables assessed *responsiveness*. On commonsense grounds we predicted that families in which members pay more attention to each other might do better in a complex problem-solving situation. The results were surprising. If we coded each person's statement according to whether it acknowledged—in any respect—the content or intent of the preceding speaker, we did indeed find families of normals highest, families of schizophrenics lowest, and families of character disorders in between. Surprisingly, we found just the reverse when we coded each statement as to whether or not it very explicitly acknowledged *both* the intent and the content of the preceding statement.

A third set of variables measured the ways family members attempted to *control* one another. In the problem-solving setting a very abrupt and obvious form of control is to interrupt another speaker. Somewhat less forceful, perhaps, is to directly order someone to do something. Interruptions are very decisive actions in that they often accomplish a change in someone else; commands are only requests for change, not change itself. Even subtler is to ask a question; this last, unlike the others, attempts control by indirectly or passively trying to draw attention away from one topic and onto a concern of the speaker. We examined these variables because several theorists and clinical observers had posited that families of schizophrenics constantly conceal their efforts to control each other and thereby reduce their effectiveness as problem-solving groups. As a consequence, we expected to find the subtler control efforts in the poor problem-solving families. Instead, our only discrimination variable—interruptions—showed families of character disorders to be the lowest.

The final set of variables was originally used to measure anxiety, but research published after we designed our own project suggested that these same measures assess *flexibility* instead. Included here are a variety of indices, combined for purposes of the present report; they include several measures of breaks in the fluency of speech: incomplete sentences, repeated words, laughter, and mean-

TABLE 1.7   CODING PROCEDURES USED TO PRODUCE THE PROCESS VARIABLES OF THE CARD SORTING PROCEDURE

Name of code	Type of interaction measured	Examples	
Information processing			
Task-related	The attention to the specific task materials and their problems	Unrelated: "Hey, what about that ballgame last night." "Look at those mikes."	Related: "Put those cards over there." "They both have Ps."
Abstract	The expression of general rules or patterns	No abstraction: "Here's one P." "Now you gotta K."	Moderate abstraction: "Both these cards got Ss." "They both begin with P." High abstraction: "All the ones with Ts go together." "Put that one in V pile."
Explicit	The clarity with which materials and ideas are expressed	Implicit: "They both got the same thing." "I just donno about this one."	Explicit: "They both got Ps." "I don't know about all these MSs."
Responsiveness	The degree of responsiveness: to the immediately preceding speaker (S, speaker; R, respondent)	No responsiveness: S: "I think the card goes over there." R: "My dress is getting tight." Low responsiveness: S: "I think the card goes over there." R: "Mmm."	High responsiveness: S: "I think the card goes over there." R: "No, I'd put it in another pile."

	Definition			
Control				
Breaking	The number of attempted and completed interruptions			
Interruptions	The number of acts prematurely ended by the speech of an interrupter			
Commands and questions		Affirmations: "You're doing it good." "This one has an L."	Questions: "How would you do it?" "Should this pile begin with a T?"	Commands: "Put the NH down." "Just leave it like that."
Flexibility				
Disrupted speech	The degree of disrupted speech flow	No disruption: "V should be down at the bottom there." "You don't count that N and B."	Moderate disruption: "I, I thought this was was right." "You have to go er John put it there."	High disruption: "Well, well I think you see what I . . ." "He said that that he I mean you can't . . ."

TABLE 1.8   PROCESS VARIABLES FOR THE CARD SORTING TASKS

Variable	Family type			Statistically sig. difference	
	Normal	Character disorder	Schizophrenic	Overall	Pairwise
Information processing					
Task-related acts	High	High	High	No	No
Abstract acts	Medium	Medium	Medium	No	No
Explicit acts	High	Low	Medium	No	N > C D
Responsiveness					
All types	High	Medium	Low	Yes	N > S
High	Low	Medium	High	No	N > S
Control					
Interruptions	Medium	Low	High	Yes	N > C D, S > C D
Commands	Low	Low	Low	No	No
Questions	Medium	Medium	Medium	No	No
Flexibility					
Disrupted speech (parents)	Medium	Medium	Low	No	N > S
Speech sequencing (dispersal of disrupted speech)	High	Medium	Low	No	N > S

Note: The data presented combine speech measures from both card sorting tasks. For *information processing variables.* Kruskal-Wallis analysis of variance was not significant for all three variables, but Mann-Whitney for explicit acts showed a trend, $p < .22$, for the difference between the normal and the character disorder groups; this last comparison, at the family level, was replicated by fathers, mothers, and patients. For *responsiveness variables,* "all types" showed a Kruskal-Wallis significance, $p < .20$, and Mann-Whitney, a difference between the normals and schizophrenics, $p < .056$; the finding was replicated by all four roles. For high acknowledgment, Kruskal-Wallis showed no significant difference, but Mann-Whitney showed a difference between normals and schizophrenics, $p < .10$. The finding was replicated by mothers, patients, and sibs. For *control variables,* only interruptions show any significant group differences. For successful and unsuccessful interruptions, Kruskal-Wallis was significant, $p, < .20$, and Mann-Whitney was significant for normals and character disorders, $p < .10$, and character disorders and schizophrenics, $p < .22$. The finding was replicated by all four roles. For successful interruptions alone (where the interrupter effectively silenced the person previously talking), the significance levels dropped; only Mann-Whitney showed a difference between normals and character disorders, $p < .22$; the findings were replicated by all four roles. For *flexibility variables,* Kruskal-Wallis and Mann-Whitney tests were insignificant for family-level analysis of disrupted speech; however, for mothers, Mann-Whitney showed a trend

TABLE 1.8   (continued)

between normals (high) and schizophrenics, $p < .22$. For fathers, Mann-Whitney between normals (high) and schizophrenics (low) was significant, $p < .22$. Patients and sibs did not replicate parental role analyses; for them, the schizophrenic group was the highest, as shown by both Kruskal-Wallis and Mann-Whitney tests. For speech sequencing, Kruskal-Wallis was insignificant but Mann-Whitney showed a difference between normals and schizophrenics, $p < .10$; the finding was replicated for fathers, mothers, and patients.

ingless words and phrases. All these are called "disrupted speech." In addition, there is a special index of continuity of codable acts. In essence this reflects whether disrupted and fragmented speech is bunched together or scattered throughout the family's discussion. Drawing on the work of Goldman-Eisler (1961) and Mishler and Waxler (1968), all these indices were interpreted as measures of special quality of family discussion—namely, its capacity to permit unplanned changes, new directions of thought, changes in topic, and just plain uncertainty. This quality of speech—if not excessive—was viewed by both Goldman-Eisler and Mishler and Waxler as a significant verbal contribution to formulating and solving problems. Table 1.8 shows that, in general, the findings for both these measures paralleled success in arriving at a good card sort solution.

In the lattice task, variables were derived to assess process directly from the sequence of messages sent and received by all members of the family. Recall that in this task families of normals and schizophrenics did well but families of character disorders did poorly. The major process measures for this task were those of *strategy*. As Table 1.9 shows, the families of character disorders were deficient in the use of the edge strategy, where senders and receivers use letters drawn from the lattice edge in order to improve each other's chances of obtaining a useful message. However, this difference was obtained in the first of two test problems we gave the families. The three groups of families differed in overall effectiveness of information exchange on the second lattice. There an insignificant trend showed superiority of the families of schizophrenics in the use of the pointer strategy (that is, family members used messages to point to their empty circles). Some families used a more complicated strategy on this second task. They seemed to be sending messages that ruled out particular edges, as far as the recipient was concerned. For example, in the twenty-one circle lattice illustrated in Figure 1.7, if patient sent mother the message (v) T-U he would be saying to her, in effect, "You can rule out the S-U-X edge for me, it's full." Five families, none of which were in the character disorder group, clearly used this strategy on the second task. Taken together these data suggest that the inferiority of the character disorder group arose from its inability (or unwillingness) to use one of several strategies as consistently as the other two groups. It may be that individuals in such families get desperate. Instead of trying to keep all channels open by sending messages to everyone else, they pick a single person in the family as the recipient. Table 1.9 shows that the magnitude of this behavior is very much higher in families of character disorders. (It is of course

TABLE 1.9   PROCESS VARIABLES FOR THE LATTICE TASK, BY FAMILY TYPE

Variable	Family type			Statistically sig. difference	
	Normal	Character disorder	Schizophrenic	Overall	Pairwise
Strategies					
Edge	Medium	Low	High	Yes	N > C D S > C D
Pointer	Low	Medium	High	No	S > N
Edge ruleout	Three families	No families	Two families	No	N > C D S > C D
Person selection	Low	High	Medium	Yes	C D > S C D > N

Note: Data shown are those from combining both problems, except for edge ruleout which is from problem 2. However, in this note we will indicate findings from the two separate tasks. For *edge,* Kruskal-Wallis was significant, $p < .20$, with Mann-Whitney showing differences between the normal and character disorder group, $p < .22$, and character disorder and schizophrenic, $p < .056$. Approximately the same significance levels were achieved for problem 1 but there were no significant differences for problem 2. The findings were precisely replicated only for sibs. For *pointer,* Mann-Whitney showed a significant difference between normals and schizophrenics for both problems combined and for problem 2, $p < .22$; the difference between normal and character disorders on problem 2 was also significant, $p < .22$. Kruskal-Wallis was not significant for any of these. The findings were replicated for fathers, patients, and sibs. For *edge ruleout,* we used an arbitrary cut-off score of 50 in a numerical measure to designate a family as showing evidence of use of this strategy; Mann-Whitney showed a difference between normal and character disorder, $p < .22$, and schizophrenic and character disorder, $p < .22$. For *person selection,* analyses for both problems together showed Kruskal-Wallis significant, $p < .01$; this pattern was attributable to differences on problem 2. For problem 1 there was almost no difference among the three groups. The findings for both problems together were replicated by fathers, mothers, and patients.

possible that this selectivity preceded and was in some way responsible for the character disorder group's failure to develop consistent and effective strategies and was ultimately responsible for their poor information exchange product.)

UNDERSTANDING THE RELATIONSHIP OF PRODUCT AND PROCESS

Not surprisingly, the families of normals stand out as the most competent group. They were successful in all three phases of information processing: gathering, interpretation, and exchange. The family processes supporting this competence appear to be a sharing of ideas during hypothesis testing (high exchange of idea scores), a willingness to take risks, a modest level of acknowledgment of each other's remarks, flexible speech styles, and the use of effective information-exchange strategies. In contrast, families of schizophrenics have a much more restricted skill. They are capable of exchanging information within the family. Indeed, they seem quite sensitive to the details of each other's behavior; they copy or imitate each other's hypotheses and, more frequently than others, acknowledge with great care the intent of each other's statements. This sensitivity to one another may help them elaborate efficient strategies for information exchange. However, when dealing with information from outside the family they are timid, avoid risks, and are quite rigid in speech style. The families with character disorders emerge as a distant third group; they are not simply halfway between the other two. Their unique difficulty is highlighted by the information-exchange tasks, where they are slow to reach completion and do not elaborate effective exchange strategies, in comparison to the other two groups. In the information-exchange puzzle they develop a maladaptive tendency for members to pick just one other person with whom to communicate. In general, the isolation of members in these families seems confirmed by the findings of vagueness in verbal discussion style (fewer explicit acts — see Table 1.8) and the infrequency of clear control attempts (interruptions).

In sum, we found three distinctive modes by which families processed information. The first was *collaborative effectiveness* with externally given information. Here, families melded information gathering, interpretation, and exchange to rapidly and accurately formulate a shared conception of the puzzles' solutions. Our families of normals fell into this group. A second mode was an *isolated independence* of family members dealing with externally given information on their own. Our families with character disorders, falling into this group, were probably held back in their ability to gather and interpret information by their inability to exchange ideas and observations among themselves. The third mode was a *closed-in hyperresponsiveness* of family members to one another. The families of schizophrenics, falling into this group, seem impaired in their capacity to gather and interpret outside information because they were so highly attentive to the details of each other's verbal and nonverbal behavior. All in all, families did seem to function as information processing groups. They had distinctly different modes — each mode characterized by a particular configuration of strengths of deficits in gathering, interpretation, and exchange.

The broader question that prompted this inquiry into information processing concerned schizophrenia. Recall that our studies of information processing were meant to fill a critical gap that existed between studies of the psychological function of parents and the developing schizophrenic syndrome in the offspring. We had found a distinctive mode of information processing in our families of schizophrenics. Could we now go back and begin to fill in the missing link? By the time this first phase in our work was completed we felt this question was becoming moot. Indeed, in our subsequent work we have never gone back to re-address this question. Instead, we have pursued the substance of our first findings in which we could see distinctly such different modes of group information processing in families. These processes seemed arresting in their own right, whether or not they helped unlock the riddle of schizophrenia.

Beyond Family Information Processing:
The Family Construes the Laboratory

Beginning with our first findings on family information processing, it would have been possible to piece together a set of hypotheses on how these family patterns might explain the symptomatology in character disorder and schizophrenia. We might have pursued our initial objective: to relate a pattern of skills and deficits in family information processing to a pattern of skills and deficits in the identified patients within those families. However, a great many observations we made of the first sixteen families we tested in our laboratory gave us serious doubts about whether we were indeed measuring a pattern of family skills or deficits. We became quite intrigued, instead, with a different explanation of what we were observing.

The concept of "skill" implies that all test subjects are equal in their wish to do well but some do better than others because of an intrinsic superiority of some kind. Our families were motivated, to be sure. The word "embroiled" might better describe some. They all became heavily engaged in the task: they listened attentively to instructions, worked without slack, and seemed to leave, in many cases, quite reluctantly. However, many families seemed to have their own objective—and it was not always to do as well as possible. For example, in the Friedkin family, father, Frieda, and Betty seemed to work together as if their principal objective was the exclusion of mother. Mother's scattered behavior might reflect a complementary objective—to be excluded by the others. This family's objective took precedence over the objective to do the task as well as possible. Our excitement began when we realized our procedure was capturing the consequences of these family-produced objectives with great clarity. The data from the Friedkins—the changes on the inventories and the patterns of hypothesis testing—clearly revealed the splits and alliances in the family and their devastating effect on family problem solving. We sensed that our families were writing their own script and playing it out with intensity while leaving a vivid, objective record of their deeds in the quantitative data of the laboratory procedure.

We became more attentive to the details of their reactions. From the moment we met these families at the door of the laboratory or in the lobby of the hospital building in which they were tested, things started to happen. Some families were clearly out to have a good time; the visit was something of an adventure. These families seemed to be the ones that had the least difficulty understanding the experimental instructions. If someone didn't quite understand, the others quickly provided him with useful assistance or encouraged him to ask the tester. Later, when they talked about the instructions (during those procedures when they were permitted to talk), they had no misperceptions of the instructions. In contrast, other families seemed to dread the procedure. They came to the laboratory out of, it seemed, a sense of duty. Nothing was interesting or intriguing, but much was frightening. These families typically had difficulty understanding the instructions. If one member seemed uncertain another would offer a distorted version that often was much more severe than the original. For example:

Son: Did he [the tester] say we had to agree?
Father: Yes. He said we *had* to agree.

The Raab family provides a clear example of this kind of reaction. The Raabs felt that they could never be successful, never prove themselves in the outside world. Paradoxically, father, aged fifty-one, had done quite well as a patent lawyer in several industrial concerns and was now teaching law at a small local university. However, he always thought he was a failure as a father and was concerned that his children—a daughter and three sons—would fail. Mother, also fifty-one, was an anxious and preoccupied woman. She too considered herself and her family to be a failure. Like father, she constantly goaded her children, from their earliest years, and always anticipated the worst. In fact, the children's performance ultimately confirmed the parents' conception of the family. Susan, twenty-six, had left home several years earlier to work as a secretary, a position that frustrated and disappointed her, after graduating from college. Dick, twenty-four, had been hospitalized for a serious depressive episode, and Peter, twenty-two, was currently in the hospital with a diagnosis of acute schizophrenia. Frank, twenty-one, had trouble staying in school and was receiving psychotherapy; his brothers thought it inevitable that he would be hospitalized. Despite the family's long-standing pessimism, now more clearly justified, they presented themselves to strangers with a swagger and verbal boisterousness. They seemed, superficially, to be cocky and competitive and able to take on anything. Some of this pattern was clear in the early minutes of the family's arrival in the laboratory. We tested the foursome of the parents, Dick, and Peter. When they arrived in the laboratory, the two boys ostentatiously fingered all the equipment and brazenly poked their noses into closets and around curtains. There was much verbal banter between parents and children. The magnitude of the family's underlying anxiety in the test situation was only revealed after one of the puzzles—the hypothesis-testing task—was over. During that task the Raabs tried hard to maintain closed and cocky ranks. All except Peter had tested a restricted range of hypotheses. Further, although the rest of the family stopped testing very early—apparently to convince themselves and the tester how easy the task was—Peter continued to test his rather wild hypotheses (did not turn on his "finish" light) for many trials. Peter's private inventories, the assessment of his own grasp of the problem, showed that he was, in fact, having great difficulty—more so than the rest of the family. His solitary and obviously inept behavior posed a real problem for the family. They could not accept it as a reflection of his genuine difficulty with a complex task. Instead, they grew angry at him, believing he had shown the whole family to be weak. Mother arose from her seat, furious. "You traitor," she yelled, "you screwed us up purposely." She struck him hard across the shoulder. Peter looked dazed and intensely mortified. The physical attack was terrifying to watch. The word "traitor," however, carried even greater significance. It conveyed that in the testing situation the family once again felt besieged; they felt, indeed, that they faced an overwhelming enemy. They protected themselves with brashness before the procedure began and—except for poor Peter—with quick, decisive, and uniform behavior in the test. Peter was just too confused to go along with this. He tried to cover it up by using another component of the family facade—zaniness. But the family perceived him as breaking ranks and exposing them all.

It would have made matters much easier if we had been sufficiently observant to note—even informally—some systematic relationships between the feeling states of the families and their performance on the procedures. We were not. At best we came to suspect strongly that there was great variety among families in the kind of feelings they had about the test situation but not much change in such feelings during a single family's problem-solving efforts. We wondered if we might go backward. Could we reconstruct, in some way, what the family might be feeling about the laboratory from its performance on the problem-solving task?

One approach was to study the interrelationships between the major variables assessing the family's problem-solving product (the quality of the problem's solution) and its process (the strategies and approaches used by the family to produce a solution). We used principal components factor analysis.[15] We thought we might identify, by their common loading on one or more factors, a group of variables which might be especially likely to suggest what the family's underlying feeling states were. We had to reduce our sample size to fourteen, since this was the total number of families tested by all three procedures (recall that one family dropped out for the information-exchange task and was replaced by another who had gone through a pilot version of the first two tasks). Thus, our factor analysis, which had to use fewer variables than families, was a very preliminary, tentative analysis. Nonetheless, the results proved interesting. We selected the following twelve variables for analysis:

1. Shipley-Hartford intelligence score. This was the full-scale *raw* score; thus, this is a measure of ability—uncorrected for chronologic age—and not IQ.

From the hypothesis-testing task we chose:

2. Concept change score. This score, not described previously, was a numerical equivalent of qualitative changes (penetration, sharpening, no change, dulling, and reversal).

3. Simple copying score. This measured the degree to which an individual's hypotheses were identical, or nearly so, to those generated by others in the preceding turn.

4. Risking change. This score measured the frequency with which an individual tested a hypothesis different from the immediately preceding one if the preceding one was right or constructed a similar one if the preceding one was wrong.

From the card sorting task we chose:

5. Card sorting score. This was a numerical equivalent of the qualitative distinction among the effective and ineffective sorts we made in Chapter 2.

6. Level of abstraction—organization score. This was the proportion of task-related acts which expressed some idea about how to group the cards. Examples: "All the ones with Ts go together." "Put 'em in a pile so that they make a pyramid."

7. Level of abstraction—implicit score. This was the proportion of task-related acts for which the referents were not clear. Examples: "Those two things go together." "Put 'em here." A listener with nothing else to go by would have no idea to which cards the speaker refers. An explicit act is: "Put the three with the NHs here."

8. Acknowledgment score. This is the proportion of codable acts which show any acknowledgment of the preceding statement.

9. Disrupted speech. This is the proportion of acts which show any disruptions in speech fluency such as repetitions, fragments, and filled pauses.

From the lattice task we chose:

10. Turns to completion. We used the number of turns to fill in the lattice required by the person last in his family to finish. We used the score only from the second lattice task because it best discriminated among the three subsamples of the study.

11. Edge score. The proportion of total messages sent by an individual, before he completed his lattice, in which both letters were drawn from an edge. This score should reflect, to some extent, the individual's general propensity to use information-exchange strategies.

12. Person selection score. The degree to which an individual selects just one recipient for all his messages.

For the factor analysis we computed mean scores on each of the twelve variables for all fourteen families. These family means were the data for the principal component factor analysis. In other words, our sample was fourteen families where the family was treated as a single sampling unit and with the family mean as the principal datum. Intercorrelations showed 11 of 66 correlations significant beyond the .05 level (and 4 of these 11 beyond the .02 level). Table 1.10 shows the results of principal component factor analysis followed by varimax rotation.

Factor I contains a product variable (turns to completion) and two process variables (acknowledgment and person selection scores). All three reflect the effectiveness with which the family dealt with cues or information from others within the family. We dubbed this factor *within-family responsiveness*; an ungainly

TABLE 1.10 PRINCIPAL COMPONENT FACTOR ANALYSIS WITH VARIMAX ROTATION OF TWELVE SCORES DRAWN FROM THE THREE PROBLEM-SOLVING TASKS (N = 14)

Procedure	Variable	Factors			
		I Within-family responsiveness	II Environment responsiveness	III Abstract expressive style	IV Explicit expressive style
	Variance accounted for	23.53	23.25	19.07	14.06
Shipley-Hartford	Intelligence	0.16	**0.71**	-0.45	-0.19
Hypothesis testing	Concept change	0.52	**0.71**	-0.18	-0.17
	Simple copying	-0.12	**-0.74**	-0.43	-0.02
	Risking change	0.36	0.43	0.15	**-0.77**
Card sort	Solution adequacy	-0.01	**0.92**	-0.08	-0.11
	Organizing comments	-0.09	-0.05	**-0.85**	0.07
	Implicit comments	-0.12	-0.21	-0.37	**-0.66**
	Acknowledge response, all types	**0.87**	0.06	0.25	-0.06
	Disrupted speech	0.30	0.26	**-0.81**	-0.01
Lattice	Turns to completion	**-0.81**	-0.02	0.41	-0.22
	Edge messages	0.39	-0.12	-0.32	**0.72**
	Particular person selection	**-0.84**	-0.28	0.10	-0.04

Note: Factor loadings greater than .60 are shown in boldface.

name, perhaps, but not inaccurate. Factor II contains two product scores, card sort and concept change. Intelligence (or, more properly, intellectual skill), also loading on factor II, is also a product score. One process score, simple copying, has a negative loading on this dimension. Those product scores all refer to the family's ability to gather or interpret information or cues from outside the family, so we call this factor *environment responsiveness*. The negative loading for simple copying implies what we already know: families where members just copy or imitate each other's hypotheses cannot effectively deal with external cues. Factor III contains two process language scores: level of organization and disrupted speech. High scorers are always talking about organizational schemes, based on some kind of abstraction or another. Psycholinguistic studies conducted by Goldman-Eisler (1961) suggest a relationship between cognitive abstraction and disrupted speech: individuals usually show disrupted speech (pauses, stutters, and so on) when they are trying to formulate and express an abstraction. Thus, level of organization and disrupted speech may be different aspects of the same underlying process. We call this factor *abstract expressive style*. Finally, factor IV has negative loadings for risking change and implicit acts and a positive loading for frequency of edges. This was and is a perplexing factor. We suggested that the nature of the dimension was best conveyed by the negative loading on implicit speech. In other words, this factor assessed an explicit expressive style. In the lattice task, edge messages also support clear communication. A close study of their role in that task shows they were used early, primarily in the first task, as a means by which family members oriented themselves to the task. Factor IV and factor I both refer to communication within the family but in different ways. Factor IV emphasizes clarity of communication from the perspective of the outside observer, who can easily guess the referents of communication. Factor I, within-family responsiveness, measures how well family members understood one another. In particular, number of turns to completion on the lattice task assesses how well each member understood the others, whether or not an outside observer understood what they were up to. With this contrast in mind, then, we can label factor IV *explicit, orienting expressive style*. How does risking change fit in? Frankly, not easily. We can only speculate that if one member fails to imitate the hypothesis of the member who preceded him, he is introducing ambiguity and unclarity into the communicational stream. This may be particularly true if a member imitates a hypothesis that was wrong; the member being imitated might say to himself, "I wonder what he saw in that bomb."

The factors divide into two relatively neat subgroups. Factors I and II emphasize the quality of experience within the family, the clarity and precision of family members' sensitivity to one another and to the outside world. Factors III and IV have more to do with surface manifestations of the family, how the family appears to the outside observer. A reexamination of the specific variables bears this out. Factors I and II have loadings from all but one of the nonverbal measures. All these variables take into account the particular stimuli facing the family at the time the measurement is made and serve as an estimate of his subjective experience of the presence and patterning of these stimuli. For example, the concept change score assesses the patterning the family sees in an objectively specified array of stimuli. Number of turns to completion on the lattice task reflects the extent to which members came to comprehend the location of the empty circles in each other's lattices. Even the one measure, the acknowledgment score, depends on assessment of the intent of the previous statement (the stimulus) and, then, whether this intent was perceived by the responder. The reverse is true for most of the variables that have high loadings on factors III and IV: organization and implicit level of abstraction scores; edge messages and disrupted speech. These scores reflect frequency counts of certain forms of expressive behavior. The score does not depend on our knowing the stimulus situation faced by the subject or his subjective grasp of that situation.[16] We were also intrigued that three of the four measures of verbal behavior had high loading on factors III or IV only. We had already known that on the card sorting procedure most of the variables of verbal interaction were not very discriminating among our three groups of families. Indeed, we have already commented that most verbal interaction sounded as if it were strictly business: it almost always referred to puzzles, observations, ideas, conclusions. To judge from their verbal interaction, all families have set as their own objective the successful completion of the task. In fact, however, words may be a smokescreen, as experienced family therapists have known for years. Conventional "task talk" in our laboratory may have hidden major differences in families' orientation toward and feelings about the task. At the time of their original publication, these were the first studies to compare systematically verbal and nonverbal measures of family interaction; we came away with an impression that words conceal and actions reveal. Thus, factor analysis did seem to yield an interesting and relevant discrimination among variables. This discrimination was supported by data, presented in Table 1.11, which showed that of the four factors, only factors I and II distinguished among our three groups of families.

TABLE I.II   PROFILE ANALYSIS OF FACTOR SCORES

	Factor				
Group	I	II	III	IV	Mean
Normal (N = 5)	+.221⎤	+.170⎤	+.072	+.082	+.136⎤
Character disorder (N = 5)	−.182⎦	−.039⎤	+.061	−.131	−.073⎦
Schizophrenic (N = 4)	.042	−.183⎦	−.118	+.098	−.040

	Analysis of Variance				
Source	df	MS	F	Full df	Cons. df
Tests	3	.003	<1		
Groups	2	.234	5.70a	2,11	2,11
Groups X tests (profile)	6	.041	1.17	6,33	2,11

Note: Brackets connect pairs of means significantly different by the Tukey test at the .05 level.
a. $p < .025$.

Since factors I and II emphasize the family's perceptions and experience, it seems reasonable to use these two factors in an effort to reconstruct how the families felt about the laboratory environment. How does it feel to be a member of a family as it enters and works in our laboratory? Consider a family who achieves high scores on factors I and II. These scores suggest that while working together the family members are very responsive to one another and, at the same time, are increasingly able to detect the subtle patterns and regularities in the stimuli of the laboratory puzzles. If each member is responsive to his environment and each member is in turn sensitive to all the others in the family, the cumulative, subjective effect is one of amplification. I know the world through my own senses but also through those of my family. Put somewhat more passively, the environment flows in through all members. There is no sense of a boundary separating us from the outer world. My sense of being able to detect order in the world is enhanced by my family membership.

Consider the subjective experience, by contrast, of being in a family high on factor I, within-family responsiveness, but low on factor II, environment responsiveness. In this family I am exquisitely sensitive to others' percepts and thoughts as they are sensitive to mine but none of us can perceive the structure and pattern of the outer world. There is here a very different form of amplification. I know the percepts and thoughts of others directly by my own experience, but also because their thoughts and percepts reflect, in part, responses to yet other family members. This intensifying exchange goes on in the absence of any successful apprehension of the environment. In time, my sense of my family comes to dominate me; it comes to constitute, while I am with them, a preemptory and bounded sensory world with the outer environment in the background, distant, pale, and unordered.

A third type of family also attracted our attention, the ones low on both factors I and II. Here, members fail to grasp any significant ordering in the environmental stimuli and are clearly unresponsive to and probably isolated from one another. We can imagine each member lost in his own world with a sense of being overwhelmed by an environment that seems capricious and chaotic.

Table 1.11 shows that these three types correspond to the three types of families — classified by the psychopathology of offspring — used in this study. Families of normals were high on factors I and II; families of character disorders were low on both; families of schizophrenics were high only on factor I.

The component scores of each of the factors were derived, of course, during the procedures or at their conclusion. It is highly speculative to suggest that those scores could be used to reconstruct feeling states the family had as they entered the laboratory. Nonetheless, our subjective impression, drawn from experiences with families like the Raabs, was that such feelings often — if not always — existed from the family's first moments and persisted in some measure throughout the testing. Moreover, clinical data indicated that such feeling states characterized the family when they met with therapists other than professionals.

The Concept of a Shared Construct

Our assortment of intuitive hunches, informal observations, and data fragments suggested that some shared feeling state in the family was reflected in their performance in the laboratory, particularly in their nonverbal behavior. Their feelings about themselves, the task, and its objectives were so different from family to family that our first model, which embraced a concept of family skills, seemed very incomplete. We developed a new model, a model which drew heavily on the work of others. Although the new model remained tied to our laboratory observations, it tried to consider the relationship between these observations and the family's everyday life.

Some aspects of the model were drawn from individual psychology. The concept of set which had been carefully and systematically investigated in the great German psychology laboratories by the turn of the century, refers to a relatively fleeting attitude or conception of the task which can be induced in subjects by instructions and then has a major governing role on their behavior. For example, colored nonsense syllables were shown tachistoscopically. The experimenter used special instructions to induce a set or expectation for perceiving the color or the syllable, or the number of letters, and so on. Subjects saw what they were prepared to see. At about the same time, in neighboring Vienna, Freud introduced the concept of transference. Freud found that the subject's past experience, from years before, was brought to the observational setting; it highly colored his view of the setting, particularly of the psychoanalyst. However, until the psychoanalytic treatment had progressed, the patient could not remember these experiences; only their indirect influences on the patient's conscious perceptions of the psychoanalyst were known. The concept of transference has had a major influence on our work, though it did not explicitly enter this newer model. A third concept, much more recently elaborated by George Kelly (1955), was that of the personal construct. Kelly proposed that each individual builds up, through experience, his own conception or personal construct of his world. The content and formal properties of these constructs can be determined by objective testing. The constructs determine behavior in almost any setting by serving, for the individual, as guiding conceptions about the underlying nature of that setting and how it must be dealt with.

Kelly's concept was appealing. Our families seemed to have shared constructs of the laboratory setting which they had readied before they came or formed almost instantaneously after they arrived. Some families felt the situation was safe and masterable; others felt it was overwhelming and dangerous. Most families did not seem to recognize the subjectivity of their views.[17] On the contrary, they believed that their concept was objective, factual, based on evidence. Frightened families thought that we, the researchers, were really up to some kind of mischief, and confident families trusted us, though they had no iron-clad evidence that we were not, in fact, connivers.

Despite the charms of the concept of shared construct, however, it is immediately apparent that there are problems with it. The first problem is the concept of "shared." Constructs or beliefs or conceptions are entities ordinarily residing in the heads of single individuals. To be sure, we are familiar with groups acquiring shared beliefs and convictions, adhering closely to them and indeed having their behavior with one another and with other groups dominated by such beliefs. Kluckhohn and Strodtbeck have shown quite clearly that subcultures within a Southwest community were so dominated (Kluckhohn and Strodtbeck, 1960). Political parties and political action groups that are ideologically pure and committed share a distinct view of the world which shapes their strategies. There was even some evidence that shared sets or shared conceptions could be induced through experimental instructions in ad hoc laboratory groups. Olmstead (1954), for example, told one set of groups to work together to solve a puzzle in a way that made everyone happy and contrasted their behavior with groups told to work at the same problem in a way that would produce the best solution most efficiently. When the concept of shared constructs was applied to families it raised the question of in what sense the family members share a conception of the test situation. If a family is frightened and suspicious, their shared views may reflect, for example, the powerful influence of a single paranoid member whom everyone else is humoring. Or the family might be split; is it not possible for the parents to be frightened and the children confident?

Our conception is that families do develop genuinely shared constructs in which all members believe. A construct may have originated in the strident or impassioned beliefs of a particular individual, but when we see the family, everyone has come to experience and construe the test situation in similar terms. It will seem paradoxical to allow that some families do not agree on certain, perhaps more superficial, aspects of the test situation. For example, families disagree on which is the best strategy for solving a problem or what constitutes the best solution. However, these disagreements are more apparent than real. We propose that such splits are sustained by an underlying agreement on the nature of test situation; that is, the test situation itself permits such splits. One shared formula might be, "There is no single or realistic way of solving this puzzle; several views are correct." A more extreme formula of the same is, "This place is one way for some of us and another way for the rest. The staff here are hostile to me and my brother but are really pretty nice when it comes to Mom and Dad."

The concept of "construct" presents a second problem. This term is borrowed from the language of science and usually refers to a rationally fashioned set of hypotheses about the outside world based on careful collection of data. In the present context it can mistakenly suggest an unemotional and dispassionate theory that the family—functioning as a team of scientific co-investigators—develops over time. This is most emphatically not the sense in which we use the term. Most of the premises undergirding the family's view of the test situation—their conscious, existential grasp of the laboratory—consists of emotionally toned and fleeting attributions of intent to the research staff ("What did he really mean by that smile?"); brief and fragmented fantasies about what is happening (what will happen to the data, what's going on in the room next door, what will the apparatus really do?); and a conception of what will happen to the family (will it succeed or fail, stay together or split apart?). The underlying construct that unites these attributions of intent, fantasies, and conceptions of the future is probably rarely conscious or articulate. It is certainly never expressed verbally to the research staff. It is intensely emotional.[18]

A Typology of Shared Constructs

Our model sketching out three phases of information processing in families was primarily descriptive: it served mainly to highlight and group certain aspects of observable family interaction. Our newer model starts out with descriptive intent: it attempts at the outset only to classify the constructs families may form in a test situation. The model goes beyond the descriptive in three significant ways, however. First, in classifying shared constructs, it is concerned with aspects of family life that lie below the surface, aspects that must be inferred from surface behaviors, and—most important—aspects that serve a controlling function. Families form a shared construct of the laboratory first; this construct then serves to shape the family's particular information-processing patterns and problem solutions. The proposition that shared constructs act as control factors is a rudiment of a truly explanatory theory. A second extension beyond the descriptive is our attempt to characterize families by the kinds of constructs they form in the test situation. The feeling state with which the family enters the laboratory persists relatively undiluted, throughout the testing. This, of course, is part of the theory, not a hard fact. We posit that the persistence of this state is no accident but reflects some fundamental feature of the family. However, it can be argued that the shared construct is a feature that may be clearly revealed only in a laboratory or, of even more concern, only in a laboratory connected with a psychiatric hospital. This last is, of course, entirely possible, since all people—whether in families or not—have strong, though highly variable, feelings about psychiatric hospitals. Our theory contends otherwise. It posits that the laboratory elicits such constructs because it is ambiguous, novel, and challenging, and—perhaps most important—because it presents the whole family with an externally given problem to which it must provide some solution. The shared construct which emerges in the laboratory, we propose, tells us something about how the family may react to a variety of novel, challenging problems in its everyday life. Examples of these might include moving into a new neighborhood, traveling to strange places, dealing with schools—especially during the novel period just after the first child matriculates—and negotiating with various family-oriented agencies such as churches, welfare programs, and neighborhood associations. In other words, a family's shared construct tells us something about how the family deals with problems in its own social world. Thus, our typology of constructs becomes, at least in a limited sense, a typology of families. This postulate is fundamental to testing the model.

A description of our typology must begin with the three types of families which emerged from our speculations using combinations of factor I, within-family responsiveness, and Factor II, environment responsiveness. Recall that we speculated about three such combinations: a family high on both factors which seemed to embrace and amplify the environment for each of its members; a family high on I and low on II which seemed embroiled in its responses to one another; and a family low on both which seemed to consist of individuals helpless and isolated in their own worlds. In putting more flesh on a theory of shared constructs in families we extended these distinctions; our new proposals assumed that these different types of family experience were typical for them and occurred in other settings as well.

One additional set of observations was included in the shared construct model. As we began pilot testing with a new group of families, a third dimension — in addition to within-family responsiveness (factor I) and environment responsiveness (factor II) — seemed important. Some families were quick to change their approach as new data became available to them; others rigidly stuck to the provisional solutions they formulated early in the task. From an experiential point of view, the latter seemed to have their experience of the immediate present dominated by their sense of their own past; the former were constantly experiencing the problem situation as novel and without precedent. We have added this third dimension to our description of family types. We call it *closure*. The descriptions of family types are generalizations of those provided by the combinations of factors I and II and the addition of closure.

Environment-sensitive.[19] In most situations, when a problem is presented, family members jointly perceive the problem as "out there," and its analysis and solution have no personal relevance for the family. The search for a solution can be governed by general principles of logic. This fundamental consensus on the nature of the problem has two consequences. First, the family jointly experiences a need to observe as many cues as possible. Each individual recognizes that the others' percepts and thoughts are a response to or an understanding of the externally given problem. Therefore, if they are different from his own, he will include them among the various approaches or solutions he is considering. He will accept or reject them based on their objective accuracy — not simply because the other has made a strong case for them. Because individuals share their observations and ideas completely, they have a broad and common base of cues and provisional solutions upon which to base their final conclusions. Thus, the family will agree on the final solution to the problem because it is based on a fully shared set of cues and hypotheses. Since each member depends exclusively on information from the environment, gained by his own efforts or vicariously through another member, the family will delay closure until it has examined as much evidence as possible. Each individual recognizes that the solution he agrees to is a result of sharing ideas within his family as well as of his own efforts to solve the problem.

Interpersonal distance-sensitive.[20] In these families there is a joint perception that problem analysis and solution are simply a means by which each individual can demonstrate to the others his independence from the family and his own decisiveness and mastery. Each individual experiences accepting suggestions, observations, or ideas of others as a sign of his own weakness. At the extreme, each member sees the externally given problem as a segment of his own personal universe, which operates according to laws and values unique for him. According to this formulation, his actions and their consequences simply cannot be useful to or be evaluated by others in the family. In order to demonstrate their independence, individuals may reach decisions quickly based on little information, or they may accumulate information indefinitely and refuse to come to closure until long after others do.

Consensus-sensitive.[21] In this kind of family there is a joint perception that the analysis and solution of the problem are simply a means to maintain a close and uninterrupted agreement at all times. Even transient dissent is not tolerated. This is a consequence of viewing the laboratory and its tasks as potentially harmful and disruptive of inter-member ties. It is postulated that the problem is experienced "in here." Family members will quickly surrender their ideas or have others accept them without reference to the externally given cues concerning problem solution. Thus, each individual's personal experience with the externally given problem and its cues is not fully expressed in the family nor fully developed by the individual on his own. The family reaches its hastily forged consensus early in the task. If cues and information continue to be provided, the family distorts or oversimplifies them in order to justify its initial collective solution. Each individual may continue to respond to this inflow of cues. When working with his family, however, he is likely to regard cues from without as unpredictable and indecipherable. His sense of regularity and structure will be derived from the predictability of his family's response to each new piece of information, not from his own scheme for ordering and patterning the cues themselves.

Distinctions analogous to those we made between environment and consensus-sensitive families had been made by others. (Here we will consider research done in nonclinical settings with families who are not in a treatment program. In Chapter 2 we will focus on clinical research, which is a critical bridge to the next phase of our own empirical work.) Strodtbeck (1958), in his study of family values and achievement, summarized a world view typical of Jewish families in Eastern European *shtetl* culture: "The external world for the Jews was hostile, to be sure, but it was by nature solvable . . . Old culture Jewish beliefs appear to be congruent in many, if not all, respects with such a belief in a rational mastery of the world" (p. 151). Strodtbeck stressed that the families were intensely aware of and open to the wider community and to the technical, impersonal aspects of culture. In contrast, families in Southern Italy viewed the external world as unpredictable and unmasterable: "The unpredictable intervention of fate may be for good or for evil, but *Destino* is omnipresent. If a man works all his life for something which *Destino* may deny him, well then, why should men look so far ahead?" (p. 151). Describing the boundedness of the Southern Italian family, Strodtbeck wrote: "*La famiglia* in the Southern Italian culture was an inclusive social world. The basic mores of this world were primarily family mores; everyone outside the family was viewed with suspicion. Where the basic code was family solidarity there was a strong feeling that the family should stay together—physically close together" (p. 150). These distinctions, in terms of beliefs about order and mastery of the external world and solidarity among members, bear a strong similarity to our own: Jewish families from the "old culture" are environment-sensitive and, to a degree, Southern Italians are consensus-sensitive. There are some respects in which there is not a specific similarity. For example, we discuss the interdependence among members as a prime constituent of the family world view; Strodtbeck, however, discusses power relations as instrumental in maintaining such collective views. These differing formulations are not logically incompatible and might profitably be combined in future theoretical work.

It is significant that Strodtbeck formulated the distinctions between Jewish and Italian families in an effort to explain the ingredients of success and upward social mobility in the American culture. Indeed, similar distinctions have been made in another study relating the experience of family membership to success in the

American culture, where success is broadly defined in terms of attained socioeconomic class. In two large-scale questionnaire survey studies, Kohn found that working-class parents typically view the outside world as unchangeable (see Kohn, 1969). Middle-class parents view the world as masterable by their own efforts. This orientation is expressed in the parents' attitudes toward their children. For example, working-class mothers more highly value obedience in their children and punish them when their behavior violates standards of society, no matter what the intent of the child. External standards are thought to be fixed and uncontrollable by the family. Middle-class mothers more highly value curiosity in their children and punish them according to the intent of their misbehavior. In effect, working-class parents value conformity, middle-class parents value initiative, and each punishes accordingly.

In their study of families, Hess and Handel (1959) developed concepts that overlap ours. Our concept of interpersonal distance-sensitive families corresponds to a group of families that Hess and Handel allude to as "disconnected." Using the case study method supplemented by several psychological tests, these investigators intensively studied thirty-three families drawn from a nonclinical population and presented five families in detail because each "represented in its interactional aspects a cluster of families of the total group." A family selected as representative of the disconnected group is described in part as follows: "The Littletons offer a fragmented pattern of family goals and standards. Preferences and ambitions affecting the family do not constitute an image upon which the group has achieved consensus. The image is lacking in clarity; it is not explicit; it is not shared . . . the family feels it is not working together as a unit towards group objectives" (p. 129). And continuing about the same family: "The avoidance of intimacy which characterizes the Littletons springs from a basic mistrust of the reciprocity and stability of affectional intimate exchange" (p. 161). In our formulation concerning the interpersonal distance-sensitive family, we proposed the dominant family experience as arising from each member's wish to demonstrate independence and mastery. This dynamic is not as central in Hess and Handel's formulations. However, there is a most important similarity in the existential description of family ambience: the sense of separate experiential universes, one for each member.

Dimensions of Family Constructs

In our next phase of theory construction we attempt to articulate three underlying dimensions which can be used to distinguish our three family types. Specifying values for each of these dimensions would completely describe any particular family type; we will demonstrate, somewhat later in this section, how that may be done. Since we phrased the dimensions in operational terms, insofar as possible, the specification process played a large role in designing new laboratory procedures and putting the model to an empirical test. Specifying these dimensions also helped us see that the three types of families we had described were only a subset of types drawn from a total set which might — theoretically — contain at least eight types composed by all combinations of high and low values for three dimensions.

Configuration.[22] Families differ, as we have said in several contexts, in their ability to grasp subtle and complex patterns in their environment. Some families are quick to perceive these patterns; other families can only recognize superficial and coarse similarities or forever experience their world as chaotic and unpatterned. *Configuration* refers to this difference in experience. On an operational level, this dimension refers to the contribution that the family, working as a group, makes to the problem's solution. It is conceptualized as independent from the problem-solving skills each individual may be able to apply by himself. Consider, for example, a family moving into a strange neighborhood. Each member might make some exploration of the neighborhood on his own to develop his notions of the structure of human relationships and nonhuman resources in the new location. This individual exploration would reflect a range of cognitive, perceptual, and interpersonal skills. Family problem-solving effectiveness would represent the additional contribution the family group makes to whatever the individuals could achieve by acting separately. In some cases the family's "contribution" is negative — that is, the family may interfere with exploration.

In the experimental setting, we can present problems of various kinds to individual members and measure or assess their solutions. Then we can present the same or similar problems to the family groups. The difference between the average solution of the individuals and the solution of the family is a measure of family problem-solving effectiveness. Roman designed such a study using the Wechsler Adult Intelligence Scale (WAIS), giving it first to each member of a marital pair and then asking the couple to respond jointly (Roman et al., 1967). Several of our previous experiments have had a similar design.

Unlike Roman, we would not equate an effective problem solution with an accurate one. We conceive everyday problems as solvable by a variety of alternative solutions. It is relatively uncommon that there is a clear standard of accuracy against which an individual's or a family's solution may be judged. Therefore, rather than viewing the poles of this dimension as "accurate" versus "inaccurate," we conceive of them as "subtle, detailed, and highly structured" versus "coarse, simple or chaotic." In the former, the family construes events and people as complex, and their relationship to each other is seen as conditional on many factors. In the latter, events and people are classed according to simple attributes, and their perceived relationship to each other is incomprehensible or is very stylized. The term "configuration"—with its emphasis on order, organization, and coherence—is meant to emphasize this distinction.

Hess and Handel (1959) have conceptualized five "processes that give shape to the flux of family life, coherence to the extended array of events, perceptions, emotions, actions, learnings and changes which the members experience or undertake." Among these notions is one of "establishing boundaries of the family's world of experience"; it is similar to our concept of configuration. "The family maps its domain of acceptable and desirable experience, its life space . . . Limits to experience—broad or narrow—are established in a variety of ways and along several dimensions . . . The family determines how deep or how shallow experience . . . how many kinds of life and action are conceived of, known of, or understood" (p. 14).

According to our definitions, we would expect environment-sensitive families to score high on measures of this dimension and consensus-sensitive families to score low. Interpersonal distance-sensitive families, lacking the richness and stimulation inherent in cooperative problem solving, would also have low scores.

Coordination.[23] The coordination dimension refers to family members' ability and willingness to develop problem solutions similar to each other's. It is a distinctly different dimension from configuration, since family members may effectively share solutions that are either coarse and simple, or subtle and detailed. The concept refers to those situations in which the family is working as a group and extends beyond the notion of simple agreement. It refers to a more pervasive experience by all members that they are, for the moment, in the same experiential universe, and the principles and patterns of that universe are equally true and equally relevant for all members. In this sense, agreement on a problem's solution follows from a more basic experience in the family that consensus is possible. Therefore, in our attempts to assess coordination, we would measure more than agreement within the family. We shall also require evidence of a more basic or primary sharing process in both formulating solutions and believing in them.

Interpersonal distance-sensitive families should clearly score very low on this dimension. Interestingly, consensus-sensitives and environment-sensitives should be high but for very different reasons. Environment-sensitives will effectively and collaboratively explore the problem and its relevant context in the environment. Because of continuous sharing of percepts and ideas, their solutions should be in good agreement. Supporting this process is the family's shared belief that the problem's solution is governed by general, impersonal laws of logic. This sense of the problem as impersonal emphasizes the belief that the laws are applicable to and discoverable by all members of the family. Consensus-sensitive families have a shared view of the environment arising from a more fundamental need to cohere in the face of an uncertain, unmasterable, and at times threatening environment.

Closure.[24] The closure dimension refers to the family's proclivity for suspending or applying order and coherent concepts to raw sensory experience. On one extreme are families who rapidly apply structured explanations to all incoming stimuli. Not only may the world be experienced as ordered; it may be experienced as continuously ordered, and the current structure is experienced as derived from the past in an uninterrupted way. Each individual has a clear experience of how his family has responded to similar input in the recent or remote past. This remembrance of things past forms a central basis for the structuring of current experience. These families struggle to apply past explanations to new data, or, failing that, apply new explanations as quickly as possible; they avoid periods or episodes where stimuli seem uncanny or inexplicable. On the other extreme are families who, for the most part, experience stimuli as continuously novel and, at times, chaotic. They cannot utilize or cannot remember the family's previous approaches or solutions to similar problems. Their sense of the present is very intense. Stimuli are experienced as immediate and transient.

The present concept is meant to refer to continuity of experience over short time spans such as the hour or two a family might spend in a laboratory. At one extreme are families who have a clear sense of how they might have solved the problem previously and hold to a similar solution without change, throughout the task. At the other extreme are families who experience each phase of the problem as entirely novel and continuously change their solution in response to every slight variation in the quality of stimuli or information relevant to the problem. However, continuity of the family's structure and interpretative style may be conceptualized as occurring over much longer periods of time. Bossard and Boll (1950), in a study of family ritual, showed how patterned group practices provide a family with a sense of permanence through many phases of its development. We also have fragmentary reports of eminent families, most with unusual political or literary gifts, who experience a clear sense of how their forebears would have responded to a great range of problems in the environment. Indeed, the members could often say, in effect, "I see the world through the eyes of my ancestors." However, the experience of continuity over long time spans requires considerable theoretical and empirical examination before it can be related to that hypothesized for comparatively brief intervals.

Our characterization of environment-sensitive families implies that they show a good deal of delayed or suspended closure. Most important, they experience the problem as "out there." The sought-after solution will be a product of logical connections perceived in an existential space outside the family; there is no necessity to experience them as continuous with the family's own previous solutions, in the recent or remote past. There is a prime valuation on evidence rather than explanation, and so a maximum exposure to ambiguity and uncertainty is sought in order to strengthen and generalize any tentatively held hypotheses. In sharp contrast are consensus-sensitive families, who experience and utilize explanation and solution itself as major mechanisms for maintaining family coherence. Thus, they strive to sustain unbroken continuity in their explanation of events; closure is early and often premature, even when they are confronted with the most unusual problems. The situation is much more complex for interpersonal distance-sensitive families. Here, there is no sense of a common family universe of explanations and viewpoints. The isolation of each individual provides him with little family "heritage" even in the short term, to permit him to build his present concept of his notions of his family's previous explanations. Nonetheless, each member may show a good deal of premature closure when operating in relative isolation. This is one good way to shut the others out of one's own personal world: "My mind's made up; I don't need to listen to you." We can see that distance-sensitive and consensus-sensitive families both strive for early closure but for different reasons. Distance-sensitive families use early closure to maintain a personal sense of isolated continuity and solidarity through time; this is a continuity of family experience only in the sense that each member is aware that each of the others is fortifying himself in isolation. Consensus-sensitives use early closure to jointly barricade themselves, as a besieged group, from the outer world.

Table 1.12 summarizes the three dimensions, the problem-solving behaviors by which they can be assessed, and the positions

TABLE 1.12 DIMENSIONS OF FAMILY CONSTRUCTS AND THE LOCATION
OF THREE FAMILY TYPES

Coordination	Closure	Configuration	
		Low	High
High	High	1	2 Environment-sensitive
	Low	3 Consensus-sensitive	4
Low	High	5	6
	Low	7 Distance-sensitive	8

of our three types of families in the resulting matrix. The table emphasizes the potential existence of five other undiscovered family types. These are theoretically intriguing, but at this point in our work we had not pursued them.

2 | Family Problem Solving and Shared Construing

Our fundamental hypothesis — that a family's problem-solving style, as measured in our laboratory, is a direct consequence of the family's typical approach to construing its social world — is difficult to test directly. For example, there are no accepted ways to measure directly a family's tendencies or approach to construing its social world. Most investigators have not considered the possibility that families perform such a function; understandably, the concept of shared construing in families has never been operationalized.

In this chapter, working with this limitation, we use three different strategies to examine the hypothesis. The first strategy is indirect. We compare the problem-solving performance of three groups of families who have very different modes of construing their social world. This enables us to make detailed predictions of how the groups should differ. A second approach is more direct. We make an effort to operationalize the concept of shared construing in families and develop three new family testing procedures which, on their face, are more direct measures of shared construing. Using our ideas about varieties of shared construing, we then predict relationships between a family's problem-solving style and its construction of particular social environments. Finally, we use a third approach to examining the basic hypothesis. In order to test the strength of the main hypothesis we consider several rival hypotheses that could account for the variations in family problem solving we have already observed. As we will explain later in this chapter, the most important rival hypothesis asserts that differences in families' styles and strategies of problem solving simply reflect differences in the skills of family members.

Strategy One: Comparing Three Groups of Families

The basic requirement of this strategy is to distinguish three types of families on the basis of their tendencies to construe the social environment in particular ways. Our discussion in Chapter 1, indicated two possible approaches. The first, suggested by the work of Strodtbeck (1958), would be to contrast problem-solving patterns in different ethnic groups. For example, Jewish families from eastern Europe could probably be classed as environment-sensitive. They should show high configuration and coordination and delayed closure in our problem-solving setting if that setting is, in fact, a measure of shared construing. Likewise, Italian families from Sicily could be classed as consensus-sensitive. If our basic hypothesis is correct we would expect low configuration, high coordination, and premature closure from them in our problem-solving setting. We did not use this approach, however, because we expected difficulty in obtaining pure cultures of these ethnic ideal types and we could not identify an ethnic subtype that was typically distance-sensitive in its orientation. Another plausible strategy, following Hess and Handel (1959), would be to classify a family according to its dominant orientation toward its environment as revealed through the interview and observation approach. This approach, although illuminating for the heuristic program carried through by Hess and Handel, was too cumbersome and subjective for the kind of quantitative effort we contemplated.

The most conservative approach seemed to be to use our own findings that the presence of psychopathology in the family is a good index of the family's mode of construing the social world. Our data suggested that families free of serious psychopathology would have an environment-sensitive orientation; families with schizophrenic offspring would have a consensus-sensitive approach; and families of offspring with some form of serious character disturbance would have a distance-sensitive orientation. The presence of psychopathology in the family was to have a very different function in this new study. In the first series of studies we had a direct interest in pathogenesis. We hoped our work would help provide a link between observations of family process and the development of an information-processing deficit in schizophrenic patients. In the current study, psychopathology played a peripheral role. It was a marker of the probable mode by which the family construed its social world. In effect, our plans were to replicate our first set of studies. However, the current effort at hypothesis testing went beyond a simple replication. To begin with, we carefully reviewed clinical and quantitative research on families of psychiatric patients to see if they justified our supposition about the link between particular forms of psychopathology and the family's typical mode of construing the social world. This review, summarized below, permitted us to sharpen our specification of what psychopathologic conditions to select for our sample. It also permitted us to make more detailed predictions of the pattern of the relationships between family problem solving and psychopathology that we might observe if our basic hypothesis, linking problem solving and construing, were true. Second, we revised and simplified our problem-solving measurements. We modified the card sorting procedure (see Chapter 1) so that it became an effective measure of closure as well as configuration and coordination; we had not measured closure directly in our first series of studies.

Our review of the literature published by the time of this next study supported the notion that middle-class families free from serious psychopathology might indeed be classified as environment-sensitive. Kluckhohn (1960) and Parsons (1965) had suggested that this kind of American family is relatively isolated from its kin and is a strongly bonded social unit that depends very much on itself for its successful social and economic adaptation to its cultural surroundings. A strong ethic favors academic and professional success. There is a clear orientation, Kluckhohn points out, toward mastering and dominating the environment. Strodtbeck suggests that a component of this orientation is the family's shared view that the universe external to the family operates according to a predictable order. It is plausible that this shared orientation of successful American middle-class nuclear families greatly facilitates, if not entirely motivates, their continuing success in a technically complex and socially competitive society. Our data from the first studies suggested an additional aspect—that each member continued to rely on the other's struggle to master problems in the environment as an integral part of his own efforts to do the same. Our data suggested that in families where the children are at least of adolescent age this is a shared family process: the children's efforts are as important to the parents' attempts at mastery as the parents' are to the children. In Chapter 1 we suggested that in these families each member serves to amplify for the others the patterning and change in the environment. In another experimental study, Mishler and Waxler (1968) compared the performance of middle-class, white American families without known gross psychopathology with families of schizophrenics. A pattern of findings suggested that normal families permitted the continuous influx of new ideas into the family's shared awareness, in contrast to some families of schizophrenics who showed overcontrol of ideas and premature closure. Thus, in a diverse body of anthropological, sociological, and experimental findings we can discern themes corresponding to the components of the environment-sensitive family: mastery, cooperation, openness to fresh experience.

A voluminous literature addressed to the causes of character disorder, particularly delinquency, attempted to show that parents of delinquents were more argumentative and dissatisfied with each other, had higher divorce rates, and set fewer limits on their children. Although these statistical data painted a picture of general turmoil and decrepitude in the family life of delinquents, they did not directly suggest the experiential quality of family life that might be distinctive for delinquents, their sibs, and their parents. However, in separate clinical studies Kaufman et al. (1963) and Minuchin et al. (1964) found a pervasive sense of isolation and subjectively experienced interpersonal distance in members of families of delinquents. Both studies pictured the parents as preoccupied with their own lives and feelings or, in our terms, with their own personal universe. Kaufman suggested that this personal universe is pervaded by each parent's profound sense of loss and his continuing search, often impulsive and self-defeating for gratification and nurturance. In an experimental study of families of delinquents, Stabenau et al. (1965) provided data suggesting open conflict between family members each preoccupied with obtaining their own "self-centered satisfaction." Our previous laboratory findings using psychiatrically hospitalized character disorders — some of whom were impulse-ridden delinquents — suggested, for each member, considerable isolation and lack of knowledge or concern about the others' thoughts and percepts, as well as a moderately reduced capacity of the family to master problems in its environment. In a review of psychoanalytic studies of delinquents, Bilmes (1967) emphasized that delinquent behavior in an adolescent is often motivated by the adolescent's attempts to establish his own universe and in Erickson's words, to "destroy the eyes of the world." In his own world, sometimes shared with delinquent peers, the delinquent adolescent can live down intense feelings of shame which are a part of adolescence and are, putatively, especially intense in delinquents. It is plausible that the delinquent's attempts to fashion his own world, with its own standards and uncontrolled by conventional adult morality, proceeds from a family ethos in which all members — to a greater or lesser extent — collaboratively fashion their individual and unique experiential universes. This is consistent with findings in the family studies of Kaufman, Minuchin, and Stabenau, and in ours. These themes from studies of families and individual patients suggested that families of delinquents were similar to our prototypical interpersonal distance-sensitive families. In particular they showed isolation and a reduced mastery of their environment. Thus, we would expect low configuration and coordination in our problem-solving setting. Evidence was not as clear with respect to closure. It seemed reasonable, nonetheless, to guess that members in these families might use premature closure to keep themselves separate—that is, they would keep themselves separate by being less involved in the task.

A large clinical literature emphasized that families of schizophrenic patients feel estranged from their immediate social environment. A dramatic example was presented in Fleck's description of a family who collectively believed in a mystical cult which they felt set them off as distinct from, and superior to, their neighbors (Fleck et al., 1965). For shared, delusional experiences of this kind Fleck used the term *folie en famille*. A similar example was presented by Laing (1964): he described a family that permitted its customs and home furnishings to remain thoroughly Victorian and buffered its pervasive anachronisms from the community by an overgrown thicket of weeds, plants, and trees around the house. More subtle but equally pervasive boundaries between the family of the schizophrenic and its social environments were described by Wynne et al. (1958) as a "rubber fence" which enforced, for each family member, the experience of his family as all-encompassing. The extraordinary mutual "involvement" and "embroilment" among members in these families have been widely described (see, respectively, Scott and Ashworth, 1967; Hoover, 1965). It may be intensified or generated by a pervasive fear of the environment as threatening or potentially disruptive of intermember bonds (Hill, 1955). A paradox has been the repeated laboratory finding that communication among members in these families is "poor." The paradox is apparent when one considers how delicately members of the family must be tuned to each other's experiences in order to maintain a vivid and precisely shared *folie en famille*. In this connection, Searles (1959) has suggested that a schizophrenic patient and his mother may be exquisitely sensitive to each other's unconscious experiences.[1]

Our first laboratory studies supported the notion that members of these families were indeed very sensitive and responsive to the details of each other's communicative acts. Recall that families of schizophrenics tended to copy each other's hypotheses, scored highest when measured for their acknowledgment of the intent and meaning of the immediately preceding speaker's statement, and did very well on the lattice task, a measure of the efficiency of information exchange. We argued that our data showed that families of schizophrenics could communicate well with one another with information that was entirely contained within the family. Although we never measured it directly, they were probably very deficient, as other studies have shown, in communicating their ideas and observations about the outside world to one another. Thus, our own data and literature are reasonably consistent in suggesting that families of schizophrenics should show high coordination.

Other evidence suggests that these families become preoccupied with their idiosyncratic experiences and filter out or foreclose the possibility of extensively or intensively experiencing stimuli from outside the family. An earlier experiment in this series showed that families of schizophrenics cannot, when working together, perceive subtle patterning in environmental stimuli. Mishler and Waxler (1968) showed that verbal communication in families of good premorbid schizophrenics is monotonous and invariant: "The unbroken quality of the good [pre-morbic schizophrenic] family's speech reflects a high degree of predictability in the sequence of events; there is little uncertainty or ambiguity and also little opportunity for the family member to break out of the rigid sequence and to change the order of events" (p.189). Mishler and Waxler suggest that this makes the family unable to adapt itself to changing environmental situations; in effect, the family has maintained premature closure in response to a continually changing environment.

In sum, the clinical work of Lidz, Laing, and Wynne suggests that families of schizophrenics form idiosyncratic or inaccurate estimates of their environment (their configuration is low, in our terms); the work of Hoover, Scott and Ashworth, and Searles and the previous experiments in this series suggest a tightly knit group that is exquisitely sensitive to the meaning of each other's communication (high coordination); the work of Mishler and Waxler suggests premature closure or excessive conservatism of response to changing environmental stimuli. These three features—low problem-solving, high coordination, high premature closure—are the cardinal attributes of our prototypical consensus-sensitive families.

Table 2.1 summarizes our predictions for three groups of families. The literature and our past findings permit reasonably secure predictions for all dimensions and types except for closure and the families of delinquents. We could not locate, at the time of study, any data bearing on closure in these families. Thus, on theoretical grounds alone—using the assumption that early closure assists in maintaining the interweaving isolation characteristic of these families—we tentatively predicted early closure for these families.

From a methodological point of view we had two objectives. First, we had to develop a sample of three matched groups of families—a normal, a delinquent, and a schizophrenic group. Sec-

TABLE 2.1   SUMMARY OF PREDICTIONS FOR THREE TYPES OF FAMILIES
ALONG THREE PUTATIVE DIMENSIONS

Type of family	Dimensions		
	Problem solving	Coordi- nation	Closure (delayed)
Normal (environment- sensitive)	High	High	High
Delinquent (interpersonal distance-sensitive)	Moderate to low	Low	Low
Schizophrenic (consensus- sensitive)	Moderate to low	High	Low

ond was to design problem-solving tests in which all the surface family problem-solving variables, representing the underlying dimensions of experience, could be assessed.

Sample.[2] Our sample had twenty-four families, each containing two parents and a child, which could be divided into three groups of eight each. In the first group there was no history of professional diagnosis or treatment for any psychiatric disturbance for parents, tested child, or his sibs (if any); in the second the child was a delinquent; and in the third the child was a schizophrenic patient. In half the families in each group the child was male.

The criteria for inclusion in the study were: (1) children — aged fifteen to thirty, living at home, single, and in good physical health; (2) parents — living together, biologically related to the child, aged sixty or under, white, in good physical health, completed high school, and born in an English-speaking country. In the normal group no child or parent in the families tested (includes siblings of tested child) had had any kind of psychiatric treatment or counseling. In the delinquent group the child had a history of frequent solitary delinquency and was not schizophrenic. In the schizophrenic group the child had an unequivocal diagnosis of schizophrenia, had a life history of less than three years of hospitalization, and had less than one year continuously prior to testing. Premorbid history and symptomatology were heterogeneous. Only by length-of-hospitalization criteria could the schizophrenics be regarded as homogeneously acute.

We attempted to match the three groups of families, who were drawn from a slightly larger pool of tested families, for education and intelligence. We also compared the families on a number of other variables, as shown in Table 2.2. The significant differences obtained here were: (1) for the whole family—a significant sex effect for Shipley-Hartford verbal and Shipley-Hartford total intelligence, with males higher than females; (2) for fathers—the same; (3) for mothers—a sex effect only for Shipley-Hartford verbal; and (4) for children—the schizophrenics were older and better

TABLE 2.2 CHARACTERISTICS OF THE SAMPLE FOR COMPARING PROBLEM SOLVING IN FAMILIES OF NORMALS, SCHIZOPHRENICS, AND DELINQUENTS

Variable	Variable mean	Significant effects
Family scores		
1. Shipley-Hartford verbal	31.7	M > F[b]
2. Shipley-Hartford abstract	28.8	M > F[a]
3. Shipley-Hartford total	60.1	
4. Mean family age	37.6	
5. Mean parental education	14.1	
6. Occupational rating-father	2.0	
7. Total family income	18,612.5	
8. Family size	6.2	
Fathers' scores		
1. Shipley-Hartford verbal	34.4	M > F[b]
2. Shipley-Hartford abstract	29.8	
3. Shipley-Hartford total	63.8	M > F[a]
4. Age	47.7	
5. Education	15.0	
Mothers' scores		
1. Shipley-Hartford verbal	31.8	M > F[b]
2. Shipley-Hartford abstract	27.2	
3. Shipley-Hartford total	59.1	
4. Age	45.6	
5. Education	13.0	
Children's scores		
1. Shipley-Hartford verbal	29.1	
2. Shipley-Hartford abstract	29.3	
3. Shipley-Hartford total	58.4	
4. Age	19.1	S > D[b]
5. Education	12.1	S > D[c]

Note: M = Male; F = Female; S = Schizophrenic; D = Delinquent.
a. $p < .10$.
b. $p < .05$.
c. $p < .01$.

educated than the delinquents. There was no significant difference in birth order. By almost any criteria this must be regarded as a very closely matched sample.

Method. In our first studies we were interested in three aspects of family process: information gathering, interpretation, and exchange. We designed three procedures, each of which had a special emphasis on one of these. In the present study we are still interested in three aspects of family process: configuration, coordination, and closure. We decided, however, to try to assess all three with a single procedure. This shortened the total testing time and eliminated problems of order effect. We modified the original card sorting procedure, to be called henceforth the revised card sorting procedure, so that it could assess all the pertinent problem-solving variables. The three major changes were: to separate individuals in booths, giving each his own deck of cards and allowing him to communicate with others over a telephone-like apparatus; to add a card sorting task before and after the family task in which each individual worked alone; and to require that the family go through the family task one card at a time. We will explain below how these modifications yield all the pertinent variables.

When the family entered the laboratory they were seated in booths such as those shown in Figure 2.1. Each booth had a deck of cards, a set of signal lights, and a ruled and numbered sorting surface with seven columns. Family members could talk with one another on an earphone-microphone arrangement, and their behavior could be heard and seen by an observer on the opposite side of an observation mirror. During the major phase of the procedure each member received a deck of cards as shown in Figure 2.2.

As in the first version of this procedure, families were told to sort the cards in any way they wished, using any number of categories or piles for sorting up to and including seven, and any method for distributing the cards into the piles that made sense to them. Almost all families who have worked with these cards seem to recognize only two fundamental approaches to sorting. One approach is the length system. The ideal or most systematic carrying-through of this system is shown in Figure 2.3. Here all cards with three letters go in one pile, those with four in the next, and so on. The seventh column is for all those with nine or more. The second approach is more sophisticated and subtle: it is to sort the cards by pattern of letters. Figure 2.4 shows an ideal working-through of this system. Three piles are used; at the top of each is a nuclear letter sequence which can be expanded by repeating certain letters at particular locations. The family was permitted to talk through the

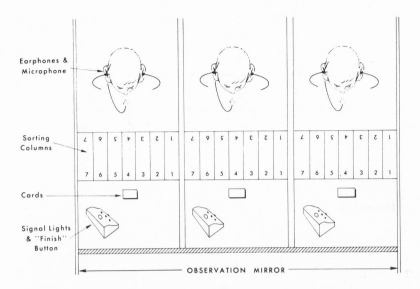

Figure 2.1. *A bird's-eye view of the apparatus for the revised card sorting procedure. Each subject is assigned to a booth: child in the center, father to the left, and mother to the right. Sorting surface, cards, signal system, and one-way mirror are in the front of each subject.*

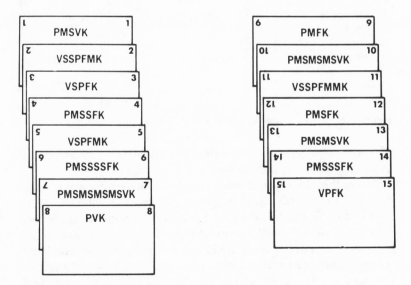

Figure 2.2. *Revised card sorting procedure, family deck*

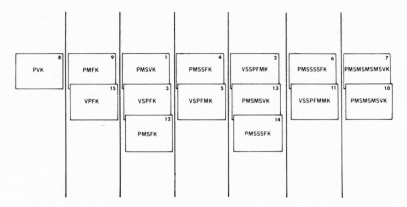

Figure 2.3.   *Length system for sorting cards*

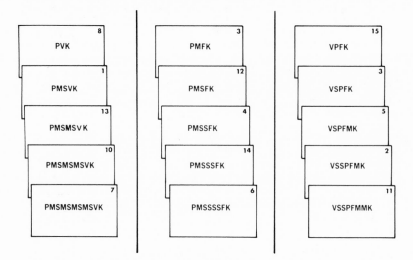

Figure 2.4.   *Cards arranged in the pattern sort arrangement*

microphone-earphone connections when working on this deck; hence they could, if they wished, work together.

Before this phase of the task, however, each member was given a deck of fifteen cards with a sequence of nonsense syllables, as illustrated in Figure 2.5. Each member worked alone here; his sort gave us an idea of which sorting system he could recognize on his own and how effectively he could carry it through. The individual sort was followed by the family sort, where members could talk to one another; the family sort was followed by a second individual sort, where members could not speak to one another. In all three

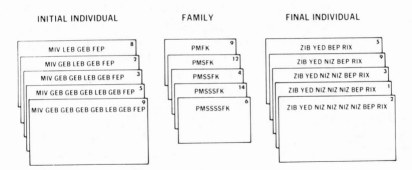

Figure 2.5. *Schematic illustration of the three phases of the card sort procedure*

sorts, sequences of nonsense syllables were used. The underlying patterns had the same general form for all three decks: three nuclear sequences which could be expanded by repeating specific elements at specific locations. The underlying patterns differed slightly in terms of the size of the nuclear sequences, the permissible location for repeating elements, and whether single or paired elements were repeated.

After seating family members in booths, the tester told them to sort the deck of cards in any way they wished, using as many piles as they wished, up to and including seven, as soon as they saw a white start signal light. When each felt satisfied that he had the best sort possible, he pushed a finish button which lit a red light on his signal box and those of other family members and the experimenter. The start and finish signal were recorded on an event recorder, which enabled precise recording of this and subsequent trial times. After all three members had finished they were instructed to pick up a second deck of cards when they saw the white signal light. However, they were told to sort only the first two cards and to press the finish button when they were satisfied they had done their best. They were to go stepwise through the remaining thirteen cards one at a time, producing fourteen separate trials to sort all fifteen cards. After each card, members were to press the finish button when each felt he had the best sort possible; when all three had pressed the button, the family was given a white signal to pick up the next card. We specifically omitted from the instructions any reference to whether the family had to agree on the card sort or on the timing of pressing their finish buttons. Any family questions were answered by rereading the most pertinent part of the instructions; thus, specific questions on the necessity for members to agree with one another were never answered. They were told they could rearrange their sorts from trial to trial if they wished. They were encouraged to discuss the puzzle among themselves. After the family sort was completed, the family was instructed to pick up a third deck and to sort it without discussion; all fifteen cards were to be sorted at one time as in the initial individual sort.

Scoring. This single card sort procedure enabled us to derive all the pertinent problem-solving variables to assess the dimensions listed in Table 2.1.

CONFIGURATION. The nature of the sorts themselves provided all the data for the configuration variables. For each of the three phases of the task, we formulated an ideal length sort, as pictured in Figure 2.3, and an ideal pattern sort, as pictured in Figure 2.4. For any sort we could ask, "How closely does this approximate ideal length or ideal pattern?" We used an algebraic system to assign a sort score of 1.000 if the sort was a perfect match, and 0.000 if it was maximally different from the ideal. It was possible to form sorts which achieved sizable above-zero scores for both pattern and length. To avoid the confusion of two different scores, we developed an algebraic conversion procedure which established a sort score for length that was unmistakably length and not pattern and a sort score for pattern that was unmistakably pattern and not length. These minimal scores for pattern and length are called "threshold scores." As so far described, this scoring approach does not distinguish the relative crudeness of a perfect length system from the subtlety of the pattern system. However, our change scores do just that. Let us say a subject used a length system initially but, after working with his family in the second phase of the task, he used a pattern system. He has clearly given up a simple system in favor of a more sophisticated one. We give him credit for this advance by computing his change score as the sum of his problem-solving scores on the initial and family task. In other words, he gets credit for giving up his length system (the magnitude of length problem-solving score), which is added to the credit for acquiring a pattern system (the magnitude of his pattern problem-solving score). Thus, if he got a problem-solving score of .700 on the initial task and .850 on the family task, his change score would be $+1.550$. The reverse of this procedure is followed if a subject gives up a sophisticated system and acquires a simpler one. The change score is the sum of both problem-solving scores multiplied by -1. Thus, a subject with a .900 pattern problem-solving score on the initial sort and a 1.000 length problem-solving score on the family task would receive a change score of $(.900 + 1.000) \times -1 = -1.900$. If a subject does not change his system from phase to phase, the change score is simply the difference between the two phases. Thus, a subject with a .600 pattern score on the initial sort and a .900 pattern score on the family task would receive a change score of +.300. This general approach to scoring produced variables which correspond to those specified in Table 2.1.

— Trial-by-trial pattern score. For each subject we computed the approximation of his sort to the ideal pattern sort for each trial, summed this score, and produced an unweighted mean by dividing by 14. We used the raw sort score and not the conversion which depended on the threshold score; thus, a subject who used the length system predominantly but used some pattern principles would get a low score but not a zero. This score measures the sophistication of the family solution; because it is unweighted with respect to the number of cards being sorted in any trial, it has the effect of giving special emphasis to the early trials. A family scoring high on this variable would clearly have achieved a sophisticated solution early in the task.

— Problem-solving score, initial to family. This is the change score, computed as explained above, describing the family's change from initial individual sort to the end of the family sort. (The score for the family sort is that from the fourteenth or last trial.) This change score is, presumably, a measure of the family's contribution to what the individual could do by himself as shown in the initial sort.[3]

— Problem-solving score, initial to final. This is an identical score comparing initial and final individual sorts. Our proposition emphasizes that gains (or losses) contributed by the family should stick with the individual when he faces similar situations alone. If this is true, this score will correlate highly with the first two.

COORDINATION. A small change in the algebraic scoring system permits us to compare one subject's sort with that of another rather than with an ideal sort. In fact, we can compare two, three, or any number of sorts. A score of 1.000 indicates that the sorts being compared are identical; 0.000 implies that they are maximally different. We call these similarity scores. Another form of data, referring to coordination, is available to us. This is how close in time members push their finish buttons at the close of each trial.

— Similarity score, family. This score is computed for the member's sorts of the fourteenth trial.

— Trial-by-trial similarity. This is the mean of the member's similarity score for each of the fourteen trials except the first two (where there are insufficient cards for a meaningful score).

— Similarity score, final. If the agreement achieved by the family when the members work together is carried over by the individuals when they work alone, this score should be high.

—Trial time, standard deviation. Figure 2.6 shows a trial time record from two families (for purposes of clarifying contrast we show family foursomes). In the family represented in the top panel of the figure, each member carefully pushes his finish button at almost the same time as the others. This simultaneity usually requires explicit effort. Father may say to one child, "Dick, are you ready to push your button?" Dick may reply, "Hold on a sec. I'm not quite ready." A moment later Dick says, "O.K. now. How about you, Mom?" Mom: "I'm O.K." Dick: "You, Jane?" Jane: "O.K." Dick: "O.K., now. Everyone push when I say three. One, two, three, push." In the family shown at the bottom of Figure 2.6, the trial endings are separated by as much as by a minute or more. In the laboratory procedure a minute or two seems like an eon. Differences of this magnitude are often associated with almost no talking among family members. In pilot testing we saw that when a subject pushed a finish button he was not really indicating his satisfaction with what he had done as much as he was conveying to the experimenter and other family members that he was ready to look at the next card. Simultaneity of button pressing in a family expressed a shared pacing or a simultaneous request for permission (in the form of a white light) to go onto the the next card. Thus, this simple act—simultaneous button pushing—conveys the family's linked pacing of the efforts to explore an unknown situation; we have already proposed that this is a crucial component of coordination. We can measure the simultaneity of button pressing by computing, for each trial, the standard deviation of trial times. In practice, such standard deviations are summed across the fourteen trials of the family phase; a mean is obtained by dividing this by 14.

CLOSURE. The same algebraic system that was used to obtain

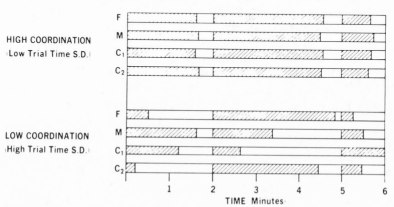

Figure 2.6. *Examples of highly coordinated and poorly coordinated trial endings*

problem-solving and similarity scores can be used for a third purpose. We can compare, for any subject, the sort he has presented on trial *n* with his sort trial *n* − 1. In effect, the sort on trial *n* − 1 is treated as the ideal sort. A score of 1.000 in this case is used to imply maximum *difference* between the two sorts; 0.000 implies they are identical.

— Radicalism. For each subject and for each trial we compared the sort to one he arranged during the previous trial beginning with the third trial. All above-zero scores are summed across trials and divided by 12 to produce a mean. A score of zero means that the subject never rearranged his cards from one trial to the next; once a card was assigned to a pile it was never moved. This might be considered "conservative" behavior. Conversely, a high score implies that the subject constantly rearranged his cards from pile to pile. These profound changes in system and approach are called, quite innocently, "radicalism." A dramatic contrast between conservative and radical sorting decisions is illustrated in Figure 2.7. We show a sorting system building up over the first five trials. It is, apparently, invariant and depends heavily on an alphabetizing approach: "Put all cards beginning with P in one column and those with V in another" (this is a very rudimentary pattern sort). However, the seventh card—seen for the first time at the start of the sixth trial—poses a problem for all families. They all see the repeating M S pairs. This card regularly calls attention to the patterned aspect of the sequences, if this hasn't been obvious from the start.

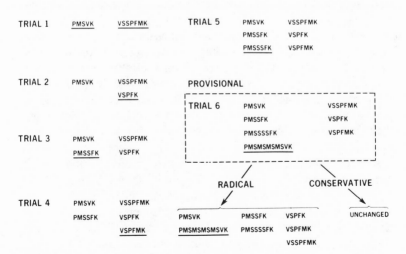

Figure 2.7. *A radical shift in card placement in contrast to a more conservative approach. The new card added in each trial is underlined.*

When faced with this interesting card, many families are tempted to change a preexisting and oversimplified sort, such as the alphabetic system. Often they switch to a true pattern system; this is the radical choice shown in the figure. Alternatively, they may take a conservative tack and simply force the novel card into a preexisting system.

— Trial time, first seven over total. In our efforts to link underlying dimensions of closure to surface problem-solving behaviors, we drew special attention to the early phases of problem solving. We reasoned that a family which seeks early closure, when it is confronting a new situation, will try to establish convention and approaches as soon as possible. Thus, we might expect in the revised card sort procedure that the family with a drive toward closure might spend most of its time in the early trials trying to work out a system to guide its work in later trials. Once this system — whatever it is — is established, the family would proceed quickly, confident that "we've already worked this one out." A simple index of this is the proportion of total time in the family task which the family spends on the first seven of the fourteen trials.

Factor analysis using principal components and varimax rotation, confirms that these variables can be grouped as we have suggested (see Reiss, 1971b). In other words, all the variables we have specified as measuring configuration do have the highest loading on one factor; variables thought to measure coordination load on a second factor; closure is measured on a third. There were two expectations in this study: the highest loading for trial time, standard deviation, was on the closure dimension, and the highest loading for trial time, first seven over total — and this loading was negative — was on the configuration dimension. This suggests that variation in the time of trial ending may be necessary to allow sufficient independent thinking to avoid early closure, which occurs when group process forces everyone to finish simultaneously. Also, the negative loading of trial time, first seven over total, suggests that families who spend most of their time working on trials when they have little evidence (they are working with fewer cards in the first few trials) do poorly.

Results. Table 2.3 presents the major predictions and findings for our three groups of families. The table shows findings from representative variables; other variables, reflecting the same underlying dimensions of shared experience, gave comparable results. The analysis was a 3 × 2 analysis of variance with three diagnostic groups each equally divided between families in which the index tested was a male and those in which the index was a female. The table shows the overall group means, combining male

TABLE 2.3 A COMPARISON OF THE FAMILIES WITH NORMALS, THOSE WITH DELINQUENTS, AND THOSE WITH SCHIZOPHRENICS ON THE MAJOR PROBLEM-SOLVING VARIABLES. THE DATUM ANALYZED IS THE FAMILY MEAN.

Score	Group			Analysis of Variance, F values		
	Normal	Delinq.	Schiz.	Diag.	Sex	Diag. × Sex
Configuration (prediction: Normal, high; Delinquent and Schizophrenic, low)						
Problem solving, init. to family	+.80	−.04	+.07	8.00[a]	0.15	0.03
Problem solving, init. to final	+.58	−.11	+.23	17.92[b]	1.48	0.08
Coordination (prediction: Normal and Schizophrenic, high; Delinquent, low)						
Similarity, family (14th trial)	.98	.81	.90	3.25[c]	2.11	0.08
Trial-by-trial similarity	.96	.77	.88	3.00[d]	0.23	0.44
Trial time, S.D. (low score high coordination)	2.84	8.26	7.01	3.43[e]	2.39	1.08
Closure-delayed (prediction: Schizophrenic, low; Delinquent, low; Normal, high)						
Radicalism	.030	.034	.023	0.48	7.51[f]	0.66

Note: Brackets connect means significantly different ($p < .05$) by Duncan's test.

Analysis within roles across groups: Separate analyses were performed comparing fathers, mothers and children from the three groups for configuration and closure variables (coordination variables do not have individual scores). The findings at the family level were replicated in each of these analyses except for mothers on problem solving, initial to final, where a trend replicated the family findings but group differences did not achieve significance.

a. $p < .001$; $\eta = .69$; $\eta^2 = .48$.
b. $p < .01$; $\eta = .82$; $\eta^2 = .67$.
c. $p < .10$; $\eta = .52$; $\eta^2 = .27$.
d. $p < .10$; $\eta = .52$; $\eta^2 = .27$.
e. $p < .10$; $\eta = .53$; $\eta^2 = .28$.
f. $p < .05$; $\eta = .54$; $\eta^2 = .29$.

and female, and the *F* values for the effect of diagnosis, sex, and the interaction between the two. In this analysis, for the configuration and closure variables, the basic datum was the family mean. For example, for the problem-solving score, initial to family, we computed a score for each of the three individuals in the family and obtained a mean of these three scores. This mean score for each family was entered into the appropriate cell and twenty-four family means were then subjected to analysis of variance. The coordination variables yield only single score for the family unit. In addition, as in Chapter 1, we performed comparable analyses for each role: father, mother, and child. In this case we used individual scores. For example, we compared the problem-solving scores, initial to family, of fathers of normals with those of fathers of delinquents and fathers of schizophrenics. These analyses replicated those performed on family means. This indicates that the overall differences between families did not simply reflect differences between the children or the fathers or the mothers; differences between the performances of all three contributed equally to the overall family differences.

The findings are not a precise confirmation of predictions. The configuration variables conform most closely to predictions. Families of delinquents were lowest and families of schizophrenics tended to lie midway between the other two, rather than at the same extreme as the delinquents. The coordination variables confirm predications about sharp differences between normals and families with delinquents. Instead of equaling normals in coordination, however, families of schizophrenics are again midway between the two other groups. Finally, our one measure of closure does not show any significant differences among the three diagnostic groups, although there was a sex effect. (Families with females sought closure earlier than families with males.) Further analyses to test the adequacy of the model were indicated.

The actual findings for configuration and closure could have been explained by an interpretation diametrically opposite to a major proposition of the model. Our model states that coordination has two very different functions in families of normals (environment-sensitive) and families of schizophrenics (consensus-sensitive). In the former, coordination serves to facilitate cooperative exploration of the environment and hence is positively correlated with problem-solving scores reflecting configuration. In the latter, it protects the family from interaction with the environment and hence is negatively correlated with configuration scores. Our findings show families of normals high in coordination and configuration and families of schizophrenics intermediate in both. It might be argued that had they achieved the same levels of coordination, families of schizophrenics would also have achieved the same high levels of configuration. If that, indeed, turned out to be the case, it would indicate that coordination serves the *same* function in both families — a substantial refutation of our hypotheses. From current data we cannot be sure about what would happen, but extrapolation is possible by correlating configuration variables with coordination variables separately for each of the two groups of families. We arbitrarily chose three coordination variables: similarity, family; trial-by-trial similarity; and trial time, standard deviation. We also picked five configuration variables: trial-by-trial pattern score; problem solving, initial to family; problem solving, family; problem solving, initial to final; and problem solving, final. The first three of these five reflect the family's performance on the family task; the second two reflect performance on the final task. Thus, we have 3 × 5 = 15 pairs of correlations. We would expect, very generally speaking, that correlations within the group of normals would be much more positive than those within the group of schizophrenics. Ideally, the sign of the normal correlations should be positive and that of schizophrenic correlations should be negative. However, it would roughly conform to our hypotheses if the correlations for the normals were positive and those for the schizophrenics were more or less zero, or if the normals were approximately zero and the schizophrenics extremely negative. In all three cases, however, the magnitude of the correlation, including sign, would be greater for normals than schizophrenics.

Table 2.4 shown an interesting pattern of findings. Seven of eight paired comparisons for the family task are in the direction predicted by our model. Three of these are significant.[4] However, for the final task four of the six paired comparisons are contrary to predictions, and two of these four are significant. These data suggest that, relative to the normals, coordination in families of schizophrenics is disruptive to problem-solving effectiveness, as our model predicts. However, the more coordinated families of schizophrenics do considerably better in the final task than their less coordinated counterparts. We can propose an answer to the question that originally prompted this secondary analysis. If families of schizophrenics had been as coordinated as those of normals, they would have done *worse* than they did on the family task — as predicted by the model. Under the same circumstances, they would have done *better* than they did on the final task — a finding not predicted although not necessarily at variance with our overall model. Our analysis is summarized in Figure 2.8; here one sees that problem-solving scores of families of schizophrenics "corrected" to values they might have achieved had they equaled the normals in coordination. We will return to a discussion of this analysis in a moment.

First, let us examine closure processes in the three groups of families. Our factor analysis yielded only one clear measure of this

TABLE 2.4   AN ANALYSIS OF CONFIGURATION AND COORDINATION IN FAMILIES OF NORMALS AND FAMILIES OF SCHIZOPHRENICS

Configuration variables	Coordination variables		
	Similarity, family	Trial-by-trial similarity	Trial time, standard deviation[a]
Family Task			
Trial-by-trial pattern score	Norm. > Schiz. $p < .20$	Norm. > Schiz. $p < .20$	Norm. < Schiz.
Problem solving, initial to family	Norm. > Schiz.	Norm. > Schiz.	Norm. < Schiz.
Problem solving, family	Norm. > Schiz.	Norm. > Schiz. $p < .20$	Norm. < Schiz.
Final Task			
Problem solving, initial to final	Norm. < Schiz.	Norm. < Schiz.	Norm. > Schiz. $p < .20$
Problem solving, final	Norm. > Schiz.	Norm. > Schiz.	Norm. > Schiz. $p < .05$

a. High scores indicate low coordination. Thus, the prediction is Norm. < Schiz.

dimension — radicalism — which failed to distinguish among our three groups. It occurred to us subsequently that a simple measure — the mean of all fourteen trials of the family task — might reflect closure. A family seeking early closure might try to keep its trial times short; just the opposite might be expected for families delaying closure. We added mean trial time as another problem-solving variable and redid our factor analysis. The new factor matrix looked very much like the original; the added variable — mean trial time — loaded equally on the coordination and closure factors. Its joint loading on both factors made it inappropriate as a discriminating variable for distinguishing among our three groups of families. However, the fact that it did load on the closure factor makes it useful for another secondary analysis using separate correlations for each of our three groups of families. Like the secondary analyses on coordination and configuration, the present analysis begins with that part of our model which proposes a different function for closure in our three groups of families. The analysis also depends on the quite plausible assumption that both mean trial time and radicalism reflect an underlying dimension of closure.

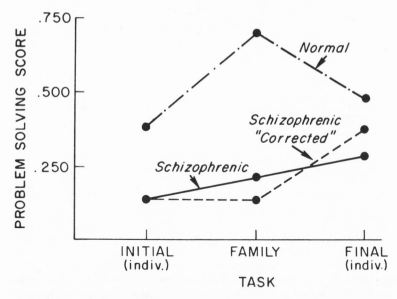

Figure 2.8. *The problem-solving scores for the families of normals and families of schizophrenics. The curve for the families of schizophrenics has been "corrected" by using the regression equations computed between measures of coordination and configuration (problem solving). The most significant estimates of this relationship were used (trial-by-trial similarity and problem-solving score, family task; trial time, standard deviation, and problem-solving, final task).*

In normals, trial ending (that is, closure) should be delayed in order to consider a variety of evidence and solutions and to reorganize the cards by a new sorting system, if necessary. The more substantial reorganizations of the cards would lead to more accurate problem solutions. However, since the collaborative work of these families is always well coordinated, delayed trial ending would not necessarily be associated with increased coordination. In sum, for normals we predict that increased trial time will be associated with increased radicalism; increased radicalism in turn will be associated with more effective family and final (individual) problem-solving situations. These predictions are indicated in Figure 2.9 by dark arrows. The direction of the arrows implies causality: "TIMEMN → RADICA" means increased mean trial time causes increased radicalism. These predicted associations will be tested by correlations which can only confirm the strength of association and not, of course, its direction.

Our model suggests that a major mechanism by which coordination is kept low in the delinquent group is that trial times are kept

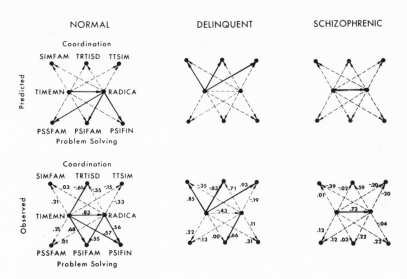

Figure 2.9. *Schematic representations of predicted and obtained correlations between trial time, mean (TIMEMN), radicalism (RADICA), measures of coordination (trial-by-trial similarity, TTSIM; trial time, standard deviation, TRTISD; and sort similarity, family task, SIMFAM), and measures of problem-solving effectiveness (problem-solving, family task, PSSFAM; problem-solving initial to final, PSIFIN; and problem-solving, initial to family, PSIFAM). The predicted relationships are shown by heavy arrows and the obtained relationships with correlation coefficients. For those .52 (27 percent of the variance accounted for p < .20, two-tailed) or over (except for relationships with TRTISD where those less than − .52 are shown), we use heavy arrows. The direction of relationship, implied by the arrows, cannot be considered as confirmed or not confirmed by the correlation coefficients.*

short. Short trial times make it nearly impossible for a family to exchange observations and ideas when it has little inclination to do so anyway. However, even in those families who delay trial ending, the degree of coordination reached, although higher than in families of delinquents with short trial times, should not be great. Moreover, there should be no greater tendency to reorganize the sorting system or achieve more effective problem solutions. This is because the family *depends* on isolation for its stability. Coordination is confusing and disruptive. In sum, in families of delinquents short trial times are viewed as a mechanism that curtails coordination to an absolute minimum, and it is on this basis that a positive relationship between mean trial time and the three measures of coordination is predicted; mean trial time is predicted to be unrelated to radicalism or the measures of problem solving since even at higher levels mean trial time does not enable these highly competitive families to reorganize their sorts and improve their problem solutions.

For the schizophrenic group, increased trial time is predicted to permit a more intense search for consensus on a stylized, simplified, and distorted solution. It may permit the family to doubt its early solution. This doubting may in time reflect its experience of being overwhelmed by its environment. Therefore, the family may reorganize its sort but with the same striving for consensus at the price of accuracy as in the original sort. Thus, although increased mean trial time permits increased radicalism, increased radicalism will not lead to improved problem solutions. Moreover, since coordination is desperately sought, it is unlikely that increased trial time will materially increase it; that is, the family is as likely to achieve coordination with short trials as with long ones. In sum, we predict only a positive relationship between mean trial time and radicalism for the schizophrenic group.

The findings are shown in Figure 2.9 in the same form as the predictions. All correlations greater than $+.52$ ($p < .20$, two-tailed, and 27 percent of the variance accounted for) are represented by heavy arrows, except for correlations involving TRTISD, where all correlations less than $-.52$ are reported (since TRTISD is inversely proportional to coordination). In general, the predictions are confirmed except for: normals, the correlations of mean trial time × problem solving, initial to family, and problem solving, initial to final × trial time, s.d., were not predicted and that of radicalism × problem solving, family, was not observed; delinquents, the correlation of radicalism × problem solving, initial to family, was not predicted.

We may examine closure process from yet another perspective. Recall that we had hoped that a simple measure of the distribution of trial times across trials might reflect closure. We rather arbitrarily picked the ratio of the time spent by a family in the first seven trials to its total time in the family task (trial time, first seven over total). Factor analysis did not confirm this as a measure of closure. Perhaps a simple ratio is too crude an index of a subtler trial time distribution process, or perhaps seven was too arbitrary a cut-off point. The basic idea still seemed good. It was reasonable to suppose that families of schizophrenics, in a frantic effort to establish stable conventions in a new situation, would spend a disproportionate amount of time in early trials, whereas families of normals, in a true environment-sensitive approach, would spend most of their time later in the task, when most of the evidence was available. Predictions on closure remain less certain for families of delinquents. In general, they are expected to keep all trial times relatively short to accomplish the twin aims of disengagement from the task and from each other.

To assess this distribution of trial times we calculated the median trial time, for each trial, for each group of families. Our hypotheses are graphically represented in the top half of Figure 2.10. Families of schizophrenics are shown with a predicted early peak, families of normals with a later peak. The most conservative prediction for families of delinquents seemd to be a straight line. In pretrials we had noticed that some families spent a long time on the final trial in an effort to check out their final position. They probably said something like this to themselves, "Hey, this is the last trial. Let's make sure everything is O.K." In making predictions before testing the actual sample, we reasoned that such fastidiousness would characterize only an environment-sensitive approach to problem solving and hence drew into our predicted curves a "terminal check-out" peak in the fourteenth trial. It must be emphasized that the magnitude of predicted peaks and slopes is entirely arbitrary.

The bottom half of Figure 2.10 presents the actual findings. The early peak for families of schizophrenics and the late one for families of normals are shown, as are a number of unpredicted peaks; in particular, we see all groups have a first and last trial peak. The first trial peak seems to reflect the families' efforts to orient themselves; the last is probably some kind of "check-out" for all groups. It is clear that these unpredicted first- and last-trial peaks make the simple ratio score (trial time, first seven over total) an overly simple measure of closure.

FITTING THE MODEL AND THE FINDINGS

We predicted that the normals would behave like the pro-totypical environment-sensitive families: high on measures of family probelm solving, coordination, and closure. The first two were directly confirmed by the findings in this study. The third was only indirectly confirmed. There were no significant differences between normals and the other two groups on radicalism, our measure of delayed closure. However, measures of trial time distribution showed a late peak only for this group. This group, moreover, had the only clear pattern of positive correlations between mean trial times on the family task and radicalism, on the one hand, and problem solving scores, on the other. This suggests that, where it was used, delayed closure functioned to improve problem solving only in this group. These findings and the delayed peak of trial time were consistent with our a priori notions of the function of closure in these families.

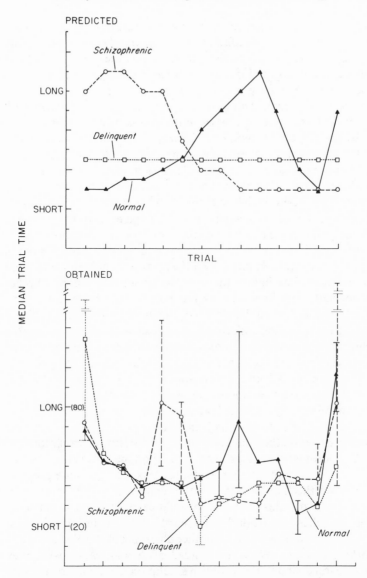

Figure 2.10. *The predicted and obtained distribution of trial time across trials for families of normals, delinquents, and schizophrenics. Actual trial time, in seconds, is shown in the y-ordinate of graph for obtained findings. As a rough estimate of variance, interquartile ranges are shown for critical points in each of the three obtained curves.*

Families of delinquents, we predicted, would perform like prototypical distance-sensitive families, although previous literature made predictions on closure more difficult. We could predict that they would be low on coordination and family problem solving. This prediction was confirmed. Correlations between mean trial length and radicalism, on the one hand, and measures of problem solving and coordination, on the other (see Figure 2.9), suggested that families may keep trial times short in order to keep coordination at a minimum. This proposed mechanism is consistent with our model of closure processes in distance-sensitive families.

We predicted that families of schizophrenics would perform like prototypical consensus-sensitive families. Not all of the predictions were confirmed and some unpredicted findings were obtained. As predicted, families of schizophrenics achieve low problem-solving scores on the family task, but they receive higher scores than predicted on the final (individual) task. Although as a group they failed to equal the normals in coordination (contrary to prediction), within-group correlations suggested that coordination served a function for these families very different from that in normals: here coordination may impair family problem solving; among families of normals, coordination may facilitate it. The evidence for this was that correlations between coordination and family problem solving were, in almost all cases, more positive for normals than for schizophrenics, where it was generally negative. Therefore, the evidence supports the prediction about the quality of coordination—it interferes with problem solution—but it does not support the predictions concerning the quantity of coordination.

Two other unpredicted findings for the schizophrenic group appear to be closely related: (1) the greater than expected problem-solving scores on the final task, and (2) the positive correlations between coordination and problem solving on the final task. It is suggested that coordination on the family task may facilitate problem solving on the final task (hence the high positive correlations between the two). This relationship could be explained if members in these families, particularly the most highly coordinated ones, learned a good deal from each other about problem solutions while working together. However, instead of demonstrating what they have learned about the problem's solution from others in their family, they delay applying this learning during the family task and wait until they perform alone in the final (individual) task. Therefore, we failed to predict the relatively good performance of families of schizophrenics on the final task (they were still significantly lower than the normal group), because our predicting model did not take into account this covert attentiveness and learning. Bleuler (1950) described an apparently similar phenomenon: "It is remarkable how many of the events which the patients seem to ignore are registered nonetheless . . . One of our catatonics, who for months on end had been constantly occupied with pantomiming toward the wall, showed after some improvement that she was fully familiar with what had happened in the Boer War during the period of her illness . . . Others can relate to perfection what was heard or seen, even though throughout the entire time of their listening, they were constantly in conversation with their 'voices.' *Even attention can be split"* (pp. 68–70).

Bleuler was talking of attention and learning in schizophrenic patients — he termed these features "double registration" — but we have found that these features are also characteristic of both parents as well. It is possible to suggest for our experiment the equivalent of pantomiming toward the wall or conversing with voices. These behaviors are expressions, in Bleuler's terms, of the patient's preoccupation with his own "autistic thinking." Likewise, as we have already proposed in somewhat different terms, the low family problem-solving scores may be behaviors representing the family's preoccupation with its own autistic experience, that is, family members' shared experience of a need to protect themselves against a hostile environment. The data suggest, however, that individuals in families of schizophrenics do not succumb entirely to this experience. They retain throughout their work with their family a hidden and more problem-oriented perspective which emerges when they work alone on the final task. It is tempting to explain this away by saying that each individual maintains a degree of "rationality" despite the irrational family pressures. In Chapter 7 we present another perspective which may account for findings of this sort. We can anticipate it here by emphasizing that each subject is actually a member, simultaneously, of two groups — the family group, and a group consisting of him and the laboratory staff. One way of representing this dual membership is shown in Figure 2.11. It is plausible that the group which includes the laboratory staff is dominated by an environment-sensitive approach or construct of the laboratory setting. In this instance, the staff's construct competes with the consensus-sensitive constructions of the family. The environment-sensitive approach has a hidden influence while each individual is actively engaged with his family. However, when an individual is released from this group in the final, individual task, the environment-sensitive perspective of the subject-staff group dominates his behavior.

In sum, the main thrust of our findings does not seriously challenge our central hypothesis, namely, that family problem solving reflects the family's underlying construction of the laboratory as

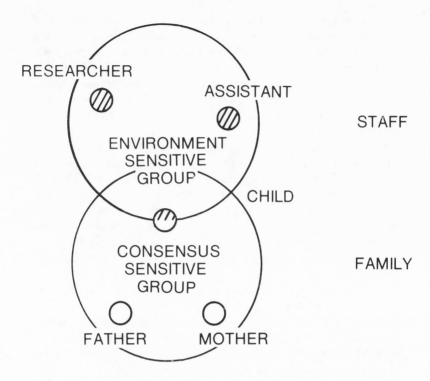

Figure 2.11. *Schematic illustration of the competition between the staff-subject group and the family group. The illustration is drawn from the perspective of the child, although each family member—as an individual—may be included in a staff-subject group.*

a social setting—but do the data *prove* it? The next two sections of this chapter provide more data.

Strategy Two: Direct Assessments of Shared Construing

The inferences we drew from comparisons of families of normals and those with schizophrenic and delinquent patients were indirect; they rested on the assumption that three groups did indeed construe their social world differently and in just the ways postulated. A more direct test of the core hypothesis—the relationship between family problem solving and shared construing—requires a direct assessment of shared construing in families. We are unaware of any theory or method which operationalizes these processes. In carrying out this second strategy, then, we had to frame additional theory as well as to develop suitable objective methods of measurement.

In pursuing this second strategy we turned again to a sample of families of psychiatric patients.[5] We wanted to take advantage of a particularly important juncture in the life of each family: the few weeks following the first admission of its adolescent child to a family-oriented psychiatric inpatient facility. Since the family itself is actively engaged—on almost a daily basis—in the treatment program, it must make its own adjustment to the new social community comprised of the ward, its staff, other patients, and their families. We have argued that a family's shared perception of a new and ambiguous social setting determines its behavior in that setting. This principle ought to apply with particular relevance to a family's adjustment to an inpatient ward community. There is much that is strange and unfamiliar about such a setting; at the same time most families have a high investment in dealing with it and managing its relationships with the ward in one way or another.

Our first step was to select two major aspects of the ward community and to compare families in their construction of these aspects. The first aspect was the ward staff and the practices, principles, and regulations that were connected with their management of the ward. The second segment was the group of families of other patients. Families of patients were brought into frequent contact with one another through regularly scheduled multiple family therapy groups as well as frequent informal contacts. Our theoretical task was to think through plausible links between two phenomena: the family's performance on each of our basic dimensions of problem solving—configuration, coordination, and closure—and the family's construction of the ward staff and the families of other patients. This additional theory permitted us to develop two new procedures—the ward perception Q-sort and the family perception procedure. It also helped us derive scores from these procedures and to predict how families would perform—as measured by these scores—from knowledge of their problem-solving style in the laboratory. In our first efforts, pursuing this more direct strategy, we focused on only two of our three dimensions—configuration and coordination.

THE FAMILY'S PERCEPTION OF THE PSYCHIATRIC WARD

The first task was to define a set of dimensions for distinguishing among families' perceptions of the ward staff and practices.[6] Three criteria guided this process. First, the dimensions should be clearly pertinent to our basic notions of coordination and configuration. Second, they should be measurable through objective assessments of family behavior; we wanted to adhere to our basic style of measuring family process, which relied more on what families do in a test situation than what they say about themselves. Finally, we wanted to select dimensions that might play a significant role in regulating the family's actual engagement and transactions with the new community of which they were becoming a part. Our success in achieving this last criterion will be more fully reviewed in Chapter 8, when we return to a different aspect of our studies of the family's encounter with the hospital.

The first dimension of perception of the ward has a straightforward relationship to the concept of coordination. We call this dimension *synchrony*. It assesses the extent to which family members reconcile their separate images of the ward community. Members in families high in synchrony regularly and effectively compare and reconcile their individual impressions of the ward community. As a consequence, when they are asked to convey their impressions in a test situation which does not permit them to communicate with one another, the impressions will be quite similar. We expect families high on coordination in the laboratory problem-solving situation to have high scores on measures of the synchrony of their perceptions of the psychiatric ward. For example, members would agree on relatively objective perceptions such as, "Staff tend to change their assignments [in the hospital] frequently," as well as more subjective perceptions such as, "This is a very well organized ward," or personal assessments such as, "Staff members work to help patients because they may gain raises or promotions by doing so."

A second set of variables fits more closely with configuration. We have defined configuration as reflecting the family's sense of optimism and mastery in a novel and ambiguous social setting. Families high on configuration have an immediate sense that any new social world is ordered and discoverable. Their initial approach is exploratory. They discover a good deal about the new environment, are sensitive to subtle cues and innuendoes, and, as a result of the enlarging grasp of the new setting, quickly feel engaged and at one with it. Three specific variables, then, suggest themselves; high-configuration families should score high on all of them. The first we have called *information accuracy*. Because they are good explorers, high-configuration families should discover, for example, that it is true that "Important ward decisions are shared among staff," but that it is not true that "The psychiatric service is less than five years old." A second variable is *subtlety of perception*. Here we reasoned that families might be distinguished by the kinds of cues that were most important to them in characterizing and understanding the ward. High-scoring families should prefer the more subtle social and emotional cues which convey a sense of the quality of the ward as a social community. They should pay special attention to what Moos has called "ward atmosphere" (see Moos, 1968, 1971, 1974). Thus, they attach special importance to attributes like these: "It is not hard to tell how patients are feeling on this ward"; "Staff sometimes argue with one another." (High-scoring families might either agree or disagree with such items but would select them as most salient for characterizing the ward.) Low-scoring families would pick as most salient for characterizing wards much more concrete elements such as, "Staff all have professional school experience." A third variable in this set is *engagement*. As we defined it, this variable refers much to the actual content of the family's perception of the ward and much more to the fit between the family's perceptions and judgments and to those which prevail among most of the families. Our assumption here is that engagement or involvement in the ward community is paralleled by an acceptance of the community's prevailing conception of itself.

A final dimension intrigued us. Influenced by the work of Kohlberg (1964) and his associates, we were curious about the moral judgments the family made of both patients and staff on the ward. On the low end of this scale would be a family who perceived the actions of patients and staff as motivated by a simple wish to avoid punishment or receive immediate rewards: "Staff members work to help patients in order to avoid trouble from supervisors." On the upper end of the scale are perceptions of patients and staff motivated by a genuine concern for one another: "Patients comply with ward rules because they see it's in everyone's best interests to do so." For this dimension, we reasoned that neither high configuration nor high coordination alone would be enough to produce a high score. High scores in both would have to be present. There are two reasons for this. First, we reasoned that low-configuration families would have difficulty seeing the ward community as an ordered and safe setting. This perception of disorder and unpredictability would extend to their moral judgments. They would tend to see individuals as motivated by impulsive, unpredictable, and selfish interests rather than by an external, clear, and dependable moral order. Our high-configuration, low-coordination families (we have termed these "achievement-sensitive families," as will be explained below) also should achieve low scores, but for a different reason. Their high configuration permits them, in general, to perceive order and coherence in a new social setting. This would not, we reasoned, extend to moral judgments. Although these families achieve high scores on configuration, their low coordination scores appear to reflect intense competition, rather than cooperation, between their members. We reasoned that members in such families would compete for the attention and praise of staff as well as other patients and their families as they appear to compete for approval and praise in the laboratory. This would lead each member to be concerned about competitive alliances others in his family would forge with members of the community; this fear would undercut each member's confidence in the trustworthiness of members of the ward community. As a result, they would make relatively low moral judgments of them. Thus, we predicted, only high-configuration, high-coordination families (our environment-sensitive group) would score high on this variable.

Sample. The sample consisted of thirty families each consisting of two parents and an adolescent child just admitted to an inpatient psychiatric service for the first time. Most parents were biologically related to the child; each of those who were not had lived in the home for at least five years. As soon as possible after admission of the adolescent, each family was tested in the card sorting procedure. The testing was done at another institution, entirely separate from the hospital, and the results of the testing were never disclosed to the hospital staff or the family. Families were classified according to four separate problem-solving scores. For configuration we used two change scores: the problem-solving score, initial to family task, and the problem-solving score, initial to final task. For coordination we used similarity of sorts in the family and in the final task. Four groups were created: those high on both dimensions, environment-sensitives; those low on both, distance-sensitives; those high on coordination and low on configuration consensus-sensitives; and those low on coordination but high on configuration, achievement-sensitives. This last group was not described or conceptualized in Chapter 1 although it occupied cells 6 and 8 in Table 1.12. These families show a mixture of confident engagement in the task and high levels of competition among family members; the competition focuses on who will achieve the most. Thus, we have called them "achievement-sensitive."[7] These four groups were comparable in a number of important respects: mother's and father's age, intelligence of mother, father, and child,[8] mother's and father's education, father's occupation, and total length of stay in the hospital. The clinical diagnoses were roughly comparable for the four groups, but the children in consensus-sensitive families had, more frequently, a prior hospitalization in another institution.

Table 2.5 shows the predictions for these families. The top half of the table shows the predictions in terms of the dimensions. The same predictions are recast in terms of family types in the lower part of the table.

TABLE 2.5 PREDICTED RELATIONSHIPS BETWEEN FAMILY PROBLEM-SOLVING BEHAVIOR AND THE FAMILY'S SHARED VIEW OF THE PSYCHIATRIC TREATMENT PROGRAM. PREDICTIONS ARE SHOWN FOR THE DIMENSIONS OF PROBLEM SOLVING AND ARE RECAST TO SHOW THEM FOR FAMILY TYPES.

| Problem-solving behavior | 1. Synchronization of individual perceptions | Perception of the treatment program | | | |
| | | Experienced mastery | | | |
		2. Information accuracy	3. Subtlety of perception	4. Engagement	5. Motives of others
High coordination	High	n.s.	n.s.	n.s.	n.s.
High configuration	n.s.	High	High	High	n.s.
High coordination × High configuration	n.s.	n.s.	n.s.	n.s.	High
Environment-sensitive (high coor/high conf)	High	High	High	High	High
Consensus-sensitive (high coor/low conf)	High	Low	Low	Low	Low
Achievement-sensitive (low coor/high conf)	Low	High	High	High	Low
Distance-sensitive (low coor/low conf)	Low	Low	Low	Low	Low

Procedure. Approximately six weeks after doing the card sorting procedure, each family was given the ward perception Q-sort. In the first phase of the procedure each mother, father, and child worked alone to sort a deck of cards; in the second phase the family worked together on a single deck identical to the one on which the individuals had worked previously.

Each of the thirty-six cards in the Q-sort deck contained a statement about the ward. These statements were equally divided into three categories: first, statements about the ward's atmosphere; second, more straightforward factual statements about the ward; third, statements about the motives of patients and staff which reflected each of Kohlberg's six levels of moral judgment.

Family members were asked to sort the cards into seven columns on a ruled surface. The written heading of a column indicated the meaning attributed to placing a card there ("most characteristic," for example, meant, "Placing a card here means you think its statement is most characteristic of the ward") and the number of cards to be placed in that column. From left to right the columns were labeled: "most characteristic, one card"; "quite characteristic, four cards," "fairly characteristic, eight cards," "neutral, ten cards," "fairly uncharacteristic, eight cards," "quite uncharacteristic, four cards," "most uncharacteristic, one card."

Scoring. 1. Synchrony was measured by the agreement of the sorts of individual members in the first card using an algebraic formula roughly comparable to that used for the similarity score in the card sorting procedure.

2. Information accuracy was a measure of the weighted sum (see below) of correct items placed in characteristic columns and incorrect cards placed in uncharacteristic columns.

3. Subtlety of perception was measured by noting the number of ward atmosphere items put in any of the four most extreme columns (in comparison to the neutral, "fairly characteristic," and "fairly uncharacteristic" columns).

4. Engagement was measured in two steps. First, we determined the "modal sort" of the entire sample of families by determining the average position of each card. Then we compared any given family's sort to this modal sort using a formula comparable to the one used for measuring synchrony.

5. The critical moral judgment score concerned the placement of the low-level items (for example, "Staff members work to help patients in order to avoid trouble from supervisors"). Families who rated statements of this kind as characteristic of the ward seemed to see the community as rife with self-interest, impulse, and personal aggrandizement and needing constant external monitoring. Thus, a

low moral judgment score was accorded to families who placed low-level items toward the characteristic end of their sorting surface.

A weighting system was used to reflect the great care and concern family members used in selecting the cards for the extreme columns (most and least characteristic). These two columns received a weight of 36; then the next two columns (quite characteristic or uncharacteristic) received a weight of 6; the next, a weight of 1; and the neutral column, a weight of 0. Thus, if a family put one ward atmosphere card in most characteristic and another in quite characteristic and the remainder in neutral it would receive a score for subtlety of perception of 42.

Results. Table 2.6 summarizes the results of this study of family perceptions of the ward. The first part of the table shows how families were classified according to their configuration and coordination scores on the problem-solving task. The remainder of the table summarizes the findings for these groups. For synchrony, low scores reflect closeness between individual sorts on the first phase of the task; thus, low scores reflect high synchrony. The high-coordination families have significantly lower scores, as predicted.

Three measures related to experienced mastery by the familes of the ward social setting show different patterns of results. Indeed, the intercorrelations among these three variables are low, which suggests that they measure different aspects of family experience. Scores for information accuracy are all negative; this indicates that all groups of families, on the average, made more erroneous than correct placements of the information cards. The environment-sensitive group made the fewest errors, in accord with predictions; the distance-sensitive group also had fewer errors—which was not predicated. The findings for subtlety of perception conform to predictions. Engagement scores, like synchrony scores, reflect closeness, this time between the family's sort and modal sort for all families. Thus, *low* scores reflect engagement. The findings for engagement show environment-sensitives high as predicted; unpredicted was the high engagement for consensus-sensitives and the low engagement of achievement-sensitive families.

Moral judgment scores reflect the placement of the two lowest-level cards. Thus, negative scores reflect the family's rejection of these items as characteristics of the ward (they put them in uncharacteristic columns). As predicted, environment-sensitive families are least inclined to see the ward as governed by low-level morality. However, the consensus-sensitive group is also low, contrary to predictions.

Many of the findings confirmed predictions; there were two sur-

TABLE 2.6 COMPARISON OF THE PERCEPTION OF THE WARD AND ITS STAFF BY FOUR GROUPS OF FAMILIES CLASSED ACCORDING TO THEIR PROBLEM-SOLVING STYLE. FINDINGS FOR SYNCHRONY ARE TAKEN FROM THE FIRST, INDIVIDUAL PHASE OF THE Q-SORT. THE REMAINING FINDINGS COME FROM THE SECOND, FAMILY PHASE.

	Configuration	
Coordination	**Low**	**High**
High	Consensus-sensitive	Environment-sensitive
Low	Distance-sensitive	Achievement-sensitive

Synchrony (prediction: environment- and consensus-sensitive high)[a]

High	593	637	$F_{coor} = 3.15$
Low	655	648	$(p = .09)$

Information accuracy (prediction: environment- and achievement-sensitive high)[b]

High	-27.0	-14.9	$F_{coor \times conf} = 7.87$
Low	-17.2	-35.2	$(p = .01)$

Subtlety of perception, ward atmosphere items (prediction: environment- and achievement-sensitive high)

High	17.0	38.9	$F_{conf} = 4.85$
Low	23.0	28.8	$(p = .038)$

Engagement, closeness to modal sort (prediction: environment- and achievement-sensitive high)[c]

High	149	142	$F_{coor} = 6.00$
Low	183	178	$(p = .023)$

Moral judgement, placement of low-level cards (prediction: environment-sensitive low)

High	-10.6	-17.0	$F_{coor} = 5.02$
Low	-4.8	9.0	$(p = .035)$

a. Scores reflect closeness; thus, low scores reflect high synchrony.

b. Negative scores reflect placement of incorrect items in "characterisitic" columns or correct items in "uncharacteristic" columns. Thus, a highly negative score means many errors of either kind; low negative scores mean the family avoided errors but made few, if any, correct placements.

c. Low scores reflect closeness; thus, low scores reflect high engagement.

prises, however. First, coordination appears much more important as a predictor than we anticipated. Specifically, it predicts a family's experienced engagement with the ward community as well as its tendency to reject low moral judgment items as characterizing the ward. Second, distance-sensitive families had surprising success in rejecting incorrect information items. They nearly equaled the environment-sensitives and were far better than the achievement-sensitives, who we thought should perform well here. Clearly the predictions, as derived from our core hypotheses, do not precisely fit the findings. It will be easier to discuss the problems with the fit after we consider another component of the family's perception of the ward community: its perceptions of the families of other patients.

THE FAMILY'S PERCEPTION OF OTHER FAMILIES

Our study of the family's perception of the ward and its staff had a larger aim at its center. To be sure, we were interested in families' adjustment to a psychiatric treatment program, but we had a greater and more general interest in families' adjustment to a broad range of social settings. Within this broader aim, psychiatric hospitals stood for a larger class of formal organizations. In that sense, the study just reported ought properly to be considered the first in a series of studies of the families' perception of and transactions with a variety of organizations: schools, churches, government agencies, and so on. In a similar vein our study of how families perceive one another uses a psychiatric sample but has broader aims. We see this first study as a steppingstone to studying interfamily perception in many contexts.[9]

As with our study of the family's perception of the ward, the central task of theorizing was to define meaningful dimensions for distinguishing among families on the basis of their perception of other families. The same three criteria guided our development of these dimensions. First, the dimensions should be meaningfully linked to coordination or configuration; second, they should be objectively measurable; and third, they should be important enough to influence the families' actual interaction with other families. Our success in achieving this last criterion is explored in Chapter 8.

We defined three dimensions. We call the first of these, once again, *synchrony,* with a meaning very similar to the meaning in the ward perception study. It refers specifically to the efforts expended by family members to reconcile their individual images of other families. In the ward perception study we focused on the outcome of such efforts at reconciliation: our primary interest was the similarity of perceptions after a process of reconciliation had a chance to go forward in the family. In the current study we focus more on the process of reconciliation of separate images. As the family formulates its views of other families, do individuals take careful account of the views and impressions of each other or, by contrast, do they ignore the impressions of others and convey little of their own? As in the ward study, we expect high coordination families to show synchrony and low coordination families to show very little.

A second dimension we call *depth and variety*. These are two closely related characteristics of the family's concept of other families. "Deep" concepts or perceptions are those that refer to underlying, shaping, or motivating features of family life. Some families' perceptions of other families focus on the quality of the relationships, the patterns and maneuvers, and the underlying feelings. Other families focus on more superficial and obvious features: physical appearance, whether the family is noisy or quiet. "Variety" refers to the range of attributes a family considers as it elaborates its conception of other families. We would expect high configuration families to show both depth and variety in their conceptions of other families.

With a third dimension, which we call *conceptual framework,* we are interested in exploring how the ideas or concepts a family uses to understand other families are related to one another. This is the analog of the pattern and coherence which characterizes the percepts of the laboratory and its puzzles by high configuration families. In some families, percepts and ideas of other families have some definable (although probably implicit) relationship. In this sense they constitute a system of ideas, a framework, or even, as Heider (1958) has termed it, a "naive psychology." For example, when families live at close quarters (as in an apartment house with thin walls), noisiness is an attribute of families that will be important to all. Families will differ, however, in the extent to which this attribute is linked to a set of other concepts about families. For some, noisiness will have a simple relationship to a single other idea such as "unpleasant." Other families will share (almost always implicitly) a much richer set of connections between the concept of noisiness in other families and other attributes of families. For instance, they may think that sometimes noisiness is related to boisterousness and high spirits, at other times to deep conflict within the family, and at still other times to the age of the children. In other words, families who perceive other families in this way not only develop simple percepts or concepts about particular other families, they also work together to develop a system or framework of interrelated ideas which can be applied to many families. We would expect such a framework to be better developed, to have richer interconnections between concepts, in high configuration families than in low configuration families.

Sample. The sample of families was almost identical to that participating in the ward perception study. One family did not properly complete the family perception procedure, so our overall sample had twenty-nine instead of thirty families. The sample was divided into the same four groups, using the card sorting procedure, just as in the ward perception study. Again, these groups were comparable on a variety of demographic and clinical variables.

Procedure. The family perception procedure[10] was given during the same testing session as the ward perception Q-sort, about twelve weeks after the adolescent had been admitted. During this period the family had been involved in intensive multiple family therapy groups at least twice a week, and had had a great deal of exposure to other families. The exposure of each family to the others was about the same. This study provides a unique opportunity to standardize such exposure prior to comparing families on their perception of other families.

The family perception procedure had four steps. (1) Each family was presented with a set of cards. Each card contained a photograph of a patient — currently on the unit at the time of testing — or a member of his immediate family. All patients and their families — including the family being tested — were represented in the card set. (2) The family was asked to go through the entire set to pick out the six families they knew best.[11] Each family was required to include itself in this group of six. (3) Families were then asked to consider each of these six in turn. For each family they selected, the family being tested was asked to identify which members in that family were most like one another. They were then asked to agree on a single descriptor that best described those individuals they regarded as similar. The aim of this part of the procedure was to stimulate the family to think about each of the six families they selected. Their discussion was used to measure the synchrony, depth, and variety of their perceptions. This phase of the procedure did indeed yield rich discussion from the subject families; it also yielded six final descriptors — one for each "known" family — which the family wrote on a special form provided. (4) The last phase of the procedure assessed the conceptual relationship or structure connecting these six final descriptors. We wanted to know which among the six were more or less equivalent — from the family's perspective — and which were distinct. In order to determine this, all the cards, representing the members in the six "best known" families, were shuffled and re-presented to the family as a single deck. The family was asked to divide the deck into two equal stacks. One stack was to consist of individuals who were most _____; the other half, individuals who were least _____. The tester filled the blank space with the descriptor the family agreed on after reviewing the first "best known" family. For example, consider a family who had agreed that the similar members of the first family were alike because they were "hostile." In this second part of the task, they were asked to divide the whole deck into most hostile and least hostile individuals. The process was repeated for the remaining five descriptors. If the family split the deck in almost the same way for the six descriptors, these descriptors must be, in a functional sense, equivalent. If the family divided the deck in different ways each time, then the descriptors are relatively independent for the family—each must have a different meaning from the others.

Scoring. Measures of synchrony, depth, and variety were obtained from coding typescripts of the family's discussion during step (3) above. Table 2.7 summarizes these codes and provides the scoring reliabilities and examples for each code. Each statement, utterance, or speech of each member was separately coded on each of the three codes. Conceptual framework was measured by comparisons of how the family split the whole deck in step (4).

SYNCHRONY OF ELABORATION. This code measures how carefully each person pays attention to what the others are saying during the family discussion of other families in step (3). We use Mishler and Waxler's acknowledgment code in ways similar to that described in Chapter 1. Each statement uttered by a speaker is coded for the extent to which it acknowledges both the content and intent of the previous statement. The statement being coded may agree or disagree with the previous one and still be rated as high acknowledgment. We assume that families with members who pay attention to each other's views will be highly likely to synchronize the elaboration of those views. Thus, high levels of acknowledgment are predicted for our high coordination families. In addition, findings reported in Chapter 1 suggest that very high levels of acknowledgment tend to interfere with subtle and probing observations of families in a problem-solving setting; very high acknowledgment means people are paying more attention to one another than to the problem at hand. In contrast, moderate levels of acknowledgment are much more likely in task-oriented families. Thus, we expect low levels of index 1 (high acknowledgment) in our task-oriented, high configuration families but high levels of index 2 (mid-acknowledgment).[12]

DEPTH AND VARIETY. Two codes measure this aspect of family performance. The depth of intrafamily perception code rates each statement for the degree to which it expresses the speaker's awareness of an underlying rather than superficial aspect of the family he is discussing. Table 2.7 provides examples. It also shows that we use a single index derived from these code categories: internal descriptors (index 3) is the proportion of statements which express perception of an underlying family attribute. Higher values for this index are expected for high configuration families. The descriptive variety code measures various aspects of the descriptors each member offers during the family discussion in step (3). Descriptors are brief phrases describing another family or some of its members — for example, "They're woman-haters," or "They're both very dependent." We are interested in three different aspects of the descriptors. First, are they all synonyms and hence show little variety? Does each member of the family offer about the same number? Does the family seem to become preoccupied with itself (recall that it must include itself among the six "best known"), as reflected in a heavy proportion of the total number of descriptors being used when it discusses itself? We would expect that our high configuration families — who we predict will develop sensitive and subtle percepts of other families — would offer a variety of descriptors (ones that are not simply synonyms or antonyms), would encourage each of its members to generate ideas in the form of descriptors, and, finally, would not become preoccupied with itself. Specifically, we predict that high configuration families will show low scores on indices 4, 5, and 6, and high scores on 7 (see table 2.7).

CONCEPTUAL FRAMEWORK. Following Kelly (1955), we assume that if a family divided the deck in step (4) in identical ways using two different descriptors, then those two descriptors must have the same meaning or be seen as closely related by the family. Consider a family who has produced, during step (3), the descriptors "quiet" and "troubled." When the family comes to step (4) they are asked to divide the whole deck into those who are most quiet and least quiet, and then those who are most troubled and least troubled. If the deck is divided in almost or exactly the same way, the family must see a close relationship between troubled and quiet. Using Bannister's equation (see Bannister and Mair, 1968), perfect agreement receives a coefficient of agreement of 1.0 and perfect disagreement receives −1.0 (for example, if all the most quiet people are sorted as the least troubled). Whether the coefficient is positive or negative, a value close to 1.0 expresses a high degree of relationship. The average strength of a relationship can be computed by averaging the fifteen possible pairwise coefficients, neglecting the sign; this is the unsigned mean score. We expect high configuration families to develop a system of relationships among their ideas about other families. That is, some of their ideas will be clearly

TABLE 2.7 A SUMMARY OF THE MEASURES OF SYNCHRONY OF ELABORATION AND DEPTH AND VARIETY OF PERCEPTIONS OF OTHER FAMILIES. THESE MEASURES ARE DERIVED FROM CODING OF DISCUSSION AS THE FAMILY WORKED ON THE FIRST PHASE OF THE TASK.

| Code | Reliability[a] | | Coding levels | Examples | Indices |
	kappa	p <			
Acknowledgment	.81	.0001	1. High 2. Moderate 3. Minimal 4. None 5. Uncodable	*Synchrony of elaboration* Level 1: *Son:* Put him there, I think he'd like to be there. *Father:* I disagree. I don't think his feelings are relevant. Level 3: *Son:* Now you can do the whole thing if you want. *Father:* Well.	1. High Acknowledgment $1/(1 + 2 + 3 + 4)$ 2. Mid-Acknowledgment $(2 + 3) / (1 + 2 + 3 + 4)$ 3. Internal descriptors $(4 + 5) / (1 + 2 + 3 + 4 + 5)$
Depth of intra-family perception	.83	.0001	1. Physical attributes 2. Easily visible behaviors or skills 3. Feeling or attitudes requiring inference 4. Qualities of relationships 5. Underlying personality dynamics or interpersonal strategies 6. Uncodable	*Depth and variety* Level 1: Put John and his father together because they look alike. Level 3: Both of 'em are woman-haters. Level 5: She tries to act strong but she's dependent. They become aggressive toward men because they don't want to get close to them.	

Descriptive variety   .59   .01

a = No. descriptors used for own family

b = Total no. descriptors for all families

c = Total no. descriptor pairs which are syn. or ant.

d = Total no. descriptor pairs which are close syn. or ant.

e = Total no. descriptor pairs = (b × b − 1) /2.

Close synonyms: talkative-verbose

Close antonyms: happy-sad

More distant synonyms: passive-dutiful

More distant antonyms: aggressive-quiet

4. Synonyms (antonyms) c/d

5. Close synonyms (antonyms) d/c

6. Own family descriptors a/b

7. Equality of contributing descriptors, all family members

a. The reliabilities are computed using Cohen's kappa statistic, which corrects for chance agreements. The computations are based on a recoding by a second coder of 8 percent of all materials coded by the primary coder.

linked to one another; others will not be linked. A family might regard "quiet" and "self-controlled" as similar but perceive no relationship between "quiet" and "flexible," for example. The perceived relationship may be relatively descriptive in the sense that the family has noted simply that demeanor and self-control often go together. The perceived relationship may go deeper: self-control, the family believes, is the personality structure that produces a quiet demeanor. In either case, it is important that "quiet" has a selective relationship with just some but not all other attributes. For example, if the family relates "quiet" not only to "flexible" but also to "pleasant," "content," and "helpful," we could infer that the family has only one underlying concept, which might be roughly synonymous with "good" (versus "bad"). In general, we expect high configuration families to have moderate unsigned mean scores reflecting a mixture of high and low pairwise coefficients and to show interpretable and selective relationships between selected pairs of dimensions.

Results. SYNCHRONY. Table 2.8 presents the results of index 2, mid-level acknowledgment. Our hypothesis on the effect of coordination is supported by a very significant comparison of family means (there is also a significant difference) when parental means and father and child scores are compared. Only for mothers was there not a clear superiority in high coordination families. Table 2.8 also shows clear superiority for configuration. Within-role analysis for this effect shows the means of mothers and children to be significantly different. The results for index 1, high acknowledgment, show, in the main, the reverse findings—as predicted. Low configuration families show higher scores than do high configura-

TABLE 2.8   MID-LEVEL ACKNOWLEDGMENT; THE DATUM ANALYZED IS THE FAMILY MEAN. (PREDICTION: HIGH SCORES FOR BOTH HIGH COORDINATION AND HIGH CONFIGURATION FAMILIES)

| | Configuration | | Significant |
Coordination	Low	High	F values
High	.58	.64	$F_{coor} = 6.40$ $(p = .018)$
Low	.46	.60	$F_{conf} = 9.64$ $(p = .005)$

Note: Analysis within roles across groups. As in Table 2.2, separate analyses were performed using the mean of both parents' scores, father's, mother's, and child's scores separately. These four additional ANOVAs revealed the same pattern of findings as that for the whole family mean, shown above. The *F* value for configuration achieved significance for the parent, mother, and child analyses; the *F* for coordination was significant for fathers and children.

tion families ($F = 7.240$, $p < .02$). However, contrary to prediction, low coordination families show higher scores than do high coordination families ($F = 3.845$, $p < .10$).

DEPTH AND VARIETY. All five indices of this aspect of the families' conceptions show trends in the predicted directions but do not reach satisfactory significance levels. Struck by this consistent pattern of trends we examined the data more closely. We found that families could be divided into three groups. For purposes of exposition, from this point on, we will regard a high score as that end of each dimension which signifies greater depth or variety—that is, the upper end for index 3 (Table 2.7) and the lower end on indices 4–7. On analysis, one group of families had low scores on all five measures of descriptors and varied descriptors. Another group had mid-level scores on all of these. Finally, a group of families had very high scores on at least one of the five variables and a moderately high score on at least one other. Computationally, we define a high score as one in the top two deciles and a moderately high score as one above the median. High-scoring families, defined in this way, were distributed into the four cells of our family classification as shown in Table 2.9. All five of the high configuration–high coordination families (the environment-sensitive) are in the high-scoring group, as are about half of the low configuration–high coordination (consensus-sensitive), and half of the high-configuration–low coordination (achievement-sensitives). None of the low configuration–low coordination families (distance-sensitive) are in the high-scoring group, however. Fisher's exact probability test, comparing the balance of high-scoring and other families for all possible pairs of family types, shows the environment-sensitive group to be significantly different from the distance-sensitive group and the achievement-sensitive group; the environment-sensitive group is marginally different from the consensus-sensitive group.

CONCEPTUAL FRAMEWORK. Table 2.10 shows that high configuration families have unsigned mean scores in the mid-range between 0.0 and ±1.0, which are significantly greater than those of low configuration families. Additional data suggests these mid-range scores of high configuration families do indeed reflect organized relationships rather than lack of differentiation between the descriptive dimensions. For example, we examined the specific pattern of relationships between coefficients of agreement to search for an underlying structured relationship between the dimensions. Somewhat arbitrarily we chose the range from .20 to .55 (neglecting sign) as an undifferentiated range. We reasoned that any coefficient above this range (neglecting sign) suggested a strong relationship between two descriptive dimensions. Any coefficient below (neglecting sign) clearly suggested no relationship. If a family has a

TABLE 2.9   THE DISTRIBUTION OF FAMILIES SCORING HIGH ON AT LEAST TWO DIMENSIONS
OF DEPTH OR VARIETY OF DESCRIPTORS.

	Configuration			
	Low		High	
Coordination	High-scoring[a]	Low-scoring	High-scoring	Low-scoring
High	3	3	5	0
Low	0	3	3	5

Fisher's exact test:

Comparison	$p <$
High-high[b] vs. high-low	.05
High-high vs. low-high	.10
High-high vs. low-low	.025

a. A high-scoring family is one who achieves a score in at least the upper two deciles on one dimension of depth of variety and above the median on at least one other.

b. First adjective in pair refers to configuration; second adjective in pair refers to coordination.

TABLE 2.10   CONCEPTUAL FRAMEWORK: THE UNSIGNED MEAN OF THE FIF-
TEEN COEFFICIENTS OF AGREEMENT BETWEEN ALL PAIRS OF THE
SIX DIMENSIONS PRODUCED BY THE FAMILY.

	Configuration		Significant
Coordination	Low	High	F values
High	.297	.364	$F_{conf} = 7.04$
Low	.268	.364	$(p = .014)$

definite system of relationships, it should show evidence that it clearly regards some dimensions related and, by contrast, regards some others as unrelated. What is a reasonable number of high coefficients (greater than .55) to set as a minimum? Let us consider the minimum of three. Three high coefficients can be used to express the balanced relationships among three different dimensions, as shown on the left in Figure 2.12. Or three high coefficients can express the linear relationship between four dimensions, as shown on the right of the figure. If a family relates three or four dimensions in this way we can be more confident it has a *system* of relationships among dimensions than if a family relates only two. Thus, the minimum of three high coefficients, although arbitrary, appears reasonable. The structures shown in Figure 2.12 take on

MINIMUM STRUCTURE

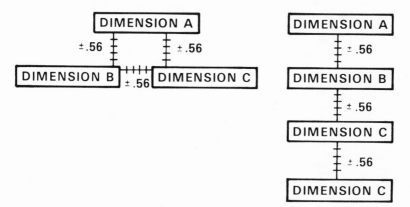

Figure 2.12. *Two possible structured relationships between families' concepts in the family perception procedure*

added meaning if we know the family sees little or no relationship between at least a few pairs of dimensions (that is, the relationships it *does* indicate are clearly contrasted with relationships it regards as slight or absent). A reasonable though arbitrary minimum number for coefficients less than .20 is two. We counted the number of families each of whom had at least three coefficients greater than .55 and at least two less than .20. Importantly, nine of the sixteen high configuration families and none of the low configuration achieved this minimum evidence of structure ($\chi^2 = 6.48$, corrected for continuity, $p < .01$, one-tailed). Further, as might be expected, the mean value of the unsigned mean scores for the nine families with the minimum values implying structure ($\bar{x} = .39$) was significantly greater than the mean for the remaining twenty without the minimum ($\bar{x} = .30$, $t(df = 27) = 2.73$, $p < .01$, one-tailed).

A second and most revealing analysis of the structural implications of the moderately high unsigned mean scores is to examine the specific dimensions selected by the families and how the family related them in their scoring. We examined all nine families who met or exceeded our minimum requirements; the relationship among descriptors for seven of these are depicted in Figures 2.13 and 2.14. Figure 2.13 shows all five families who met our requirements and whose final set of dimensions included the descriptor "quiet" (or, in the case of family #93, its antonym "verbal"). In each of these families the descriptor "quiet" or its antonym was

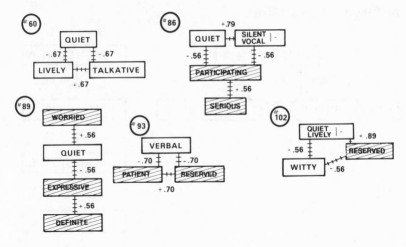

Figure 2.13. *Family conceptual structures containing the concept "quiet" or its antonym "verbal"*

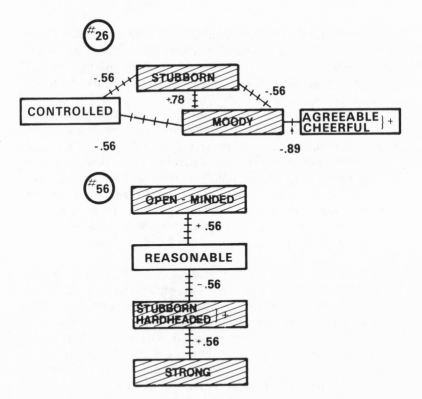

Figure 2.14. *Family conceptual structures which included the concept "stubborn"*

related to other descriptors; However, the patterns of these relationships differ from family to family and suggest different shades of meaning for "quiet." To aid in the analysis we have shaded those descriptors which received a score of 3 or more on our code for depth of interfamily perception, implying the perception of a deeper or more internal characteristic. "Quiet" is a superficial descriptor in that it refers to an attribute which requires very little inference. Its meaning to each family can be inferred from its relationship to other superficial descriptors and, more important, to the deeper descriptors.

Family #89 links "quiet" to "worried"; this pair is opposite in meaning to another linked pair, "expressive" and "definite." Thus, for family #89, "quiet" may be a signal of underlying personal trouble. Family #86 has another view of "quiet"; it is the antithesis of "participating" and "serious." Since the families came to know each other in a multiple family group, we may infer for family #86 "quiet" assumes importance as an indicator of lack of serious participation in the group. As in family #89, "quiet" is an indicator of trouble, but it is trouble of a different shade: more social than affective. The complex of relationships depicted for family #93 suggests a more positive view of "quiet." "Verbal"—the opposite of "quiet"—is negatively linked to the quality "reserved" (neutral from an evaluative perspective) as well as to "patient," a quality most people value. Thus, family #93 seems to view "quiet" (or, more precisely, "not verbal") as an indicator of a valued underlying characteristic, "patient." Families #60 and #102 have more superficial structures. They seem to be characterologies rather than psychologies. Family #60 seems to be noting, rather simply, that quiet people are not lively and talkative; family #102 observes that quiet people are often reserved but rarely witty.

Figure 2.14 shows the two families whose descriptors included the word "stubborn." Once again, the relationships each family makes with this core word yield distinctly different shades of meaning. For both families stubbornness is a form of strength: in family #26 it is negatively correlated with "controlled" and in #56 it is positively correlated with "strong." However, for #26, stubbornness has a more affective quality; it is associated with the deeper attribute of moodiness and is manifested, more superficially, by an absence of cheerfulness and agreeableness. For #56 stubbornness is more an attitude: on a deeper level it is positively related to hardheadedness and manifests itself, more superficially, by an absence of reasonableness. The latter quality is clearly perceived as an attitude; it is positively associated with the deeper attribute of openmindedness. Of the nine families who met our standards for structure, the remaining two (not represented in either Figure 2.13 or 2.14) showed evidence of characterologies similar to families #60 and #62.

THE FIT BETWEEN MODEL AND DATA

Table 2.11 summarizes the predictions and results from our two direct assessments of family construing. The fit is good but not perfect. What are the implications for our core hypothesis of this good but imperfect fit? In order to answer this question let us review the logic of the specific predictions. The core hypothesis is that a family's problem-solving style in the laboratory reflects its general approach to construing novel or ambiguous social settings. In order to fashion specific predictions for testing in these two studies we followed a specific path. First we defined a set of dimensions which could distinguish among families according to how they construed their social world; these dimensions could be recast as family types (as shown in Table 2.10). Then we selected a special social community — the psychiatric hospital — for directly observing family constructions. We developed additional theory in order to clarify how families might differ, with respect to their constructions, in this setting and how these differences ought to relate to the basic, laboratory-measured dimensions. Finally, we had to design, from scratch, two new methods for directly assessing shared construing in families.

Reviewing this chain helps clarify two points. First, there are many theoretical and methodological problems — other than the validity of the core hypothesis — which could have produced a poor fit between predictions and data; indeed, from this perspective the fit we actually achieved seems quite acceptable. Second, it is parsimonious to reexamine the later steps in this sequential process of theory and method construction — theories about family experiences in the hospital and our methods for measuring it — to understand why not all our predictions were confirmed. In the overall structure of our investigations, our core hypothesis lies at the logical center. Altering that hypothesis means recasting a large number of other propositions and interpretations. Reexamining — and perhaps revising — the more restricted hypothesis about the family's experience of the hospital has less direct consequences because fewer other interpretations and propositions depend on these more peripheral concepts. To be sure, a systematic failure to match predictions to findings would seriously question the core hypothesis itself. Clearly, we are not in that state with respect to the contents of Table 2.11.

All our failures to match predictions and outcomes are fun-

TABLE 2.11　THE FIT BETWEEN DATA AND PREDICTIONS FOR DIRECT STUDIES OF FAMILY CONSTRUING. THE TABLE INDICATES THE PREDICTIONS MADE FOR EACH OF THE FOUR GROUPS OF FAMILIES. AN ASTERISK INDICATES WHERE PREDICTIONS WERE NOT CONFIRMED; IN THOSE INSTANCES, THE ACTUAL FINDINGS ARE INDICATED IN PARENTHESES.

Variable	Family type			
	Environment-sensitive	Consensus-sensitive	Achievement-sensitive	Distance-sensitive
Perception of the ward				
Synchrony	High	High	Low	Low
Mastery				
Information accuracy	High	Low	High* (Low)	Low* (High)
Subtlety of perception	High	Low	High	Low
Engagement	High	Low* (High)	High* (Low)	Low
Motives of others	High	Low* (High)	Low	Low
Perception of other families				
Synchrony (Acknowledgement)	Very High	High	High	Low
Depth and variety[a]	High	Low* (Moderate)	High* (Moderate)	Low
Conceptual framework	High	Low	High	Low
Number of predictions				
Made	8	8	8	8
Obtained	8	5	5	7

a. We used the combination of five scores, as shown in Table 2.9.

damentally attributable to three surprising findings. First, in our study of ward perception, high coordination was associated with high scores on our measurement of engagement and with the placement of low moral judgment items in the "uncharacteristic" columns. We had expected that high configuration would have been related to high engagement and that only environment-sensitive families would see others' motives as reliable and inner-directed.

Second, also in our study of ward perception, we had expected high configuration to predict information accuracy; instead, distance-sensitives did better than expected and achievement-sensitives did worse. Finally, in the study of family perception, we had expected configuration to predict clear-cut differences in depth and variety. Only environment-sensitive families showed a clear-cut superiority over the others, and this could be delineated only by combining a number of separate measures.

Let us turn first to the surprising relationship between coordination and the ward perception variables, engagement and moral judgment. Reexamination of the meaning of these two variables themselves offers an explanation for this surprise. Initially, our predictions rested on the untested assumption that engagement and moral judgment measured two different dimensions of a family's experience of the ward. However, examining all the dependent variables in this study shows that this pair had the highest intercorrelation ($r = .51$; $p < .01$). Thus, these two variables may be measuring the same dimension of the family's experience; both may measure the family's sense of comfort in the ward. Originally, we proposed moral judgment as an index of the family's experienced comfort in the ward setting — particularly the predictability, from their vantage point, of the social order. Let us redefine comfort as a feeling of being a part of the ward community. According to this revised concept of comfort, high scores on moral judgment reflect a sense of being part of a system of ordered and altruistic relationships, and close fit with the modal view reflects a sense of being with the majority. However, it is quite possible that comfort, as we are redefining it, arises in two different ways. When a family is effective in perceiving subtle cues in the environment, the sense of comfort may reflect the family's successful exploration and mastery of the new environment. This would most clearly be the case for our environment-sensitive families, who have high scores on our measure of successful exploration on the ward perception Q-sort: information accuracy and subtlety of perception. They also seem to form rich and organized conceptions of other families, as indicated by high scores for depth and variety and conceptual framework on family perception procedure.

However, comfort may also be a result of conformity. A family may have strong need to feel a part of a larger group out of a sense of its own inadequacy. In this case a family's experience of fit would be compensatory or protective rather than a consequence of mastery. One deficit which the family may feel is an inability to grasp, in an accurate or subtle way, some of the main features of the ward community. This would be the case for consensus-sensitive and distance-sensitive families: they both have low scores on information accuracy and subtlety of perception on the ward perception Q-sort. Likewise, on the family perception procedure they have low scores for conceptual framework and only modest (consensus-sensitive) or low (distance-sensitive) scores for depth and variety. The two groups differ, however. The distance-sensitive group, we have posited, feels discouraged about itself as a group; members have a fundamental pessimism about gaining anything of substance from their association with one another. Consensus-sensitive families feel a clear and omnipresent sense of themselves as a group. Following Strodtbeck (1958), we can argue that they seek to be part of a greater order they do not believe they themselves can understand or fashion. Thus, according to this line of reasoning, they are much more likely than distance-sensitives to seek the kind of compensatory comfort, through compliance, that we are proposing.

Our second surprising finding concerned information accuracy and the particularly low scores achieved by achievement-sensitive families. We had assumed that information accuracy on the ward would be equivalent to pattern recognition in our laboratory task. Thus, since high configuration families are defined by their ability to recognize patterns in the laboratory, we had expected they would have comparable high information accuracy scores on the ward. It may be, however, that learning accurate information about the ward is a more sustained, complex, and exploratory process than the more focused pattern recognition of the card sorting task. If this is true, then information accuracy may not reflect the family's sense of optimism and mastery; instead it may reflect the freedom each member has to explore and understand the new environment. The most pertinent "freedom" is freedom from distraction by an embroiling and absorbing family. This new interpretation of information accuracy would explain why achievement- and consensus-sensitive families have the lowest scores. They are, according to our present understanding, the most embroiled families. The former is embroiled in competition, the latter in consensus-seeking. In effect, the boundaries of the achievement- and consensus-sensitive families are more impermeable to the outside community. Chapter 8 presents evidence that these two groups of families do indeed have impermeable boundaries. On the ward, this shows itself in the families' seating patterns in a multifamily group (clumped rather than dispersed), and on sociometric choices (families much more often choose each other, rather than nonfamily members, on a standard questionnaire asking whom in the group they know best). This interpretation clarifies the unanticipated finding of high information accuracy scores with the distance-sensitive families, who are also relatively less embroiled with one another.

The third surprising finding was the lack of clear distinction among our three groups on our measures of depth and variety of perceptions of other families, as measured by coding the family discussion. We had expected clear-cut superiority of high configuration families; in fact, we had to combine all five scales and then found only that environment-sensitive families had a clear-cut superiority over the others. In other words, when we measured the number and variety of descriptors each family produced, there was not a clear separation among our groups of families. However, when we measured how the families organized these descriptors into a coherent conceptual structure, high configuration families did have a clear superiority (see Table 2.10).

Pertinent here is a study by Barenboim (1977) of interpersonal perception in children and adolescents. He learned that as a child matures he first develops a set of clear descriptors or dimensions for distinguishing among people he knows. He then organizes those dimensions through a set of relationships which become, for him, an implicit or personal psychology. Comparable concepts of development have been applied to group and family process and may be apt here.[13] Some families mature in the sense that the relationships between members become more complex and subtle. For example, as children become adolescents they develop an increasingly complex appreciation of their parents, and in healthy families this is often reciprocated by their parents. As relationships flower, individuals become increasingly sensitive to each other's views, including, presumably, their views on other families. The mutual appreciation involves the continuing integration of each individual's view into a common set of understandings and conceptions. The structured conceptions of other families, which many high configuration families showed in our study, may serve as the simplest example of such common conceptions. By contrast, "immature" families — ones that are less adaptive or healthy — may fail to reconcile the varying perceptions and conceptions of its members. This would certainly be consistent with the low scores on mid-range acknowledgment found in our low configuration families. While the family may be capable, when it chooses to or is forced to work together, of generating many ideas, they cannot integrate these ideas into any coherent whole.

Overall, these findings and those of the previous section do not seem to offer a serious challenge to the core hypothesis. They have, nonetheless, encouraged us to think more specifically, and presumably more accurately, about the ramifications of this hypothesis. Our studies comparing families of normals, schizophrenics, and delinquents encouraged us to think about the limits on the influence of the family's shared perception of the laboratory on the behavior of its members. For example, in seeking to explain the relatively good performance of families of schizophrenics when performing in isolation on the second task, we speculated that shared constructions of the laboratory staff might offer a countervailing influence and that each member was simultaneously a member of at least two groups. As another example, in our ward perception studies we thought through more clearly the components and mechanisms underlying a family's feeling of comfort in a social setting. Finally, in our family perception study, we began to think of the parallels between family development and the progressive integration and synthesis of their experience of their social world. These findings, in large measure, have supported the core hypothesis while serving as a stimulus for more specific theorizing about shared construing in families.

Strategy Three: Pursuing Significant Alternate Hypotheses

The third approach to examining our core hypothesis is to assess plausible and important rival hypotheses. There may be other ways to explain differences in families' problem-solving styles than to find differences in their underlying approaches to construing the social environment. Do data support these alternate explanations rather than the core hypothesis? There are three theoretical domains to consider in formulating alternate explanations: external or macrosocial forces that shape family process (social status, ethnic and cultural background, and so on); other kinds of internal family process (various aspects of family structure, styles of conflict management, power relations, values, prior experience with problem solving in general and logical puzzles in particular); and, finally, the skills of the family members considered as individuals.

The first group of alternate explanations remains plausible. Strodtbeck's work (1958), already discussed, suggests major differences in the problem-solving styles of southern Italians and Eastern European Jews. Straus (1967, 1968) has shown important differences between working-class and middle-class families. We chose not to pursue this area systematically, because in our data there were no relationships between social class or ethnic background, on one hand, and families' problem-solving styles, on the other.

The second class of alternate hypotheses, which remains important for us to consider in future work, has for the moment been placed on the back burner for two reasons. First, it is not clear in what sense these are truly alternate explanations. For example, shared construing may be understood as a method by which families regulate internal conflict, assign roles, and establish norms and rules about interaction among members. Other explanations that seem at first blush to be different or alternate might also be subsumed under the concept of shared construing. Even if they are not subsumable, some of these concepts may in fact be equivalent in terms of their meaning and logic. For example, the concept of family values (that is, what the family regards as most important) may be roughly equivalent to the ideas of shared construing. A second reason for not pursuing this class of presumably alternate hypotheses is that the problems of measuring the critical variables are at least as severe as the problems of measuring various aspects of shared construing. The efforts of many scholars to measure power in families (who is more powerful than whom) have nearly run aground since the correlations among scores from the many different instruments are very close to zero (see, for example, Cromwell et al., 1975). Nonetheless, recent theoretical and methodological work in this area makes it a more inviting source for rival hypotheses.

We chose the third domain—individual skills of family members—to explore intensively. Family problem solving seems to involve an enormous number of skills from each family member: basic intelligence, vigilant and selective attention, great skill in pattern recognition, a personal confidence in one's ability to master a test situation, and sensitivity and attentiveness to the views and experiences of others. Indeed, as we have already argued, family problem solving per se may merely be an epiphenomenon; how the family performs as a group may simply reflect the presence or absence of individual skills in its members. For example, it seems reasonable to suppose that—all things being equal—a highly intelligent family is more likely to perform in an environment-sensitive fashion than a family of low intelligence. If intelligence or related problem skills accounted for most of the variation in family problem skills, a serious blow would strike our core hypothesis. Our methods would have to be regarded as little more than a crude group intelligence test. The scores they yield would reflect little about family process—the process of shared construing or any other.

The particular developmental course of our work gave us another reason to attach high priority to this alternate hypothesis. Our first two series of studies (reported in Chapter 1 and the first section of this chapter) concerned families of psychiatric patients. For the past fifteen years there has been mounting evidence that some forms of psychopathology may be inherited. The evidence is strongest for schizophrenia.[14] Thus, we might expect the biological parents of our schizophrenic patients to be afflicted with serious psychopathology themselves (although the odds were against their ever having actually been schizophrenic). It was quite plausible to argue that the behavior the parents and children showed in our problem-solving setting reflected nothing more than genetically transmitted and biologically based information-processing deficits they all shared. The enmeshed, self-protective patterns might be viewed as a *socially adaptive* response to a pervasive impairment of this kind. This same argument is more difficult to render for our families of delinquents, although some forms of this disorder may also be genetically transmitted.

A third reason also led us to intensively explore this area. The study of how individuals interpret and construe their environment had for years been a productive vein of research in individual psychology. We were attracted by the work of Kelly and his successors (which found its way into the family perception procedure), as well as Rotter's exploration of individuals' perceived control over the environment and the work on cognitive controls by Gardner, Holtzman, and their group.[15] It was easy to posit that individuals with certain types of perceived control, modes of construing the environment, and cognitive controls might—when they aggregated to form a family—shape family process in just the ways we had been observing.

We took two general approaches to studying the relative influence of individual skills on family problem solving. The first approach was simple and straightforward but not definitive. Families were grouped according to whether they were high or low on the three basic dimensions of problem solving (configuration, coordination, and closure); this produced eight groups. The groups were then compared on measures of individual intelligence, perceived locus of control, and a variety of perceptual style variables (such as field articulation, leveling/sharpening, tolerance of ambiguity, physiognomic perception, and category width). We used a number of different samples. Some of these samples included families with psychiatric patients. Other samples consisted entirely of nonclinical families. (In Chapter 8 we will explain more fully how and why samples of families without any manifest psychopathology show the same variation and varieties of problem solving as samples of families with psychopathology.) In general, the findings have been quite negative. Occasionally a finding showed some significant relationship between family problem solving and an individual skill variable, but then in another sample this relationship seemed to disappear (or, in one case, a finding in the opposite direction was obtained). Many of these findings have been reported elsewhere (see, for example, Oliveri and Reiss, 1981). Our overall impression is that the findings are pervasively and reliably negative.

Our second approach to studying the relative influence of individual skills on family problem solving was more direct and precise. True experiments were conducted—that is, we brought under direct experimental control certain information-processing sequences in individual members and observed the impact on family problem solving. Two experiments will be described here.

The first experiment directly controlled the level of individual skill in a single member of the family. The agent of control was 175 mg of secobarbital, which in previous studies had been shown to produce a short-term, entirely reversible deficit in the kind of information processing likely to be crucial for solving our laboratory puzzles. We reasoned that if family problem-solving styles were critically dependent on the individual skills of its members, this experimental manipulation should have a clear-cut effect on several of our critical measures of family problem solving. On the other hand, if family problem solving was a reflection of the family's shared view of the laboratory, including—in this case—its view of the drug-placebo aspect of the study, then its problem-solving style should remain unaffected. In fact, the family should show some evidence of compensating for the information-processing deficit produced in the individual receiving secobarbital.

The second experiment directly controlled members' access to one another during the problem-solving period. We assumed that as this access was reduced, members would feel more and more isolated from their families. This was the first study to use computer-controlled on-line techniques for studying family interaction. The computer was required for a special and precise kind of experimental control. We wanted to reduce each member's access to the others and yet keep constant the amount, quality, and pacing of information he was receiving. We reasoned that as a member's access to others in his family was cut off, he should feel less and less like an active member of the family group. If family problem solving is a reflection of individual information-processing skills, as argued by the alternate hypothesis, then reducing a member's sense of being in a family should not influence his performance; that is, our manipulation should produce no effect. This would be particularly true if the timing, amount, and quality of information could be kept constant as intermember access was reduced. Maintaining this constancy is difficult, however. In the card sorting procedure we isolated members in the initial and the final tasks. But in doing so we not only cut individuals off from a sense of involvement with their family, we also cut off a critical source of information supply — the ideas and observations of the other members. This confounds change in access to other members with change in information inflow. For example, using an individual skills approach, we could explain the improvement shown by families of schizophrenics in the first study reported in this chapter. This explanation would begin with a reasonable assumption that all members in the family have a mild attentional defect. They do well in problems when they are not distracted by information arriving unexpectedly but get distracted when unbidden information arrives without warning. The unbidden quality of information inflow does in fact characterize the family interaction phase of our card sort. The deterioration of families of schizophrenics in this phase might be due to the phase's informational characteristics rather than its social ones. Our computer-based method was designed to duplicate the unbidden and unexpected aspect of information inflow and thereby to maintain a constant environment of information as intermember access was reduced. It thus provided a crucial test for the individual skills hypothesis, which would predict constant performance under constant conditions in the informational environment.

CONTROLLING INDIVIDUAL SKILLS: THE SECOBARBITAL EXPERIMENT

The study compared the effects of secobarbital with a placebo, in a double-blind fashion, on the critical problem-solving variables assessing configuration and coordination.[16] We used a pretest/post-test, between-subjects design. Two subsamples of subjects — families of psychiatrically hospitalized adolescents and families of children without psychiatric disturbance — were distributed equally in the drug and placebo conditions.

Subjects. We used twenty-four families, six in each of the groups. Each family had a child in late adolescence who received the medication. The children who were psychiatric patients were almost evenly divided between those diagnosed as having schizophrenia or a related disorder and those with a severe impulse disturbance. The most critical comparisons in the design were between the drug and placebo groups in the post-test. Since the sample was small, we could be sure that random assignment to drug or placebo conditions would demonstrate a true drug effect. We needed to be as sure as possible that the problem-solving performance of the two groups would have been identical, or nearly so, if an active drug had not been administered. The best way to assure this was to match the twenty-four families, within diagnostic groups (normal or psychiatric), on the basis of their problem-solving performance on the pre-test. We used the problem-solving score, initial to family, and trial time, standard deviation, to produce twelve pairs of families. At random, one member of each pair was given the drug; the other received the placebo. In fact, this procedure not only produced a drug group and a placebo group precisely matched for problem solving (on the pre-test), but produced almost perfect matching between the two for intelligence, age, education, Hollingshead-Redlich occupational rating, family income, and family size. This comparability was preserved when we analyzed parental means and individual scores of fathers, mothers, and children for these six variables. The only discrepancy between drug and placebo—of the seventy-two comparisons made among the problem solving and other variables—was that fathers in the drug group had significantly more education than those in the placebo group. A variety of secondary analyses failed to reveal any effect of this discrepancy between the two groups on the important dependent measures.

Procedure. (1) Each family was given a card sorting task on night one. This task used sequences of numbers rather than letters, but was otherwise identical to that described earlier in this chapter. (2) On the following afternoon, the normal children were admitted to the research hospital for an overnight stay; the psychiatric patients, on another ward, had been admitted several weeks to several months previously. (3) Two hours after eating, the adolescent (patient or normal) received either 175 mg of secobarbital or a placebo on a strict, double-blind basis. (The guesses of parents, children, and observer as to whether a placebo or active drug had been given were often inaccurate.) (4) An hour later the parents were seated in the booth assigned to them in a way that minimized or eliminated any contact between parents and child. (5) The post-test card sort was administered. This used the conventional letter/nonsense-syllable form of the test. All speech in both pre-and post-test problem-solving sessions was tape-recorded and then transformed by a polygraph to a visual record.

Results. Figures 2.15 and 2.16 show that there was no effect of the drug, in either patient or normal group, on two critical measures of family problem solving; problem-solving score, initial to final, and trial time, standard deviation. This is confirmed using an analysis of variance (2×2; diagnosis $\times$ drug status) for the post-test data or analysis of covariance using the pre-test problem-solving scores as the covariate. However, the apparent difference

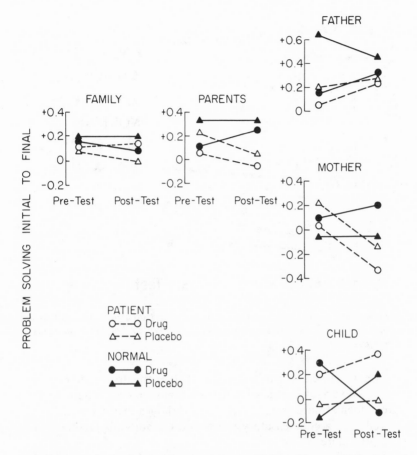

Figure 2.15.   *The effects of drug and diagnosis on problem-solving scores, initial to family. The only statistically significant effect was the difference between the normal and patient parents on the post-test.*

between patient and normal groups, shown in the figures, is also revealed in ANOVAs of post-test data (for parental problem-solving score, initial to final, F for diagnosis $= 4.66$; $p < .05$; for trial time, standard deviation, F for diagnosis $= 3.88$, $p < .10$).

The findings revealed the predictable differences between normal and patient families. For a mix of impulsive and schizophrenic disorders, we expected both a measure of configuration (problem-solving score) and coordination (trial time, standard deviation) to be lower in the patient group. The results, however, showed no effect of the drug. Could this be due to the fact that our procedure was insensitive to an otherwise significant drug effect?

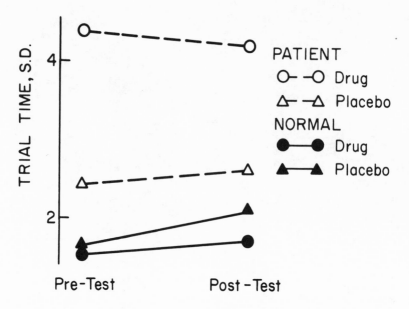

Figure 2.16. *The effects of drug and diagnosis on trial time, standard deviation. Individual analyses for fathers, mothers, and children cannot be computed.*

One way to explore this is to see whether the drug had an effect on other variables which in turn may have compensated for or overridden a more direct effect. Two variables that may well have served such a compensatory function are readily obtainable from this procedure.

The findings for *speech rate* are shown in Figure 2.17. Speech rate is computed by dividing the total number of seconds in which speech was recorded by the total number of seconds of experimental time (start of trial 1 to the end of trial 14). Ferreira and Winter (1968) have shown that this variable is highly correlated with family communication effectiveness and efficiency. Figure 2.17 shows there is clear tendency for all families to decline from pre-test to post-test. However, drug families decline at a much slower rate; this produces a clear difference between them and the placebo families on the post-test, although these groups had almost identical scores on the pre-test. An analysis of covariance shows this quite clearly (ANCOVA F[drug] = 4.82 (1,19), $p < .05$). The pattern of findings is repeated examining parental mean scores (ANCOVA F[drug] = 4.74 (1,19), $p < .05$), and individual scores for fathers (ANCOVA F[drug] = 5.36 (1,19), $p < .05$), mothers (nonsignificant trend), and children (nonsignificant trend).

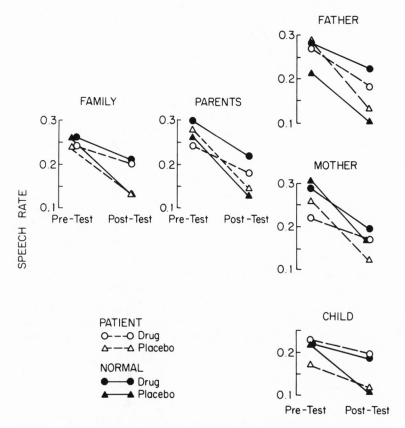

Figure 2.17.   *The effects of drug and diagnosis on speech rate*

Although only the first two of these are statistically significant, it is clear that all three individuals contribute to the overall family differences.

The second variable, *overlap percent,* is computed by dividing the number of seconds of speech in which there were two people talking simultaneously by the total number of seconds in which any speech at all occurred. Overlapping speech has been thought of as disrupted and disruptive. The commonsense notion here is that if more than one person is talking simultaneously, speech is hard to follow. Although a simple index like this may reflect many different sociopsychological functions, recent evidence suggests that an absence of overlapping speech in family conversations is a sign of *inadequate* communication. Mishler and Waxler (1968) found, in families of acute schizophrenics, that low overlap percentage, measured somewhat differently, indicated an overcontrol of spontaneity. We have found low overlap percent, measured as by Mishler and Waxler, to be an index of frigid politeness and interpersonal distance (see, for example, the low values obtained by the families of character disorders in Chapter 1). It is quite likely that there is an inverse U-shaped relationship between levels of overlapping speech and communication effectiveness so that at very high levels — where speech becomes incomprehensible — and at very low levels it reflects or causes poor intermember communication. On the pre-test, our normal families had a level of 20 percent; on the assumption that communication patterns in normal families are effective, we may surmise that this figure approximates an optimum, the apogee of the inverse U-curve, under the conditions represented by the experiment. Figure 2.18 shows the normals were higher than the patient families (pre-test ANOVA $F = 4.1666$ $(1,20)$, $p < .10$). Combining normal and patient, the two drug groups maintained their level of overlapping speech on the post-test (from 17 percent to 16 percent), whereas the placebo groups fell sharply (from 18 percent to 12 percent). Analysis of covariance shows a significant drug effect (ANCOVA F [drug] $= 10.52$ $(1,19)$, $p < .005$).

The resilience of family process. The data strongly suggest that the drug might have influenced family problem solving, but the family actively countervened in order to prevent this effect. We can get a clearer glimpse of this process by posing three more questions to our data. First, might the drug simply, through its well-known disinhibition effects, have allowed the child to talk more? The parents' increase in speech rate and even overlap percent might simply have been a passive, imitative response (not actively compensatory) to the disinhibited speech in the child. Two sets of data argue against this. First, it is primarily the parents, not the child, who show most of the effects of the drug in the first two trials of the task (that is, the difference between drug and placebo groups shows up later in the task for the children than it does for the parents). Moreover, cross-lagged correlations between the speech indices of parents and children on the first two and last two trials of the post-test family phase show that the parents' speech indices on trials 1 and 2 predict the child's indices on trials 13 and 14, but not the reverse. In other words, the parents seem to detect some change in the child in the first two trials, and they speak and interrupt more from then on.

What are the parents detecting? Might they have consciously guessed their child was drugged and then consciously spoken and interrupted more to offset that effect? This is unlikely for two reasons. First, many parents in both groups guessed wrong. Se-

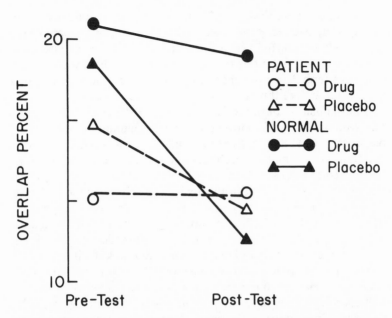

Figure 2.18.   *The effects of drug and diagnosis on overlap percent. Individual analyses for fathers, mothers, and children cannot be computed for this variable.*

cond, there was no relation between correct guessing, in either the drug or placebo group, and speech rate or overlap percent. Thus, the parents were, in all likelihood, unconsciously detecting subliminal cues very early in the task. Since parents had no opportunity to see or talk informally with their child between drug administration and the problem-solving test, these cues must have been conveyed by the child's speech over the intercom system. The speech changes must have been subtle indeed. The children were not obviously somnolent, nor was their speech obviously slurred. Indeed, an experienced psychopharmacologist who observed one-half of the testing sessions often could not distinguish the children with the active drug from those with the placebo.

Let us assume that the parents could detect, on a subliminal level, that their offspring had received a drug. Let us further assume that the parents' increase in speech rate and overlap percent was a result of this subliminal detection. What function might have been served, for the family, by this increase? One hint is to examine the correlates of speech rate and overlap percent. We might argue that the drug had a tendency to produce a deficit in configuration, coordination, or both, and that the parents' increased speech rate was a compensation for this deficit: it maintained coordination and configuration at pre-drug levels. Unfortunately, we cannot examine this hypothesis directly. We know that the speech rise in parents of drug children occurred very early—within the first two trials. Our measures do not permit us to determine whether there was any actual short-term deficit in either coordination or configuration in the drug group before this rise in speech rate and overlap.

An examination of the correlates of speech rate and overlap percent with measures of coordination and configuration, in this sample, does provide some suggestive clues. These clues center on coordination. For example, speech rate and overlap percent both show positive correlations with sort similarity, final trial ($r = .47$, $p <$ $.05$, and $r = .29$, nonsignificant trend, respectively) in the post-test only. This finding suggests that speech rate and overlap percent may compensate for deficit in coordination but not in configuration. To substantiate this further, we constructed, post hoc, another index which should reflect coordination. A significant component of coordination, as we have thought about it, is the sensitivity of members to the internal states of one another. Thus, in well-coordinated families the parents should be able to correctly detect the drug status of the child. Accordingly, we constructed a score which credited parents if they successfully guessed the drug status of the child. This perception could be direct (for example, for parents of drug children: "I think he/she had the drug") or indirect (again for parents of drug children: "I think we did better last night than tonight"). This drug perception score had positive correlations for the drug sample ($r = .52$, $p < .05$, for speech rate, and $r = .29$, nonsignificant trend, for overlap percent) and for the placebo sample ($r = .71$, $p < .01$, for speech rate and $r = .65$, $p <$ $.02$, for overlap percent). The correlations for the drug perception score have the same significance as those for sort similarity. They are consistent with a notion that *if* the active drug reduced family coordination—through its impact on the adolescent—then increased overlap percent could have compensatorily returned coordination to its original, pre-drug level.

In sum, the data argues for the efforts—probably most of them unconscious—to which families go to maintain problem-solving patterns in the face of a sudden change in the problem-solving skills of one of its members. Beyond that, these data would argue that our problem-solving setting reflects a family process—not some simple summation of the skills of individual members.

CONTROLLING ACCESS OF MEMBERS TO ONE ANOTHER:
THE TELETYPE EXPERIMENT

This study examined the individual skill hypothesis from a very different perspective than the secobarbital study.[17] In the secobarbital study we reasoned that if family problem-solving styles reflect a simple summation of individual skills, then a sharp reduction in the skills of one member should have a noticeable impact on the overall level of family problem solving. The teletype experiment takes a different approach. If individual information-processing skills play a preeminent role in a family member's performance, then the overall effectiveness of that member should depend on two factors. The first is the level of skill itself; good problem solvers—it is almost tautological to assert—will perform more effectively than poor ones. A second factor is the quality and availability of problem-related information. Holding skill constant, a member's performance should improve as the quality and availability of information improves.

Our card sorting procedure cannot, by itself, adequately explore the individual skill hypothesis. It cannot readily disentangle information-processing skill from quality of information factors. Recall that in the card sort we compared each member's performance on the initial, individual sort with his performance on the family sort, where he worked with other members. This comparison, among others, is used to draw inferences about the impact of the family on its members. However, as we move from individual to family sort, the informational characteristics of the task also change. Each member has access to ideas and observations from others. In some families this may support effective problem solving. In others, this access may be hindering—particularly if ideas come rapidly, sporadically, or unexpectedly, thereby distracting or annoying the members. Suppose, however, we could keep the informational characteristics of the task absolutely constant as we went from the individual task, where individuals have no exposure to one another, to the family task, where the exposure is highest. Under these conditions, the individual skill hypothesis would argue that family performance should remain the same; the basic skills of each member remain constant; further, the procedure assures that the quality of the information remains constant. However, if there were significant shifts in an individual's performance as intermember access was increased or decreased—despite constancy of information across these shifts—then the individual skill hypothesis would be weakened.

The most critical objective of the methods of this experiment, then, is to maintain the constancy of the quality and character of information inflow to each member during the problem-solving period. This was the task of the computer-automated procedure. We used a slight modification of the hypothesis-testing task described in detail in Chapter 1. To review briefly, it is the task of each member to discover the pattern behind a sequence of letters like this one: C T T T T C. Each subject gets a clue or an example sequence at the start of his work and then can test his own sequences by submitting them to the experimenter. If they conform to the underlying pattern rule, he receives a plus (+); if not, he receives a minus (–). After his hypothesis is submitted and rated, it is circulated to other family members. Thus, each member can learn not only from his own experience, but from those of others in his family. Further, he can use others' experience to formulate his own strategy for testing hypotheses.

In the present experiment, the computer-automated procedure was used both to rate and to return the hypothesis to each member testing one as well as to circulate the rated hypothesis to other members. Members communicated with one another and with the computer by computer-controlled teletypes. The procedure operated in three modes. In the *public mode,* each member's hypothesis was circulated immediately to all other members with a symbol clearly identifying which member had typed in that sequence. In the *anonymous mode,* the hypothesis was also circulated to the others; however, the identity of the author was concealed. In the *standard mode,* each member's hypothesis was sorted in the computer. A sequence of similar informational value, with a (+) or (–) correctly assigned, was then distributed to the others.

We compared two groups of families: environment-sensitives and consensus-sensitives. These families were classified according to their performance on the card sorting task. We have argued that environment-sensitive families perceive the puzzles we present them as out there: a vivid, masterable component of a verifiable and discoverable world. Within this frame, we reasoned that in environment-sensitive families, when faced with novel problems in the environment, a member's prime utility to the others is his capacity to provide them with information for their own problem-solving efforts. Thus, if the member – as a source of information – is replaced by another nonfamilial source (in the present study, a computer), the information will be utilized in the same way. In other words, information is valued for what it conveys about the problem in the environment and not for what it conveys about the member providing it. Thus, if we provide each member with the same amount of information about the environment, as we cut off access to his family, he will continue to be an effective problem solver. In contrast, we reasoned that members of consensus-sensitive families would treat information from each other primarily for what it informed them about the others' thoughts and attitudes. This would be in the service of achieving an agreed-upon rather than a correct interpretation of the environment. Thus, if we replace the other members by substituting a nonfamily source of information about the environment, each member in the consensus-sensitive family will treat the information itself differently. Since the information can no longer inform him about the ideas and attitudes of other members, its function changes. There are at least two logical possibilities. He may discard it altogether, using only information he himself gains, or he may utilize it for its value in identifying properties of the environment rather than properties of his family. In the text accompanying Figure 2.11 we discussed findings which can help us in predicting which of these two alternatives is more likely. We argued that, free from the influence of their families, members of consensus-sensitive families will learn from their own efforts and from the efforts of others. Thus, we predict that consensus-sensitive families will improve as they move from a mode with close connectons between members to one where there are no such connections.

Sample. The overall sample consisted of fifteen families, although we will focus here on the results from eight families divided into four closely matched pairs labeled (a) through (d). Each family comprised two parents and two adolescent children. In this pilot study four pairs were just sufficient to achieve the acceptable significance level of .06 — using the binomial theorem — if the direction of findings was the same for all four pairs. One family in each pair was environment-sensitive, the other consensus-sensitive. Four scores from the card sorting procedure, in which all families had participated prior to the teletype study, were used to make this distinction: problem-solving score, initial to family; absolute problem-solving score, last trial of the family task; for coordination, trial time, standard deviation, family task; and sort similarity, family task. All eight families were high on the latter two. The environment-sensitive families all had positive change scores of .200 or better and absolute problem-solving scores of at least .375. The consensus-sensitive families all had absolute scores below this level or negative scores or both. Paired families were closely matched for intelligence, parental mean education, total family income, parents' age and children's age. In three of the four pairs each environment-sensitive family had offspring without serious psychopathology and each consensus-sensitive family had an offspring diagnosed as schizophrenic or adjustment reaction of adolescence. In the fourth pair, both families had an offspring with the diagnosis of adjustment reaction of adolescence.

Procedure. When the family arrived in the laboratory they were seated at teletypes between screens, as shown in Figure 2.19. They were told that each member would be designated by a letter: A =

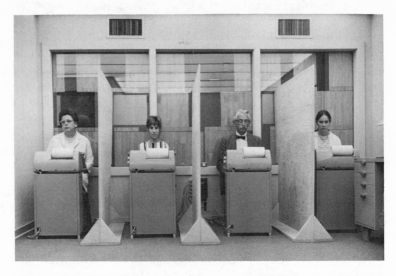

Figure 2.19.   *View of apparatus with screens pushed between subjects according to the procedure for experimental puzzles. One-way observation mirror is directly behind the subjects. (The individuals pictured were members of the professional staff of the National Institute of Mental Health and were not actual subjects.)*

mother, B = patient (or patient-control in normal families), C = father, and D = sibling. (These letter designations should not be confused with designation of family pairs, also by letter.) When the experimenter read the instructions the screens were moved away, thus permitting eye and voice contact between members. The entire procedure was controlled by a fifth teletype in an observation room immediately behind a one-way mirror.

Each of the four pairs worked in each of three modes: public, anonymous, and standard. The order was different and randomized for each pair. In each mode, the family was given the hypothesis-testing task. To review, this task had the following steps: (1) Each member received an example sequence; parents had examples drawn from one principle of sequence construction; children had sequences constructed by a different principle. (2) Each member received a private inventory composed of twenty sequences from which he had to select a subset he believed was correct. (3) Each member tested his own sequences when it was his turn. (4) When each member felt he had discovered the underlying principle or principles, he indicated this to the experimenter (in this procedure by pressing a special key on the teletype). (5) When all four family members were done, they received another private inventory to assess changes, if any, in their concepts of the underlying pattern rule.

The three modes differed from each other during steps (3) and (4). In the public mode (see Figure 2.20) each member's sequence was distributed to the others immediately, with its rating of (+) or (−), and a notation indicating who had authored it (A = mother, B = patient-child, and so on). In the anonymous mode the authorship of the sequence was concealed by omitting the appropriate symbol as well as by delaying and randomizing the redistribution of the sequence. In the standard mode the member's sequence was never redistributed. A sequence from a standard library, constructed by computer, was circulated as soon as the member received feedback, (+) or (−), from the computer. The library was made up to contain the kinds of sequences an average family would construct. In fact, a number of measures of the quality and usefulness of information in these sequences showed that sequences distributed to the family in the standard mode were comparable to those in other modes. Most important, there were no within-pair differences with respect to the comparability of the information distributed to the family in the standard mode and that produced by the family's own sequences in the other modes.

The success of the experiment depended on the family's clear

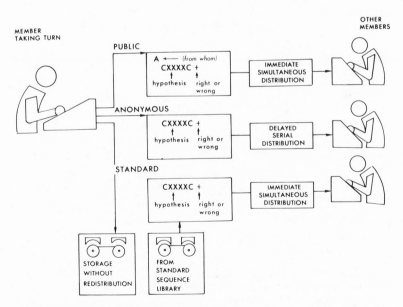

Figure 2.20. *Schematic representation of the three modes by which sequences were distributed among family members*

understanding of the differences among the three modes. Thus, each mode was preceded by a sample puzzle by which the family was instructed in the operation of that mode. Further, a variety of programming techniques—such as programming the teletypes to produce an auditory signal confirming the mode of distribution—reinforced these instructions. At the conclusion of each mode, a careful, exhaustive, and standardized questionnaire confirmed that almost all subjects thoroughly understood the differences among the three modes; there was no difference within pairs of families in the level of this understanding.

Results. The results of fundamental importance are shown in Figure 2.21. We used two measures of problem-solving effectiveness to measure the impact of the three different distribution modes. These scores reflect each member's change from the initial to final private inventories given in the three modes. The first score,

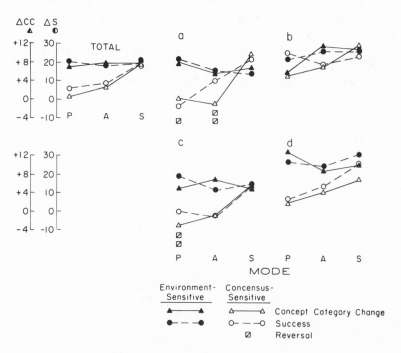

Figure 2.21. *Change in performance from initial to final private inventories for all three modes. The unit datum is the family mean. Graph at left compares means from the environment-sensitive and consensus-sensitive groups; four graphs at right shown individual family pair. In all graphs changes in concept category (ΔCC) and changes in success scores (ΔS) are represented.*

change in concept category, was described in Chapter 1. A maximum score of $+12$ is assigned for a change that shows the most growth in the understanding of the patterns: at the conclusion of the task a subject still holds the concept based on his own example *and* he has also learned the concept underlying the example of the other generation. In Chapter 1 we referred to this as *penetration;* it was the kind of change the Friedkin family could never achieve. The lowest score of -4 is assigned to the change showing the most slippage from the first to the second private inventory, a change we call *reversal.* Here, the individual gives up a concept he clearly (and validly) perceived, at the start of the task, from his own example and which he expressed on the initial private inventory. In addition, he accepts *only* the concept of the other generation. The second score, called the success score, is less sensitive to qualitative shifts in concept from start to finish. A success score is simply the total number of correct sequences accepted and the total number of incorrect sequences rejected on an inventory. The change score shown in Figure 2.21 is the difference in this score between the first and second inventories.

Figure 2.21 shows the mean, for both scores, of all four members in the family. The graph in the upper left shows the data for all eight families combined. This pattern of changes follows our predictions precisely. An examination of each of the four pairs shows that, for at least one of the two measures of concept change, change in concept category or success score, each of the consensus-sensitive families shows a progressive increase from public to anonymous to standard mode, whereas none of the environment-sensitive families show that pattern on either measure. Of special interest are the instances of reversal. There are five instances of this, all occurring in consensus-sensitive families and none of them in the standard mode.

In sum, the results of the teletype study would argue against a theory of information-processing based on individual skills as adequate for explaining family problem-solving behavior in our laboratory. The poor performance of consensus-sensitive families, when they are actively engaged with one another in the family phase of a problem-solving situation, is probably not due to informational characteristics of the family phase, the unbidden nature of the rated hypothesis and its timing. These qualities of informational inflow are preserved by our computer-automated procedure in the standard phase, but the consensus-sensitive families do very well in this phase. The more likely explanation for poor performance of consensus-sensitives in the family phase would involve some kind of family-level process.

SUMMARY OF THE EVIDENCE

Three independent sets of data together argue very persuasively against an individual skills hypothesis. First, when we divide both clinical and nonclinical samples into eight groups based on our three problem-solving dimensions—configuration, coordination, and closure—we can find no consistent differences between these groups on a large number of measures of individual skill: intelligence, perceived locus of control, and perceptual style. Second, when we systematically—under experimental control—reduce the individual skill of a family member participating in family problem solving, the basic style and competence of the family is not thereby altered. In fact, the data strongly suggest that the family actively compensates for the deficit of one of its members. Finally, when we reduce family members' access to one another while keeping information inflow to each member constant, we can actually reverse problem-solving deficits in consensus-sensitive families. This finding is not easily explainable by an individual skills concept.

Part II
Family Crisis and
Family Paradigm

3 | The Role of the Family in Organizing Experience

Personal Explanatory Systems

At every moment the inner world of our body and the outer world of our environment bombard us with stimuli—endless in their variety, unchanging, unique, and infinitely complex. No filter, no system of sampling, no percept or theory is orderly or efficient enough to comprehend the manifold connections and patterns of this universe of stimuli. In this "blooming and buzzing" confusion we might drift with terror and then dissolve in uncertainty. But we do not drift; we do not dissolve. From the very moment of conception we develop filters to shield us from most of the manifest complexity of our inner and outer worlds. Further, we can organize those stimuli which pass through our fields. We can detect patterns among the stimuli and gain a measure of understanding; we can relate them to ourselves and gain a measure of meaning. In the history of Western civilization—particularly in the increasingly homogeneous subculture of the postindustrial middle class—we will argue that the family has come to play a central role in providing understanding and meaning of the stimulus universe for each of its members. The family has come to offer a set of explanations of the world to each of its members that serves as the primary organizer of internal and external experience. This reduction of uncertainty is immensely rewarding. The "fuel" which establishes and maintains these family explanations is the profound satisfaction provided by their capacity to reduce uncertainty. Let us examine this basic argument step by step.

From uterine days onward, each individual acquires experience to distinguish between stimuli from his own body and those from his environment, and to make finer discriminations within these groups of stimuli. Sometimes internal and external stimuli are of significance because of their physical properties: a blanket provides warmth and is sought out; the hot sun can burn and should be avoided. Most stimuli, however, achieve significance not from their physical properties, but because they contain information relevant to an individual's survival or, more generally speaking, to his well-being. A young child learns that a dog's growl signals the animal's anger and that his own stomach's growl indicates his own hunger. Not all stimuli perceivable by the individual can be dealt with. There are too many. Selective mechanisms are required to control and organize incoming stimuli. Broadly speaking, these mechanisms can be divided into two classes.

Elementary controls include a wide range of mechanisms which selectively sample and provide simple organization to incoming stimuli. These include such elementary mechanisms as the differentiation of the receptor function of the nervous system into discrete receptor systems (vision, hearing, and so on) responsive to different classes of stimuli; the development of thresholds for these receptor systems (thereby excluding all low-intensity stimuli); the development of peripheral pattern recognizers within the receptor organs or their primary receiving area in the brain; the development, through regulation by the central nervous system of strategies of attention and stimulus organization. This last group of mechanisms includes cognitive controls (see Gardner et al., 1959, 1960). It also includes the mechanism of defense as elaborated by Sigmund and Anna Freud.[1] Among these more complex elementary mechanisms are those which transform sensations and simple percepts into a perceptual world. Emerging from these processes are highly selected and intricately organized sensations of stimuli which are apprehended as animate and inanimate objects occupying a specifiable location within a span of apperception whose boundaries are established by attentional mechanisms.

Elaborated controls add a new dimension to the reduction of uncertainty and to the establishment of structure in the experiential world. These mechanisms accomplish two things. First, they provide some unifying principles of relationship which tie together the unfolding events and objects in the perceptual world. The separate components of the perceptual world—which are themselves products of highly selective reception and organization of stimuli—are experienced as standing in some relationship to one another. Inner and outer stimuli—organized into bounded entities, usually in the form of concrete objects—become connected by explanations. For example, consider two external events facing the driver of a car: the accelerator pedal on his car and a moving lamp post. The driver connects the two by an explanation. Depressing the pedal increases gasoline flow; this increases the frequency of gas explosions in the cylinders of his car engine, which in turn increases the speed of his car, which produces decreased transit time of a lamp post across his field of vision. Internal events may also be connected. For example, a runner experiences the following sequence: running, shortness of breath, end of running, return of breathing to normal. These events are connected by an explanation: running is linked to oxygen consumption by his muscles, which require increased respiratory activity.

Elaborated controls provide not only understanding but an experience of meaning to the perceptual world. Specifically, we are referring to a sense the individual has of his own place in his perceptual world. Principles of relationship yield an understanding of the perceptual world and, secondarily, some measure of prediction and control. An experience of meaning provides a more transcendent outcome; it yields a sense of the significance to the perceptual world, thereby providing answers to questions such as: "Why am I here?" "What is the significance of my love and my labor?" "What is the meaning of my death?"

Elaborated controls usually consist of a set of interrelated and hierarchically organized explanations. A stark example of a personal explanatory system is that of the paranoid; a well-organized and well-differentiated paranoid person may evolve a complex, highly interrelated system of personal explanations based on a few selected premises. Heider (1958), however, showed that each of us, paranoid or not, develops an elaborate and intricate "naive psychology," a system of explanations that we use to understand the behavior of others. Naive psychologies are personal explanatory systems concerning a restricted range of phenomena in the perceptual world—human behavior and its relationship to its human and nonhuman context. However, personal explanatory systems covering a much broader range of phenomena are now coming to light and are being systematically studied. Developmental psychologists have recognized for decades that a child develops highly elaborate explanations of both animate and inanimate connections. Freud recognized that children can develop idiosyncratic physiological theories about the reproductive process. More recently, investigators have begun to study systematically individual conceptions of the structure of people's physical environment—a neighborhood, a city. In the last decade several theorists have provided more comprehensive theories of personal explanatory systems. Berger and Luckmann (1966) have argued that virtually all experience is organized, interpreted, and understood according to personal systems developed by individuals and projected into their stimulus world.

There are fundamental continuities between elementary and elaborated controls. Since these continuities play a crucial role in our model of family paradigms, we will consider some of them here. Psychoanalytic theorists have offered one concept that bridges these two domains, the notion of character; cognitive theorists have offered another, that of style. In both cases, the central concept is that elementary controls are combined into a configuration unique for each individual. This configuration serves to shape how an individual attends to the fullest range of his experience, how he connects the various elements of his experience, and what he concludes about his own position in his perceptual world. The fact that elementary controls are organized into individual and unique configurations means that certain characteristics of this configuration depend on its structure: the particular relationships of the component elementary controls. However, and more important for our present purposes, there is also a continuity between the characteristics of elementary and of elaborated controls. Thus, if we know something about the characteristics of an individual's elementary controls, we can predict a great deal about the form and function of his elaborated controls.[2]

A single example can illustrate this continuity. Silverman (1967) was interested in assessing differences in the approaches and attitudes of different psychotherapists. He was attracted to the dichotomy noted by Whitehorn and Betz (1960) who classified therapists as *A* or *B*. *A* therapists were empathic and tried to see the world from the perspective of their patients; they felt their role in the therapeutic process was to help the patient find a loophole in his problematic world, to help the patient use his own skills in the areas that would give him the most reward. *B* therapists operated more by their own perceptions; they kept a greater emotional distance from their patients, were sensitive to inconsistencies in their patients' behavior, and conceived of their role as working with patients to sort out these inconsistencies and discover underlying psychic conflicts. Pertinent to our discussion here, *A* and *B* therapists can be distinguished not only on their attitudes and approaches to therapy but also on the basis of a test of an elementary control mechanism, field articulation. Operationally, this mechanism is measured by assessing an individual's ability to resist the distracting influence of a tilting frame which surrounds a rod whose verticality the subject must accurately assess. It is a test of the subject's sensitivity to and distractability by peripheral cues. *A* therapists were more sensitive than *B* therapists to these peripheral cues and hence were less accurate in their judgment of verticality.

Silverman argued cogently that this sensitivity to peripheral cues—cues that were inanimate in the field articulation test—was critical to a sensitivity to personal cues. Interpersonal sensitivity, he argued, is the core of the *A* therapists' stance toward their patients. In other words, sensitivity to peripheral cues becomes elaborated into an attitude and approach toward psychotherapy as well as a meaningful grasp of a therapist's position in the life of his patient. Likewise, the *B* therapists' ability to resist distraction, the ability to pay attention to the most "salient" cues in the stimulus field, becomes elaborated into a more distant and analytic stance with patients.

The correlation between elementary and elaborated controls is undoubtedly complex. The simple, monotonic, and positive correlations in the therapist example are appealing but may not be representative. However, later in our argument, we shall find it extremely productive to keep these relations in view.

Let us return to elaborated controls, particularly personal explanatory systems. Specifically, let us examine the criteria they must meet in order to serve as an elaborated mechanism for dealing with stimulus complexity—in particular, to provide understanding and meaning.

First, the explanatory system must be felt to be external to the individual—*it must have an objective quality*. Cautious and scholarly scientists can afford to entertain tentative and relativistic constructs of the limited range of phenomena they study in their laboratories. In everyday life, explanatory systems are guides for choices and decisions in a complex stimulus world. They work effectively only when they enable the individual to be convinced of the system's objective reality. This is not to say that some uncertainty and trial-and-error cannot occur; but the underlying explanations tying separate elements of the perceptual world together must be thought to be objective and "out there." Take, for example, a car that develops a flat tire on a steep hill. The driver may not be certain of exactly how he will change the tire and prevent the car from rolling; through trial and error he might try using wheel blocks, repositioning the car, chaining it to a tree, and so on. However, any action in an analogous situation depends on the driver's absolute belief in explanatory principles including the effect of air pressure on tire curvature, the effects of friction on keeping wheel bolts in place, and the principle of the lever which enables him to jack up the car. Serious doubts about any of these would immobilize him in such a situation. He must perceive these various connections as properties of the car, tires, and jack, not as organizing principles in his head.

A second requirement of a useful explanatory system is that is be *consistent or internally logical.* Individuals will vary in the complexity of their logic, but major inconsistencies within an explanatory system render it relatively useless. For example, consider a simple polytheistic religion; among experiential events it helps a believer to explain, it is useful in helping him understand the passage of the seasons. In this religion there is a God of Spring, a God of Summer, a God of Autumn, and a God of Winter. Suppose this mythology (of course, a believer would not *think* it was a mythology) states simply that each god lives on his own mountain top and comes to earth whenever he feels like it, and when he's around the corresponding season occurs. An explanatory system with such little inner coherence would provide no understanding, no reduction in uncertainty. It will vastly improve things if this mythology contains more of a story. Let's imagine a titanic dance of the gods. These gods are four brothers; the youngest, the God of Spring, is still a child. When the earth was created, the four brothers began to dance arm in arm, but the youngest soon tired and fell to earth. There he drew strength; in three months, thus restored, he returned to the dance only to find the next youngest brother, Summer, tiring and about to fall. On it goes, year after year, the never-ending dance with a fall and a restoration. Clearly the internal consistency of this explanatory system renders it much more useful.

A third requirement is the *stabilization of the system*. A system works best if it does not change or its changes are slow. From cosmologies to auto mechanics, an explanatory system works best if it serves as an anchor or reference point for grappling with a constantly changing stimulus universe. We will introduce here a notion that becomes a conceptual cornerstone later in our exposition. Explanatory systems are stabilized by their relationship to very general or *framing assumptions*. In other words, the stability of an explanatory system arises from its applicability to a wide variety of events, its generality. In most cases personal explanatory systems cannot deal with the fine texture of everyday experience; ad hoc derivations are almost always required to make decisions. A driver has no explanatory system that will determine, a priori, how he will change the tire of his car on a hill. He has to put together some knowledge of mechanics and gravitation, and then there will still be room for trial and error. This is also true for the four-brother cosmology. Ad hoc variations in the image of the brothers' dance will be required to explain why this year's spring is so rainy and last year's was so dry.

Personal explanatory systems are severely challenged when one individual engages in a sustained face-to-face encounter with another.[3] By "face-to-face" we mean those encounters between two or more individuals in which there is relative freedom in each person's experience of the other: freedom from convention, freedom from stereotypes, freedom from highly simplified conceptions. In a face-to-face encounter, each individual has an immediate, emotionally charged sense of uniqueness of the other. The most important ingredient of a genuine face-to-face encounter is that each individual accords to the other the power of independent regard.[4] Each individual (ego) senses in the other (alter) the power to observe independently and understand ego; ego recognizes that he cannot fully predict or control alter's perception or understanding of him and that alter will perceive and understand ego according to alter's systems of organizing and understanding the perceptual world, a world in which, at the moment, ego is an important stimulus object. Many human encounters are not of this kind, particularly in complex, technical societies. People often perceive one another as technically functioning objects in a stimulus world which often is experienced as infrahuman if not inanimate. Thus, when I board the bus for work in the morning, I perceive the bus driver as a complex machine for directing the course and speed of the bus. The man sitting next to me is "one of those uptowners" about whom I feel, because of my own limiting stereotypes, I already know everything. When I reach my office building, the elevator is crowded with unknown "business types" whom I don't know but whose dress tells me "everything." In this stream of typical, brief encounters with other humans, I do not feel that I am perceiving others as unique individuals or that I am being personally perceived, explained, and understood. However, when I arrive at my office, an old friend of mine whom I have not seen for several years is waiting for me. As soon as he sees me his face becomes lined with concern. I cannot dispel the powerful experience that he has perceived something in me which I cannot see and is already formulating a worried explanation. He tells me that he has noticed that I've lost weight, and I sense he is formulating a tentative explanation: "The poor fellow has some terrible illness." No matter how *I* may perceive and explain his concern ("he always worries about me"), I cannot dispel the impact of my awareness of his independent regard of me.

Face-to-face encounters have, as their sine qua non, this disarming quality, which always contains the potential for seriously challenging any element of a personal explanatory system. If I accord to the other the power of independent regard of me, I must include his power of independent regard of my explanatory system. Experientially, my explanatory systems — a few, many, or most of them—undergo an immediate and radical transformation; they become a stimulus component of the other's perceptual world. For the instant in time when I accord the other the power of independent regard of my explanatory systems and do not know whether his own system is in accord with mine, my own system loses its preemptive, explanatory quality. In short, I feel that profound existential doubt about which theologians have written so eloquently. I cannot tolerate such a state for long. I have three options. First, I could withdraw my attribution of independent regard by explaining away my friend's reaction. In other words, I can include his behavior as a component of my stimulus world and fit it into some overarching explanatory system of my own. At this point I have ended my face-to-face encounter. Being psychologically minded, I might say to myself, "You know, the poor fellow's always been a bit jealous of me. He'd be quite eager to find some pretext for worrying about me, for thinking I've come upon hard times." Second, I could try to convince him to subscribe to my explanation. I might say (out loud to him), "You know, I've been dieting recently and feel like a million bucks." Finally, I might try to elaborate de novo with him an explanation that neither of us had thought through initially but which we develop as part of a continuing series of face-to-face encounters between us, encounters which interweave with an evolving explanation that satisfies us both. To be sure, such a shared explanation will be influenced by our prior knowledge of one another; we will already have a sense of the kinds of explanations each of us might accept.

Thus, knowing that like me his is given to psychologizing, I might tentatively offer, "Well, it's been surprisingly easy to diet. I really haven't had much of an appetite."

He might counter, "Well, I kind of wondered whether you might have been a little depressed."

I would add, "I have been a bit concerned that the business would do badly once old J.B. retired."

"Aw, come on, now," he would say (getting enthusiastic), "you know how attached you were to the old codger. You really miss him and feel bereft without him."

Reluctantly, but with relief, I'd conclude this little joint elaboration. "I guess you're right. I'm depressed that he's gone. I have been having trouble sleeping, too."

Face-to-face encounters, as this vignette suggests, are not only proving grounds for personal explanatory systems; they are also a major source and continuing fuel supply for such explanations. As Berger and Luckmann have described, there are two distinct modes by which face-to-face encounters stimulate and sustain such systems. In the first, two individuals encounter one another for the first time. There is an opportunity for them to develop a truly shared system, a system to which each contributes and in which each believes. Even though we already know one another, the psychological explanation (my depression) that my friend and I elaborate together exemplifies this. Suppose, instead, I had gone to a doctor out of concern about my weight loss. And let us suppose, to give added emphasis to this point, he had called in his colleague in the next office. They examined me, asked a few medical questions and then (quite tactfully, of course) a few personal questions. They then left the room to confer and returned to inform me, "We believe you're depressed and think that some pills might be of help to you." If I am like most people, I will accept such an explanation; the word "succumb" might be more accurate because it emphasizes that I have (voluntarily, to be sure) passively accepted an explanatory system offered to me by others. My acceptance of it, with faith and conviction, enhances — to some extent — the conviction of my doctors. I might have resisted it with a plausible counterargument: "You know, doctor, I went through the war and lost several buddies. And then my brother died. And a year ago my house burned down. I was sure sad, but never depressed. I didn't lose my appetite and have trouble sleeping." More than one doctor, faced with this kind of reluctance in a patient, will reapply himself to the diagnostic task and — once in a while — will come up with something new. "Sure enough," he might report a few days later. "Those new tests we did showed you had a rare chronic infection called Brucellosis."

This last sequence, beginning with the doctor's reexamination of his own convictions, never would have happened had I accepted the explanation handed down to me by someone whom I recognized and who recognized himself as an authority. We would have come to share an explanation of my weight loss. However, unlike the one I elaborated with my friend, this explanation would have been given to me by decree not mutual elaboration.

Now that we have some sense of the role of face-to-face encounters in the development of explanatory systems, let us reconsider the three criteria for effective personal explanatory systems: objectivity, coherence, and stability. Each of these three aspects can be severely challenged in a face-to-face encounter. Alternatively, each of these three can be established and enhanced through particular social mechanisms.

Objectification, as we have said, means that I do not think my explanatory system is in my own head; I think it reflects reality or — from a more existential perspective — the system resides in reality.[5] It is often assumed that, as we grow, we master intellectual mechanisms that help us "learn about reality." These mechanisms permit us to perform little experiments in our stimulus world from our childhood years, when we build up notions of shape, color, and volume, to later years, when we tinker with cars, gardens and sex. However, our systems are not built up de novo out of raw experience. Explanatory systems, as we have said, serve to guide explorations much as they themselves are products of exploration. We contend, however, that in the ordinary course of daily living, objectification comes less from solitary personal experiments with nature and more from social concord. In other words, my belief in the objectivity of my explanations of my stimulus world depends, in an essential way, on the fact that my explanations are shared by others.

Let us return, again, to the four-brother cosmology. Suppose a nonbeliever is told the outlines of the simple cosmology. He seems ready to believe but is not convinced. The believer and nonbeliever are at the moment herding sheep in the twilight hours of a late June day, a day, incidentally, which has been the first truly warm one since the previous year. As the sky darkens and the sheep settle down for the evening,the whirring of the crickets lulls the believer off to sleep. But the nonbeliever, alert and pondering the believer's stories, remains awake, his gaze riveted on a thicket of eucalyptus in the distance, bowing and straightening gently in a light evening breeze. Suddenly, in the last dim rays of the sun, a black shape passes across the waving trees. Was it just a shadow across the breeze-bent trees? No! He can see its human shape—its arms, its legs, and its head, bent slightly with fatigue. He excitedly shakes the believer awake. "It is him, the God of Summer!" The believer sits up with a start and looks toward the grove of eucalyptus. But "he" is already gone. The believer does not doubt the nonbeliever's observation. Indeed, the believer is quickly off to sleep again, dreaming of the warm days to come now that the God of Summer has come to rest.

Coherence, too, can be enhanced by specific social mechanisms. In the course of daily life the coherence of an explanatory system depends on the capacity of another individual to fill in a missing piece. We might call this *social interpolation*. Thus, the believer tells the nonbeliever about the four brothers. He focuses on the youngest being the God of Spring and mentions the next youngest being the God of Summer. He also talks about fatigue, falling to earth, and restoration. Although the believer stops there, the nonbeliever will be able to quickly see that the God of Autumn must be older still (and has greater stamina) and the God of Winter oldest and strongest of all. The sense of coherence in the believer's explanation of the seasons will be strengthened because the nonbeliever has been able to interpolate from the part of the explanation the believer gave him. By a kind of poetic implication, the nonbeliever might even sense that because they are gods, the four brothers might have *ages* but yet be *ageless* in the sense that they do not get older. This would be further interpolation accounting for the perpetuity of the seasons and their sequence. As the nonbeliever fills in the missing pieces, both he and the believer become more enthralled, more engrossed in an explanation that grows—for both of them—more vivid, more organic, and more whole. The nonbeliever becomes a believer; the believer becomes even more convinced by the power of his cosmology to enthrall a nonbeliever through its capacity to sustain interpolation.

Closely related to interpolation, of course, is extrapolation. The capacity to extend a circumscribed set of principles to cover a broad range of phenomena depends on the generality of the principles themselves. Thus, the explanation using the four brother gods may encounter difficulty in its extension to explain the *content* of the four seasons. It works well only to explain their unvarying sequence. Why should spring show warming weather, summer hot weather, fall cooler, and winter coldest? The believer has claimed that the seasons reflect a process of physical restoration of a tired god. He will have to formulate a clearer concept—or, more precisely a more generalizable concept—of what is meant by restoration and why it should take different forms for brothers of different ages. Suppose, however, the nonbeliever can quickly "see" that the youngest boy restores himself by recreating the warmth of his mother's love; the older by the first heats of sexual passion; the older still through the exhilaration of battle where cold steel mixes with the fading warmth of those dying in battle; and finally the oldest, just as he is passing the zenith of his strength, finds restoration in defying the rigors of wintry winds and snow. In effect the gods set the temperature that matches the needs they require to restore themselves to full strength. The nonbeliever has "seen" in the nucleus of the believer's explanation a cosmologic psychophysiology of divine restoration and thereby explained the principle content of the seasons, the change in temperature. In effect, the potential for generalization did not reside within the believer; he could not "see" the possibility for extension. It did not reside within the nonbeliever; he required the nuclear explanation offered by the believer before providing the crucial extension. In an experiential sense the full potential for generalization—perhaps we may call it the hidden or implicit framing assumptions of the four-brother cosmology—resided in the relationship between believer and nonbeliever. Their relationship served as a repository for the framing or most generalizable aspects of a personal explanatory system they had come to share and into which they could fit or interpolate the missing pieces.

Shared explanatory systems—whether mutually elaborated or transmitted by authority—play a crucial role in organizing and maintaining group process. They define the boundary of a group, clarify its objectives, foster the allocation of roles, and establish norms for interaction. The believer and former nonbeliever now jointly share a conviction in the reality of the brothers. The first believer's prescience has outlined this novel cosmology and the second believer's vision has confirmed it. Will they keep this secret to themselves? This is unlikely. The vivid excitement of their discovery demands proclamation. Indeed, the existence of nonbelievers—particularly if they are engaged in face-to-face encounter—threatens the objectivity, coherence, and stability of the emerging cosmology. The believers will seek converts to their nascent religion and ipso facto—as Berger and Luckmann have also discussed—they will have an institution. Their new institution, of course, will fare badly if their sheep-herding society already has a religion with which it is well satisfied. Indeed, at the very mention of an unorthodox version of an explanation for the seasons, they might risk serious harm to themselves from believers in another cosmology. In fact, the organization of society into overlapping and stable groups—each defined, organized, shaped, and nourished by a unique set of shared explanations—puts serious constraints on originative elaborations such as this cosmology.

It is beyond the scope of this book to inquire into the large-scale social processes which both constrain and encourage the development of originative and share explanations—particularly on the grand and cosmologic scale of new religions. Even the most restrictive, coercive, orthodox, and ideologically monolithic societies permit some latitude to both individuals and groups to develop their own conceptions of a broad range of events in their perceptual world. Our concern, more specifically, is with the family. We shall want to know whether in some sectors, at least, of current American society the family itself plays a significant originating function in the elaboration of significant personal explanatory systems. More specifically, we will want to know how much latitude members of a family have in formulating, for themselves, shared explanations of significant events in their perceptual world. In particular, are families a source of or a strong influence upon those very general modes or styles of organizing perceptual experience?

The Family as Originator of Explanatory Systems

Let us compare two societies: one in which the family had very little latitude to originate for itself any significant and novel constructions of events in its perceptual world, and one in which there appeared to be very great latitude. An example of a society permitting very little latitude is the Puritans in seventeenth-century New England. In contrast stand the families who settled the Great Plains during the mid-nineteenth century and saw themselves as the originators of culture and civilization.

John Demos referred to the Puritan family as "the little commonwealth";[6] this epigram emphasizes that on many levels the family served as a microcosm of the entire community. As the new Puritan civilization spread out over New England it was organized, very strictly, into towns. By explicit law, families were required to build their homes within a half-mile of the town's central facilities, its meetinghouse and church. The basic unit of the Puritan town was the household. It was the basic economic or productive unit (in formal, sociological terms this was the "corporate family"): a family, as a working unit, engaged in farming or a craft. The family house itself served both as a shelter for family members and as the primary focus of their economic productivity. Perhaps more significant than its economic function was the family's social and religious function. Social functions performed by families included care of the indigent and the sick and the "moral reeducation" of wayward youths. The family also had explicit and assigned religious functions. Father was charged by law with instructing his children in the reading of Scripture; fines were levied for dereliction of this duty. Beyond that, family worship services and household meditation were common and encouraged. Out of this matrix of social, and religious functions grew a more crucial function for the family. It became the significant concentrate of the full range of human life and emotion that were obtainable or immaginable in Puritan civilization. Work, love, sex, illness, and death were concentrated in the family and its household. Indeed, so much of the actual life and work of the entire civilization were concentrated in the home that the growing child could sample all there was to know within his family. Whatever explanatory systems developed within the family—systems for understanding God, nature, morality, the vicissitudes of human relationships—were themselves microcosms of the broader orientation and conceptions of the Puritan town and the Puritan civilization from which it grew. The family played a central and indispensable role in this civilization. No single family could have a major originative role without enormous opposition from the community at large. Instead, families had a representational role. For each of its members, the family rendered into vivid, intense, and personal terms the more abstract tenets of Puritanism.

The families of the mid-nineteenth-century Great Plains were a sharp contrast. Many of them had been encouragd to move westward by the Homestead Act of 1862, which ushered in a new phase of American history. All citizens—and aliens intending to become citizens—were promised up to 160 acres of land in large, designated areas of the Great Plains. The land was free; the only requirement was that it be continuously occupied and farmed for five years. Thousands of families streamed from the Northeast and Southeast, and from Europe as well, out to the broad and lonely plains. Once they established homesteads, many of the pioneers of this last wave led very solitary existences. Rich and vivid pictures of plains life have been given by Hamlin Garland (1914), Willa Cather (1949), Laura Ingalls Wilder (1937), and others. The dominant theme was isolation and the profound sense that the family was its own greatest resource. Accompanying this isolation was a continuing ambivalence about pushing on to the great unknown or returning to the comfort and familiarity of the settled East Coast. Garland recalls:

> One of the songs which we children particularly enjoyed our mother singing [was] a ballad which consisted of a dialogue between a husband and wife on this very subject of emigration. The words as well as its wailing melody still stir me deeply, for they take hold of my subconscious memory—embodying admirably the debate which went on in our home as well in the homes of other farmers in the valley—only alas our mothers did not prevail.

> (Husband) "Oh, Wife, let us go; Oh, don't let us wait;
> I long to be there, and I long to be great."

> (Wife) "Dear Husband, remember those lands are so dear
> They will cost you the labor of many a year." (p. 235)

Under the surface was a strong conflict between the excitement of exploration and the promise of owning one's own land, on the one hand, and the thirst for continuity with the tradition of the community left behind, on the other. Families were careful in their new households to have remnants of their former way of living. Laura Ingalls Wilder recalled, for example, that when the family moved into a new dugout, her mother refused to sleep on the floor. Just a few willow branches placed under the bedding was enough of a semblance of a bed to give the whole family a sense of connection to its past. In addition to physical reminders, families focused intense feelings of love and support on their children. Even under the harshest conditions there was time for some of the joys of childhood. Laura Ingalls Wilder described a Christmas out on the plains where her mother produced a long-saved box of buttons so that the children could make a button string for the holidays as mother herself had done. Indeed, the children became not only the ties to the past but also symbols of a new rootedness and stability. This kind of transformation is illustrated by the central figure in Willa Cather's *My Antonia,* whose growth from childhood to old age expresses this special experience of the unfolding of childhood in pioneer families. At the end of the book we find her "a battered woman now, not a lovely girl; but she still has that something which fires the imagination, could still stop one's breath for a moment by a look or gesture that somehow revealed the meaning in common things. She had only to stand in the orchard, to put her hands on a little crab tree and look up at the apples, to make you feel the goodness of planting and tending and harvesting at last . . . She was a rich mine of life, like the founders of early races" (p. 229).

The family unit, alone on the dangerous and desolate prairies, had to summon all its physical and moral strength to break the plains, to survive, to lay claim to any sense of security. The successful family came to see itself as a well-integrated mechanism for accomplishing virtually every task of frontier living. More importantly, it had to create for itself a sense of civilization, "like the founders of early races." The family had an extraordinarily originative role in the creation of a sense of order, balance, and coherence in its life; its members could weave this out of memories of the past (their own childhood), out of the maintenance of custom (as with the willow branches), but, most important, out of an experience of their own fecundity: the vigor of their children and their survival by their own efforts.

How Prevalent Is the Originative Family?

The Puritan family was a miniature representation of a broader culture and had little latitude to originate its own conception of order and stability; the Great Plains family wove its own civilization from a variety of strands. Can we conceptualize a distinction between these two types of societies and their families? Concepts of this kind would help in characterizing the relative freedom of any set of families to originate. (We are, in our current studies, most interested in American middle-class urban and suburban families.) Are these two contrasting examples unique, or is there some underlying continuity which can be used to distinguish the two, one from the other, and both from other examples of family life which may be more or less originative? In seeking such a distinction we want to look at characteristics of the social structure in which families are embedded, since there were such conspicuous differences in the social conditions of the families. In comparison, it seems futile to ask whether there were some essential differences between the Puritan and Great Plains families as families or among their constituent members as individuals.

Our contention is that in the industrialized West, social evolution has placed the family in a distinctively generative and autonomous role. While few families can be regarded as "founder of races"—as our stylized image of pioneer families portrays—many families come reasonably close. It is for these families that the model which we describe in this book is most apropos. A family of this kind is, in most cases, a variant of the classical nuclear family—at least one parent and one child. Such families usually will live in their own household. But family and household structure are very poor indices of generative and autonomous families. Our primary interest is in families with a particular kind of relationship between its members: each member accords to the others the power of independent regard. As a consequence each member's construction of social and physical reality must be coordinated with the others'. In other words, membership in families of this kind depends on collaborative engagement by all its members in the joint construction of reality. Like their Great Plains counterparts, these families originate and maintain collaborative constructions as part of their own development. Among the Puritans, by contrast, collaborative constructions of reality derived from the history and development of the larger group: Puritan migration and civilization in seventeenth-century America.

We have lacked useful conceptual tools to understand how an individual family can elaborate and maintain its own shared construction of reality. We have not understood how the specific history of the family's own development can shape its idiosyncratic shared visions, understandings, and assumptions about the world in which it lives. The remainder of this book will be an attempt to sketch out relationships of this kind. We will focus on periods of crisis in family history as a conceptual cornerstone. We will argue that the fundamental process by which a family recovers from crisis is the collaborative construction of reality—first of the crisis itself, and then, by a process of generalization which we will describe in some detail, of a broad range of social and physical reality. The main lines of our argument are laid out in the next three chapters.

Our model rests on a picture of family life which will come as a surprise to many readers. We are arguing, as we have said, that social evolution has placed the family in a position of strength, originality, and creativity. We are picturing the family as an active initiator: a historian of its past, an interpreter of its present, and a designer of its future. On the surface, this picture seems at variance with a notion that the family is now in a period of decline. Many have argued that rising divorce rates, pervasive intrafamily violence, increasing illegitimacy rates, and many other indicators reflect the dissolution of the family. Popular reaction to these statistics often seems based on the assumption that in times past, families were somehow stronger, more cohesive. It is not the function of this book to perform the comprehensive social analysis which would justify our fundamental image of the contemporary family as a resilient and active group.[7] Indeed, such analysis is not necessary. Even a brief survey of modern scholarship of the family reveals a fascinating portrait of the kind of resilient, generative, and initiating family for which our model is best suited.

Recent demographic and historical analyses point to one major conclusion: contemporary families compare quite favorably along many dimensions with families of the recent and remote past. More important for our purposes are studies that convey the evolution of the *quality* of family relationships. In this work we can identify some fundamental themes which delineate the rise of the autonomous and generative family. Three themes in particular are worth noting. The first is a theme underscoring the gradual separation of the family from the wider social world in which it functions.[8] The contemporary family cannot be viewed, according to this line of inquiry, as simply a component of large social organizations: neighborhood, city, socioeconomic class, or culture. Families are bounded social groups with their own internal dynamics. Much of what a family does arises from within itself and is not simply a passive reflection of social process around it. A second theme focuses on the active conservation of culture within family generations. Here "culture" is to be understood in both a stricter and a broader sense. In a strict sense, families in many Western industrialized nations have become the crucial medium by which ethnic particularity is transmitted from generation to generation.[9] In this country, for example, the conservation of Irish, Italian, Jewish, or Serbian ethnicity now relies on processes internal to the family. But families are also the originators of their *own* cultures with their attendant secular rituals and world views.[10]

These cultures, intrinsic to each family, can only be shaped and then transmitted to the next generation by an active, resilient process within the family. Finally, a third theme clarifies the continuing heterogeneity of family initiative. Overall historical trends and social evolution, to be sure, point to a growing autonomy and initiative in family life. But within any Western industrialized nation, there are still vast differences between families in this regard: some are indeed almost passive effector organs of a large social body. Others, like the Great Plains families, stand as a universe unto themselves and as founders of a new race.[11]

We can argue that our own work—focusing intensively on generativity, and autonomy in family life—comes at a historically opportune time. Social evolution has presented to us millions of families who play a larger role in shaping their own destiny than did their forebears. At the same time, we must acknowledge that our model is least applicable to those families—perhaps as numerous or more so—who function as rather passive components of a larger social order.

4 | Crisis and the Development of the Family Paradigm

Outline of a New Model

In previous chapters we have proposed that families develop shared explanations of a wide range of events in the perceptual world. We have suggested, without providing an explicit account of just how it happens, that these explanatory systems are shared because (a) the sharing process itself strengthens the system, and (b) sharing avoids the severe challenges that intense face-to-face encounters (characteristic of at least some classes of contemporary families) would provide for explanatory systems which were fashioned and believed in by individuals alone. We have given examples of how such sharing may go forward. We have listed three mechanisms (although there are probably many others): social concord, social interpolation, and social extrapolation. We turn now to a more focused description of the nature of these shared family explanatory systems.

In our first laboratory studies we were struck by specific shared explanations or understandings which families developed. We reported a particularly dramatic example (see the Raab family in Chapter 1). We described one family's intense fear of being humiliated in our laboratory and the swagger and zaniness they used to conceal that fear from us (and perhaps themselves). More generally, we defined a concept of *shared construct* to refer to the family's shared images of the laboratory. These constructs contain, at a minimum, the family's fantasies about the nature of the research and its procedures and conception of what would happen to the family in the research setting. These shared experiences all have the same characteristics: they are *situation specific*.[1] In other words, they all refer to particular situations in which the family finds itself. A second characteristic of the components of shared constructs — attributions, fantasies, and self-conceptions — is that they are *representational* or *depictive*. They are mental events, shared by all members of the family, which are felt to portray the situation as the family defines it.

In contrast, we are introducing the notion of paradigms as a concept of greater generality.[2] We focus now on a shared set of operations within the family which shapes and controls both the form and content of these situation-specific, representational images. They emerge in the life of a family in two ways. First, they operate as *framing assumptions,* specifying — with great generality — certain fundamental properties of the perceptual world, properties which are given, are not subject to dispute, and cannot be either verified or disproved with experience, analysis, or discussion. These framing assumptions specify how the perceptual world is to be investigated, what conclusions are permissible from those investigations, and how such conclusions are used to shape a full range of family action, especially further explorations of the perceptual world. These assumptions do not, in a way, guarantee agreement or consensus — as these two terms are ordinarily used — in family life. With respect to family consensus, these assumptions function more as a meta-rule providing broad answers to questions such as, "In this family is genuine disagreement even possible?" or "In this family what are the grounds on which agreement can be built or how can we even recognize when we have disagreed?" Paradigms also manifest themselves in the family's *organizing patterns of daily living*. These patterns shape the family's relationship with its social environment, synchronize each member's action and planning with others in the family, and maintain the family's continuity with its own past. In Chapter 6 we will describe these patterns in the family's daily life and their relationship to the family's paradigms, and the framing assumptions by which they are sometimes manifest. Taken together these next two chapters map out a relatively new approach to exploring family life: the close coordination between enduring shared experiences in family life and patterns of interaction between members that persist over time.

We will also show how the concept of paradigm helps explain the stability of ordinary constructs. In other words, it helps explain why, in any particular family, ordinary constructs might have different content from situation to situation but have distinct formal similarities. For example, a family that tends to see a new situation as patterned and masterable will construe a new neighborhood in this way, a new school situation, and a new country when it travels. The paradigm, functioning both as a set of shared framing assumptions and patterns of family action, shapes each ordinary construct of neighborhood, school, and foreign country. However, the concept of paradigm, as a set of underlying framing assumptions or interaction patterns, has—by itself—very limited explanatory power. Logically speaking it might be reduced to a sentence such as, "Formal similarities between ordinary constructs are explained by a stable underlying tendency to form constructs of a particular kind." This is nearly tautological unless we can say something more about how paradigms arise and why they persist.

In order to provide a more truly explanatory model, we are introducing several concepts of family stress and disorganization. These concepts serve two important and closely related functions in our model. First, they give us some indication of how paradigms become established in family life. Our concept of family disorganization attempts to explain how the family's established and traditional conceptions of its environment are lost and how conditions are created which favor the creation of new and very general conceptions of its environment. Briefly, we argue that severe family disorganization entails the failure of previous modes of construing the environment. Second, and even more important, these concepts of stress and disorganization explain why the family adheres to its new paradigm once it is established. In other words, the model provides us with propositions about *motives* in family life. Briefly, we are positing that these new paradigms make their first appearance during grave family disorganization. At first, paradigms are themselves shared constructs; they are constructs not of ordinary or everyday puzzling or problematic events. They are, at the outset, constructions of the stressor event, the family's initial response to it, and the solution required. This construct emerges as the family's active response to extreme stress and the origins of the stressor event as well as its own efforts to restore integrity in the wake of disorganization. *The central idea in the entire model is that a construct that successfully deals with such a grave crisis in the life of the family stands out as an extraordinary achievement to all members of the family.* Its dramatic success means that the family will attempt to apply at least some aspects of its construction of severe crisis to more ordinary problematic events of daily life. This idea is the essence of what we are borrowing from Kuhn's concepts. Like Kuhn, we are arguing that a group cleaves to a particular mode of explaining its world because the essential elements of that mode of explanation were dramatically successful attempts to deal with a severe crisis.

By introducing concepts of stress, disorganization, and crisis, we can, metaphorically speaking, change the direction of our theorizing. Until this point we have been reasoning "backward." We have started with ordinary constructs which we can observe in our laboratory. Then we have talked of similar shared constructs of other social environments. We have said that we expect formal similarities between these two as a consequence of very general shared assumptions the family holds for this entire perceptual world. In other words, in a causal chain, the general assumptions entailed in the paradigm come before the specific features of the ordinary constructs. Thus, inferring the nature of the paradigm from what we know about ordinary constructs is going backward in the sense of inferring a cause from an observed effect. Concepts of stress and family disorganization enable us to reason forward. We can formulate our model around what is known or can be plausibly conceived about stress and family disorganization. Beginning at this point, we can reason forward to the next step in the causal chain: the family's construction of its own crisis situation. We then follow the process by which the family selects certain key aspects of this construction for everyday use.

Family Stress and Disorganization

Family stress. Most conceptualizations of family crisis and disorganization begin with a notion of family stress. The most influential of these approaches is that articulated by Hill (1949, 1958). The elusive phenomenon, most of these conceptual approaches suggest, begins a chain reaction which may sooner or later lead to family crisis and disorganization. We will follow the form of this basic argument, but, in our view, stress, crisis, and disorganization in family life are almost never sequential links in an orderly chain of events. On the contrary, they interpenetrate one another, enhance, distort, reinforce, and mute each other in endless varieties of chain reactions and feedback loops in immediate sequence or after long periods of time.

Family stress is an elusive phenomenon because it is difficult to define. At an elementary level, we distinguish it from family crisis and disorganization. Stress is something that happens *to* the family; its origins lie outside the family's boundaries. Crisis and disorganization are processes that happen *in* the family. Yet traditional theories of family stress cannot define family stress without observing the relationship of some external event to a change within the family.[3] More particularly, a stressful event is defined, by these theories, as one that somehow changes usual family patterns. For example, a father is called away for six months of military service; many patterns of family life are—as a consequence—changed. However, this definition of a family stress is ambiguous because it relies for its definition on the magnitude of its impact within the family. This approach is understandable because it is so difficult to define family stress by an examination of the stressor events themselves. To be sure, some events are almost universally stressful for families: sudden loss of income, death of a child, prolonged separation. However, many other events are more neutral: the unannounced arrival of old friends, a flat tire, a declining Dow-Jones average; these events are stressful for some families and are inconsequential for others.

We can examine the notion of stress from another perspective, one more consistent with the tenor of our argument so far. Stress can be defined independently from its impact on the family by assessing general or conventional constructs of stress. In looking for these general contributions, we can take the perspective of the culture or community in which the family lives. In so doing we are following (although this is by no means obvious) in the footsteps of the life events studies of Holmes and Rahe (1967), the Dohrenwends (1978), and others. Perhaps the most intriguing findings of these studies is that people with the same culture or social class can agree quite precisely with one another on the magnitude of stress that various life events usually engender. It is not simply a matter that most people can agree that death of a child is much more likely to be stressful than loss of a job. More important, they can agree on how to rank order or assign a very specific weight to various life events according to their potential for producing stress.[4] This agreement probably reflects a shared conception of stressful potential of a wide variety of events by members of the same culture or social class. In effect, the reliability with which life events can be scaled for a stress, by a representative sample from the same subculture or class, reflects a common social construction of the nature of these events.

Our proposed definition of stress is this: an event is stressful by virtue of a common social construction that it will produce a substantial change or alteration in the life patterns of an average family. Of course, Holmes and Rahe and the Dohrenwends were not interested in what is stressful for *families.* Nonetheless, it requires only a minor modification of their procedure to ask a representative sample of individuals to scale life events for their stress potential for families rather than individuals.

Family disorganization. Family disorganization in response to stress is ugly. Blame, hatred, tyranny, and exploitation rise and fall with staggering swiftness and according to unfathomable patterns. Each member feels as if the center of his life is loosening, that his unseen ties to others and to his past have become highly visible, vulnerable, and finally torn. The family, as a group, loses its most precious possession: an extended and dependable repertoire of background understandings, shared assumptions, traditions, rituals, and meaningful secrets which made it possible for them to function implicitly. Anyone who has ever been a member of a family knows the texture of this implicit function. On the surface it consists of:

- The familiar joke that one member needs only tell a line of to set the rest to laughing;
- The epigrammatic reference to a problem neighbor that sets off in everyone a cascade of images and memories;
- The broken, code-like command which seems like a Greek password to the outside but which the family understands, whether or not it obeys;
- The brief and muffled angry outburst which everyone – on some level – knows reflects an underlying and forbidden sexual tension that must be resolved;
- The never-ending ritual before a trip of triple-checking the gas stove to be sure it's off – the ritual which means, "We're finally off," with all the joy and fear that everyone knows will follow;
- That little sign – father touching mother's shoulder – that everyone knows, when it occurs on a trip, means, "There's danger lurking, be careful!"
- The automatic understanding that one child is to be available for a long phone call when one grandmother calls and another when the grandmother from "the other side" calls.

Everyday family life is distinguished by this fine texture of implicitly understood gestures and codes. As we shall try to show in the next section, these are unified by their capacity to abstract and retain certain coordinating concepts – shared by the family – of its perceptual world. This texture of implicit function is woven gradually by a family. The newly married couple may carry over such a texture from the parents of husband or wife; usually one side predominates. Or the couple may, more laboriously and over greater time, weave a texture of their own. We contend that for most families this texture is gradually developed. It is rarely altered over time. Much of it goes on outside the family's awareness. Only occasionally does a severe crisis occur that rends this texture, destroying its integrity with such devastation that it is impossible for significant coordinating implicit functions to continue. We posit that it is only at these times of major family disorganization that fundamental changes are possible in the coordinating texture of its life. We propose that family disorganization may be thought of as occurring in three separate phases. Our analysis owes much to Kantor and Lehr (1975), although we have substantially altered many of their concepts to make our own conception of family disorganization more logically consistent with our overall model. The three stages are: (1) The emergence of rules as the implicit quality of family life disappears;[5] (2) the emergence of an explicit family as a tyrannical social construction; (3) the rebellion of individual members against a tyrannical power they now feel is external to them. Let us review each in turn. They are summarized in Table 4.1.

1. THE EMERGENCE OF RULES. The first sign of a disorganizing family is the falling away of implicit regulation and coordination. In a smoothly running family, shared objectives, understandings, role allocations, and norms do not often have to be stated. Even when they are, limit-setting messages can be very brief and can often be conveyed gesturally. When a family finds it is engaged in laying out verbally explicit rules for itself, it is already in the midst of a stressful situation — although it may still be far from a full-

TABLE 4.1 STAGES OF FAMILY DISORGANIZATION

Stage	Central features	Possible outcomes
1. Emergence of rules	Family's first response to stress. Simple rules, usually verbal, are articulated to deal with unclear events, coordinate planning between members, or monitor family's response to an unusual challenge.	This stage is very frequent in the life of a family and almost always is essential for them to return to level of implicit function. This may also be the first stage of a deeper slide into disorganization.
2. The explicit family	The simple though explicit rules begin to coalesce into more rigid systems of control. All family members now become aware of their family as a working, struggling, combative, or defeated group.	Family interaction patterns are losing their capacity to implicitly shape experience and provide meaning. More severe disorganization is possible.
3. Rebellion and action	The family or someone in it (the scapegoat) is now perceived as a tyrant or a malevolent source of enduring difficulty for most members. Individuals fail totally to perceive their own contribution to the status of the family.	Family dissolution is near; the interventions of outsiders (including aspects of members themselves, aspects which have not been part of the family before) is often crucial. If dissolution is avoided, major family change is possible during reorganization from this stage.

blown crisis. The family may find it necessary to articulate rules when it is in a strange setting or engaged in unusual activities. For example, when an ordinarily stable family travels to a foreign country it may have to articulate certain rules for itself in dealing with hotels, customs agents, foreign languages, and totally unexplored physical settings. Daily routines, coordination of schedules, fantasies, hopes, and plans may all require some explicit, verbal working-through with a product being a set of rules, plans, and principles elaborated ad hoc for the special circumstances.[6] The stressor is the strangeness of the foreign country. Most families in such a setting experience momentary disorganization as they perceive that few of their routine behaviors are suitable to the new surroundings. When the family returns to its familiar surroundings and its ordinarily stable existence, the rules become null and void. A few of the new rules, developed during the time of stress, may not be entirely shed. They may be transformed into more implicit patterns within the family if they do not challenge the cardinal texture of life to which the family has become accustomed.

For example, consider a family traveling to Italy. Only the older of two daughters, Marilyn, can speak Italian (which she has been learning in high school). One of the explicit rules developed for this trip could be stated in this way: "It is important, each time we have to deal with an Italian official, to make sure Marilyn is with us and to indicate that she is to speak for us." On the return home, Marilyn's linguistic skills were no longer required, but her spokesman's role, legitimized by the ad hoc travel rule, was nonetheless retained in some measure. One evening at dinner father announced he was too tired to go to that night's PTA meeting; mother recognized that she too was unusually tired. Simultaneously, they both got the idea: "Marilyn, why don't you go represent us?" Father leaned slightly toward his older daughter and said with a sly wink, "You know, Marilyn, treat them like Giuseppe." The family laughed. Giuseppe was the Italian customs official who had wanted to examine every nook and cranny of the family luggage. Marilyn, with great flourish, had taken charge. She noticed the official's name plate (Giuseppe Gambini) pinned to his smart blue uniform, and began her plea for the family by addressing him by name, "Signore Gambini." With subtle skill she explained how carefully the family had packed after a magnificent stay in Italy. She drew particular attention to the presents, especially to a magnificent gift for her maternal grandmother who she implied (deceitfully) was also Italian. This last was enough to melt poor Signore Gambini, who let the family pass without so much as opening a bag.

The temporary rule about Marilyn the spokesman was probably effective because it rose from a more implicit texture of family life that had already accorded Marilyn increasing responsibility as an effective, skillful, maturing adolescent. It was not difficult to transform such an explicit rule into a more informal modification of family texture with an increasingly autonomous role for Marilyn. In this sense the emergence of an explicit family rule does, indeed, imply family stress—as occasioned by the strangeness and challenge of a foreign country. Yet it serves as a temporary, ad hoc support to a family whose basic organization remains firm. The emergence of rules can be ominous and presage a slide into more chaotic states of disorganization. One of the most chilling examples in the published literature is provided by Wynne and his colleagues (1958) in their classic paper on pseudo-mutual families. In that paper, a family is described in a more advanced state of disorganization: a family with severe interpersonal strains where no one's intimate wishes or striving for autonomy were being recognized. A particular victim was the young son, whose needs were now secured by an explicit family rule stating that on one day each week, every request of the son would be honored. This day was explicitly (and tragically) enshrined as "Little Boy Day."

A point of confusion may arise here. Many family theorists regard all family behavior as rule governed. They usually are referring to the precisely repeated patterns of interpersonal behavior that characterize all families. The regularity and invariability of these sequences makes them appear to be governed by a set of rules. But these rules are *implicit* in the sense that they are never stated explicitly by any family member and may even be unconscious for all members. In contrast are the *explicit* rules which characterize family crisis. These are often clearly stated verbally and come in the form of clear commands and expectations.

2. THE EMERGENCE OF THE EXPLICIT FAMILY. As explicit rules multiply in the disorganizing family, they coalesce. If they are to have any effect whatsoever—as desperate attempts to forestall further decay or as temporary supports against a passing stress—they must have some internal consistency. For example, a rule forbidding children to go alone to the store made its appearance in the Michaels family soon after the father died in an automobile crash. This can be recognized as an attempt to prevent more losses. An apparently contrary rule developed: "Everyone now has to make his or her own breakfast." This rule expressed the family's desperation more directly: the remaining adults—mother and grandmother—already feel too burdened with grief and are signaling that

they have no resources to tend to one another or the children. So far these two explicit rules were not in conflict. However, the second one—as crisis and desperation grew worse—was generalized: "No one around here should make any demands on the adults." How then were the children to go to the store at all? They could not. Moreover, they became more boxed in by yet another general rule: "Children are not to go out at all." Very rapidly an explicit regulatory system is developing. The rules may represent a caricature of the style of implicit functioning that was typical of the family before the crisis, as Kantor and Lehr have shown. For example, the Michaels family was a relatively closed, self-protective family all along, although in a subtle way. After the father's death a set of interlocking, explicit rules arose to tyrannize over the life of each individual in the family. The rules became the repository, and the caricature, of all that was formerly felt. More important, the new set of interlocking rules transformed a family—implicitly experienced as a texture of suggestive, fleeting gestures before the crisis—into an encroaching, all-too-explicit family.

3. REBELLION AND ACTION. The family has deteriorated to a phase that is most ugly, bitter, and dangerous. Each individual begins to evolve a grave, though explanatory, fiction for himself. He makes a new distinction between himself and his newly explicit family. He fully participated first in the creation of the implicit family—and its informal, partially hidden constraints. Further, he fully participated in its caricature—the construction of the explicit, tyrannical family. He now regards the family as his enemy and struggles to destroy or escape it in a desperate effort to protect himself. This phase of family deterioration is all to familiar to clinicians. It is recognized most easily in critical dyads that make up a family. For example, clinicians have described the "trading of dissociations" which go on in deteriorating marriages. For example, consider Fred and Ann at the end of two years of marriage. Each came from a family where the issues of aggression and passivity remained problems that could never be entirely embraced, worked through, and regulated by an implicit texture of conventions. Indeed, Fred's family encouraged aggressive behavior, on the implicit assumption that people who did not assert themselves would get nothing. By contrast, Ann's family encouraged passivity, on the assumption that aggression was always potentially dangerous to others. During their first month of marriage, the new couple built a somewhat tenuous fabric of implicit conventions around the issue of aggression and passivity. Manifestly, Fred became the aggressive one and Ann the passive one. Suddenly, Ann's mother—still a young woman—suffered a severe and totally disabling stroke that

left her permanently paralyzed and unable to utter or understand speech. Fred and Ann each felt a fleeting but intense and unspoken experience of guilt; Fred had a sense that somehow the stroke was a consequence of his agressivity and Ann thought her passive inadequacy was to blame. In the months following the stroke, the marriage began to deteriorate. Fred began to find Ann too passive, too dependent on him. He felt both drained and furiously frustrated, and began to verbally and then physically attack her. At the same time Ann became preoccupied with an image of Fred as aggressive and dangerous, and secretly feared he would kill someone. In an effort to restrain her own anger she began to offer certain rules. "Look," she said, "each time we're angry, let's not say anything. Let's go off by ourselves and try to cool down." Soon more rules were suggested. Explicit schedules were aimed at getting Ann to take more responsibility and others were aimed at forestalling the potentially murderous effects of Fred's anger. Each one came to feel trapped and overwhelmed by an engulfing, unproviding "marriage" for which each blamed the other. Neither individual could recognize his own contribution to the edifice. Each sought to escape it, or — more dangerously — to destroy it. The explicit, opaque, and constraining rules — that last vestige of family order and cohesiveness — were defied, circumvented, unilaterally enforced, or capriciously modified. It is at this phase that the family, through desperate efforts to repair itself, had lived out its own destruction. The family, as a set of durable and familiar conventions for coordinating the lives of its individual members, was nearly dead.

As the family moves from implicit processes to rule-governed behavior, then to explicit constraints and finally to rebellion, several important parallel shifts also occur. Three of these are most important and we will, very briefly, describe them here. We will focus on the role of the family in providing shared explanations of social reality for its members, the family's awareness of its own processes, and the increasing role of outsiders.

The family functions as a matrix of explanations and social constructions when it functions implicitly. We are hypothesizing that many, if not most, of the family's daily routines do not routinize or deaden the family's experience of its social world. Rather they serve to emphasize, highlight, and color certain aspects of the family's experience of itself in the world. Thus, to cite a previous example, the daily routines of a pioneer family reinforced its sense of being a world unto itself, the founder of nations, whereas the daily routines of the Puritan family emphasized its status as a microcosm of a larger order. Implicit family processes are effective in shaping these shared conceptions precisely because they are implicit. They highlight and color each member's experience without calling attention to themselves. It is this background feature of implicit social process that gives social constructions their objectivity. Members do not say to themselves, in any sense, "My family is doing-thus-and-so; therefore it is likely that the social world is constructed thus-and-so." However, when the family's social processes become more explicit or obvious to its members, their capacity to sustain objectified social meanings diminishes.[7] Each member suffers a decentering. His attention begins to shift away from objectified conceptions of social reality to a preoccupation with the now obvious processes of his disorganizing family. This decentering probably did not occur in Marilyn's family. The temporary imposition of rules remained focused on the family's optimistic efforts to manage a strange although basically intriguing and pleasurable situation. However, the Michaels family has become preoccupied with itself. Mother and grandmother feel the drain of keeping household routines going and of the incessant demands of the children; in a complementary sense the children are preoccupied with the inaccessibility of the adults and the enormous restrictions of their own activities. The preoccupation with family process is even more intense with Fred and Ann. They blame a great deal in their lives on the very bad marriage and are reaching a conviction that their only recourse is to "get out." Both these families have ceased to provide their members with an orientating set of explanations of social realities. Quite the contrary; each member experiences his family as blocking him from engaging in his social environment.

In effect, as disorganization proceeds, the family becomes, in Olmstead's terms (1954), process oriented. The family—as a group—withdraws its investment in managing identifiable tasks and instead struggles with itself. Bion (1959) has referred to a similar state of process in therapy groups and calls it "basic assumption" functioning. In using this term he emphasizes the archaic fantasies members in this phase of group life have about one another; these fantasies dominate the life of the group, which loses its grasp on the major tasks that once held great promise and meaning for group members. As we will show in the next section, the family's preoccupation with itself, although maladaptive in many respects, contains the seeds for healing and the recovery of implicit function.

As the crisis deepens, the family disorganization becomes more severe and outsiders take on a more significant role in family life. The concept of outsiders should be broadly conceived here. We use the term in two senses. In the first sense we refer to individuals who have not previously been intensely engaged in the inner life of the family. These could be members of the extended family or friends, or they might in important instances be total strangers. In the second sense, we apply the term to denote certain attributes of the family members themselves. In particular, we refer to aspects of a family member's personality which had, for one reason or another, been suppressed or excluded from ordinary family life in the days when the family functioned at an implicit level. For example, a family was thrown into severe crisis by the acute medical illness of a teenager while the family was camping in a remote area. The father, who had always been a self-effacing and boyish prankster in family affairs, rose to the occasion in a way no one in the family had ever seen or had thought possible. He became serious, mature, comforting, wise, and extremely effective in getting help and organizing the family's return to a settled area where medical care was available. This aspect of father was — in an important experiential sense — an outsider to his own family. In either or both senses of the term, outsiders occupy a more significant place in family affairs as the crisis deepens. This can occur in one of two ways. First, as the family becomes bound and constrained by an oppressive system of explicit rules, outsiders are likely to become engaged, because one or more members of the family are doing poorly in some area of work or school. In the Michaels family, the mother's performance at work as well as with her friends show a marked downturn. Lisewise, both children began doing poorly in school. In fact, one child's teacher was so concerned that she insisted on a course of psychotherapy for the child (which had only modest effects since it did not address the family issues which so burdened the child). When the family is in open rebellion one member or another may take more initiative in bringing outsiders into the family fold. Indeed, Fred and Ann both came for marital therapy, though each was quick to try to get the therapist to take sides in their dispute.

Vulnerability to Stress and Disorganization

There is a very inexact relationship between stress and family disorganization. At times a family may be subjected to severe stress and show little disorganization. At other times we come upon very disorganized families and have difficulty locating any set of external circumstances discrete enough to be called stress. Also, there may be a very long delay before a stressful event has its full impact on the family. Consider, for example, the Jacobs family with two parents in their forties and a son about to become Bar Mitzvah. When the father himself was in the midst of his Bar Mitzvah observations his father had died suddenly of a heart attack. As the current Bar Mitzvah approaches the family becomes tense, irritable, combative, and feels overwhelmed with fatigue. Clearly, some families are vulnerable to stress whereas others resist it. Further, as in the case of the Jacobses, families may be vulnerable to stress at some periods in their development and not at others. What characteristics distinguish vulnerable from invulnerable families?

We posit two underlying factors of primary importance. The first is the family's level of organization at the time of stress. The second is the quality of its ties with its social environment.[8]

We have already listed three fundamental changes which parallel the stages of family disorganization. As the family moves from smooth, implicit function to life labored by external rule systems and rebellion, it loses its capacity to provide explanations and meaning, it becomes preoccupied with its own processes, and outsiders take on an increasing importance in shaping its experiences. Along with these changes comes a general and pervasive sense that ordinary life tasks are an extraordinary burden for the group. Routine events such as household chores and regular marker events such as birthdays and graduations are perceived as onerous duties requiring great energy. They no longer serve, in Kantor and Lehr's terms (1975), a re-fueling function of their own. If further burdens face this depleted family — an illness, a death, an economic reversal of some kind — the effect will be substantial. Severe disorganization is much more likely to ensue.

The family's social environment plays two different but related roles in the family's vulnerability to stress. First, as we have already indicated, it plays a consistent and pervasive role in the definition of the magnitude of stress which inheres in an event, circumstance, or situation. The community participates in this process by providing its own frameworks, values, attitudes, and conceptions of life changes and events. It is certainly true that in all communities, certain events of human life are extraordinarily stressful: severe illness, unanticipated death, the mysterious disappearance of a loved one, economic privation. However, some communities soften the blow of these events by providing a coherent explanation or approach to these events, usually accompanied by a profoundly engaging set of rituals in response to those events. For example, the Navajo "sing" brings an entire community together for a religious and social ritual when there is a serious illness. Although illness is thought to be caused by supernatural forces (for example, ghosts), healing is understood to flow from a carefully prescribed social ritual which is believed by the Navajo to correct the disordered relationship between the patient and the supernatural.[9] Illness is a community event; its cure is the responsibility of a collective healer, the community. Framing these specific views of health and illness is the Navajo's conviction that it is current life, not the life hereafter, that matters most and things must be set right now by those who have the power to do so. A similar conception frames the Jewish response to death. Jews, like the Navajo, have only hazy notions of a life after death.[10] Life, as it is lived right now, is fundamental. Among many rituals which express this community conviction is the seven-day mourning after death. While the impact of death may not be lessened by such a ritual, the community is mobilized to support the living by helping them first to experience the death fully and to grieve for the lost family member, but, even more important, to return to the earnest engagement in present life while it is here to be lived. In this sense, Judaism helps shape the meaning of death not by influencing the immediate magnitude of the stress involved but by helping to transform this stress, as rapidly as possible, into a resolve to continue life.

The family's social environment contributes to its invulnerability to stress in a second and equally important way. We will discuss this special role in more detail in Chapters 7 and 8. To anticipate that argument, we propose that this supporting function is performed in two ways. First, the community—in concert with the family itself—forges links or bonds of a particular quality with the family. The nature of these bonds supports and sustains the family. In particular, they can support the family's typical or characteristic conceptions of its social reality as well as the implicit interaction patterns with which such conceptions are intertwined. In Chapter 7 we will describe patrician or "old line" families who maintain high status, centrality, and influence in communities and how these high status links help to perpetuate the family's sense of itself as bounded, removed, ongoing, and confident. Second, as in the case of the Jews and the Navajo, social communities have their own values, outlook, and conceptions of social reality which can strengthen and support corresponding constructions in individual families. For example, as we have described in Chapter 1, Strodtbeck (1958) has shown that Sicilian religious and community conceptions give strong support to cohesive families who place their fate in the hands of God and destiny. In contrast, the ethos of community and religious life in Eastern European Jewish communities supported families who collectively explored, understood, and mastered the nuances of their intellectual and social environment.

In sum, we are proposing several factors which can intervene between stress and family disorganization. Thus in many cases a stressful event may not be the necessary and sufficient cause of serious and sustained family disorganization; nonetheless, it can play a prominent role in family disorganization. Paradoxically, as we will show in the next section, stress can be an important component of the family's recovery from disorganization. Stressful experiences—whatever their actual ties to family disorganization—can become a nucleus of the family's own conception of its predicament. In other words, we are positing that many families come to terms, at least in part, with their own crisis and disorganization by selecting or highlighting certain events as stressful even though those events may actually have played only a minor role in their downward spiral.

Consider, for example, the Jennings family. The father is a successful architect in a Midwestern industrial city. Twenty years before he had married his secretary and soon had three sons. The marriage had always been stressful; indeed, Mr. Jennings carried on a well-concealed affair for the duration of his marriage. At the time the third son left for college, the marital strain became worse and could no longer be ignored by the couple. As they saw it, maintaining a house in the downtown area of the city was a difficult experience. They began to attribute their marital strain to the house and its neighborhood. Their shared view that they should not be living so close to blue-collar whites or blacks was never stated. Such proximity, they felt, was a daily source of strain. Indeed, this construction of what constituted the significant stress in their lives formed the nucleus of an elaborate effort to reorganize their marriage. They decided to buy a suburban riverside mansion which had once been owned by one of the grandest old line families in the area. This enabled them to live out their own fantasies of being part of their aristocracy, although their origins had in fact been quite humble. Had their kin, the new community, and father's architectural firm then accepted this shift as an indicator of rise in social prestige and reinforced it (that is, treated them as if they were aristocrats), the Jenningses' solution to their own crisis might have achieved some long-standing success. It is unlikely that this shift would have improved the quality or satisfaction of their relationship with one another, but it might have facilitated a smooth coordination of their lives in a marriage which rested on a shared sense of lineage, superiority, and privilege.

Family Reorganization

THE CONSTRUCTION OF CRISIS:
FIRST STEPS TOWARD REORGANIZATION

As we have discussed, three major changes in the family parallel its slide from implicit function to constraint by a system of explicit rules and rebellion. The first of these is a reduction in the family's capacity to highlight and explain the structure of the social world; second is the family's increasing preoccupation with itself; and third is the substantially enlarged role of outsiders in shaping family life. Increasing family disorganization can be the core of a chronic state of rigidity and misery, a prelude to final dissolution of the family, or the basis for its redemption. The factors which determine which path is followed—chronicity, dissolution, or reorganization—are important but will not be considered in detail here. Suffice it to say that a combination of personal resources of individual members and resources available in the family's immediate social environment can contribute to redemption rather than dissolution. In Chapters 7 and 8, we will continue the discussion begun in the previous section, of the ways in which the family's social environment—particularly its kin, its community and important organizations (including therapeutic ones)—can shape and help maintain its recovery from crisis. Here, we will simply assume that sufficient internal and external resources support the family's recovery or reorganization. We wish to focus on the steps of this recovery and on the role of what we call the *crisis construct* in initiating and shaping that recovery.[11]

The path to recovery or reorganization of the family begins with the crisis construct, a new form of construct; the family recognizes—on some level—that it is in crisis and begins to develop some shared concept of that crisis. This crisis construct, however, is unlike any other shared construct we have so far considered. First, it is a construct or shared (although usually implicitly so) conception of the family process itself. Most constructs, however shaped or toned by family process, have—as their central focus—some aspect of life outside the family; where they concern the family they focus on the family's position in its social world. The crisis construct focuses more on the family itself; it includes some percept of its disorganization. It is, in effect, the family's growing conception of its own crisis and the pathways, if any, open to it for resolution of that crisis.

A second unique aspect of the crisis construct is that it is often relatively cut off from the system of explanation and understanding which guided the family during its better days of implicit function. It needn't always be so. Even in the depths of crisis, a family may grapple with its own difficulties in terms that are quite similar to those of better days. Thus, the Michaels family, grappling with the sudden death of the father, had always been a proud, independent family which set itself apart from the rest of the world (they lived, for example, in the penthouse of an office building, which—in a spatial sense—expressed the family's sense of superiority and distance from other families). Its concepts of its own crisis—if that had developed — might have been toned by his family's ways of viewing itself in the world. (In fact, the Michaels family remained in a chronic state of stasis, with little resolution, for years. They never recognized their own crisis as a group.) The central point here nonetheless is that the crisis construct has a particularly good chance of being independent from previous systems of explanation and meaning because these have been so badly shattered through the family's crisis. The Jenningses' conception of their marital discord — which they attributed to living "downtown" (a euphemism, in their lexicon, for "among the working class") — was toned with an aristocratic and patrician cast that had not been a fundamental theme in the family's life until then. It had existed in a subdued or peripheral form in the fantasy life of father and one of his sons but had not before served as an organizing force or theme in family affairs. In that sense it had, until the marital crisis was recognized, an "outside" location.

A third unique aspect of the crisis construct is the involvement of outsiders or outside aspects of individual members. Because outsiders now enter the family system in a new way, they have the opportunity to influence and participate in the family's experience of itself in a manner that in better days would have been impossible.[12]

The fact that the crisis construct may be separated from the family's prior system of explanations and understandings and is under substantial influence of an outsider means that it may be different — in many essential attributes — from any significant construct the family has previously shaped. In other words, the crisis construct constitutes a basis for family change. Equally important, if the construct does form the nucleus of the family's recovery from crisis, it stands as a dramatic achievement. It takes a special place among the family system of constructs: it is the one that initiated redemption. As such it becomes a model, a paradigm in the true grammatical sense of the word. In the future, other solutions to other lesser problems, other constructions of ambiguous and disconcerting events, are patterned after this one. Thus, the crisis construct forms a motivational core of the family's conception of itself in a social world.

Subject to the influence of outsiders, the crisis construct can take one of many forms. Indeed, we are positing that the differences between families' crisis constructs leads to corresponding differences in families' underlying systems of shared constructs. This is because all constructs in a family system are shaped in some way to follow from the crisis construct, which comes to serve as a dramatically successful paradigm. It is now of interest to follow this process forward, to conceive how differences between families in crisis and —

most important—differences in their crisis constructs—might lead to much broader differences in their underlying systems of explanation. We have already, in Chapter 1, argued the merits of paying special attention to difference in form rather than in content. Further, we have found it best to identify a small number of dimensions which can be used, conceptually and methodologically, to make such formal distinctions. We will follow the same strategy here. We are proposing that three dimensions will clarify many of the differences among the types of crisis constructs developed by families—under the important influence of outsiders—at times of severe disorganization.

In describing these dimensions, and thereby delineating some of the possible differences among families in their crisis constructs, we will use as examples rather clear-cut crises. In each case, the stressor event is distinct and bounded, and the crisis and disorganization in family life has a close relation to this stressor. This makes it possible to clearly show how the crisis construct can become organized around an explanation of the stressor event and its impact on the family. It is important to remember that severe family disorganization may have no clear-cut relationship to a specific stress in the family's experience or anyone else's. Moreover, whether or not there is a clear-cut stressor, the family's construct may focus on quite another set of events which they regard as the critical stress, or invent one, or not focus on any discrete, continuous, or amorphous stress of any kind.

When we consider stressful events that can, in fact, lead to serious family crisis, we can turn to two universal categories of human suffering: prolonged illness and death. We chose the former and picked a special form of that: sustained disability in a young child. Recent evidence suggests that severe prolonged disability, particularly congenital disabilities that cannot be treated, pose a major stress to families—even those families without a history of difficulty prior to the birth of the child.[13] We also know that these children produce a family crisis precisely because they disrupt usual family routines and make it impossible for families to function on the implicit level (see Korn, Chess, and Fernandez, 1978). Finally, we know that families differ remarkably in their long-term responses to these stresses: in time, some families become more loving, confident, and effective, whereas others remain caught in rigid, unhappy lives.

1. *The template for reorganization:* recognition and growth through experience versus revelation and solidity through meaning. At end-stage deterioration, the family consists of a set of individuals who have emerged from the family by an illusory process of

externalizing the family and divesting themselves of emotional holdings and commitment to the old and egregious order. Reorganization will be shaped first by an evolving, unspoken, and implicit template or set of standards. At the very outset two distinct possibilities lie before this collection of individuals. The first is a template for reorganization that joins two modes of resolving the crisis: processes of recognition and growth through experience. This approach is most likely to begin with some form of identification of the disorganizing stress itself: this includes an attempt to demarcate it from the routines of ordinary life.

For example, consider the Roberts family. Both parents worked as full-time professionals. They had a healthy two-year-old son. After an uncomplicated pregnancy Mrs. Roberts delivered a daughter with severe birth defects which impaired heart and respiratory function. The child's prolonged stay in the hospital, her ultimate discharge into the care of her family, and subsequent severe difficulties constituted an enormous and ongoing stress. The parents' sleep was continuously interrupted; their sexual relations were seriously hampered. They could delegate child care to no one but themselves. The needs of their healthy two year old were often ignored. Visits into the house by any non-family members were very limited. The family went on virtually no visits of its own, no vacations. Their relationship with friends and family was seriously impaired. Their financial resources were seriously drained. Somehow, they also felt stigma was attached to their situation. Friends, neighbors, acquaintances, and relatives began to deal with them in new ways: they became overinvolved or withdrew and sometimes vacillated unpredictably from one to the other.

However, as the crisis deepened, the seeds for recovery were also sown by the family. This process seemed to begin with the couple's efforts to clarify that it was indeed this externally given crisis—the birth of their daughter—that set into motion the family's own futile attempts at self-healing and ultimately its disorganization. Closely related was a shared realization that this tragedy was, at first, unfathomed but fathomable. More than that, the couple developed a commitment to piece together evidence and to learn through experience about an unknown and unprecedented event. Their passive gathering of facts—which were the products of the experience of others (doctors, geneticists, embryologists)—was only the nucleus of a more active phase of this approach to recovery. The couple allowed themselves, at unguarded moments, a direct experience of the unknown aspects of the crisis. First, the stressful event itself was directly experienced. While the deformed baby was in her early days, she was visited often by both parents. She was seen, smelled, and touched.[14] The parents were initially overcome by the bewildering and chaotic experience of the intensive care nursery for newborns, of the infant herself, and of their own emotions of disgust, pity, guilt, anger, and humiliation. Ultimately, they were able to acknowledge and bear these feelings. They began to recognize that other families were suffering similar crisis; they also saw, on their own, that the nursing staff could tolerate the anguish of their own role without becoming emotionally leathery and insensitive. They began to see, through repeated experience, that their doctor fully intended to take the ultimate responsibility on himself for the decision about continuing the heroic treatment to let the baby live or to stop treatment and let her die. Equally important, they learned of their own emotional capacities, their capacity to be helped by an understanding doctor, to support the grief of other families with infants on the same medical unit, and most important—despite their disgust and humiliation—to love their own child. At this point recovery was set in motion. Emerging from all these intertwined experiences of the couple was their clear perception of their child, with all her weaknesses, as well as a conception of their own capacities and deficiencies. This conception was built up over weeks and months of experiencing, questioning, and learning.

For the Roberts family this evolution constituted a fundamental change. The couple had been heavily invested in their careers. Both had come from families with a long line of academic and business success and both had thrown themselves into their own professions out of a strong commitment to traditions and expectations and their own parents and extended family (Chapter 7 provides a more detailed account of influences of this kind). Following this sustained crisis, partial disorganization, and reorganization, the couple had a fundamentally new sense of confidence in their own competence at personal as well as business relationships.

In contrast to this template for recognition and growth is one that centers on revelation and the discovery through meaning. The central characteristic here is that the chaos experienced by the family—now a collection of individuals—is transcended by a rich and personal meaning attached to the crisis events. In this template for reorganization the emphasis—at the outset—is not the acquisition of new experience, knowledge, and skills. Rather, the family becomes engaged in decoding the symbolic meaning of the crisis and subsequent disorganization. The group strives for the emergence of a sense of solidity around a common perception of the revealed significance in the crisis. The disorganizing stress itself is not carefully delineated. If its role in the family's disorganization is perceived at all, usually only a single aspect or very circumscribed part of the total stress situation is singled out for special attention.[15]

In contrast to the Roberts couple, consider the Weavers. The Weavers were in their early forties and had two adolescent daughters. Mr. Weaver worked for a large computer company; Mrs. Weaver had returned to school part-time, hoping to finally finish college. She had left school when she had her first pregnancy eighteen years previously. Now, in her early forties, she had an unplanned pregnancy. She gave birth to a girl with defects similar to the Roberts child. The Weavers, like the Robertses, became partially disorganized as a consequence of some of the same factors: financial stress, altered relationships with neighbors and extended family, inability to tend to the needs of their adolescent children, and the need to take continuing responsibility for the care of their sick child.

The Weavers' response to the crisis was from the outset different from the Robertses'. They felt that this event was somehow foreordained. Mrs. Weaver even became convinced she was destined never to complete her schooling but that in the end she would be consigned to follow in the footsteps of her mother, dead now for five years, who had been a loved and devoted housewife but had stifled many of her own talents. The family visited the newborn baby very infrequently although she was in the hospital for many months. They relied heavily on a single nurse in her early sixties for information about how the child was doing. Mother, along with the rest of the family, struggled with her conflicting feelings from a much greater distance from her child than the Robertses. She became preoccupied with the fact her baby had been born on her mother's birthday. She talked of this often with the rest of the family. Although they discounted the almost magical significance that Mrs. Weaver attached to the coincidence of birthdays, there was talk in the family about Mrs. Weaver's mother, how she might have handled this situation, what she might have said, what her feelings would be.

The birth of this very sick infant clearly reawakened strong feelings in all four family members about the dead grandmother. At one time or another everyone commented that the hospital and its staff reminded them of the hospital in which Mrs. Weaver's mother had spent her last days. When their own child died even the funeral and burial reminded them strongly of grandmother. After the death of the child there seemed to be little open grief. During the years before the crisis everyone in the family had been intensely engaged in activities that were advancing or promoting their interests. The father, a very hard worker, had received a number of promotions in a short time. The oldest daughter had been selected as valedictorian just before her sister was born, and the younger daughter, also a good student, was the only sophomore in the high school to make the girls' varsity basketball team. After the death of the child everyone's ambition seemed to flicker. Mother left school and never returned. Father developed a strong interest in a fundamentalist Christian group. The academic careers of both adolescent daughters never lived up to the promise of their high school days. However, the family remained close and visits by members of the family to Mrs. Weaver's aging father became more frequent.

The contrasting reactions of the Robertses and the Weavers to a similar stress and ensuing family disorganization exemplify the fundamental differences between the recognition and revelation crisis constructs. The Robertses, at first without any clear intent to do so, embarked on a long and painful road of building up experience. The construct which developed over time included an enlarged conception of themselves as individuals and as a couple, a clear and vivid set of images and understandings of the physical plight of their baby, a growing knowledge of the intricacies of the medical staff taking care of her, and an informed appreciation of the reactions of other families. There was, in an important sense, no end to this crisis construct. Even years later, the Robertses would consider some new aspect of the experience and come to a fresh understanding of what they had been through. By contrast, much less of the Weavers' reaction involved direct experience. As a group they seemed to find significance in the experience, not through a direct exposure to it, but because it took on intense symbolic meaning for all of them (we can see this symbolic meaning most clearly in Mrs. Weaver's response). In a way the family could only dimly perceive, the birth of this very ill infant connected them to a woman, now dead, who had been very important to all of them. All members of the family felt there was some unseen force lurking behind the events. This feeling may have had its origin in the family's reactions to Mrs. Weaver's pregnancy. It surprised everyone; the entire family felt somewhat out of control of events. The feeling of being out of control solidified after the birth of the baby and the long illness. All members shifted their pattern of decisions and ambitions without being sure why they were making changes.

The most proximate influences that account for the difference between the two families are not clear, since there was a considerable shift in family patterns as a result of crisis and partial disorganization. Our vignette of the Roberts family suggests that a strong involvement with an open and supportive medical staff had a major impact on how the couple dealt with the sustained crisis. A signifi-

cant influence on the Weavers was Mrs. Weaver's incomplete griev-
ing of her dead mother; her sustained ties to her mother may have
been reactivated by her pregnancy and the birth of the child. These
processes, partially sequestered inside her in the five years since the
death of her mother, had a particularly strong impact on the rest of
the family at a time of crisis.

2. *The enactment of reorganization:* collective versus personal
action. Relatively early in its efforts at reorganization, we contend,
a family establishes a template for reorganization. The clearest distinction among families is highlighted and demarcated by the distinction between the recognition and revelation approach. As the
family reorganizes itself, these overall approaches—recognition or
revelation—become further differentiated. During the first phases
of the family's effort to restore itself these distinctions are very
subtle. They are overshadowed by the family's efforts to learn
through experience or to grasp the hidden or symbolic meanings in
the crisis. Nonetheless, as the family's reconstitution goes forward,
further differentiation—in response to crisis—plays a larger and
larger role. When resolution is complete, they make an equal contribution to the form of the paradigmatic solution and, therefore,
to the subsequent course of family life.

The first such differentiation concerns the balance between collective versus personal action. As family disorganization proceeds,
the family has become a collectivity of individuals. The resumption
of group life, as reorganization takes place, permits a new balance
between the individual and the group. Let us compare how this
equilibration proceeds in recognition families and in revelation
families. As this process goes forward, we contend, families will
begin to diverge.

The recognition families engage in developing their own pain-
stakingly constructed conception of their immediate circumstances.
In time, this conception becomes complex. Both explicitly and implicitly the family begins to link together the stress, its own response, and its reorganization into a coherent system of events. As
any family grows in experience through crisis it acquires many diverse observations, ideas, and concepts. The total accumulation
soon exceeds the capacity of any single member to grasp, remember, digest, or integrate. Let us return to the Roberts family. As the
crisis was prolonged Mr. Roberts became concerned with problems
of medical insurance, with economic problems occasioned by his
absence from work, with the impact of the events on his family.
Mother, by contrast, focused on her healthy two-year-old son, on
her prolonged amenorrhea in the months following the crisis, on
the sudden worsening of her sister's asthma which was now return-

ing after being dormant for many years. The two-year-old son had his own intensely personal world of action and reaction: whispered conversations, sudden changes in daily routines, intense emotion in his parents, and their prolonged absences. How shall such separate worlds be united? Some families, we propose, will retain coherence by a sense that each member is a family specialist: each member *represents* the family in a specialized world in which he has particular expertise. Wherever possible, the family will fashion some general underlying principles to guide the specialists in their daily activities. Thus, ultimately the special experiences of each individual may add — at least in part — to the family's overall growth of understanding, to the development and detail of their emerging conception of crisis. By contrast are families — still engaged in the recognition approach — who become individualists. Family members implicitly acknowledge among themselves that personal experiences in the crisis are too unique to be fully reconciled. Thus, father's occupational problems or stresses with his own family might be regarded as ones for him to handle because their subtlety and complexity are too great for his wife to manage. His individual occupation and family experience become a nidus for fashioning his own model of the crisis — much of which is never reconciled with his wife's. What unites him with his wife is their shared valuation of recognition, particularly their valuation of growth through experience. They may reinforce and support each other's efforts to gain in understanding through direct experience. The experiences themselves are never brought into concord, never reconciled. More important, there is a fundamental acceptance and conviction that they can never be.

Families whose initial mode of recovery — its template for reorganization — is primarily one of revelation and meaning may also diverge from one another. One group of these families will see themselves as a single unit in a field of inexplicable forces and meanings. All will feel connected to the events of crisis as a unitary element. Other families whose recovery begins in the same mode may show a progressive pulling apart and isolation of its members from one another. Our vignette of the Weaver family is not clear on this point. One direction this family might take is for all members to have some shared sense of reliving their relationship with Mrs. Weaver's dead mother. Our brief picture of their reaction suggests this might be the case. In ways they could not explain, all members of the family felt, in this crisis, a reconnection to someone they all had loved and depended upon. Further, the event served to reestablish latent ties with extended family. However, the course of recovery and reorganization might have taken another turn. Mrs.

Weaver might have been left alone to grapple with the reemerging feelings toward her own mother. Indeed, she had several intense experiences during the crisis she never shared with anyone: at moments when she least expected it she thought she heard her mother calling her name. This more isolated private experience of an inexplicable phenomenon might also have colored the experience of other family members as they recovered from the sustained crisis. Mr. Weaver, unable to share his wife's intensely personal reaction, might have thrown himself back into his work, sensing, without understanding, that this crisis had somehow erected a wall between himself and his wife. The daughters, without sharing their feelings, might have blotted out the intensely pleasurable fantasies of marriage and childrearing which were propelling them into early adulthood. In short, the prolonged illness and death of the child would have had intense but deeply personal and private symbolic meanings for each member of the family. The life of the family and the lives of each member might show significant change, but included in this change would be an increasing isolation and distance between the members.

3. *The resources of reorganization:* environment versus family. However families may differ, reorganization involves effort and energy for them all. The process of recovery from crisis and deterioration involves the expenditure of immense energy, and families include, in their construct of the crisis, an experience of the sources of energy which fueled their recovery. Kantor and Lehr (1975), to our knowledge, have been the first to conceptualize energy in families. They concern themselves with what they call "mechanisms of fueling" (social operations by which the family draws on resources outside itself) and "mechanisms of investment and mobilization of energy" (social operations for controlling these resources of energy once they are obtained). Our emphasis, though related, is distinctly different. We do not ask how a family gathers or distributes energy. We are asking how a family comes to understand the sources of energy or strength for its own redemption. Again, we may distinguish families engaged in recognition from those engaged in revelation.

The recognizing families, as their experience of their own crisis develops, can be distinguished from one another according to what they experience as the wellspring of effective action. Some families will begin to focus on their own reactions to the crisis, will come to perceive more clearly their own potentialities and strengths, will learn through experience that they can depend on themselves in a way they had never expected. The Roberts couple, for example, learned it could love its ill child and, in the midst of its own crisis, could sense the intense preoccupation of other families in similar circumstances. Such experiences, we contend, become the experiential cornerstones of a newly emerging sense or construct of the crisis which highlights or underscores the family's discovery of its own strength. Other families may direct their attention to the configuration of the outer world. The Robertses recognized in their doctor a person of great experience in the care of ill newborns, a person who would struggle to save life but who also knows when the struggle has gone far enough. The Roberts couple also devoted extraordinary attention to the possibilities or impossibilities for the survival and development of their ill child, of her incapacity to sustain her own life without heroic medical support. Indeed their enlarging concept of crisis may have included both a detailed conception of the precise biological limits of their child and the dependability of the doctor. In sum, the Robertses show a mixture of the two possibilities here: seeing themselves as a resource, as they gained in self-awareness and confidence, and seeing the environment as a resource, as they grasped more of the significant patterns and details in their immediate world. Many families, we contend, will clearly emphasize one or the other response here.

There is a corresponding divergence in the patterns of reorganization in revelation families. In the Weaver family, the ill infant is seen as a link with a dead grandmother. In this example the family's experience of crisis becomes organized around a connection between its own disordered and chaotic present and a past that is seen as a touchstone of strength, reliability, and infinite resource. In contrast, reorganization in a revelation family may center on a person or circumstance outside the family. The doctor, again, may be the focus of attention, but the family will view the doctor with more awe than would the recognizing family. The revelation family will view him as a savior, as endowed with miraculous powers of healing and balm, of representing traditions and forces which can endow the family with the strength they need for reorganization. The recognizing family also will show trust and admiration for the doctor but their trust and admiration are built up slowly as they come to take full measure of his capacities and experience.

The dimensions of the crisis constructs we have just reviewed are summarized in Table 4.2.

We have drawn particular attention to family process at the time of grave crisis. We have specified that extreme crisis cuts the family off from its own past — the traditions and conventions of its own life which prior to the crisis served to heal family disorder but which now only speed the family toward its ultimate dissolution. The time of disorganization is a time for something new. In this

TABLE 4.2 REORGANIZATION OF THE FAMILY AFTER CRISIS AND DISORGANIZATION: THREE DIMENSIONS FOR SPECIFYING DIFFERENT MODES OF REORGANIZATION

Dimension	Poles of the dimension	Characteristics of the poles
1. The template for reorganization	a. recognition through experience	Family's reorganization is shaped by its growing experience, knowledge, and understanding of the external stresses, its capacity to deal with them, the resources it can draw on from others, and the experience of other families.
	b. revelation through meaning	Family's reorganization is shaped by the symbolic significance of the immediate stressor and its context.
2. The enactment of reorganization	a. collective action	Each member experiences his own efforts at reorganization as part of the efforts of the group.
	b. personal action	As reorganization takes place, each member focuses on the tasks he must accomplish and on his own accomplishments or understandings.
3. The resources of reorganization	a. family	The family experiences itself as the wellspring of reorganization; the *recognizing family* learns about its own inner resources, whereas the *revelation family* becomes symbolically tied to its own past.
	b. environment	The family experiences the environment as the wellspring of reorganization; the *recognizing family* experiences its enlarging grasp of critical people and events in its experiential world while the *revelation family* derives a central strength from a venerated person or meaningful event.

section we have specified the underlying dimensions that can be used to distinguish the various forms the new approach can take. We will continue, in the next chapter, to show the long-term implications for the family of each particular form of these patterns of reorganization from crisis.

5 | The Abstraction of the Family Paradigm

The Need for Abstraction

Once the solution for the crisis is set in motion, there is a good chance it will achieve some form of family reorganization and reconstitution. We have been arguing that initiating and shaping the process of reconstitution is an evolving construct formulated by the family. This construct serves to coordinate each member's delineation and comprehension of the crisis itself, the family's response to the crisis, the action that is required to surmount it, and the resources on which such action can depend. As the crisis resolves, the family retraces its steps. From a group of individuals arrayed against a threatening and tyrannical externalized family, they become a rule-bound explicit family once again.

The process of healing can go beyond this to what we might call — to maintain symmetry of vocabulary — full reorganization. This is a phase in the family's life where most functions of regulation and concord are carried out entirely on the implicit level. In this section we will argue that the pattern and texture of this new phase of implicit function is organized by the mode of crisis resolution itself. This is the core meaning of the concept of paradigm. The construct that guided the family's restoration is felt by all members to have been an extraordinary achievement. Thus, it serves as a model (*paradigm* in the strict sense) for guiding the elaboration of shared constructs during all stressful, problematic, or puzzling circumstances of the family's everyday life. The crisis construct also screens out or excludes from the family's awareness aspects of the crisis which were too painful for the family to acknowledge. For example, the Weaver family in the preceding chapter protected themselves from many of the thoughts and feelings that would have arisen by more frequent visits and more direct exposure to their ill infant when she was in the hospital. The same processes which shape and conserve the family paradigm maintain this exclusion process as well.

In this chapter we will try to give some account of how the dramatic achievement of crisis resolution becomes paradigmatic, that is, how the essential attributes of the construct in crisis achieve their guiding function. To do so, we will consider separately two processes which are, in all probability, completely intertwined. The first is the process by which the most critical attributes of the crisis are abstracted. It is evident that the crisis construct—in its entirety—cannot serve as an exemplar, guiding future family responses to problems and puzzles of daily living. For example, the family of a congenitally ill infant will construe a great deal about infants, neonatology, doctors, and hospitals that will have little relevance for puzzles and problems it faces later. Clearly some essential features of their experience must be abstracted if any aspect of the experience is to carry over to the future. Once these fundamental aspects of the paradigmatic construction are abstracted by the family, they must be conserved. In many families the entire crisis experience may be forgotten—using the word "forgotten" in the superficial, mentalistic sense meaning that if you asked members to recall the crisis events they couldn't respond. (We could also include here a more sophisticated psychoanalytic sense of the word "forgotten" meaning that careful psychoanalytic reconstruction is also impossible.) We will argue that memory, as conventionally understood by individual psychology, is *not* the medium or repository for the conservation of the family paradigm. On the contrary, it is the structure of family interaction behavior which is itself the primary repository and conservative factor.

The Process of Social Abstraction

A crisis construct can have enduring value to the family because it contains certain features which help organize the family's experience of problematic and puzzling situations in everyday life. A process of abstraction must occur by which the essential elements of the crisis constructs are preserved through time, to be applied again and again; the nonessential elements are discarded during the crisis period itself and do not reappear in the life of the family. We will refer to this winnowing or selection process as one of *abstraction*, in the sense in which Suzanne Langer uses the term.[1] She focuses on the processes, other than formal logic, by which individuals select, highlight, and transform essential aspects of their experience and delete the rest. The criteria applied in this selection process are more aesthetic than logical. In particular, they come close to what Gestalt psychologists have referred to as "good form."[2]

The abstraction process, although it involves a paring away of nonessential aspects of the crisis experience, paradoxically involves a building up of very different kinds of social experience, the abstracted experiences. The two common threads of this social abstraction have already been discussed briefly: social interpolation and social extrapolation. Let us examine, very briefly, how these processes serve the ends of abstraction. Social interpolation and extrapolation both involve seeing the hidden potential in a formulation and using this hidden potential to add a new piece. Interpolation usually involves seeing a hidden potential in at least two separate elements of an explanation and adding a piece that serves to unite previously unconnected elements. Recall again the four-brother cosmology. The original formulation contained several explicit elements: A God of Spring, an older God of Summer and several principles concerning a dance, fatigue, a fall to earth, and restoration. In our account of this formulation, gods of Autumn and Winter were very briefly described. Their age wasn't mentioned. A second person could "see" that Autumn must be older than Summer and that Winter is even older. This might seem like an ordinary logical act similar in form to the incomplete number series that appear on intelligence tests. However, a more critical interpolation is performed by the second person. He can also "see" that although the gods have different ages, they are ageless. Neither the original formulation or its author could clearly "see" the ageless property of the gods. Nonetheless, the original formulation, because it invoked gods and because it sought to explain an invarying of sequence of seasons, clearly implied the property of agelessness. This "implication" is not — strictly speaking — a logical one, although we can cast it in logical terms. The force generating both the implication and the consequent interpolation is much closer to an aesthetic one. The implication and interpolation bring the formulation closer to good form: a circle of brothers whose internal dynamics are somehow self-enclosed and self-generating. We use the term "closer to" good form because the story of the brothers is not complete. It is exciting because it can be meaningfully (and perhaps endlessly) elaborated through additional social interpolations and also social extrapolations. Extrapolations, like interpolations, depend on seeing the hidden potential in at least one element in the formulation. The main function of the extrapolation is to extend the formulation rather than to increase its inner coherence. Thus, after a process of interpolation, we had a cosmology with four ageless brothers of different ages united in an endless dance. We lacked an account, however, of the restoration process and its precise extension to the seasons. Extrapolation by a second individual added a new theme: each god set a temperature which his age required for thorough restoration.³ To be sure, this extension also had the effect of providing greater coherence to the entire cosmology. Indeed, extrapolation and interpolation are so closely related that we use separate terms only to give a slightly different emphasis.

As interpolations and extrapolations multiply they come to highlight certain cardinal hidden or underlying properties of the formulation. Interpolations and extrapolations will select certain hidden properties more than others. This will enable the formulation to achieve a high measure of integration. The hidden properties that are most frequently used for interpolation or extrapolation become the most crucial for maintaining the integrity of the entire system. Thus, the four brothers may be the most crucial element; they appear in every interpolation and extrapolation as the cosmology is transformed through successive face-to-face encounters. The hidden element may be the implicit and special loving competition and camaraderie between brothers. As the explanatory system becomes more and more elaborate it reaches an asymptote. It is not the particular elements of the system that become fixed. They may be replaced and endlessly modified. Indeed, a "good" system is one that is enthralling enough to invite such changes (which may be the product of experience, imagination, or both). What reaches an asymptote is the structure or form of the most fundamental hidden potentials. Thus, a still-changing cosmology may reach stability in the sense that the hidden structures of the relationship among the four brothers remain constant. In this critical sense, a process of repeated social interpolation and extrapolation serves as an abstraction of certain crucial elements of an explanatory system.

Our little ad hoc cosmology is a particularly accessible example because it is so simple. In families, matters become much more complex. An extended analysis would be required to show how a comparable abstraction process would go forward. We will confine ourselves to a few suggestive examples in family life by returning to the confused situation of the congenitally ill child, and we will deal only with partial abstraction—that is, abstraction carried out only to the point it would ordinarily reach in the first weeks after the crisis. As the family begins to reorganize, some elements of the crisis construct emerge as critical and others have been set aside; however, the selective process is still in progress. First, let us consider a recognizing family whose emerging construct of the crisis is organized by a unitary, underlying principle and which focuses on the family itself as a resource for dealing with the crisis through a modification of the environment.⁴ A family of this kind might devote a good deal of its efforts to exploring and understanding the processes of conception, gestation, and birth. On some level they will come to know and feel the crude and ineffective physiologic struggles of their infant. Their sense of their own bodies as physiologic mechanisms and as sources of rich and varied sensations may be enhanced by both their increased formal knowledge of their child's plight and by implicit and detailed experiential sensitivity to her struggles to survive. The mother and father, on resuming sexual relations some weeks after the crisis began, may have a more exquisite sense of their own and each other's bodies. The same couple, having spent many painful hours seeing and vicariously feeling their ill infant's labored breathing, may have an enhanced experience of their own routine bodily functions: salivation, breathing, cardiac palpitations, bladder pressures, and bowel movements. There may be a more sensitive physical communication established with the well child, who—as part of a family-wide process—may have changes in his own body image. We suggest that, in this family, as abstraction proceeds it begins to isolate awareness of one's own body and another's body as hidden properties of many elements of the crisis experience.

As another example, consider the Weavers. The crisis in this revelation family began to resolve as the Weavers regarded the ill infant as an unfathomable link between themselves and the dead grandmother. As isolating abstraction goes forward, almost all of the specific experiences of the crisis may be forgotten. Under the sway of a construct that is becoming paradigmatic, the family begins to center its attention on a force of deep power, transcendent mystery, a return of the dead, which has touched them through the birth and death of a child. Their reorganizing conception of themselves in the world may now take on a religious, mystical, and even messianic quality. Indeed, the hidden potential in their crisis construct is its messianic cast: the redemption of the family through the awesome and unfathomable connection of a child who, by transcending death, links them to a universal power.[5]

Certain hidden properties of any construct or explanation are emphasized by the process of social abstraction. Which properties are selected and which are left aside is determined by the frequency with which those properties are used as the crucial nidus for extrapolation or interpolation as reorganization goes forward. The differences in such frequencies may be due to an entirely random process. We have suggested, though, that some properties of good form make certain hidden properties particularly attractive. It may be that very simple Gestalt principles could be of great assistance here: proximity, similarity, good curve, common fate, closure, and the rest. For example, the four-brother cosmology may exert its appeal because of the hidden property of a circle with a missing member (unclosed) which seeks closure (the restoration of the fallen brother). The Gestalt principle of common fate may underlie the concept of a link between a dead grandmother and a dying infant. More generally speaking, we are arguing that the tendency toward good form is universally distributed among all individuals, as argued by the Gestalt psychologists. When any individual is faced with a complex pattern of stimuli, he will tend to organize these stimuli to produce good form. This universal facility becomes an integral part of a process of social simplification as well. As social abstraction goes forward, interpolation and extrapolation tend to focus on elements within the complex crisis construct, elements whose relation to one another achieves good form. To repeat our frequently quoted example: the four brothers in our cosmology remain the stable core of interpolations and extrapolations because the relationship among these elements, of all the related elements in our cosmology, most closely approximates good form, a circle coming to closure.[6]

Interpolation and extrapolation can be observed in reorganizing families as well. To follow this pattern, one must take into account not only what family members say and think but also the countless gestures, feelings, and patterns in their daily interaction. Consider the example we have just given of the recognizing family's awareness of their own bodies. Mother and father return home from the hospital where they have each spent a few minutes with their ill infant, holding her and observing her difficulties in breathing and her somewhat listless movements. Importantly, father had rarely held his two-year-old son when he was an infant; thus it was unusual for both parents to have shared the experience of holding and rocking an infant. Mrs. Roberts, drained from the experience, sits close to her husband on the car trip home, an unusual position for her. When they arrive home, the babysitter tells them that their two-year-old son does not look well. Mother sits at the child's bedside holding his forehead while father goes to get a thermometer. As gently as possible, he inserts it in his son's rectum, also for the first time. Surprised, the little boy does not protest as usual. He has a moderate fever. Mother gets him a tall glass of juice and sponges his forehead. Father searches for the baby aspirin and mother, smiling slightly, shows him where it is kept. A conversation of gestures of central significance is going on here. In holding his ill child, father was not only learning, firsthand, the physical difficulties of his ill daughter; he was also able to experience a tenderness in himself. Mother, too, can see this for the first time and sits closer to him during a routine activity in which they are ordinarily separated. By the time she begins tending her son, she already "knows" that she can count on her husband to participate in his care, even though he has never done so before. The silent acknowledgment of this change comes in her smile when he can't find the aspirin. The father also "knows" that he will be able to successfully insert the rectal thermometer in his son from his experience with his sick child, an experience that has already unveiled for him his own physical tenderness. However, his "knowledge" and that of his wife are genuine social interpolations — a rapid building-up of missing pieces which are beginning to create a solid conviction, a conviction each member of the family holds about one another, of a new physical openness in the family. After this sequence, the little boy begins to get in on this interpolated "knowledge." He now "knows" — without definite prior experience — that his father will be more approachable; specifically, he knows that his father will let him sit on his lap and will let him fall asleep on his shoulder.

The Results of Abstraction

The crisis construct itself is the family's conception of the crisis and its own response. As such it is a system of explanations and experiences that ordinarily concern relatively complex entities: people, emotions, life, death. Broadly speaking, we might envision that social abstraction would provide the family with a framework for considering less dramatic and more ordinary problematic events in its daily life. Most of these events might involve social relationships or events within and without the family. However, we shall take a different tack. We will posit that the end stage of social abstraction yields a set of framing assumptions about the perceptual world of much greater generality. The paradigm, as we have said, is a guide to the family's understanding of its world. It functions as a guide by providing the family with a set of framing or very general assumptions. The framing assumptions concern not only people and human events but extend way beyond this to include assumptions about the connection, patterning, and origins of stimuli, animate and inanimate, of the widest possible variety. In other words, we conceive of the paradigm as a guide to the family's shared conception of the relationships among complex events such as human actions (in Chapter 3 we referred to these as elaborated controls) as well as a guide to its conception of the patterning of very simple stimulus events (the domain of elementary controls).

Let us now consider the forms taken by end-state abstractions. As we have done many times before in our model building, we will specify the variety that end-state abstractions — the paradigmatic constructs — may take by specifying a minimum number of dimensions necessary for describing that variety. To arrive at a specification of these dimensions, we have, on a speculative level, carried forward the process of social abstraction. We began with the dimensions of the crisis construct itself. Then we considered how the abstraction process might go forward under the principles of good form. Finally, we pursue now the abstracting process until it seems to achieve organizing principles which deal not only with the complex elements which were the core crisis experience (people, events, places, feelings, fantasies, attributions, and so on) but also with the much simpler sensory and perceptual events that are the usual fare of the elementary control principles. Let us now consider these three basic dimensions.

DIMENSION 1, COHERENCE:
STABILITY VERSUS INTRINSIC MOVEMENT

Is there a knowable, structural coherence underlying and explaining the experienced world? Families who are on the high end of this dimension will encourage the assumption that a highly reduced set of explanations ties together all events; further, that the connections between this underlying structure and surface events are precisely specifiable. The most critical feature of the underlying structure is its stability; that is, the underlying structure will hold still until it is discovered, and the discovery itself will not perturb or destroy it. This framing assumption is abstracted from the *template dimension* of the crisis construct. In particular, it stems from the family's sense of its own experience-tested, stepwise development during the crisis. The basic principle abstracted here is that *experience is additive*. In other words, adding new experience does not change the essential nature of prior experience. Old and new experience may be added together to gain a clearer picture of an underlying reality. The underlying reality only becomes clearer and closer as it is approached; it never recedes or crumbles. Its stability and emerging clarity provide the prime motivation for continuing to add new experience to what has already been embraced. Furthermore, the fact that the family can retrace the links among the elements of their experience, and that they can arrive at a clear perception of the underlying reality, provides essential reassurance in the pursuit of other underlying realities. For example, consider the recognizing family who is piecing together a model or explanation of its ill child. A small portion of the family's conception will be derived from direct experience with the inept infant. Father visits the child in the morning and reports to his wife that the baby looks blue, her breathing is intensely labored, and her little arms are rigid and flailing. He recognizes that the baby—already in serious trouble—has been *in extremis*. Mother visits the child the same afternoon. The child looks pink, the breathing—although somewhat stertorous—is not unduly labored. In fact, the infant is rather calmly asleep. How will this family reconcile these two distinctly different experiences? They are *added*. The family, as an information processing group, combines both experiences to conclude that the underlying disease process is somehow cyclical; there are relatively bad periods and relatively good periods. The underlying process does not change: it is consistently cyclical. In other words, the couple comes to perceive a constant process whose stable and dependable feature is its cycling. (Their view may be reinforced when the doctor tells them that the baby's ups and downs are due to an infection—superimposed on her deformity—which can be controlled but not eradicated. The baby's good periods reflect a temporary abatement of infection; her bad periods, a recurrence.) The true properties of the underlying process have been approached by adding experience. It is this underlying or hidden property of the crisis experience which is carried forward by isolating abstraction and remains in the end-state paradigm: the adding of experience to approach an underlying and stable reality.

On the other end of this dimension are families who encourage the assumption that the underlying reality changes. Experience cannot be added in a systematic or reliable way. There are no canonical methods for tracing steps from experience to underlying reality. Attention to the details of experience has a very different function for these families: vigilant attention is paid to experience because experience is a sign of movement. Consider, again, the Weaver family, who regarded their ill infant as a link with—indeed, as the embodiment of—the spirit of the dead grandmother. They came to think that the baby's impending death represented the emergence of this ancestral force as it was linked to the family. Thus, each shift in the baby's status was seen as a sign of the approach or recession of the impending force, a force which moved of its own volition. Experience cannot be systematically added and distilled. Indeed each experience must be separated from all the rest so that its unique signal or symbolic function can be maximized. Thus, if a baby worsens in the morning and gets better in the afternoon, these two experiences are not added to approach a reality undergirding both. Each experience is its own unique signal: in the morning, the baby's worsening signals the approach of death, which for some revelation families may signify some kind of ancestral force. In the evening, the baby's improvement indicates the force's (thoroughly unpredictable) recession. No conclusion can be drawn from these experiences; the force can approach and end the baby's life, or it can recede forever. The hidden property of the crisis experience that is carried forward by social abstraction is: each experience is its own unique signal of the status of a moving, underlying force; two separate experiences are related by a concept that an underlying and moving force has changed position.

We can recognize some very general principles of good form at work in each of these abstractions. In the first, the principle of figure and ground[7] is operating to reinforce the selection of certain attributes of the crisis construct: structure *behind* an array of stimuli which seems—at first glance—like pure chaos. In the second, it is the *phi* phenomenon: the experience of movement that serves to connect two or more distinct stimulus events. In other words, we are proposing that two principles of good form help reduce the complexity of the crisis into a refined and abstracted set of conventions. Families on the stable end of the coherence dimension transform the experience of crisis into a sense of discovery, a sense of contact with a solid reality guided in good measure by a fundamental principle of abstracting a figure from ground. In contrast, the phi phenomenon constitutes a simplifying process in the revelation families. The field of experience, for them, becomes organized by a sense of movement of unseen forces; these movements explain or order a field in which experience is felt first in one location and then in the next.

These two contrasting family positions—stability and intrinsic movement—can influence the form of the family's situation-specific, ordinary constructs. The assumption of an underlying and stable structure encourages the family to collect and add experience in order to yield a rich, complex, and conditional conception of its perceptual world. Thus, those families positioned on the stability end of the paradigm dimension will also be located on the complex end of the configuration dimension of the ordinary construct. Likewise, a family that believes experience cannot be added will not systematically collect, compare, and record experience; they will not distill, reconcile, and organize these conceptions to formulate a complex model. They will be left with coarse and highly categorical conceptions of their perceptual world and hence be positioned on the simple end of the configuration dimension. The relationships between crisis construct, paradigm, and ordinary construct are shown in Figure 5.1.

DIMENSION 2, INTEGRATION: UNIVERSAL VERSUS PARTICULAR

Are underlying processes in the environment impersonal? Families on one end of this dimension encourage the assumption that, whether the underlying structure is stable or whether it

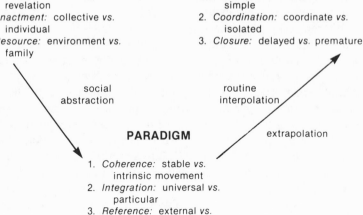

CRISIS CONSTRUCT

1. *Template:* Recognition vs. revelation
2. *Enactment:* collective vs. individual
3. *Resource:* environment vs. family

ORDINARY CONSTRUCT

1. *Configuration:* complex vs. simple
2. *Coordination:* coordinate vs. isolated
3. *Closure:* delayed vs. premature

social abstraction

routine interpolation

PARADIGM

extrapolation

1. *Coherence:* stable vs. intrinsic movement
2. *Integration:* universal vs. particular
3. *Reference:* external vs. internal

Figure 5.1. *A summary of the dimensions describing the crisis construct, the paradigm, and the ordinary construct*

changes of its own volition, all members have equal access to the underlying process. The perceptual world, whatever the nature of its underlying forces, is unitary. Families on the other end of this dimension see the world as divided into pieces—one piece for each member of the family.

We have seen the origins of these two perspectives in certain critical features of the crisis construct, particularly in the enactment of reorganization. Recall, for example, our recognizing family, the Robertses. The husband was dealing with phases of the crisis that involved his family and his occupation; his wife was dealing with her family and her own psychophysiologic response to the crisis, amenorrhea. Although subtle and complex, each individual model would never be reconciled in a family on the individual pole of the enactment dimension. This kind of family experiences the complex world of the husband as inaccessible to the wife and vice versa. The individuality on the enactment pole was seen for revelation families as well. Each member can become absorbed in his own interpretation of the symbolic significance of the crisis.

To clarify the fundamental assumption of accessibility, let us follow the process of isolating abstraction, particularly as it is governed by the principle of good form. Let us return to our recognizing family, the Robertses. Once they have established a basic template of reorganization, they have two major options: the enactment of reorganization on either a collective or an individual basis. In order to consider the consequences of this choice, let us focus on just one detail, the wife's amenorrhea. If the family takes an individualistic approach to enactment of organization, the husband is bound to ask himself, somewhat rhetorically, a question like this: "How could I possibly understand or deal with such a feminine issue as menstruation?" Judith Kestenberg (1968) contributed a very valuable article to the psychoanalytic literature on precisely this kind of question. Men, she says, have a particular difficulty in grasping the experiential and emotional import of women's sexual functions. This is not because women's sexual functions are so different from men's. Rather, it is because men are so insensitive to comparable bodily experiences of a sexual nature in themselves (for example, the internal sensations in the prostate and seminal vesicles that precede and follow ejaculation). The husband in our example *could* gain access to the full range of his wife's experiences, including her most personal body sensations. He could achieve this by finding some experience of his own which, slightly modified, could give him a picture of how things looked to his wife. He might become aware of a particular anesthesia or lack of pleasure that he himself is now experiencing during ejaculation. This very general term "empathy" is sometimes used to describe this form of seeing things from an other's point of view. However, recent research has shown that this process arises from a more specific and elementary process. Krauss and Glucksburg (1969), for example, studied the process of referential communication in young children. Many young children, when presented with a complex visual array, were able to imagine how such a display would appear to someone looking at it from a very different perspective.[8] The social capacity of taking the role of the other, a significant component of symbolic interactionist theories, may very well arise from a more elementary perceptual capacity to change perspective.

As a family responds to crisis, a genuinely collective position does not require that each individual learn and understand everything that other members of his family are feeling and thinking. What is critical for each individual is that he identify at least a single aspect of another's experience; this single aspect will serve as evidence that *if one wanted to* one could enter the other's experiential world. Once this experience of potential accessibility is achieved true specialization can go forward. Each individual can truly respect the others in his family because he and they are convinced that the others could be experiencing what he is experiencing.

The concept of good form further clarifies this line of abstraction. Each individual's emerging concept of the crisis situation may be represented by the aggregated dots on the top of Figure 5.2. Let us say we have a family of four. Let us take the perspective of one of the members of the family, say father. His image of the crisis consists of experiences and ideas he can clearly identify as his own and those of the other three which he has heard about or inferred. Let us say each of these four are somewhat different. The upper figure in the diagram represents this situation by showing four clusters of dots, each with a slightly different configuration. If father is in a family with a collective approach to the crisis, he will identify at least one element in the experience of others that corresponds to his own. (This assures him of potential access to the entire experiential world of the others.) We can represent this situation, as in the lower right of the diagram, by blackening one circle in each group at an intensity equal for all four. Immediately, by the

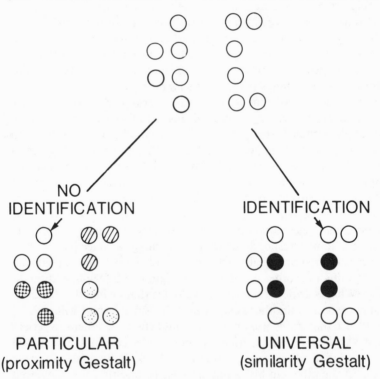

Figure 5.2. *Schematic illustration of the integration dimension of the family paradigm*

good form principle of similarity (see Kohler, 1947), a square emerges. Its most critical function is to unite the separate groups so that the entire array of dots is then perceived as a single, integrated array with four subsections. The visual diagram is meant to represent the emerging or abstracted experience of the collective family. That is, individual experience of the crisis is tied together as an integrated whole. It is this hidden potential of the crisis construct that is carried forward by social abstraction. The attraction of this aspect of the crisis construct is determined by the good form principle of similarity. If father (and presumably others in the family) cannot identify with any of the others' experiences, no blackening of any of the dots is possible. By the good form principle of proximity, the array will appear as four separate groups.

We can summarize this line of abstraction as follows. The collective approach to crisis resolution requires that individual members be able to identify with at least some of the experience of other members to assure themselves of the accessibility of the experiential world of others. This identification may employ a very elementary perceptual process of changing perspective. If identification can be accomplished, then the good form principle of similarity will enhance each member's conception that the experience of all members is universal, integrated, and connectable. If identification is not achieved, then the principle of grouping enhances each member's sense that his own world is separate from the others and that a comparable isolation exists for all members of the family. It is important to emphasize that the segregated family is *united* by its shared conception of the world as particularistic and segregated.

DIMENSION 3, REFERENCE: EXTERNAL VERSUS INTERNAL

What is the origin of sensory stimuli? On an implicit and elementary level, far below the level of conscious awareness, every family—we hypothesize—provides an answer to this fundamental question. If sensory stimuli are to be ordered into a coherent perceptual world, and if that world is to be further organized and understood, the family must provide an answer to this question. As Brunswick (1955) clarified in his famous "lens model," the grasp of the perceptual world may be considered as beginning with two major steps. The distal stimulus is the actual physical source of stimulation—for example, the light emanating from a burning candle. The proximal stimulus is the actual perturbation that is caused by the distal stimulus at the receptor site—for example, the retinal image of the burning candle. We can argue—although with technical imprecision—that individuals can, under special circumstances, become directly aware of proximal stimulation. Experientially, this is an awareness of the most unadorned perceptual data to which we have access. It is self-evident that what an individual "knows" is only the nature of proximal stimulation. The actual status of the distal object can only be inferred. These elementary inferences, as they occur on a moment-by-moment basis on a subliminal level, do not directly concern us here, although they may be apposite to family processes in a number of ways. What does concern us is a more general assumption about this relationship; here we distinguish two radically different perspectives.

The empiricist family encourages the assumption that the distal stimulus is located in a real world, external to the family. Thus, a family on the stable end of the coherence dimension, and on the empiricist end of the exteriority dimension, will feel it is adding experience together in order to approach a reality residing in an external world. In an extreme case, a family of this kind will not experience itself as a family but, instead, feel itself an integral part of a greater natural order of which it is a component indistinguishable from other components.

Consider one possible style of reorganization available to the Roberts family, our example of a family reorganizing through recognition. They might have engaged almost exclusively in learning about their child's illness, in fully appraising the strength and support available from the nursing staff, in studying—in detail—how other families reacted (where such study was not a guide for their own action), in exploring fully the resources of the community for assisting them through their prolonged crisis, and in seeking expert genetic and medical counseling about the advisability of having another child. The style of response to crisis inherent in these examples starts the family on a course whose end point will be an external or empiricist position. The family's "basic stance" or fundamental orientation remains turned toward the outside; the family believes that its success will continue to derive from careful reconnaissance and interpretation of the world outside its boundaries. The family's fundamental conceptions or reality are organized around a vivid conception of an outside world with endless mountains and crevasses to explore and understand.

Revelation families can also, through social abstraction, assume an empiricist position. (Revelation families, as we have already proposed, come to rest on the "intrinsic movement" pole of the coherence dimension.) For the Weaver family, whose template of reorganization was built around a sense of connection to the dead grandmother, an empiricist position is unlikely, since its reorganization is shaped around attachments to its own family past. However, a revelation family may develop a strong and symbolically rich tie to a figure entirely outside the family. In a medical crisis of the kind we have been discussing in our examples, such a person is often the doctor or, less often, some other member of the medical staff. Enormous powers—indeed omniscience—may be seen in the healer.[9] A few families in the midst of a medical crisis may turn to faith healers or a fundamentalist religion. As the crisis resolves, the family feels connected to a strong, and perhaps benevolent, force outside its boundaries. As is characteristic of the intrinsic movement position, the family believes the force has autonomy and free will—it moves on its own outside the control of the family.

In marked contrast to empiricist families, solipsistic families encourage the assumption that the distal stimulus resides in the family itself. The outside world does not have an independent existence; it is not perceived as having a capacity to inform or shape the family independently. "The world is what we make it." This is not to say that the world is ignored or that solipsistic families are invariably socially withdrawn. Rather, lying at the core of their understanding of the perceptual world is an assumption that every precept and concept is a distinct product of the family's own hypothesis, its own sensory process, and its own synthesis.

A more complex concept of good form helps illumine the difference between empiricist and solipsistic families. As Gestalt psychology matured, it recognized the need to account for more than order and coherence in the perceptual world; it had to account for the experience of the preceiver of himself as an entity in the perceptual world. The perceiver himself could be regarded, by Gestalt theory, as an object, and his form and boundaries were subject to the same principles that ordered the world of object outside the perceiver.[10] But the Gestalt psychologists recognized that the perceiver, as perceptual object, had a more fundamental property than did other objects. The perceiver served as a framework so that events in the perceptual world were experienced as occurring *in relation to* the perceiver. The simplest illustration of this phenomenon concerns the perception of movement. In many cases, movement occurring in the perceptual world is experienced as a property of the world itself; the perceiver experiences himself as stationary and everything else as moving past him or about him. At other times, the perceiver experiences himself as moving through a space; the outside world is then the framework and he himself is an object moving through coordinates externally established. Gestalt psychologists were fond of illustrating this perceptual choice with an example such as riding in a train. The perceiver can "choose" to look out the window and see the scenery speeding by backwards, or he can experience himself as hurtling through space *forwards*. Another example of the special role of the perceiver concerns the simple apprehension of three-dimensional space. In many instances the perceiver regards three-dimensional space as divided into four major quadrants: above, below, front, and back. Usually the perceiver himself lies at the very center of those four quadrants. Indeed, in a three-dimensional representation of space, the perceiver lies at the zero point of the three axes defining that space. The perceiver is thus simultaneously in all four major quadrants of space. At other times, however, the perceiver experiences himself at the periphery, as in only one or two of the possible four quadrants whose zero point is defined by something or someone else.

The fundamental distinction between solipsistic and empiricist families is that the former regard themselves as the framework for all movement in the perceptual world and as the center of all coordinates of the experienced space in which they live; the empiricist families, by contrast, regard themselves as the objects moving in a perceptual world whose coordinates are defined by others. The distinction is presented schematically in Figure 5.3.

We can make clearer the application of these concepts to families recovering from crisis by considering some possible lines of reorganization. Recall, again, the Roberts family. A major experience in their recovery from crisis was a series of social interpolations leading to a conviction of their own strength. More specifically, they had a sense of confidence in their own bodies: a feeling of being able to recognize subtle changes in their own and each other's bodies, of being able to affect one another and seek physical solace from one another. We have argued that this growing conviction was a crucial nidus for reorganization of the family from a point of severe crisis. It provided them with a sense of material solidity which, we are now arguing, will serve as a long-term experiential anchor point as they rebuild their relationships with their experienced world. This sense of their own solidity will yield an enduring sense that, as a group, they lie at the center of their own social world and that movement and action in the social world can be understood in reference to themselves as an experiential core. Even within this line of reorganization there are subtle and important differences. The potential for the family to become narcissistic is apparent. In that event, the family becomes more than the fundamental framework of its experienced world; it may become its own principal preoccupation. Extreme forms of this self-preoccupation are often signs of family disorganization — recall the explicit family. The Roberts family could have followed a

THE INTERNAL
PERSPECTIVE

THE EXTERNAL
PERSPECTIVE

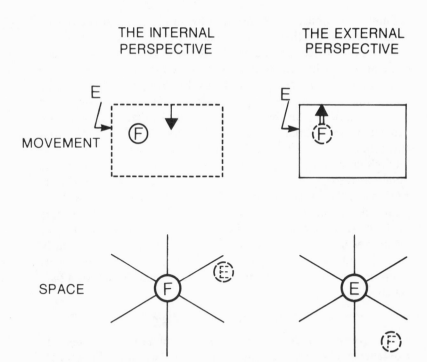

Figure 5.3. *Schematic illustration of the good form principles underlying the internal and external perspectives. Families with an internal perspective regard themselves as the reference point for all movement and for the spatial coordinates of their perceptual world. External families regard the critical junctures in the outside world as the reference point for their own movement and location in space. E = environment; F = family.*

different line of reorganization; they might have focused on grasping the realities of medical care, external resources, and biological facts. In this line of reorganization, they would have invested themselves in clarifying the coordinates of the external world and have struggled to find their place in it.

It would be a mistake, however, to think of the different lines of reorganization as simply a matter of what facts and experiences accumulated during recovery. It is much more the growing and symbolically toned integration of facts and self-experience that matters. Consider, for example, the process of exploring, with competent medical authorities, the likelihood that the congenital defect will repeat itself. Most couples want to know if the defect can happen again, but there is an important difference in how the question can be pursued. A family following the environment-as-resource line of reorganization will experience the *results* of its search as defining its options. if they are told by authorities that the risk of giving birth to another defective child is high, they will think of their options for conceiving another child as being blocked by circumstances outside themselves. A possible maladaptive error here is to take too much on faith, to be overawed by a single authoritative source. A family following the family-as-resource line of reorganization, on the other hand, thinks that its options are defined by the search for information itself. Information from authorities is a tool for reaching the family's own objectives – the family's growth, in this case. The possible maladaptive error in the family-as-resource approach is a derogation of authoritative information and the couple's denial of their inability to conceive without great risk. In subtle but important ways, the same information is used differently by the two kinds of families. Families who see themselves as resources feel that their objectives are continuously alive although the means to achieve them must be different; environment-as-resource families feel the permanent loss of a particular option.

Abstraction and Paradigm

The processes of social abstraction are summarized in Table 5.1. The table can be read and conceptualized in two ways. Coherence, integration, and reference can be seen as lines of reorganization. All families who are recovering from disorganization engage in processes through time which may be regarded as pursuing stability or responding to intrinsic movement; as employing universal or particularistic approaches; and as developing external expiricist or internal solipsistic positions. A line of reorganization, then, is a particular thread or sequence in the process of reorganization. We are proposing that, in all families, reorganization follows these three basic lines (more or less simultaneously). Within each line, some families adopt a style more characteristic of one pole or extreme, whereas other families adopt an opposite style.

The table can also be read as a summary of the dimensions by which paradigms themselves may be distinguished. Paradigms, as we have said, are end-state social abstractions. They are what remains after social abstraction is completed. Social abstraction runs a natural course. In some families it may go on over a period of years; in others it may be a matter of a few months (very rarely, we would guess, is it less than that). The fundamental group motive for continuing the process is a restoration of the family to the level of implicit functioning. Family disorganization brought uncertainty, projection of intense feelings (with the consequent impoverishment of self), and pervasive exhaustion. Reorganization

TABLE 5.1 THE LINES OF REORGANIZATION AND THE DIMENSIONS OF PARADIGM

Lines of reorganization	Poles	Critical features	Corresponding principles of good form
Coherence	Stable	Belief in an underlying structure or order in the experienced world which remains fixed before, during, and after discovery; experience can be additive.	Figure and ground
	Mobile	Underlying reality or force changes of its own volition; thus, experiences are separated to serve as signals for detecting motion.	Phi phenomenon
Integration	Universal	Belief that each member's experience is shaped by universal phenomena and thus is accessible through empathy.	Similarity
	Particular	Belief that the world has a different configuration for each member, and thus individual experience is inaccessible to others.	Proximity
Reference	External	The family's experience of its world is anchored by coordinates whose origins lie outside themselves.	The environment as perceptual frame
	Internal	The family's experience of its own solidity and/or centrality is the central orienting point in its experiential world.	The perceiver as perceptual frame

through a process of social abstraction brings surcease. The paradigm emerges as a family accomplishment shaped by exposure to hidden qualities of its members or fresh and shaping influences of the external world. Despite outside influences, it stands as an accomplishment of the family. This is so whether the paradigm has undergone a fundamental shift (as we have traced in the last two chapters) or has been reaffirmed (the paradigm in place before the crisis could be drawn on as the fundamental resource for recovery). Thus, because it is seen as an accomplishment and has restored the family to an implicit level of functioning, the family keeps it firmly in place through the ordinary activities of its daily life. The next chapter sketches out some of these mechanisms of conservation.

6 | The Conservation of the Family Paradigm

Our account of the transformation of the family's experience of crisis into a paradigm has focused on short-term, dynamic changes in family life. Family interaction patterns, the influence of outside forces, hidden aspects of members' personalities are melded, in the family group, into an emerging and refined structure. This structure serves both as a repository of the family experience of crisis and as a guide for the everyday behavior which is now becoming both more routine and more meaningful. In order to understand how the family paradigm remains the central governor of routine family process, we must account for its persistence over time. At a point when crisis and abstraction yield a new paradigm, what stabilizing forces account for its conservation?

The Temporal Patterning of Crisis and Change

Although serious research is now under way on this topic, we do not yet know with any certainty about the temporal patterning of crisis and change in family life. The new information will be central to our evolving model. At this point two possibilities can be considered. If crisis and change occur frequently, say several times a year, then the burdens placed on mechanisms of conservation are not great. In this instance, conservation mechanisms would need only be adequate to sustain a paradigm for several months or at most a year. On the one hand, if paradigms are retained over many years, the mechanisms conserving them would have to be highly structured, stable, and very sturdy indeed. We suspect that there is a great deal of variability between families in the stability of the paradigm. Most interesting for our theory construction are the cases in which paradigms persist for many years and may be perpetuated from generation to generation.

Our best examples of the long persistence of family paradigms come from examining historical reconstructions of family life. These reconstructions are of two kinds. The first set of studies uses detailed interviews of families to reconstruct their past. These reconstructions often go back one or two full generations. The second approach uses historical records—public documents, diaries, correspondence, and the like—to reconstruct several generations in the life of certain prominent families: for example, the Blackwells and Adamses in this country and the Rothschilds and Bleichröders in Europe.[1] These studies are in striking agreement on the remarkable persistence of certain fundamental themes and orientations in family life. For example, the Rothschild family retained over many generations a sense of its own special status as a distinguished, powerful, and regal family, which set it apart from but also made it the special representative of European Jewry. Strict rules for inheritance, childrearing, and marriage (Rothschilds were encouraged to marry only other Rothschilds) buttressed the family's conception of itself and of its position in the world over a period of nearly two hundred years. To be sure, this family is one of the most unusual in the annals of family studies. Yet it serves to exemplify the upper limits of continuity in family life.

In this chapter we take a middle road. We attempt to delineate mechanisms that could—in rare families like the Rothschilds—account for stability over may generations. However, the concepts that we develop are also suited to the more usual case: stability which can be observed for many years within a single generation of a family but which does not always continue for succeeding generations. Although solid empirical evidence is lacking, we assume that fundamental shifts in paradigm do not occur frequently in family life; the theoretical sketch to follow does not attend to mechanisms that maintain paradigms only in the short run.

The Medium of Conservation

Ceremonials and pattern regulators. At the core of our proposal is this simple idea: family interaction patterns themselves are the repository of the family paradigm. By "family interaction patterns" we mean something more than what one member says to another; we refer to nonlexical aspects of speech and nonverbal behavior as well. Interaction patterns, then, are patterned congeries of these three components—lexical speech, nonlexical speech, and nonverbal behavior—as they are organized into regular and recurring patterns. We shall propose that as these patterns are used in the various settings in which the family gathers, they are delicately and subtly organized to serve a memorial function. In the next section we present a very preliminary sketch of how this may occur. We will anticipate our proposal here briefly. In a very simple sketch (Figure 6.1), we picture family behavior as a sphere. At the center are episodic behaviors which are charged with feeling and symbolic meaning. They usually involve the participation of all members of the family and function to express—but sometimes to conceal—certain aspects of the family's history as well as conceptions of itself and its current social world. It is these core behaviors that bear a primary function in maintaining central threads of family life over long periods of time; they are the primary repository of the family paradigm. In contrast, at the periphery of the sphere are routinized behaviors, much more frequently engaged in by families. They can be delegated in the sense that only one or two members are necessary for their conduct. They are not emotionally charged and may not even be noticed by family members, although—as we shall point out—they play a crucial role in translating or transforming the family's paradigm into the immediate minute-by-minute experience of family membership for each member of the family.

The core behaviors—we will call them the *ceremonials of family*

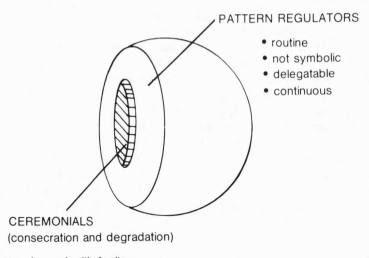

PATTERN REGULATORS

- routine
- not symbolic
- delegatable
- continuous

CEREMONIALS
(consecration and degradation)

- charged with feeling
- symbolic
- requires all members to participate
- episodic

Figure 6.1 *Schematic summary of major characteristics of ceremonials and pattern regulators*

life—include formalized and repetitive patterns that enhance the family's image of itself and express it clearly to its members and nonmembers alike. We will refer to these as *consecration ceremonies*. Included here are family rituals which were first comprehensively described by Bossard and Boll (1950) and studied systematically by Wolin and Bennett (Wolin et al., 1979, 1980). Also among the ceremonials—we will call them *degradation ceremonies*—are those whose primary function is to conceal aspects of family life which members find terrifying. We shall focus on one of these degradation ceremonies—scapegoating.

The peripheral behavior in our sphere—which, after Steinglass (in press), we will call *pattern regulators*—includes the kinds of everyday, highly routinized sequences catalogued by Kantor and Lehr (1975) and studied systematically, though from a different perspective, by Steinglass. These include the variety of behaviors which families use to regulate space and distance among themselves and between the family group and the outside world. Despite the central importance of pattern regulators in family life, the family is ordinarily unaware of them. Indeed, their subliminal quality may—as we will describe—play a crucial part in their central function for the family; it permits the pattern regulators to shape each member's experience of family membership without his or her awareness. Although there is little evidence to guide us here, we are proposing that the central ceremonials of family life both shape and stabilize the minute and subliminal pattern regulators. Reciprocal relationships between the two also occur.

The memorial function of family behavior. How can we consider interaction behavior itself as a repository for something like a family paradigm? As we have defined it, a paradigm is a deep-seated and persistent attitude or a set of assumptions about the family's social and physical world. Behavior is ordinarily thought to have an expressive and/or instrumental function rather than a *memorial* function. The repository of family paradigms might ordinarily be thought of as the memory of individual members—that is, what each member retains in memory of the family's history, myths, heroes, values, secrets, and assumptions as these are melded together into a coherent paradigm. We might more easily regard interaction patterns in families—ceremonials or pattern regulators—as expressing rather than conserving the nature of the family's paradigm or, in some sense, carrying out some plan which was shaped or toned by the family paradigm. However, we are asserting something quite different. The behavior itself is the locus, the medium, the storage place of the paradigm as well as a means of expressing it and carrying out the plans it shapes. To clarify this proposition we will want to consider properties of interaction patterns which make them well-suited for the memorial role we are proposing and then consider limitations of individual memory which make it suited, at best, for a subordinate role in the conservation of the paradigm.

In considering the suitability of interaction patterns, we want to focus on three of their properties. First, interaction behavior functions to shape and modulate *information*. Examples of this were presented in Chapters 1 and 2. Recall, for example, how the family's problem-solving behaviors modulated and shaped the information flowing into the family from the laboratory environment. The members of some families were effective in processing information from outside the family and paid close attention to each other's problem-solving efforts. We spoke of this pattern of behavior as amplifying the environment for each family member. In contrast, the members of other families paid close attention to each other's problem-solving behavior but that behavior did not effectively explore or organize the environment. We suggest that this between-member responsiveness, in the absense of strong and structured inflow of information, isolated the family from the environment; indeed, the family was more aware of itself than of the outside world. In this case, family interaction patterns could be said to amplify, for each member, the experience of membership in his own family. These problem-solving behaviors and interaction patterns were unusual for the family; they were elicited in a highly artificial laboratory setting. In this chapter, we will try to show how more ordinary interaction patterns—parts of the family's regular routines—have the same impact on shaping and modulating information.

A second important feature of interaction patterns, central to their memorial role, is their capacity to store information over time. We have encountered an almost trivial example of this function of interaction in the laboratory work reported in Chapter 2. In that chapter, we described closure process in family problem solving. Two types of behavior were important here. First, families who repeated problem-solving responses from trial to trial—despite new evidence to deal with—were clearly holding on to ideas from the past (although the "past" here was separated from the present by only a few minutes). The repetition of the previous problem-solving response was neither a simple nor a passive indicator that the family held to its earlier idea; the repetition, we have argued, reinforced or conserved that earlier view. A related behavior served the same conservative function. Recall that in Chapter 2, our families of normals went through the earlier trials of the task more rapidly, reserving their energies for later tasks when there was more evidence. The families of schizophrenics did the reverse; they had a "peak" of time investment in the early trials. This distribution of time and energy in the course of processing stimuli from the outside had an impact on closure. Families of schizophrenics came to an early decision and stuck with it; all performance in later trials reinforced, perpetuated or *memorialized* the "past"—the earlier trials. In our laboratory setting, we can say that both the identical repetition of previous problem-solving patterns and the distribution of time primarily into the earlier trials served to conserve the family's past idea—to keep it relatively invulnerable to new information or experience. We will attempt to show in this chapter that more ordinary behaviors in the family's repertoire accomplish the same ends.

The third property of interaction patterns embraces and enlarges the first two; it is the capacity to objectify the family's beliefs about itself. We encountered this concept before, in a highly suggestive way, in our four-brother cosmology (see Chapter 3). Adapting the ideas of Berger and Luckmann (1966), we see interaction behavior in the family as transforming information about the family into information about the objective world. In other words, interaction patterns in family life enable all members to experience their own values and assumptions as if they were unquestionable components of outer reality. This transformation enables the family paradigm to serve as guide or framework for action-in-the-real-world by all members, which further reinforces their conviction in the objectivity of their assumptions. As we will point out in more detail, the three functions of interaction behavior—to modulate and retain information as well as to objectify that information as a basis for action in the external world—make it an ideal candidate for a role as the major repository of the family paradigm.

The memory of individual members is a less satisfactory candidate, although it surely plays a subordinate role. The fundamental drawback of individual memory is that it lacks the compelling and coordinating force of interaction behavior itself. In clarifying this relative weakness we focus, in particular, on the role of differences between members in the memory of critical crises, resolutions, secrets, and values of the family. We propose that these differences constitute a nucleus or initial cleft marking each individual's autonomy from his family. There are also individual differences between members, of course, in their engagement in ceremonials and pattern regulators. But these differences function not so much to initiate autonomy of the participating individual from a family position; they bespeak and conserve segregation and isolation in the family paradigm itself (see Figure 5.1). Nonetheless, despite its defects, memory has an important subordinate function in conservation. Its role is particularly evident in gaps in family continuity. For example, consider a newlywed couple who establishes family patterns which are similar to those of the wife's family, even though all members of her family have been dead for years. The wife has remembered not the paradigm nor any of its direct, experiential derivatives; rather, she has remembered critical interaction patterns—both ceremonials and pattern regulators. Only when these are reenacted within a new group—in this instance, a new marital dyad—does the experience of paradigm, particularly its transformation of the objective world, reemerge.

Interaction Behavior in the Conservation of the Family Paradigm

Consecration ceremonials. Consecration ceremonials—when they are fully organized, conspicuous, and highly stable over time—may be called family rituals.[2] The following brief case history illustrates some aspects of family ritual.

The O'Hara family consists of a father and mother in their late seventies and three grown sons who moved away from the parental home years ago. The O'Haras had a dramatic and, in some ways, distinguished past. The father's grandfather had made and lost a fortune drilling some of America's earliest oil wells in Pennsylvania. The father's father had been a hardy farmer and lawyer well known for a mixture of compassion and toughness. The father himself was a newspaper editor who had successfully run for Congress but had been defeated after one term. A fundamental theme in the O'Hara family was achieving preeminence through a special blend of physical toughness and willingness to take risks (even to risk all, as in drilling oil wells, raising crops, and running for election). When the three sons were boys, the family developed a ritual response to father's return home (often after prolonged absences required by his political activity). The boys would briefly arm-wrestle with father, and mother would sit and cheer them on. A crucial component of this brief but often repeated ritual was that the fight would look tough but that father would be careful to inflict no real pain or injury on his sons. Now, when the sons return home, the ritual is still repeated, but it is now the sons who are careful to inflict no pain on the aging father.

The arm-wrestling ritual seems to encompass and symbolize the family's sense of its hard and tough past as well as its conception of itself as careful and compassionate with the weak. At each repetition the ritual consecrates a fundamental conception of what the family feels distinguishes itself as a group. Mother, as audience, symbolically expresses the family's continuing need for and sense of its conspicuousness in the community. However, there is also a component of degradation in this brief ceremonial. Mother is relegated to the role of audience. Indeed, she is in a subordinate and demeaned position in the family. Her own family traditions are in fact a source of great anxiety, since in each generation there was a member who attempted or committed suicide, and the fear of suicide in the O'Hara family has been a terror they have tried to suppress. A slight hint of degradation is also evident in the sons' care not to injure their father, which conveys fleetingly, though painfully, the father's rapid decline in strength and faculties. From a more general perspective, we can recognize in this brief vignette the dual function of interaction behavior. First, this ritual contains information in a very compelling form: it forcefully reminds all participants of the recent and remote past in the life of the family, and it expresses certain fundamental themes from the family's past. By simultaneously evoking the family's hardy past and sense of strength through combat now, the ritual reinforces a particular conception of the world: riches and victories are available to the tough. This conception is undoubtedly a component of the family paradigm.

Degradation ceremonials. The degrading aspects of the O'Hara family ritual are subtle and subordinate. However, ceremonials built around degradation are probably an occasional feature in many families and are quite prominent in some. They differ, of course, from consecration rituals in their purpose and overall tenor. They tend to be joyless and tense, and are often sprinkled with sarcasm, arrogance, and contempt. A particularly conspicuous form of this ceremonial has been studied by family observers for at least two decades under the rubric of "scapegoating."

Eric Bermann (1973) provides a particularly instructive example based on prolonged, continuous observation of a troubled working-class New England family in its own home. The family consists of two parents and five children: Deedee, twelve; Sheila, ten; Ricky, nine; Roscoe, eight; and Pamela, four. Both parents grew up in working-class families. Critical in the mother's past was a requirement that she organize her own childhood around the care of a younger brother because of her mother's full-time job. Critical to father's history was the death of his own mother when he was two and his longing to leave a strict and authoritarian father, an aspiration that was blocked when both of his father's legs were severed in an accident. During his late adolescence, Mr. A. had developed rheumatic fever, and in recent years had developed a severe heart disease which threatened his life. At the time of Bermann's observations Mr. A. faced the prospect of surgery with a very uncertain outcome. Of the five children, Roscoe was selected almost from birth as a potential scapegoat. An important reason for this selection seemed to be that after three children, Mrs. A. had begun to hope for some liberation from her role as housewife. Roscoe, an unplanned child, had put an end to her hopes and reawakened her angry feelings at her brother, whose care had so limited her opportunities.

The scapegoating ceremonials did not begin in earnest until Mr. A.'s cardiac illness became manifest and family terror grew. Then a series of interaction patterns with Roscoe as villain began to emerge. For example, Ricky discovered that Roscoe had found a crab in a nearby creek. Before the entire family he accused Roscoe of putting sand in the bucket of water which housed the crab. Everyone accepted both the accuracy of Ricky's report and the truth that sand in a bucket could kill a crab. Mr. A. ordered Roscoe to return the crab and ridiculed him by saying he "was supposed to be a nature lover." Pamela then joined in the ridicule. Similar, but not identical, ceremonials were regularly performed; it was claimed that Roscoe would ruin his new shoes, that he would break a terrarium, that he taught the family dog dangerous habits, and so on. Each sequence had similar components. Roscoe became engaged in something which interested him; someone else—often Ricky—accused him of damaging it or threatening it; one parent listened to the accusation and then passed judgment, often forcing some humiliating surrender on Roscoe's part.

As Bermann pieced these ceremonials together he saw them as a way for the family to conceal their shared terror of what might lie in store for Mr. A. and for the whole family if his heart worsened or if surgery was not successful. Clearly these current fears were deeply intensified by the deprivation, injury, and death that were so central in the childhoods of both Mr. and Mrs. A. From our perspective the ceremonials seem to have reaffirmed the family's conception of the world as being full of murderous forces and victims; genuine control, understanding, or acceptance of these forces was probably experienced as impossible. Only collective counterattack by a united family was an adequate defense.

Juxtaposing the two very brief depictions of family ceremonials helps us contrast and then integrate our notions of the special feature and functions of each. First, these two vignettes illustrate the difference in formality between family ritual and scapegoating. The arm-wrestling ritual, like many others described by Bossard and Boll, is formal in the sense that it is repeated—in almost exact form—at almost every instance of the sons' arrival. Each participant has a sense of being engaged in a prescribed sequence and senses something amiss if it does not occur. Indeed, this quality of prescription is a fundamental aspect of the experience of consecration. Each member feels engaged in something larger than himself. Blended together is a shared subjective sense of the extensity of the family (the group clearly extends beyond the experienced boundaries of each member) and the extensity of time (the arm wrestling vividly condenses, for each son, his experience as a child of his father and of now becoming father to his father).

The scapegoating ritual lacks this degree of formality and prescription. Therefore, as a ceremony it cannot provide the experiences of intensity and extensity central to the consecration of the family. The scapegoating sequence is nonetheless a ceremony. The basic components of the sequence are invariant (Roscoe's engagement in something, an accusation, a hearing, a judgment, and a humiliation). The roles assigned to individual family members are reasonably fixed. Further, there is unquestionably a high emotion and intense symbolic meaning in these sequences. The family believes in the reality created within the degradation sequence itself. For example, no one questioned—indeed everyone seemed to believe quite firmly—that sand kills crabs. Considering the vast quantity of sand in creeks and bays, where crabs thrive, this family conviction is a truly remarkable example of socially constructed reality. Examining these two ceremonials together helps us see that the arm-wrestling ritual served to provide a positive sense of belonging to a family through the reinforcement of the family's view of itself and the opportunities and possibilities in the world around them. The sequence with the crab offered a much less exalted opportunity for the family: the opportunity for relief. A murder and victim could be temporarily identified, the murder dealt with, and the victim saved; for this instant the family could protect itself from the terror of father's illness, over which they had no control. A further contrast also is apparent: consecration ceremonies probably occur during relatively quiescent periods in family life. Increasing degradation may be one signal of increasing stress and may in fact presage the sequential unfolding of family disorganization.

PATTERN REGULATORS

At the periphery of our imaginary sphere are naturally occurring and highly patterned forms of behavior we are terming *pattern regulators*. These are the regularly recurring behaviors by which families carry out their daily routine. They are the ones that would be most readily observable by a perceptive visitor to the family's home. Indeed, it is these behaviors which Kantor and Lehr (1975) attempted to catalog after extensive in-home observation of nineteen families. Steinglass (1979) studied—with great care to make precise and objective measurements—a smaller subset of these behaviors. We draw heavily on the work of these two in laying out this portion of our theoretical sketch.

Pattern regulators may be thought of as behaviors which shape the family's experience of two fundamental resources it requires for conducting its day-to-day life. These resources are time and space.[3] From what we can now observe and from the observations of Kantor and Lehr and Steinglass, we propose that families are strikingly different in their management of these two resources and that these differences, shaped and maintained by the central ceremonials of family life, play their own crucial role in the conservation of the family paradigm.

Time. Kantor and Lehr delineated two major mechanisms by which families routinely organize their experience of time: orienting and clocking.[4] Of the two, orienting requires greater inference on the part of the observer. It refers to the reference points, in time, which the family regularly uses to conduct its daily affairs. The obvious examples are explanations people give to one another for taking a position, setting a limit, or making a plan. In past orienting, some aspects of historical time—usually something in the family's own past—is the fundamental reference point or organizing principle. Present orienting focuses on present circumstances as a justification or basis for action; future orientation appeals to some prediction or divination of the future. Although not specifically described by Kantor and Lehr, we suspect that time orientation is expressed in much more subtle patterns of family life than explicit time references in family discussion; for example, it might be expressed by household furnishings, contacts with kin, patterns of friendship, what is saved and what is thrown away of the daily influx of materials into the house. Time orientation may be particularly evident in the kind of economy constructed for the household; in situations where there is a choice, the balance among savings, income from investment, and credit may reflect a difference in orientation. A household economy based substantially on credit may be clearly present-oriented; savings may reflect a future orientation; income from investments may reflect a family living on the accumulated wealth of several generations and hence constitute a strong root in the past. (See our analysis of elite families in Philadelphia at the conclusion of Chapter 7.) Finally, career planning and development—insofar as this is a major component of family process—may reflect an underlying orientation to time. Consider the differences between a son who enters his father's law firm, a son who decided — on impulse — to study for the Law School Admissions Test, and the first-born son of working-class parents who organized the family's economy to provide funds to send him to college and law school.

Kantor and Lehr delineate a second set of mechanisms they call clocking. Although they distinguish several types of mechanisms in this area, all have to do with the spacing, sequence, and timing of events in the flow of family experience. Some families order events into a linear schedule with each event neatly following the next. Not only is the sequence of events clear, but the boundaries between events are kept clear so that there is no mistaking when one is actually participating in one event and when one has gone on to the next. Thus, a family has a distinct meal preparation time, an eating time, a clean-up time, a pre-bedtime, bedtime, and so on. Activities are carefully organized so that there is clarity about which is which. Another family attempting the same sequence might typically let the various activities run together and blur. The overall order is clear enough, but neither the members or outsiders are ever sure exactly which point in the sequence they are in. Likewise, families differ in the speed of events. Some have a sense of constant rush and flurry: everything is packed into as short a time as possible. In others, time is almost frozen. There is a pace of events deliberate in the extreme: problems are fully discussed; decisions are delayed and carefully considered; interruptions are kept to a minimum; schedules are kept light; sleep cycles may be long; meal times, as well as vacation and recreation periods, may be long. Steinglass has tapped this domain with one of his in-home measures: included among a broad range of assessments is an interesting observation of the frequency with which people move about the house. In a sample of thirty-one families — observed at numerous times over a six-month period — he recorded one family whose members shifted from room to room at a laconic average of eleven times per hour, whereas, on the opposite extreme, was a frenzied family who did so at a rate of fifty-four times an hour.

Space. Space is the other fundamental resource which pattern regulators transform into distinct experiences for each family. Kantor and Lehr call attention to two fundamental functions of these patterns. The first is to establish and then regulate a boundary which separates the family's own space from that of the outside world. A variety of routines in family life — from dinner-table conversations to talks with neighbors across the fence — permit the family to chart or jointly conceptualize the neighborhood in which it lives and the boundaries which are most appropriate to establish its own territory. Once these boundaries are established the family develops patterns of transactions across the boundaries: how family members should come and go and how nonmembers should enter and leave. Some families have strict principles requiring all members to "check in," that is, to enter the family for a period each day; other families have little concern for this. Some families are constantly open to neighbors and friends; others admit outsiders only by carefully prearranged appointment. Some families are vigilant about guarding their boundaries (Kantor and Lehr call this "patrolling"). In our studies of multiple family groups—which will be described in detail in Chapter 8—we have observed significant differences between families in their establishment of boundaries. Some families, for example, sit closely clumped together during meeting after meeting and form few firm bonds with others in the group; other families, in contrast, quickly spread out through the whole group and forge quick and strong relationships with outsiders.

A second function of the spatial pattern regulators is to regulate internal spatial relationships between family members. A simple but important pattern concerns the distances individuals keep from one another. To be sure, the architecture of the house plays some role here. Small houses and apartments and rooms force reduced distances between individuals. But even where architectural variables are held constant, families differ a great deal on this important dimension. Steinglass, for example, measured the average distance between any two members of a family when they were interacting in some way. At one extreme of his measure were families whose average distance was just over four feet between members who were interacting in some way; families on the other extreme averaged over nine feet of separation. The organization of spatial arrangements within the family, however, goes well beyond simple distances between interacting individuals. For example, families differ in how they use the space within their homes. In some families individuals are accorded their own private and inviolate space. Children have their own rooms; the parents' bedroom is rarely entered by anyone but the parents. There are special dens, closets, cupboards, and seating locations at the table. Other families are much less systematic in assigning priority use of specialized area. There is a much freer flow of all family traffic into all areas of the house. A special case is the family's practices in initiating and maintaining privacy. Some families live out rigid standards of privacy; bathrooms and bedrooms are locked, special possessions are concealed, and even clothes are worn to carefully cover up sensitive parts of the body. Again, other families are much more lax about these standards.

Finally, families also develop and enact certain conceptions of the space outside their home in which they conduct their daily lives. In this respect, a fundamental distinction can be derived from the work by Merton (1949). He distinguished "cosmopolitans" from "locals." Merton developed this distinction to apply to residents of a small town who exerted considerable power and influence. However, the distinction is equally apt for families. A cosmopolitan family, to continue our extrapolation of Merton's ideas, is oriented toward a broad range of activities and interests extending far beyond the confines of its immediate neighborhood. Friends, places of employment, and schools may be scattered over a very broad metropolitan or suburban area. Beyond that, occupational planning in the family may be centered on promotions or advancements which require the family to move a great distance at frequent intervals. Locals, on the other hand, are firmly rooted to a particular place. Their roots in a particular locale often go back one or more generations. Their business or professional practice is not only in or near their home, but the business depends on a strong, local network of friends and acquaintances. Within these broad divisions, families also differ in how their principal arena of action—local or cosmopolitan—is explored and traversed. Some families develop a detailed and comprehensive chart of their personal world through constant exploration, such as visits to public agencies, commercial establishments, scenic areas, and other people's homes. Their picture of their environment is detailed, sharp, and penetrating. Other families grasp little of their surroundings. They develop a few, carefully maintained pathways which then take them from home to work and to a very few other locations; there remain large uncharted areas within their domain of which they know nothing.

The role of pattern regulators in shaping the family's experience of time and space is summarized in Table 6.1.

Synchronization in time and space. With respect to pattern regulators there is another distinction between families which is of paramount importance: the level of synchronization of their daily routines. In their transformations of both time and space, members in some families are careful to synchronize the patterned routines of their daily lives. Collective tasks and routines are executed with a good deal of effortless collaboration, unruffled assignments of roles, reasonably clear planning and evaluation of results, and outcomes in which all members share. Likewise, in highly synchronized families, delegation of tasks which do not require cooperation is done effortlessly. Individuals represent the family commonwealth in an effective although highly routinized way. Even when in-

TABLE 6.1   THE ROLE OF PATTERN REGULATORS IN SHAPING THE EXPERIENCE OF TIME
AND SPACE

Attribute	Mechanism	Description
Time	Orientation	Time references in speech; household economy (e.g. savings vs. credit; career planning).
	Clocking	The rapidity of experienced events; the degree of distinctness of these events.
Space	Boundary maintenance	Establishing separation from the outside world; regulating entrances and exits across the boundary.
	Regulation of internal space	Distance between members, privacy, etc.
	Charting	The family's evolving conception of the physical and emotional arrangements in its world. Family's arrangement of internal space clearly reflects how it as a group conceptualizes or understands the world outside the family.

dividuals pursue their own interests, apart from any agenda or interest of the family as a group, their activities are reasonably coordinated with others. In contrast to synchronized families are those who constantly fail to collaborate and delegate. In some families there is constant conflict. Routines performed by individuals are often competing for time or space with those performed by others. Collective activities cannot be effectively planned because there is disagreement about plans, competition for favored roles, dissension about standards for evaluating the outcome of collective action, and wide difference in the commitment to final decisions. Other families fail to be synchronized through extraordinary isolation of members from one another. For example, failures in delegation arise less from open conflict than from an absence of any plan or the failure to elaborate any specific role or shared criteria for evaluating action. Individual plans are carried out with only the most marginal reference to the group as a whole; indeed, each individual lives in his separate space and time.

CEREMONIALS AND TIME, SPACE, AND SYNCHRONY

The relative simplicity of pattern regulators in family life helps us to recognize how they function to organize the family's experience of space and time and how they serve to synchronize the family's behavior. However, ceremonials may also be thought of as organizing the family's experience of time, space, and synchrony. As we will detail below, their contribution to this organization is somewhat different than pattern regulators'. Because of the complexity and symbolic richness, ceremonials serve many functions simultaneously; sometimes these functions are antithetical to one another. Thus, where pattern regulators can be examined for their primary or singular function—with respect to time, space, and synchrony—ceremonials must be broken apart, analytically, to discover each of their component functions.

Time. The relationship of ceremonials to time is illustrated in the contrasting ceremonials we have already considered, the arm-wrestling ritual and the scapegoating degradation. The arm-wrestling ritual engenders an experience of time fused. Through each repetition the family reexperiences a crucial aspect of its past as if that past were present: the family's hardiness and success through competition of the remote past, and the family's more recent past, when the adult sons were children. Indeed, the fusion of past and present crystallizes around the experience of fathers: the sons, one now a father, experience themselves as fathers of their father through a ritual whose special meaning comes from memories of themselves as small sons of their father. The experience of fusion in time, felt during the few and fleeting instances of this ritual, may be thought of as a de-differentiation of past and present that enables the past to live in the present, to shape and inform it. The arm-wrestling ritual thus provides the family with a sense of continuity with its own past. This experience of the past is less explicit but also less mundane than the corresponding pattern regulator "past orienting" described by Kantor and Lehr.

The degradation ceremonials aimed at Roscoe provide, it would seem, quite a different experience of time. To be sure, the degradation ceremonials contain elements from the past: Mrs. A.'s relationship with her younger brother, the trauma of the amputation of Mr. A.'s father's legs, and—first and foremost—the terror surrounding Mr. A.'s cardic illness. These elements of the past are symbolically incorporated into the ceremonials in ways quite different from how past events are incorporated into the arm-wrestling ritual. No aspect of the A. family's past is conscious or explicitly remembered during the actual conduct of the ceremonial; the family's attention is not fixed on themselves as a group with extensity beyond each individual and a duration beyond the present instant. Indeed, the ceremonial serves to fix the family's attention on Roscoe; the parts that other family members, play in the ritual are not experienced so clearly. To be sure, Ricky plays a prominent role as accuser, the family as silent jury, Mr. A. as judge, Pamela as chorus. These crucial roles are not themselves the object of vivid experience; existentially they are in the background (indeed, it is often the job of a family therapist to make a family aware of how they develop and coordinate roles in ceremonials of this kind). In this degradation ceremonial the family as an experienced group pales beside the vivid and unyielding experience of Roscoe as soiler, spoiler, ruiner, and murderer. Thus, the degradation ceremonial—though representing the past symbolically—excludes the past experientially; moreover, by preventing the family from sustaining a vivid experience of itself as a group it blocks the family's experience of its own future as a group. The degradation ceremonial, in effect, freezes the family into a point in time.[5]

We are proposing, as an extension of this contrast, that the balance of consecration and degradation in the central ceremonials of a family's life determines the extent to which time is fused or frozen. Where consecration predominates, the past is vividly relived in the present and gives the present shape and meaning. Where degradation predominates, the present is frozen and the past actively excluded. The coordinate functions of consecration and degradation can be seen in those fundamental ceremonials which contain elements of both. Indeed, the arm-wrestling ritual is a good example of this mixture. Recall that mother serves as an appreciative but passive audience. The role of audience is not by itself a degraded role. However, the arm-wrestling ritual in the O'Hara family is the most affectively charged, meaningful, and poignant component of the way in which parents and children greet one another after a long absence. Mother's passive role in such a ritual effectively excludes her from an active role in this greeting. In this sense we can understand her role as a degraded one, though the degradation is mild and subtle in comparison to Roscoe's. The degradation here is consistent with, and probably actively serves, the family's wish to exclude anxious concerns about the history of suicide in mother's family. Indeed, it is more specific than that: mother herself had a transient depression following the birth of the youngest son (his first entry into the family), and the ritual seemed to be effectively excluding, from the family's awareness, this aspect of the family's past as well. For each subsequent entry of the sons, the ritual seems to imply, mother will be relegated to a much more passive position than when she gave birth to her sons. The fundamental point here is that a ceremonial with mixed consecration and degradation components serves to include some things from the family's past and exclude others. In this instance it seems to be excluding one entire lineage (mother's) and consecrating or enhancing another (father's). Wolin and Bennett have emphasized how often a current family will honor only one lineage in just this way; the honored lineage becomes, in their terms, the "family of heritage"; it is a primary source of the family's sense of continuity over time. The sons, feel themselves much more descendants of their father's family than their mother's.

Space. Ceremonials also play a central role in the family's experience of space. In considering this role we will concentrate primarily on consecration ceremonies, and particularly on rituals, although we believe degradation ceremonies also have an important role here as well. Four aspects of the structure or conduct of family rituals seems most important in their role of organizing the family's conception of space. First is the site where the ritual is typically conducted. Second is the regulation of family boundaries incorporated in the conduct of the ritual; this is most evident where the function of the ritual is to deal with entrances to and exits from the family of non-family members or, as in the case of the arm-wrestling ritual, of family members themselves. The third aspect, closely related to the second, concerns the ritual's embodiment of connections to or protection from the social community in which the family lives. A fourth concerns the quality and extent of resources utilized in the conduct of the ritual. In general these four aspects of ritual, aspects which can be observed and recorded, operate together to organize the experience of the same domains of space as do the simpler pattern regulators. These domains, to review, are: the family's experience of the boundary between its space and that of the outer world; the family's chart of the space outside the boundary; and the experience of the organization of space of its own territory.

First, let us consider the site of family rituals. As a rule, most rituals are practiced in the family's home. As such they serve to consecrate the home territory, to endow it with special charge and symbolism, and to create a gradient of experience between "outside" and "inside." Home-based rituals enhance all members' feeling that their home territory is familiar, meaningful, rich, supportive, and continuing. However, some families do engage in rituals outside the home. As described by Bossard and Boll, some families have regular days for shopping in which the whole family engages in a ritualized way. Other families hold annual reunions in restaurants or public halls. Some families ritualize their attendance at annual intercollegiate football games or at major social events or at church. These rituals serve to superimpose on an impersonal world a special sense of familiarity and ownership for the whole family. In effect, part of the social community outside the family's boundaries gets charted or demarcated as friendly turf.

Rituals also serve to clarify the nature of the family/nonfamily boundary itself. They can do so in at least two ways. First of all, some rituals are specifically constructed to deal with welcoming people into the family or saying goodbye to them. For example, the Brady family described in Chapter 1 had elaborate rituals for dealing with phone calls and visitors. These rituals served to screen out or defend the family against almost all outsiders who were perceived as intruders. Mother took exclusive responsibility for answering the phone and the doorbell. She met callers with great civility but handled virtually every call or visitor herself. Often son and uncle listened attentively to mother while smiling wordlessly at each other. Mother rarely let an outsider engage these two timorous men. The ritual effectively sealed the family borders against intrusion.

Rituals themselves can serve as links to the broader community and hence influence the permeability of the family boundary by quite another mechanism. For example, a home-based religious ritual serves to establish a link between the family and its coreligionists. This may be particularly true where the family is a part of a racial, religious, or ethnic minority. The ritual serves simultaneously to strengthen the bonds of the family with others in its minority group as well as to demarcate the family from the broader, and for the moment less differentiated, community of the majority. Examples here are the celebration of the seder by Jewish families and of the slava by Serbian families (see Bennett, 1978).

Finally, rituals often draw on specific resources for their conduct. For example, in some families the celebration of Christmas involves a great feast with a grand table setting, the finest food and drink, and the attendance of servants. Among other functions, a ritual of this kind serves to emphasize the family's command of resources. A central experience is of the outside world flowing into the sinews of the family: the family experiences itself as a transformer, transducer, and consumer of its surrounding community, which yields a sense of ritualized mastery and control. Consider a contrasting ritual in an American family where each year the father, born in France, reads a Christmas story in French to the entire family. Other aspects of the holiday celebration—the food served, the site of the celebration, the attendance or nonattendance at church—may vary, but the storytelling remains. Here the major resource is the family's past; the father's French lineage serves as the family of heritage. The ritual centers the family's attention on its European past and for the moment produces an estrangement between it and its American present. The family does not feel a sense of command of its immediate social community but rather a momentary sense of withdrawal and estrangement.

Synchrony. There is a third sense in which rituals parallel pattern regulators: the family's experience of its own synchrony. As we have defined them, all rituals synchronize family behavior; they require coordinated interaction from most or all family members each time they are performed. However, Bossard and Boll point out a critical distinction. Some rituals have as their primary function bringing order to broad spheres of family life. Bossard and Boll describe rituals such as the whole family going out together every Friday night or dinnertime rituals which require everyone to be present at a particular hour every day. Rituals of this kind keep the life plans of each family member very much in lock step with one another. It is not simply that once the family members come together they coordinate their behavior quite precisely in order to carry out a ritual; this level of synchrony is nearly ubiquitous in family rituals. Beyond this minimum, rituals of the kind we are discussing require all family members to dovetail their individual daily plans with one another long before the ritual starts and perhaps long after. For example, if everyone must be at the dinner table by six each evening, then each member must carefully plan his time both before and after the actual meal time in order to carry out a ritual with this kind of imperative for punctuality. Thus, planning and punctuality rituals give each family member a special sense of synchrony with, if not embroilment in, each other's lives. Other rituals such as the arm-wrestling ritual require a good deal of synchrony between family members: each must take a specific role and execute it as has been done in the past in careful concert and sequence with the performance of other crucial roles. However, the ritual does not impose on the family any broad-scale requirement for organization and synchrony beyond that required for the performance of the ritual itself.

The role of ceremonials in shaping the family's experience of time, space, and synchrony is summarized in Table 6.2.

CEREMONIALS, PATTERN REGULATORS, AND CONSERVATION OF THE PARADIGM

We have argued that both ceremonials and pattern regulators shape the family's experience of time, space, and its own synchrony. This parallel leads us to suggest how rituals and pattern regulators are related in the overall organization of family interaction behavior. Moreover, it will be a basis for our proposal that both ceremonials and pattern regulators conserve the family

TABLE 6.2 THE ROLE OF CEREMONIALS IN SHAPING THE FAMILY'S EXPERIENCE OF TIME, SPACE, AND SYNCHRONY

Attribute	Mechanism	Description
Time	The balance between consecration and degradation	Consecrations enhance the experience of the past, fusing it with the present and providing a leisurely and deliberate experience of the flow of time. Degradation blots out the past, freezing the family at a point-instant in present time. Time is felt as a rushing, fleeting evanescence.
Space	Location of ritual practice	Rituals practiced outside the home establish the outside world as encompassable, manageable.
	Welcoming rituals	These rituals allow outsiders to easily traverse family boundaries. In contrast are those rituals which screen outsiders and carefully regulate their entrance into family affairs.
	Ties of rituals to the broader community	Religious and ethnic rituals serve to connect the family to its outer world and to deepen, enrichen, and strengthen those connections.
	The resources for ritual practice	Rituals drawing on resources outside the family (money, servants, etc.) emphasize the family's mastery of the outer world.
Synchrony	Planning and punctuality rituals	These rituals require the coordination of life planning by family members; of necessity their separate worlds must, in some way, be integrated in the service of family continuity.

paradigm. Each of these two points—the relationship of ceremonials and pattern regulators and how this relationship conserves the family paradigm—will be considered in turn.

Ceremonials and conservation. Clues for the special role of family ceremonials can be gained from a closer inspection of their formal and experiential character. We have already commented that they are highly charged with affect and symbolic meaning, that they require participation from all family members and are diluted by absenteeism, that they are episodic rather than continuous, and that they enhance rather than place in the background the family's own experience of itself as an interacting group. In our analysis of the arm-wrestling ritual we could see that these features served to provide each family member with a vivid sense of membership in a group that extended beyond him, in a spatial sense, and before and after him, in a temporal sense. Indeed, Turner (1977) has pointed to features like this as a central function of both religious and secular ritual.

The formal features of ceremonials contribute to the temporary surrender of the individual to a sense of merger with the group. Perhaps two features of ceremonials are most important here. First, their affectivity and symbolic charge serves to rivet each member's attention on the unfolding ceremonial; for the moment, the rest of the world—in an experiential sense—is blotted out. In addition, the ceremonials provide each member not only with a role but with a program for carrying through the responsibilities of that role to completion. Thus, as the full range of stimuli outside the family are blotted out, so too are all the ambiguities and uncertainties and the need for active decisions ordinarily entailed in routine daily behavior. Thus, each member is deprived of two regular and crucial components of his explicit sense of himself as a self-aware, bounded, and autonomous actor. This perception of the full range of his social community is blotted out, momentarily, by the affectivity of the ceremonial. In addition, he can no longer feel himself in a field with ambiguities he must define and decisions he must make. Thus, he is deprived of a crucial substrate for feeling himself an autonomous actor.

Consider, for example, a distinguished young professor who returns at Christmas to her family, where she is the younger of two daughters (the other is a physician). A major family ceremonial is the opening of presents on Christmas morning; the youngest child, as always, is to serve as Santa Claus and distribute presents to the others. It is perhaps not enough to say that the young professor becomes a small child once again. This perspective fails to pay attention to comparable changes that everyone else undergoes (the older daughter, it might be said, is transformed from a physician to a big sister) and assumes that the role of Santa Claus in this family is necessarily "childlike." Indeed, in this brief ceremonial, Santa Claus is the distributer, the provider, and is presumed to know what is contained in each package. A necessary component of the ceremonial is bantering that Santa knows the contents of each package and is distributing the packages so that each person gets his fair share of both surprise and value. It is perhaps more accurate to say that the Santa Claus ritual blots out the "real world," which provides abundant cues as to the "real identity" of both children (and the parents too), and rivets the family's attention on a prescribed set of interactions which require virtually no complex decisions by any participant (although endless minor embellishments are constantly added).

The submergence of self in what Turner refers to as "communitas" gives ceremonials their special force of objectification. The central realities of family life—particularly as they relate to space, time, and the family's own synchrony—are reinforced at each performance of the ceremonial. We have shown how the fundamental form of family ceremonials—its collective character, its symbolic significance, and (as outlined above) its submergence of individual members—can vary from family to family. As indicated, these variations can be thought of in spatial and temporal terms as well as in relation to their synchronization of family life. It is these variations that help us see how ceremonials can account for particular forms of pattern regulation and (as we will consider in a moment) conservation of a particular family paradigm. What we are proposing is that the inner realities of family life become, through ritual, the only realities (episodic and momentary though they are). The family's shared conviction concerning this reality provides them with a guide for action in its daily routines. For example, where consecration predominates over degradation the family recreates a reality—through every ritual observance—where the past lives in the present. This conception of time, arising in ritual, remains a framework for all the routines of daily family life. Thus, past orienting—the routinized reference to the past in the course of household and other routines—is shaped by the fundamental guidelines for action established through ritual. To take another example, ceremonials practiced outside the home establish a vivid, shared conception that portions of the outside world are familiar and, in some sense, possessed by the family. This conviction—born in the intense and encompassing communitas of ritual—remains, after the ritual is concluded, as an action guideline supporting and shaping spatial pattern regulators. Indeed, we would expect that families whose ritual sites included those outside the home would show, in their daily routines, a much greater utilization of space outside the home. It would not be simply a matter of the family returning—for more routinized but less ritualized interaction—to the particular sites where formal ceremonials had been conducted. The relationship should be more general: the central fact that rituals are performed outside the home establishes a framework for action which implies that the outer world is negotiable, understandable, and masterable. Thus, for example, consider a family who shops together regularly each Thursday evening, attends church together each Sunday, and vacations together every summer (and assume that in each case the collective behavior conforms to our definition of ritual). These "off-site" rituals should establish a conviction of the manageability of the external world. In its daily routines, all members of the family will range over a wide compass of space outside the home: in the neighborhood, in an entire urban setting or in even more remote parts. The family's daily routines—its pattern regulators—are designed to permit a great deal of visiting, sightseeing, and individual and family participation in a variety of activities and organizations.

Thus, to summarize our main point here: ceremonials blot out the separate and broader experiences of family members. They intensively focus each member's attention on the experience of undifferentiated oneness with each other and, through this process of refocusing, establish and maintain the family's own conception of social reality. As we explained in Chapter 3, conceptions of reality are most important when they serve as guides for action and decision making. Indeed, it takes but one major practical challenge to an assumption about reality to turn that assumption into a criterion or a plan for evaluating or developing action. It is, in this sense, that ceremonials shape and regulate pattern regulators and thus deserve placement at the center of our imaginary sphere.

Pattern regulators and conservation. Pattern regulators, although they are shaped and guided by ceremonials, have their own fundamental role in the conservation of family paradigm. Their special role derives from an experiential attribute of pattern regulators which is in complete contrast to ceremonials. Ceremonials are vividly and engrossingly experienced by all family members. However, family members are often not explicitly aware of fundamental pattern regulators in their family. For example, they do not monitor the distance they stand from one another while talking, or the frequency with which they shift from room to room, or the extensity of their visiting and participation in the community. These are second nature, a matter of course, and so familiar as to be invisible. When a child from one family spends the night at the home of a friend he gets a good glimpse of the pattern regulators in the host family. He is often surprised at how different—in many little ways—the host family is from his own family. For example, the bedtimes of members in the host family are all different (in his own family, everyone goes to bed together); no one in the host family says goodnight to the others (in his family, this is carefully performed); no one in the host family has breakfast with another; no care is taken to exchange information as to where each member of the family will spend his day. The child is not only surprised at these differences; he is at least equally surprised to become aware of—almost to discover—the contrasting patterns in his own family's routine.

The background character of pattern regulators derive from their routinization. Indeed, the background character is the source of one of their special contributions to the conservation of the family paradigm: reification. Pattern regulators play a special role in enhancing the conviction each family member has in the fundamental assumptions which shaped those pattern regulators in the first place. Ceremonials, as we have seen, reaffirm a family's assumptions about itself and the world through explicit and intense and focussed awareness on particular family processes. Pattern regulators continue to influence and reinforce these conceptions on a much more subliminal level. They operate, in many ways, like subliminal cues in commercial advertising. Advertisements for an expensive scotch, for example, will contain a hint of the social prestige a consumer might expect if he served the brand being advertised. As long as these cues remain relatively in the background the advertisement is likely to achieve its effect. When a reader can say to himself, "Look at all those little prestige cues they're using to influence me," the spell is broken. Likewise, the patterns of family life exert a continuing though unseen and unfelt influence over the family's shared conception of itself in the world.

Joseph Howell (1973) has illustrated this effect quite nicely in his detailed contrast of family types on a single street ("Clay Street") in a Washington, D.C., suburb. He provides a vivid account of the daily routines of "hard livers" and "settled families." Families in the former group continually feel overwhelmed and disconnected from their community and struggle to maintain themselves on a moment-by-moment basis. They feel themselves to be hanging on, almost by clawing, in a world that seems precarious and ungiving and unknowable. These feelings are expressed in virtually every aspect of family routine.

Howell describes one such family, the Shackelfords. The day begins with the mother alone in a tiny kitchen at 4:00 AM, savoring the only moments of peace she can. She tries to return to bed (which she shares with her husband and daughter) and trips over her husband's paint cans on the way in (he is a part-time painter working when he is not drunk). She can't sleep and gets up to read the paper. An hour or so later her three younger children (aged seven, five, and three) demand bottles. She knows the children are too old for bottles, but she prepares them and gives them to the children anyway. She prepares breakfast first for her blind step-father, then for her children, who weave in and out of the house in a variety of play routines while still in their underpants. Then her husband appears in the clothes he has worn for a week; his only breakfast is a bottle of beer. No one knows if he will go to work to-day. The battery in his truck is dead (he knew about this the day before). He struggles for some time to replace it with another and then drives off; no one knows where.

Even this brief vignette gives a sense of the interplay of family routine and family experience. It would be a mistake to call either the routines or experience chaos. There is a regularity and expectability to many of these sequences; they recur in similar if not identical fashion at other times during other days. What we can recognize here is a fundamental fusion between events and sequences and spaces that, in other families, are kept bounded and distinct: work materials (paint cans) are in the living areas, children and adults sleep together, older children are given food in bottles the way infants ordinarily are, the sleeping time of one overlaps with the waking time of another. There is no sense of one thing leading to another, nor a sense that the first event is a cause and the second is a consequence. Most people in the family are on their own. Mother adapts passively to the routines of others and becomes the only remaining link for what remains of the synchronization of members with one another.[6]

Other families on Clay Street are in sharp contrast. These "settled families," as Howell calls them, show daily routines of a different order: the adults have the same bedtime and arising time; the children go to bed earlier and in age-graded ways (the youngest at the earliest time). Work materials are kept out of the house. The rooms in the house are clearly differentiated, with play areas and living areas carefully demarcated, and all the rooms are orderly. The houses are owned rather than rented, and the organized routines allow family members to participate actively in local organizations. The settled families have a clear and conspicuous awareness of their differences from the hard livers, whom they call "white trash." It is doubtful, however, if they are aware of how much their own routines reinforce and strengthen their sense of rootedness to, and indeed a sense of ownership of, the community in which they live. The settleds see the white trash as dangerous intruders. The hard livers have a less distinct sense of contrast between themselves and others; they regard themselves as a group of individuals nearly always overwhelmed by events beyond their control. For example, the Shackelford mother later had a hysterectomy after months of a swelling abdomen and excessive menstrual bleeding. After her operation, she did not seem to have any sense of what the surgeon had found out about her condition during surgery. She says she was never told, but it seems quite likely she never asked.

To summarize, we are positing that ceremonials play the fundamental role in establishing and reinforcing a family's conception of itself and the world in which it lives. When the family must set about its daily routines—performing actions, making decisions—these conceptions become actualized as action guidelines which then directly shape the routinized pattern regulators. Pattern regulators themselves take on any important supplementary function; by virtue of their background and routinized character they enhance a family's conception of itself and its social world. This impact is largely indirect, subtle, and often subliminal, but as a result it is very compelling.

The Specificity of Conservation

Our sketch of the organization of family behavior — a sphere with ceremonials at the core and pattern regulators at the periphery — was intended to clarify how family interaction behavior might function to conserve the family paradigm. Thus far, our sketch has given some account of the durability of these structures. It has also shown, in a general way, how both ceremonials and pattern regulators can join forces to shape the family's conception of itself, its social world, and its place in that world. However, we have not so far demonstrated that the organization of interaction behavior is specific enough to conserve the particular or idiosyncratic aspects of paradigm we have already described.

Requirements for specificity. Recall that we posited three distinct dimensions which could be used to characterize the distinguishing features of a family's paradigm (see Table 5.1 for a summary). The first of these dimensions was coherence: families differ in whether they conceive the world as governed by an underlying and stable set of discoverable principles of whether the world is shaped by invisible, capricious forces capable of moving on their own. A second dimension was integration: some families experience the social world as similar for all family members, whereas others see separate worlds with different principles for each member. Finally, we posited a dimension of reference: external or empiricist families are convinced that the coordinates of experience are in the external world, whereas internal or solipsistic families think that the ultimate coordinates of experience are located in their own family: "The world is (using *is* in the most epistemological sense possible) what we make it."

Now let us return to the original point about the specificity of interaction. If the organization of interaction behavior is to be conceived as the primary medium of conservation of the paradigm, it must not only be durable, not only be capable of shaping and reifying a family's experience of itself in the world, it must also be specific enough to conserve the location of the paradigm on each of these three dimensions. In other words, we must be able to recognize or delineate analogs of these three dimensions — coherence, integration, and reference — in the organization of behavior itself.

The concepts of time, space, and synchrony provide, we will argue, an approximate though not exact bridge between the dimensions of paradigm and the organization of interaction behavior. Let us consider each in turn.

The conservation of externality or internality. The link between interaction behavior and the paradigm dimension that we have called reference is perhaps the most straightforward and the easiest to describe. Families at the empiricist end of this dimension operate on a fundamental assumption that the ultimate origin of their experience lies in a world outside the family's boundaries. They see themselves as subordinates of external events; their constructions arise and are shaped by what they sense or know or guess about their environment. The Shackelfords are clearly in this position. However ungiving and haphazard their world may seem, they feel themselves shaped by its forces, receptive to its nuances, without any sense of their own solidity as a group or the reality of their own history as a counterbalance or source of color or emphasis in their experience. In contrast, the O'Hara family, originators of the arm-wrestling ritual, collapse their experience of past and present; the fusion of the experience of father and son — experienced alternately by the older and younger fathers — and the rich sense of the family's history shape a hardy, competitive, assertive conception of the present. In this fusion of present and past is a central feature of internal or solipsistic families. It is the shape of the family's own past which is the origin of the quality of their experience. The family's past centers the family in its experiential world. It gives the family the solidity to serve as the zero point on the world's major axes (see Figure 5.3). We can recognize, then, the emergence of one strand of a link here: the reference dimension can be conserved through the balance of consecration and degradation in family ceremony. Consecration, therefore, conserves internality or solipsism.

It would follow logically, then, that degradation would conserve externality or empiricism. However, at first glance, this seems to be an ungainly apposition. Degradation, we have argued, is that part of family ceremonial which conceals from the family aspects of its past — particularly painful aspects associated with crises. The major mechanism employed is projection. Feelings and memories are projected onto an individual or group instead of experienced and acknowledged by the family. This exclusionary and projective process — if pervasive in family life — cuts the family off from its own past and narrows its focus of experience onto the immediate present. We have described this as freezing the family at a point in time. The family's very narrow focus on the present makes it particularly enslaved to current experience and stimulation, which forces the family into a dependence on immediate experience. The family with a very limited sense of its own origins and development cannot see itself as an originator but only as a responder. Included in this experience of itself vis à vis the world is a sense that time flows rapidly; in these families the clocking routines may often show a frantic pace. This is clearly conveyed by Howell's description of the Shackelfords. Events go on at breakneck pace. Indeed, Mrs. Shackelford savors the few moments of solitude—at 4:00 AM—for their unaccustomed sense of repose. In contrast, internal or solipsistic families have a sense of themselves as stretching out in time and embracing it; what happens today is recognizably similar to what happened yesterday. At certain quintessential moments the flow of time is halted. This clearly is the case for the Santa Claus ritual. All the years that have flown by since the two daughters were children, the daughters' schooling, their graduation, their ascendancy into honored and difficult professions—all this is eradicated in a single moment of return to the past, or, to put it more properly, at the moment when the past fuses with the present. Clocking is slowed down. This is not to say that activity is less, that the family is lethargic or sluggish. Rather, it is that their sense of time in which action takes place is one of even, deliberate flow and occasional arrest together.

In sum, ceremonials and pattern regulators conserve the reference dimension. Consecration combines with deliberate and leisurely clocking to conserve a sense of the richness of the family's past and, often, an awareness of the full sweep of its development. The continuous experience of this richness and sweep consistently endows current experience with a color and a shape imposed by the family's past; this experience, in turn, lies at the core of the internal or solipsistic position. In contrast, degradation, with its exclusion of the family's past, combines with rapid clocking to focus the family on the immediate present and to bind it to the vicissitudes of current experience. The family senses its own actions are responses to vivid and immediate experience in the present; this experience lies at the core of the external or empircist position.

The conservation of coherence. We have already seen that both ceremonials and pattern regulators play a role, usually complementary, in organizing the family's conception of the space in which it lives. More particularly, we examined three regions in this space: the family's own territory, the broad reaches of space outside that habitat, and the nature of the boundary that separates the two. We propose that differences between families in how these three regions are experienced are a clear expression of underlying differences of their paradigms—differences, in particular, along the dimension of coherence. More specifically, families high on coherence will experience the family boundary as simply a marker rather than a well-patrolled fence, and internal spatial organization will be perceived as a natural consequence of the family's charting of its external space. In contrast are families who are low on the coherence dimension, and as a consequence are shaped by a vigilant attention to intrinsic movement in their environment. For these families, a charting of the social environment is not possible. The concept of charting implies that experience can be built up over time, by one or more individuals, to contribute to an increasingly more accurate and comprehensive image of the surrounding territory. To be sure, all families, simply to survive, must construct—singly or together—some schema of their surrounding community. However, some of these will be quite rudimentary in the sense that they will focus exclusively on relatively inanimate or superficial characteristics of the environment: simple acts, geographical routes, access to stores, and so on. However, other more sophisticated and more comprehensive charts are possible—those which include, for example, conceptions of how organizations function and how people relate to one another. In Chapter 2, we described two procedures by which social and interpersonal charting of this kind could be objectively measured. The ward perception Q-sort assessed the family's conception of the ward as a social community; the family perception procedure assessed the family's conception of other families in the ward community. We are contending that these charts—representations not only of spatial arrangements but also of emotional arrangements—are closely related to the family's experience of space. For example, a family organized to allow easy and frequent access of its members to the outside community (and the reverse, access of the community to the interior of the family) will be most likely to construct high-fidelity charts of this kind.

Families low on coherence, who are dominated by a sense of the world as shaped by forces with their own intrinsic principles, cannot build up charts of this kind. Indeed, the social environment is perceived as more of a signal detection field: it must be frequently scanned for changes and scanned regularly. These changes, once they occur, may have implications for the family but they cannot be predicted in advance. Thus, the family senses its own boundaries (which could perhaps be the four walls of its house) as a defensive perimeter within which a semblance of order may be experienced. The Brady family in Chapter 1, where mother monitored all incoming information, exemplified just this kind of defensive perimeter.

Differences in the experience of space outside the families boundaries, between high and low cohesion families, lead to comparable differences in the organization of space within their own territory. In high coherence families, internal spatial arrangements tend to be clear consequences of their evolving chart of the outer world. In other words, internal spatial arrangements are shaped in accord with the role the family as a group, or its individual members, take in the actively and comprehensively construed social environment. An observer can recognize, in the family's internal traffic pattern, a system well worked out to fit with its conception of the opportunities and requirements of its outer world. To cite a very simple example, space will be allocated to members based in part on their roles and responsibilities in the world outside the home. If mother returns to school for graduate studies then she is given space for studying. If son makes the football team then space is reserved for the weightlifting program he must follow. If parties and meetings are a major form of relationship within the community, the spatial arrangements inside the home will reflect this. Recall that in the Shackelford family the outside world was also represented in substantial measure in the family's own living space. For example, when mother returned to bed in the early morning, she tripped on father's paint cans. But examples like these can be viewed more as leaks from the outside world rather than representations of it. Indeed, we get the impression that flotsam and jetsam from the outside world might continuously be found in the houses of many of the hard livers. This is an entirely different matter than what we are considering for high coherence families. The inner spatial arrangements of their homes reflects an active, constantly enlarging conception of the outside world and the family role in it, a conception (or chart, as we are calling it) that is built up through time, observation, and experience. Mrs. Shackelford knew very little about her husband's work experience. No one in the family really knew where or when he worked; there were long periods of time when even Mr. Shackelford—drunk or badly hung over—had only the haziest idea. We are arguing here that the mere presence of paraphernalia of the outside world inside the home does not indicate that the internal spatial arrangements express a conception or chart of the outer world.

A fundamentally different organization of inner space was seen in the Brady family. A particularly dramatic example was the reservation of space for the continued display of father's medical books and the placement of father's unused desk. These two instances were clear examples of spatial organization unrelated to any continuing role of members in the outside world. It reflected instead a fundamental inability of the family to relinquish the sense of the dead father's presence in the family and to relinquish all ties and connections to a status the family had enjoyed when he was alive. The internal spatial organization, then, reflected not a chart of the current world but a dim, idealized conception of the way things had once been and might — under ideal circumstances — become again.

This same sort of discrepancy between the current outside world and the internal organization of a household can often be seen in refugee families. Consider the Ivanov family, a threesome. Mr. Ivanov is a businessman, Mrs. Ivanov is a piano teacher, and her maiden sister is a children's book editor. They are all in their seventies now and had come to a large city in this country after fleeing from Russia during the revolution. They live now in a large apartment house. To enter their home is to enter, quite literally, another world. The apartment house corridor is brightly lit by overhead fluorescent fixtures. As soon as one enters the Ivanovs' apartment one is immediately struck by the sense of darkness and heaviness. The windows are all but covered by heavy red satin drapes brought from Russia. Ornate but dim glass lamps, also from Russia, are in every corner. The walls are covered by dark, embroidered Russian fabric, and pictures of famous Russian composers are hung on almost every one of them. The house is a museum consecrating the family's past in Russia, where it was a member of the minor nobility. Nothing of the family's current life, its experiences or knowledge of the world around them, is reflected in the organization of the household.

In sum, we are positing that the family organization of space conserves the coherence aspect of its paradigm. For families low on coherence, the internal organization is the family's sole source of order; the outside world is movement without pattern or the possibility of mastery. Internal space is organized as a defense against the anxiety and unease that comes of living in a world that seems alien or not possessable or even threatening. In contrast, the dominant organizer of space in high coherence families is their evolving map of an external world that seems discoverable. All the pattern regulators are coordinated to promote easy access in and out of the family as well as extensive engagement, by the family, in a broad range of activities and relationships in the community. The internal spatial organization of the family reflects the continuing results of these engagements. To emphasize a fundamental point, this internal organization is *active;* internal spatial arrangements are actively designed and redesigned based on a concept. They are not, as with the Shackelford family, the results of the haphazard leakage of the outside world into family affairs.

The conservation of integration. We can turn next to synchrony and its links to universality. We have already taken a brief look at rituals which require more than simple coordination of individual behavior for their performance. Following Bossard and Boll, we have said that some rituals require a pervasive coordination of the life planning of each family member. Thus, a dinnertime ritual which requires all members to eat promptly at 6:00 PM every day of the week forces each family member to plan his entire day, before and after the ritual performance itself. Other rituals stop somewhat short of this sweeping imperative. For example, a more modest integration of life planning is implied by the ritual of leaving notes in the morning. Bossard and Boll describe this as a frequent ritual where each member leaves the others a brief accounting of where he will be during the day. A ritual of this kind does not force high levels of coordinate planning, but it does give each member a clear view of the others' life planning. When we discussed pattern regulators, following the lead of Kantor and Lehr, we recognized an analogous gradation. Some families had a dominant pattern of synchronizing the routines of its daily life. Howell's settled families displayed this feature clearly enough. In contrast, the Shackelfords displayed virtually no synchrony or any planning and punctuality rituals.

There are two ways in which punctuality, coordination of planning, and synchrony of pattern regulators can sustain or conserve the universality aspects of the family paradigm. The first mechanism of conservation occurs in high coherence families. These are families, as we have said, who assume the world is masterable and whose assumptions in this regard are sustained through their organization of space into an evolving chart of their social world. Where punctuality, planning, and synchrony are high, this evolving chart is a shared enterprise. Each member has access to the others' world and the conception each builds of his own world depends on what he has learned from the charting of others in the family. Thus, the simple ritual of exchanging notes early in the morning can be seen as a tool for dovetailing or coordinating the family's joint conception of the daily plans of each member. This involves knowing more than simply where the other members will be. The note exchange ritual will surely be supplemented by other pattern regulators and ceremonials in which the simple facts contained on each note are elaborated, related to other information, and synthesized into an organic conception. The end result is crucial to sustaining the universality aspects of the family's paradigm; the family carries through the conviction that each member lives in the same experiental world as the others. Thus, one member can take the perspective of another; he knows what the other wants to achieve, where he wants to achieve it, and what he is up against.

Punctuality, planning, and synchrony can lead to this "one world" conception by quite a different mechanism in low coherence families. These families, as we have said, do not build up and sustain a subtle and comprehensive chart of their environment. Their conception of the environment is one of disorder, change, ambiguity; in a word it is unchartable because the territories and the connections among them are not stable, articulated, or visible. In low coherence families, punctuality, planning, and synchrony serve a very different function: they tend to augment, in each member's experience, the size, dominance, and prepotence of the family group. Thus, a dinnertime ritual which requires punctuality carries a message: "You owe it to your family to be here." Planning activities or events together—in the course of ceremonials or the less charged everyday routines—likewise has its own function here: "You owe it to your family to involve them in your affairs." In high coherence families, coordinate planning—of vacations, trips to the store, school activities, and the like—are another opportunity for each family member to learn something about the life space of the others. For example, if a family has difficulty planning a shopping trip together, the difficulty itself becomes informative. The family group may learn, for example, that one daughter has a regular meeting time with a friend or that the son has been looking forward to watching a football game all week. To some degree, the personal worlds of these two children get partially integrated into a group image of the outside terrain most relevant for family members. In low coherence families, difficulties in joint planning are seen as threats to family solidarity. While reasons may be offered by individual members for their own difficulties in joining the group—and these difficulties may be, on the surface, the very same ones offered in high coherence families—the family perceives them as excuses rather than as items of information. Thus, punctuality, planning, and synchrony—in low coherence families—become a mechanism for excluding the outside world of its members. Family members come to experience themselves as living in the same world, to be sure, but this world is the family itself stretching endlessly to encompass the broadest possible range of shared experience. Lyman Wynne (1958) has talked of families of this kind as surrounded by a rubber fence.

The role of ceremonials and pattern regulators in the conservation of the family paradigm is summarized in Table 6.3.

TABLE 6.3 THE ROLE OF CEREMONIALS AND PATTERN REGULATORS IN THE CONSERVATION OF THE FAMILY PARADIGM

Dimension of paradigm	Pole	Role of ceremonials	Role of pattern regulators
Coherence	Stable	Ceremonials establish the family's connection with, engagement in, and mastery of the outside world.	Pattern regulators are organized around a chart of the outside world; internal spatial organization represents a family's vivid conception of its environment.
	Mobile	Ceremonials seal the family off from the outside world, and draw only on the family's own resources.	Family boundary is clearly established and well-patrolled; access to outsiders is limited.
Integration	Universal	Planning and punctuality rituals require a coordination of life planning in the service of family continuity.	Delegation, specialization, and coordination of routines are performed effortlessly.
	Particular	An absence of planning and punctuality rituals.	Delegation and coordination problematic. Daily routines are initiated, modulated, and monitored by each member without reference to the others.
Reference	Internal	Consecration rituals connect the family's present and past. The family's vivid experience of its own history gives it a sense of solidity and mass, which serves as the central experiential reference point in dealing with the world.	Past orientation in verbal interaction, economic strategy, and career planning supplement the connections to the past provided by consecration ceremonials.
	External	Degradation ceremonials blot out the past and freeze the family at a point-instant in present time.	Present orientation in interaction, economic and career planning and rapid clocking reinforce the experience of frenetic and fleeting time.

Part III
The Family's Bond to Its Social World

7 | Orienting Concepts in Family-Environment Organization

The core of our model, which focuses on the roles of crisis and paradigm in family life, has been outlined. Crisis makes the family particularly vulnerable to changes in its fundamental orientation toward itself and its social environment; the mode by which a family recovers from crisis contains the seeds for a more permanent form of family organization. This organization—built around the family's conception of itself in the world—becomes stabilized and conserved. We have indicated that the family's ongoing ties with its social environment play a crucial role in this sequence. First, these ties determine the family's vulnerability to crisis; second, they shape or influence its mode of recovery; and finally, they stabilize its new organization.

The next two chapters focus on the third function of a family's ties to its social world: their function in stabilizing family organization. In these two chapters we want to sketch out a mechanism by which the family becomes tied to or engaged with its social environment. We will show that these ties are complex and serve many functions for both the family and its social environment. Indeed, these ties are structured and complex enough to justify the umbrella term *family-environment organization*. By this term we mean to emphasize the interlocking and multifaceted connections between each family and the many aspects of the social environment with which it becomes engaged.

The Cycle Hypothesis

Our most central ideas about family-environment organization can be stated in a single hypothesis which we will call the *cycle hypothesis*, illustrated in Figure 7.1. The cycle hypothesis was developed as explanation of how the family paradigm is stabilized

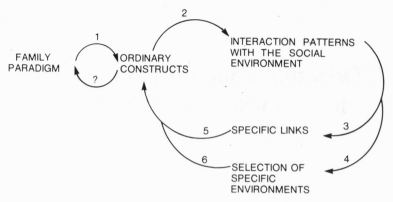

Figure 7.1.   *The cycle hypothesis*

over time. As the figure indicates, the hypothesis specifies six steps linked by a circularly causal chain.

Steps 1 and 2 are familiar to us from the preceding chapters. We have shown how an underlying family orientation that we call a paradigm shapes the family's shared conception of any specific social situation. These specific shared conceptions, which we refer to as ordinary constructs, guide the family in conducting its affairs. As we have stated, constructs can undergo progressive changes in content as the family learns more about any particular environment; moreover, family members may disagree about specific content. With respect to underlying form, however, the constructs are shared by all members of a family – and do not change despite the family's growing knowledge of the social environment.

Steps 3 and 4 contain a mixture of something that is already familiar to us and something new. We know that ordinary constructs determine in large measure a family's actual conduct in a social environment. Step 3, however, introduces a new idea, which focuses on the accumulating results of the style or strategy the family uses to deal with its social environment. After a sustained transaction with an aspect of its social environment – for example, its neighborhood community – the family will achieve a certain type of *link* with that environment. For example, the family may achieve a conspicuous position of high status and influence, or it may retreat to an inconspicuous position. Likewise, in step 4, the family will select, and then become engaged with, an aspect of social environment with particular values, orientation, or social atmosphere. Some families might select a liberal, racially integrated, relaxed, and friendly suburban neighborhood. Others may select an impersonal, racially segregated, conservative, and elite urban neighborhood. Indeed, the family's transaction with its environment plays a role in the selection of and enclosure in a limited number of social environments, each with its own values or perspectives.

In steps 5 and 6 we argue that the types of links a family forms with its environment — as well as the nature of that environment itself — exert their own influence on the family in a reflexive way, which produces the hypothesized cycle. Once a family achieves a particular position within a demarcated social environment with a particular ideology, both its position and the environment's character function to maintain the family's initial, ordinary constructs of itself in the world. For example, consider a family that achieves high status in a neighborhood. The family is perceived as influential and in fact exerts a good deal of influence. Its concept of itself (that is, its ordinary construct) as a group competent to meet a broad range of challenges should thereby be confirmed.

The cycle serves, primarily, to stabilize or conserve. When it operates smoothly and repetitively, the family paradigm can be conserved indefinitely; when it breaks down, the family becomes vulnerable to crisis.

Components of the Cycle Hypothesis

The cycle hypothesis has two major components: first, the concept of the link between the family and environment, and second, the notion of qualitatively different environments. A broad definition of these two central concepts will be developed in this section. In the remainder of this chapter, and in the next, we will discuss the hypothesis in greater detail.

DIFFERENT TYPES OF FAMILY-ENVIRONMENT LINKS

A family forms certain kinds of bonds with many different kinds of environments. A family may achieve centrality and status in its neighborhood, in its church, and in the financial and business life of the state. These are three different environments, although the character of the link is the same. Here we will emphasize the family's role in shaping these links; however, the links are — in all likelihood — a product of the environment as well. The social community in which the family lives must take some initiative for starting and maintaining links with any family. Thus, a family's tie to the local PTA is partly a result of the family's own style, values, and energy; it also reflects the energy, commitment, and recruiting zeal of the PTA. Further, the PTA may subtly encourage the participation of some families and discourage others. For example, some PTAs sponsor an annual Parents' Prom. This subtly discourages, perhaps unintentionally, single-parent families from joining fully in the life of the PTA.

We will explore three aspects of the family's links with its social environment. First, we will examine who in the family has the main responsibility of forging and maintaining the link. To cite again the PTA example, in the typical two-parent family the mother is often the most active or, indeed, the only active family member. Nonetheless she is representing her family in the PTA and representing the PTA to her family. In contrast, families participate as whole units—without the need for any single member to represent them—in organizations such as camping associations and church groups. We refer to differences of this kind as differences in the *medium* of the link. Second, whether the family's links are carried on by a single member or whether the entire family is active in forging and maintaining the link, the link takes on a stable and recognizable *architectural form*. In other words, it assumes a quality which permits us to describe how the family fits into the social environment. We have found it useful to consider three aspects of the architectural form: the centrality or status of the family in its environment; the openness of its boundaries to new information and personal relationships; and the intensity and level of engagement of the family. To complete our analysis, we will examine family-environment links from a third perspective: the *motivation* of these family ties. We will want to distinguish, in particular, what the family perceives it will gain from forging ties with the environment. For example, in coercive links the family feels forced into its ties with environment and maintains them to avoid some form of punishment. In contrast are normative ties, where the family feels ideologically committed to its environment and maintains its ties in order to support, develop, or preserve the environment itself.

DIFFERENCES IN SOCIAL ENVIRONMENTS

In this, our first, effort to map out the cycle hypothesis, we have deliberately chosen to explore only a portion of the family's social environment. First, the family's extended family or kin will be considered. Second, we will focus on the family's relationship with its community; "community" here refers to the people and collectivities in the family's immediate vicinity. Vicinity will be thought of as a spatial vicinity so that the concept of community and neighborhood can be used relatively interchangeably. Finally, we will inquire into the family's relationship with formal organizations. Our own data refer specifically to the family's relationship with the psychiatric hospital, but we will phrase our discussion here in terms sufficiently general to consider the family-hospital relationship as a prototype of many other family-organization relationships.

Several considerations motivated our choice of these aspects of the social environment for special analysis. First, we had a preference for direct observation of family-environment transactions. As Chapter 1 and 2 have indicated, we have a clear preference for directly observing the interconnecting behavior patterns in individuals in order to infer social processes in the family. We want to take the same approach to inferring social processes in the family-environment transactions—that is, to observe the interrelated behavior between family members and individuals in their social community. This interest in behavioral observations led us to select more concrete, rather than more abstract, forms of social organization. Olsen (1968) has summarized, in a comprehensive way, current forms of social organization. Of those he describes, we were much more drawn to kin, community, and organization than we were to, for example, society, culture, and class. To be sure, these six forms of social organization are highly interrelated. It can also be argued that the family's transaction with the broader and more abstract social organizations, such as class, is mediated by the more restricted and concrete social organizations, such as kin. Our concern, however, is not with these broader and undeniably important relationships between various components of the social structure; these we gladly leave to macrosociology.

Another aspect of kin, community, and organization attracts us. In some sense they are representative of various levels of social evolution. Thus, kin is clearly the most archaic form of extrafamily organization. Indeed, it was a matter of social evolution itself that nuclear and extended families became differentiated from one another. Formal organizations—particularly those with high levels of centralization of power, bureaucratization of structure, and functional specialization—are clearly creatures of the industrialized world and appeared late on the scene. Community spans the two and occupies, in an important sense, an intermediate position in social evolution. Coherent social communities were initially—and in many cases are now—aggregates or collectivities of families. They often have some of the more intense and personal ties that are typical of kinship relationships as well as the functional specialization and bureaucratization of formal organizations.

However, the evolutionary perspective reminds us of an important point about kin, community, and organization. To be sure, social evolution has created, in all societies, new forms of social *organization*. But of more interest and pertinence to our overall thesis, social evolution has led to new forms of social *relationships*.

Thus, bureaucracy as a form of social organization is typical—indeed emblematic—of formal organizations. However, bureaucratic organization of relationships, emphasizing the functional or authority aspects of relationships among people, also characterizes human relationships in communities and kinship networks as well. Likewise, kin and community relationships—characterized by what Tönnies (1957) called *Gemeinschaft*—can also be observed within formal organizations. Thus, kin, community, and organization refer to both different, and relatively concrete, forms of social organization as well as different perspectives for analyzing social relationships in many different settings. It may be even more accurate to say that kin-like and community-like relationships exist in formal organizations if one looks for them. In other words, kin and community can be recognized as analytical perspectives. Thus, the distinction among kin, community, and organization can be understood in two ways: first, as a mutually exclusive typology of concrete and directly observable forms of social organization; or second, as a set of perspectives for analyzing social process in any collectivity. This dual perspective will serve us well in this and the following chapter.

The major components of links and environments are summarized in Table 7.1.

Links between the Family and Its Social World

THE MEDIUM OF FAMILY-ENVIRONMENT TRANSACTIONS

The nuclear family rarely interacts as a group with its social environment. Adams (1968) has shown, for example, that with kin it is the mother who has by far the highest volume of direct contacts such as visits and joint activities and indirect contacts such as phone calls and letters. With formal organizations such as places of

TABLE 7.1 A SUMMARY OF THE MAJOR COMPONENTS OF LINKS AND ENVIRONMENTS IN THE CYCLE HYPOTHESIS

Major component	Constituent components or analytic perspectives
Link	Medium
	Architecture
	Motivation
Environment	Kin
	Community
	Organization

employment, it may be the father who has the greatest volume and most sustained contact over the years. Likewise, the adolescent has the most contact with a psychiatric inpatient service for adolescents. Our interest in direct behavioral observation threatens to betray us; it might lead us to look at family-environment interaction only in those instances when the entire family group is interacting with the environment. These instances will be infrequent and perhaps relatively unimportant. Even in those infrequent instances when two or more members do interact with the same social organization, they may interact with different parts of it. For example, a father, mother, and son may interact with entirely different individuals—usually same-sex peers—in the neighborhood community. If we will rarely see the entire family, as a unit, interacting with its social environment, in what sense do we consider "family-environment transactions"?

In order to advance our argument without undue complexity, we will assume that in most instances when an individual appears to be acting on his own, he is in some sense representing his family to the environment and representing the environment to his family. In their transactions with the community, individuals actually serve an ambassadorial function. The quality of this ambassadorship will vary between individuals in the same family and between different families. There are even interesting and important limiting cases in which individuals do act entirely on their own. Their transactions with the community in no sense—neither at a superficial level nor at a deeper symbolic level—represent their families, nor do their transactions with the environment have any impact on the family group. Despite these limiting cases, recognizing the ambassadorial function a single family member can serve permits us to describe four modes of family-environment linking.

The individual member as accredited ambassador. Here the individual's explicit role in the family makes him an obvious ambassador, on behalf of his family, to a segment of the social community. For example, a father represents his family in a place of employment. Perhaps the best studied aspect of this ambassadorship is how it functions to bring the quality of work experience into the home as major force shaping fundamental aspects of family life. For example, Kohn (1969) has studied how the routinization of father's work influences the life of the whole family. Consider a father whose job is heavily supervised and offers few surprises, much routine, and little self-direction. This quality of work has a pervasive influence on the attitudes and experience of workers. Father brings these attitudes home; they serve as a core of the childrearing attitudes and practices of both parents. Indeed, the experience of father reinforces a shared experience of the couple that virtually all of social life is a panoply of highly ordered sequences over which they have little control or discretion. Thus, they build into their childrearing a heavy emphasis on conformity: a child is to behave according to clear-cut external standards and is punished if he is not. Father, as an individual ambassador, has forged an important connection between his place of employment and his family.[1]

The individual as covert or implicit ambassador. When an individual member serves as an "accredited" ambassador, his ambassadorial functions themselves may be wholly or in part implicit. This is probably the case in the example just cited. The fact of father occupying an explicit role, the-one-who-works, is clear enough. The fact that this role serves to link his family to the quality of his work is much less clear. Nonetheless, most members are aware, and would endorse, father's role as the linking individual, even though none of the members may be aware of the full ramifications of this link. In contrast to this relatively explicit and accredited role, families use more covert mechanisms to assign to individuals a linking function.

Often families are intensely curious about certain aspects of the world around them but wish to conceal their curiosity because they feel it is embarrassing or shameful.[2] One member of the family, often an adolescent, is selected — perhaps manipulated is a better term — to serve an exploratory function for the family. For example, a teenager's accounts of her sexual exploits may provide a family with dramatic and titillating details about local adolescent culture. The teenager is serving as a significant link between the family and a segment of the neighborhood. However, this role is concealed. First, the information the teenager brings home finds its way into the family circuitously. Perhaps a younger brother is told first. He then lets fall a few significant tidbits in a discussion with his mother who then, behind closed doors, discusses it with father. No one is sure who knows what, but everyone has a sense that word has gotten around. A second way this role is concealed is that the linking individual — or at least part of his behavior — is officially disowned by the family. In extreme cases, the individual may be called delinquent or neurotic or impulsive by the family and referred for "treatment." In less severe cases, mild derogations referring to "adolescents" or "kids" might be used. Despite its importance, the linking role is concealed; in all its respects it remains covert.

Another form of covert linking is manifest when a member takes a more protective gate-keeping role. In seriously pathological families one individual may be covertly assigned the task of filtering all incoming information. Recall the Brady family in Chapter 1: the mother answered all phone calls and conducted all dealings with neighbors. She was the only one to read the newspaper and provided digested summaries to the rest of the family.

Direct family contact. There are occasional instances where some or all of the family makes clear and direct contact with a significant segment of the social community. In the next chapter we will summarize some research of our own on a very specialized form of this mode of contact: that between the family of a troubled adolescent and a psychiatric inpatient service. In more everyday life, various neighborhood associations such as PTAs, churches, and recreation groups bring several members of the family into transactions with the same group at the same time.

The family as a component or unit. In a few cases the larger social unit is, in effect, composed of families. The family does more than interact with the larger environment; it is itself a fundamental component of that environment. This is true in some but not all extended families. Some businesses are constructed in this way; typically, these consist of two or more nuclear families who jointly own and operate the business. Some circuses are a particularly interesting example of a type of business which incorporates whole families but which is not owned by the family. Some of the radical social experiments and utopias of ninteenth-century America were built by bringing together a number of separate family units (the more long-lived of these usually were successful in breaking down family boundaries in favor of increasing the allegiance of each member to the community as a whole). In our own research we have constructed social units of this kind: we have assembled and studied multiple family groups over many months.

ARCHITECTURAL ASPECTS OF FAMILY-ENVIRONMENT TIES

Whether ties are established by collective action or through the offices of an ambassador, the family's ties to a particular segment of its community take on a recognizable and stable form. A hint of the different forms that may exist was suggested by our brief laboratory observations. High configuration families seem engrossed in their work with our laboratory materials; low configuration families seemed withdrawn and confused. When we consider families in more long-term associations with their social environment and in a broader range of settings, we can define at least three aspects of the architecture of those relationships.

The first aspect is the conspicuousness or centrality of the family within the large social unit. We can refer to this by a familiar term, *status.* Status represents a special concatenation of the influence and prestige of the entire family unit. Within kindreds a particular member is often viewed as the family sage or patriarch or as the one wealthy enough to get the others through times of crisis. Often although not invariably, this special status is shared by the esteemed member's nuclear family. For a family's transactions with its community, Barber (1961) has delineated the concept of family status. Communities evaluate families in at least three ways. First, by using prevailing standards, the community judges families according to whether their internal relationships are in some sense good, laudable, and worthy of emulation. Is the marriage harmonious? Do the parents take adequate responsibility for the care of their children? Second, families are accorded status by their contribution to the community itself, and third, by their heritage: admired families come from admired lineages. As we will outline in the next chapter, families also differ greatly in their status within formal organizations; some families are influential, can command many of an organization's resources (for example, time and space), and are well known by everyone. In contrast, other families are peripheral and unknown. It is important to emphasize that status is the combined result of the family's skills im making itself well known to others and indispensable to the organization. It also depends on the attention and respect accorded to the family by the larger social unit. These two components of status may not always be highly correlated.

A second architectural aspect is the openness of the family's boundaries to people and experiences in its social environment. By *openness* we mean the relative freedom of people and experiences to enter the family and, in some sense, transform it. For example, families differ in the extent to which nonmembers are readily welcomed and can form, very quickly, various kinds of ties with one or more members of the family group. These families may treat information as they treat people. Information is readily brought into the family and can be used by the family group to enlarge its shared understanding of the surrounding social world. In contrast, other families have great difficulty admitting strangers, who are often rebuffed and made to feel like outsiders. Moreover, these families may not allow easy inflow (or outflow) of information. Tightly bounded families are not necessarily impervious to information from without; indeed, some such families may be vigilant and sensitive to any cues that the world around them is becoming dangerous. However, the information does not enter into the family as a basis for further exploration, nor does it enlarge the family's understanding of its world. At best it is a danger signal or an unambiguous confirmation of a belief already held by the family. In many instances families with impenetrable barriers are preoccupied with themselves. This may be temporary, as is true in many family crises. For example, when someone in the family is severely ill the entire group may become preoccupied not only with the illness but with its impact on all of them. Self-preoccupation in families may be a more enduring feature. As we will indicate in the next chapter, it can arise from chronic conflict in the family or from the family's enduring fear of and estrangement from its social milieu. In Chapter 4 we suggested mechanisms responsible for family self-preoccupation in times of crisis.

A third architectural aspect of the family's link to its environment is its intensity or depth of its engagement. Following a long tradition of research in group psychotherapy we refer to this dimension as *cohesion,*[3] although other terms such as engagement and investment would do as well. Cohesion refers to the level of the family's investment in its ties. This may be indicated simply by the amount of time or activity the family devotes to its relationship with the larger social unit. It may be reflected in more experiential aspects such as the family's sense of urgency or commitment to these ties. Cohesion differs from status; the latter refers to the success or influence of the family which may accrue to it even if the family itself puts little effort into its ties with the community. For example, "old line" families in many communities have a great deal of local status although they themselves may invest little time and energy in their current relationships with it. Cohesion also differs from openness of boundary; the latter refers to the unhindered passage of people and information into and out of the family. It does not indicate how actively, even aggressively, the family pursues its relationships with people or its search for information in its social milieu.

THE MOTIVATIONAL BASES OF FAMILY-ENVIRONMENT TIES

Why does a family link up with a particular aspect of the social environment? In considering the possible reasons we draw on the work of Etzioni (1961).

At the crudest level some families maintain ties with a larger social environment because they are forced to do so. Etzioni calls these *coercive* links. A clear example is the link between slave families and their masters. However, subtler coercions may force a family to remain in one social setting rather than others. A variety of racial and ethnic prejudices in the wider environment force families into social and geographic ghettoes. Political control, often expressed through explicit or implicit governmental threats, forces families to live in certain locales and forge particular kinds of coercive ties with the social environment. Finally, economic forces can provide very restrictive constraints on geographic and social mobility. For example, mining families deeply in debt to community stores are locked into mining villages and mining life even though their collective urge to leave may be very strong.

Coercive ties imply that the family has virtually no room for bargaining or initiative. Another type of bond—Etzioni calls them *remunerative*—implies that the family has achieved a bargaining position. Families develop ties to a segment of the social environment because they are paid to do so. "Payment" should be construed quite broadly here. Financial remuneration is, of course, of fundamental importance. Families can organize many of their links with their environment around business or occupational dealings. For example, families of local shopkeepers and families of professionals with local practices can organize many of their links around a wish to favor or support the family trade. Remuneration may come in other than monetary forms. A family may move to a neighborhood because of its physical beauty, safety, or prestige. A father (in this case serving as his family's explicit ambassador) may belatedly join an alumni association to help his son gain entrance to his own alma mater.

Perhaps the most complex ties are those Etzioni calls *normative.* Here he refers to social links that are motivated by ideological or attitudinal commitment. A family may join a neighorhood association because it is committed to racial integration (or, for that matter, segregation). Two families may form a close tie with one another that is initially based on common attitudes toward occupational commitment, the role of women, and approaches to childrearing.

The motivational base of a family's link with its social environment may change. Coercive relationships may be subtly transformed into remunerative ones; remunerative ones may further develop into normative ties. Complex blends of two, or even three, may characterize the relationship of any one family and a segment of its social environment.

Perhaps more important, these three different types of relationship should not be conceptualized in narrow observational or behavioral terms. Assessing the motivational basis of a family's ties is not always straightforward. The family's own experience of the relationship is as important as the objective characteristics more easily noted by an outside observer. For example, the strong ties a family may develop with a local community may benefit the business the family runs there. Nonetheless, the family may experience a genuine commitment to the development of its community, a sense of engagement with the future of its community that overrides or transcends the financial gain its ties may bring. Thus, its ties are more genuinely normative, although they appear to be remunerative. Likewise, a family may appear to engage in social welfare activities of its church; the family's underlying experience, however, is that such participation will bring praise and status. To take another example, there were slave families in the American South who would be regarded by casual outside observers as fully coerced but who perpetuated among themselves the conviction that they would one day be free (Haley's *Roots* gives eloquent evidence of this).[4]

By the way of summary we can identify core experiences in each of the three kinds of relationships. At the core of coercive ties is the family's sense that it is a victim without the possibility of effective initiative. At the core of remuneration is the family's experience of itself as a quid pro quo bargainer. There is a sense of autonomy and separation from the social environment. At the core of a normative link is a sense of collaborative mutuality with the social environment and the fundamental transcendence of family boundaries, as the family — along with others — fully identifies itself with a common objective or ideal. Particularly instructive examples of transformations of this last kind are contained in the historical records of nineteenth-century American utopias.[5] The successful communities were those in which individual families could transcend their own remunerative investments in communal life for genuine normative union with others. The fundamental predicament of normative ties is the threat they pose to the continued bounded integrity of the family unit itself. Indeed, many of the nineteenth-century utopias went on to thoroughly eliminate any vestige of bounded family units.

The links we have been discussing tie the family to major components of its social world. These components have their own qualities and conceptions of social reality which can, under many circumstances, help to stabilize the family's own conceptions. In the next section we will begin our consideration of these components of the family's social world: how they are structured, how they vary, and, most important, how these variations matter for the family. Before doing so, however, it is important to specify that the nature of the links themselves have a reifying function. The quality of links the family establishes with its social world do themselves corroborate, in no small measure, the family's underlying conceptions of itself-in-the-world. In other words the family's own paradigm is stabilized through routinized contacts it — as a whole group or through the medium of its ambassadors—has with corresponding social units in its environment.

We will argue that there is not a precise parallel between the characteristics of the links themselves and the type of paradigm and ordinary construct—as defined by the three cardinal dimensions of each. The characteristics of the links interact with each other—as well as with the character of the larger social unit—to reify and stabilize family structures. In other words, we have to consider the combined effects of several different aspects of the link (its medium, its architecture, and its motivational base) as well as several different attributes of the large social unit to understand how both link and environment function to stabilize a family's paradigm.

Organizing Constructions in the Social Environment

The family's links to its social environment tie it to very specific kinds of social collectivities. As we have said, our initial interest is with kin, community, and organization—among which there is a great deal of difference. These differences, we propose, influence family paradigms in ways that are just as important as the differences in the links we have just described. In our analysis of how these differences influence the family we must begin with a focus on those differences which will have the biggest impact. For example, communities differ from one another along many dimensions. Some are relatively closed to strangers, others are open; some are dominated by outside forces (government or business), others are autonomous; some have families of different social classes and races, others are homogeneous. Which, if any, of these dimensions are most pertinent to family process and, more particularly, to the cycle hypothesis? This hypothesis states, in part, that a family's paradigm is important in initiating or maintaining a family's membership in a kindred, community, or organization of a particular type. The characteristics of this particular type of collectivity serve, in turn, to stabilize in the family's disposition both to construe the social world and to transact with it in particular ways. In order to pursue this part of the cycle hypothesis we need pertinent dimensions for characterizing the social collectivity.

Of the many ways to characterize a social collectivity, the one most pertinent to our concerns focuses on the collectivity's own conceptions of social reality. Kin, community, and organization—as we will show in more detail—all build up their own integrated conceptions of themselves in relationship to the world outside their boundaries. It is these socially wrought conceptions that serve not only as starting points for our analysis but as fundamental organizers of experience and behavior within the collectivity;

they also organize its transactions with its own social environment (for example, kin with strangers, communities with other communities, and organizations with their clientele). To anticipate, we draw on Nagy's concept (1973) of the social dynamics of kinship groups to propose that they are dominated by a shared conception of justice and loyalty which we will call the *kinship code*. The code specifies what family members can expect of one another as a result of blood or marriage ties alone. The salient variations between kindreds, relevant to our model, can then be understood as arising from variations in the loyalty between members prescribed by this underlying code. In an analogous way, a community is organized by a shared conception of its layout, resources, critical distances between components, and boundaries. We follow Suttles's usage (1972) in proposing that communities are organized in part by a shared, socially constructed *community map*. The community map is a spatially oriented conception of the community's social imperatives, with several fundamental properties of the community highlighted: (1) its boundaries and embeddedness in a larger social world; (2) its resources and their locations; (3) critical distances between people and things and (4) permissible avenues for movement and commerce. Finally, we draw on the theoretical work of David Silverman (1970) to propose that structure and process in formal organizations are shaped by an *organizational objective*. This is an amalgam of the practical requirements of the organization—chiefly its need to provide goods or services to the larger social community—and the personal needs of its ruling or controlling elite (in some highly democratic organizations the "elite" may include everyone in the organization). The organizational objective is a socially constructed set of convictions concerning how to judge the quality of the product and what organizational structure and process are most effective in producing a high quality product.

The concepts of kinship code, community map, and organizational objective are subtle and complex. Our aim in this chapter is therefore restricted to providing brief sketches of these central concepts in the cycle hypothesis. The sketches are intended to convey, in a general sense, our approach to specifying crucial differences in the social environments in which families live.

KINSHIP CODE

Perhaps the most immediate, influential, and enduring social environment for most nuclear families is each family's own extended family or kindred. As we will detail in the next chapter it is not a simple matter to identify, for any nuclear family, exactly which individuals to include in its kindred. It is possible to approach the problem form a simple demographic position and identify all "first-degree relatives," or "all living first-degree relatives of husband and wife." An approach of this kind is of limited value for our own analysis. Our primary interest is in a kindred family with a rich and significant influence on our nuclear family. Some living first-degree relatives may have no impact on a nuclear family even if they live in the same city. In contrast, more geographically remote relatives living thousands of miles away may have much more impact on their lives, in many cases even if the relatives have long been dead. It is this "effective kindred" that probably plays the most crucial role in the cycle hypothesis. Chapter 8 details one approach to identifying and studying kindreds of this kind. To anticipate that section briefly, we asked family members to identify for us which members of their family were important to them. All the members in some families gave us nearly identical lists; members in other families gave almost entirely different lists, which shows that the "effective kindred" may be different for different members of the same family. This approach probably falls short of fully identifying the effective kindred. Some relatives may have a major impact on members of our target nuclear family, an impact which the members cannot or will not identify. For example, an uncle may have committed suicide. Although this act had an enduring effect on the family, it has also produced so much shame and guilt that the act may be repressed and the uncle momentarily forgotten (or, more accurately, repressed) when the family lists its relatives. Or, to cite another example, a daughter in an orthodox Jewish family who married a Gentile may not be listed because of the entire family's highly coordinated commitment to regard her not only as dead but as having never existed.

For most families we can identify an extended family, or perhaps several extended families, which it has identified as being in some way important to it. We can presume that this subjective sense of importance of just these relatives is accompanied by some sort of link with those individuals, a link whose properties can be described from the three vantage points of medium, architecture, and motivation we described in the previous section. Our task now is to sketch out concepts which permit us to understand and specify how kindred groupings, identified in this way, can differ from one another, and how such differences matter for the nuclear family which is tied or linked to them.

The concepts of Nagy (1973) give us a start by directing our attention to fundamental properties of the relationship between members of the same kindred. We propose that the differences between kindreds, most salient to the cycle hypothesis, is the nature of the sense of loyalty each member feels toward others in the kindred. Sense of loyalty functions as a code which governs each member's sense of what he owes his family and what obligations they have to him. While the loyalty code may be interpreted and enacted somewhat differently by different family members, depending on their personality and role within the kindred, the loyalty code is the property of the kindred itself and has a central role in regulating the behavior of one member to another. Nagy's fundamental point, as we see it, is that this code is hidden and often inaccessible both to casual observers of the extended family and to the members themselves. Nonetheless, the strength and endurance of the code can be inferred from closely observing the bonds that develop between members of the same family as well as the guilt, and defenses against guilt, that are stimulated by these relationships.

These processes are well illustrated in a family of Belgian origin. The history of the family, which is summarized for this century in Table 7.2, extends back several centuries to a time when the family played a central role in the commercial life of a large Belgian city. At the turn of this century there were two parents, a son, and three daughters. The father owned a small business which was never very successful. The family lived in an old and elegant house which had been handed down in the family for many generations. It was a constant reminder of the family heritage to which the father felt he could never measure up. The mother had been attracted to the father, when they were young, by the glamour and daring of his wildly optimistic schemes for making great commercial ventures and recapturing for the family name the prestige and power it had once held. She herself was raised in a poor, working-class family which had little hope for the future and no fond memories of the past.

Early in their marriage it became clear to the couple that father could never mount the commercial successes they both had dreamed of. Although bright and imaginative, he could not confront his competitors at crucial moments. He backed down or avoided conflict and thus lost opportunity after opportunity to establish his business ventures. The mother felt intense disappointment as well as guilt at having, in some way, abandoned her own lackluster family. She could sense that her marriage, and the fantasies surrounding it, were an oblique criticism of her own parents. Indeed, she remained chronically estranged from her parents, seeing them only once or twice a year until their death. She buried her disappointment in a concentrated effort to keep her family going on a very tight budget. She cleaned, baked, scrubbed, and mended

TABLE 7.2   FOUR GENERATIONS OF A BELGIAN FAMILY

Time period	Family members and their characteristics
18th and early 19th	The original family heroes: great commercial adventurers who accumulated conspicuous fortunes in manufacturing and international trade.
1st generation	*Father.* Early showed considerable musical talent. Wooed his wife with extravagant plans for commercial success. His small business faltered through five decades.
	Mother. Left a lackluster working-class family for her husband; was filled with dreams of excitement and wealth. When her husband's business faltered, dedicated herself to lifelong household drudgery. Three daughters, one son (below).
2nd generation	*Oldest daughter.* Married at the outbreak of World War II and cared diligently for her ill and dying parents. No children.
	Younger daughters. Never married. Finally left home after World War II.
	Son. Brilliant and a great academic success, he married an American and moved to New York City just before the outbreak of World War II. Three daughters (below).
3rd generation	*Oldest granddaughter.* Remained in New York City; married the son of a Belgian family. No children.
	Middle granddaughter. Remained in New York City, had three unhappy marriages, and lived many adult years with her parents.
	Youngest granddaughter. Married the son of a North African family to help him start a highly successful women's wear wholesale business in Nevada. Most active in maintaining ties with her three Belgian aunts. Three daughters (below).
4th generation	*Three great-granddaughters.* Now teenagers, they are very much engaged in their Belgian past through frequent trips and stories written by their grandfather.

tirelessly and meticulously year after year. She derived, perhaps, some sense of absolution in her endless chores.

The four children came quickly — in less than five years. At first there were three daughters and then — at long last, both parents thought—a son. From their earliest years all the daughters were warm and loving but not outstanding in any way. The son, however, was clearly distinguished. He taught himself to read at the age of three, to add, subtract, and multiply when he was four. He entered school at five and in a few years his extraordinary achievements became known not only to his school but to the whole town as well through a series of prizes, commendations, and small scholarships. His father began to see in his son the hope of restoring the family name, which he had, with a sense of bitter failure, recognized he could not himself reestablish. Mother saw in her son a vindication, at last, for the apostasy of leaving her own family. Thus, the treasured son was carefully protected from the drudgery and anxiety of a large household constantly short of money. He was free to study while mother and sisters laundered, scrubbed, and cooked.

As the mid-1930s approached the son was admitted with great fanfare to the outstanding university in the country. His immediate success continued to buoy his parents' spirits even as the clouds of war began to darken over western Europe. In the early spring of 1939 the son announced to his family that he had fallen in love with an American woman studying at his university. In a few weeks they were married and left for America, not to return to Belgium for eight years. The son became an American citizen and spent the rest of his life living in a large brownstone house in Manhattan. Just a few weeks before Hitler pushed across the Polish border, the eldest of the three daughters announced that she too had fallen in love. There was a second wedding and the new couple purchased a house in a town thirty miles away from the parents. A short time later the Nazis began their five years of occupation.

The Belgian wing of the family, now in two households, endured the ravages of war, although both parents, in their late sixties, became frail from the poor diet of wartime living. At the conclusion of the war, the two daughters remaining at home secured full-time work and recognized that their frail parents could no longer maintain the big family home. It was sold to an American relief agency on the condition that it be maintained, without major change, as a historical landmark. The parents went to live with their married daughter, whose life for the next decade was organized around caring first for her father as his health continued to deteriorate and then for her mother, who died three years later.

The son and his American wife meanwhile had three daughters—we will call them granddaughters to locate them in the proper generation—during the war. It was not until 1947, when the youngest American child was five and the oldest was eight that the five journeyed back to a Belgium still dark, cold, and hungry after the ravages of war. The three American grandchildren, who had heard endless stories about their Belgian relatives, developed an intense love for their father's family, particularly his sisters. This love was to take several different forms during the next generation. The youngest granddaughter, like her father, was clearly intellectually gifted from her earliest years. She duplicated his academic achievements and, like him, married while still a student. Also, like her father, she married an outsider, a dashing and dark-skinned son of North African parents whose grandparents had been deeply religious Moslems. They moved to Nevada where the husband established the region's most successful wholesale dress company. The other two granddaughters also graduated from college—but without distinction—and continued to live close to their parents in New York City. One daughter had a happy marriage to the son of a Belgian family who had come to New York on the same boat as her father had in 1939. The second American granddaughter went through a series of three brief and tormented marriages and spent many of her adult years living with her parents.

What interests us most here is the strikingly different relationships between the three American granddaughters and their Belgian aunts. The eldest two continued to feel great love for their Belgian aunts but rarely wrote or saw them, though the aunts all lived well into their eighties. The youngest daughter, although living a much greater distance away, made strenuous efforts to keep the relationship with her aunts alive. She and her husband, with their own three children, traveled to Europe often. Invariably the trips were organized to spend many days with the Belgian aunts. Quite often the family went from Nevada to California and then over the North Pole to Brussels. The three Nevada great-granddaughters wrote and performed a little musical about their trips. The final song, "Over the Pole to See Our Aunts," was learned by everyone in the family on both sides of the Atlantic (although it was never once sung in the home of the two New York granddaughters).

This four-generation family history offers striking evidence of a family whose relationships were shaped by a strong, although partially hidden, loyalty code. In the first generation the father's adolescent fantasies, the style of his courtships, and his first ventures as a young adult were shaped by a strong sense of loyalty to his past. His own father had also felt, and transmitted to his son, a deep sense of guilt over his failures as a businessman in a family made famous by its commercial success. The father—in the first generation of our history—had been a fine violinist and, had he been free of this pervasive sense of responsibility to his family, he might never have ventured into business at all. Mother also buried her sense of having violated a code of loyalty to her own lackluster family by subjecting herself to a lifetime of self-punishing housework. Thus, for the children—the talented son and the three daughters—there was a rich heritage of both obligation and guilt. The one daughter in the second generation who left home for marriage made up for this mild apostasy by caring single-handedly for her dying parents. Indeed, her two sisters felt forever indebted to her, and when, years later, her husband became chronically ill and died, they took endless care of her. The talented son did not leave his family behind in wartime Europe without an enormous sense of obligation (his sense of obligation had already grown through the privileged position he occupied in his family while he was a child). He himself never directly paid back to his family—particularly his sisters—what he felt he owed them. Unaware of his own motives, he squared accounts by being less in his profession than his brilliant academic achievement in school indicated he might be. Further, he had many inhibitions which bordered on phobias, the most notable of which was great anxiety about crossing bridges. His sense of great obligation to his own family was clearly passed on to his own daughters and granddaughters. His two oldest daughters remained geographically and emotionally close to him for the rest of his life; their sense of obligation was discharged in this way. The youngest daughter, who made a more complete break with him, was the one who resumed the Belgian connection through her own and her husband's activity and through her children.

In this kindred, marriages are particularly helpful in illuminating the loyalty code, particularly true when the marriage provides an opportunity to build a new set of successes and traditions rather than maintain the old lineage. The mother—in our first generation—clearly was separating herself from her own family through marriage. The eldest daughter in the second generation was not so much establishing a new life with her husband as she was leaving the anxiety and drudgery to her mother and two sisters and, in that sense, abandoning them. In the third generation the youngest American granddaughter seemed clearly to be breaking away from the family through her marriage to a cultural outsider and her move two thousand miles away from her parents. (It stood in sharp contrast to her older sister, who married the son of a Belgian and remained geographically close to her father.) Thus, all three marriages were a form of apostasy or abandonment and incurred an obligation with each of the three women met in their own way: mother through self-punishment, the oldest daughter through caring single-handedly for her ailing parents, and the youngest

American granddaughter by being the one child in her generation to maintain active contact with the Belgian wing of the family and also, importantly, by passing down the adoration of the Belgian lineage to her children.

We propose that the loyalty code is a good conceptual starting point for examining how extended families differ. In other words, we can develop dimensions along which such codes vary. These dimensions can be used to characterize the quality of relationships in any particular extended family, which in turn will permit an empirical study of the portion of the cycle hypothesis that posits a reciprocal relationship between the paradigm of the nuclear family and the loyalty code of the kinship groups to which it is linked. From our own data it seems reasonable to say that many nuclear families will be linked to several different kindreds, although one may be most important. It is possible to imagine competing influences from kindreds of different types, that is, kindreds structured by different loyalty codes.

Our history of the Belgian family — and particularly its loyalty code — suggests three interesting dimensions which may be pertinent for comparing kindreds and their impact on family paradigms. The first dimension is *intensity*. Clearly, the sense of loyalty in our Belgian family remains strong and undiluted over many generations. All members of the family do not necessarily act in a loyal way. Rather, everyone feels a strong sense of loyalty; for many this feeling may be mostly unconscious. It may engender a great deal of guilt; a family member may deal with this guilt by distancing himself from others in his family or by personal inhibitions and displacements. However, in contrast, there are kindreds much more loosely bound. In these kindreds, distant and tenuous ties between members are a straightforward expression of the absence of any experienced loyalty, rather than a defensive distancing.

A second dimension distinguishing different loyalty codes concerns the *character of action which can satisfy the obligation* incurred by the code (whether the obligations are intense or only moderate). The original heroes of this family — great commercial adventurers in the eighteenth and early nineteenth century — achieved great success for themselves, and prestige for their families, by conquering the world in which they lived. Our history began with the Belgian father's futile attempts to pay off some strong emotional debt to his forebears through achieving comparable success and mastery in his own community. The academic achievements of his own ultimately served, in part, this function. This, then, was a family that could glory in the external achievements of its members; loyalty accounts could be balanced, in part, through achievement of this kind. In other families there is no shared glorying in outside achievement. Indeed, in extreme cases, if a member seriously invests in a life outside the family, his investment is experienced as a treasonous act. In a family of this kind, accounts and obligations are met through direct emotional investment of members in one another.

A final dimension is suggested by the conspicuous *historical orientation* of our Belgian family. Everyone in the family had some knowledge and a great deal of pride in the great commercial heroes of the family's past. It was a tragedy for everyone when the ancestral family home was sold. Indeed, the American son wrote stories for the Nevada great-grandchildren about the "Great House" and all the events that had happened there through the centuries. The stories were a mixture of fact and fantasy, but they transmitted to the fourth generation, the Nevada great-grandchildren, a vivid image of the family's past. To be sure, this history took on different meanings as time passed. For the original parents and children, living their whole lives on meager resources, it was a comfort and support. It helped them feel a release and distance from their daily pressures. For the American son, this image of the past tied him to his Belgian family whom he had so ambivalently left. Amid the transient, superficial, and amoral community of a mid-size Nevada city, the American son's daughter found a sense of rootedness in her Belgian forebears. This historical sense in an extended kindred comes, of course, very close to the sense of past in nuclear families whose paradigm reflects a rich sense of its own past. Indeed, it is probably almost invariably the case that a nuclear family draws on the historical traditions of its kindred to develop its own sense of its historical past. However, there are many kindreds without a sense of a long and vital past. Thus, a dimension of historical past orientation may be useful in clarifying significant differences in loyalty codes. Some codes will be rooted and indeed legitimized by a rich sense of the family's past (which, as in any historical reconstruction, will be an amalgam of accurate information and contemporary interpretation or distortion). Other codes will have no such roots.

COMMUNITY MAP

Communities are a collectivity of a very different quality than kindreds, although in the extreme some communities may function like kindreds and vice versa. Life in a community is governed not by a sense of loyalty but rather by the details of its geography, its boundaries, who lives in the community and how close they live to one another, how the community's space is marked out, and how interaction patterns between individuals are regulated and coordinated. These last, following Kantor and Lehr (1975), could be called interpersonal "traffic patterns." Indeed, just as an ethical and legal metaphor (the "code") seemed appropriate to describe essential attributes of kindreds, so a spatial metaphor seems most salient for communities. Drawing on Suttles's work (1972), we employ the concept of community map to denote a central social organizer of community life. Our goal here is the same as that already pursued for kindreds and to be pursued for organizations: to delineate a central social organizer in communities in a way that yields several dimensions by which such collectivities can be compared. This, in turn, will serve our exploration of that part of the cycle hypothesis which specifies a reciprocal relationship between family and community.

The term *map* can be deceiving unless its metaphorical and allusory aspects are grasped. By map we refer to a shared experience, by members of a community, of the fundamental layout of the community. We propose that although the map is experienced in primarily spatial terms, it represents important experiences in the history of the community as well as views people have about one another.

We can illustrate the evolution and character of a community map with another case illustration. Consider the community of Mariner's Grove. It is a subdivision located in a suburb of a seaside city, at least ten miles from the shore itself. It was built ten years ago by a developer as the last and most elegant of four adjoining middle-class subdivisions of individual homes. The other three were Hickory Hill, Wingate Village, and Willow Farms. Figure 7.2 is a schematic map of all four. Mariner's Grove's elevated position among these four communities comes from four sources. First, it had been built around several very large and expensive older houses which became incorporated into the Mariner's Grove community. One of these was the former home of a governor and is designated as a state historical landmark. The other three subdivisions consist entirely of houses constructed by developers within the last fifteen years. Second, the newer houses built by the developer are larger than those in the other three communities and are located on bigger lots. Third, Mariner's Grove contains the high school which serves all four communities. Fourth, it is closer to the major shopping areas.

The central spatial feature of the community map is Wingate Creek, which forms a natural boundary separating Mariner's Grove from the other three communities. It also represents a threat,

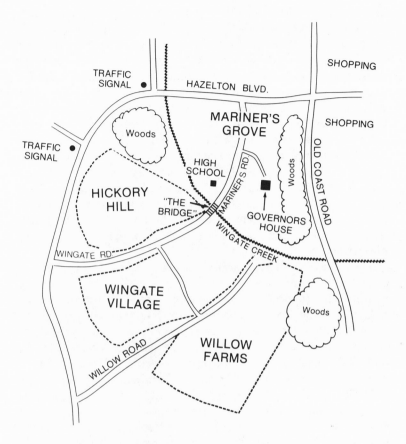

Figure 7.2. *Mariner's Grove*

however. From the first years of these four communities, many of the residents of Hickory Hill, Wingate Village, and Willow Farms had petitioned the suburban government to build a vehicular bridge across Wingate Creek. (A narrow footbridge had crossed the creek for many years.) The usual appeal from these communities emphasized increasing their access to the high school, which served them as well as Mariner's Grove. The residents of Mariner's Grove viewed these appeals quite cynically. They argued that parents of the other three communities seldom needed their cars to get to the high school since it was within walking distance of all three. They felt that the other three communities wanted easier access to shopping. The residents of Mariner's Grove feared that if a vehicular bridge was constructed a great deal of traffic would flow through their community as a short cut around the two traffic signals on

Hazelton Boulevard (see Figure 7.2). Indeed, several members of the Mariner's Grove Citizen's Association argued that a through street, which would be created by joining Mariner's Road and Wingate Road, would create "security problems." Housebreakers in Mariner's Grove, they argued, could escape in either direction (north or south) rather than being cornered in a community with only one exit. As time went by and the appeals of the three other communities became more strident, many residents of Mariner's Grove felt that their somewhat more privileged status was the real target of the bridge appeals. They felt the other three communities purposely wanted to deface their community with through traffic and all the noise and risk that went with it. For their part, residents of the other three communities came to look on Mariner's Grove as a community of self-indulgent idle rich (although the average family income in all four communities was quite high, with no major differences among the four).

The struggle between Mariner's Grove and its three neighboring communities continued for several years until, after a series of hearings, the suburban government ordered the construction of a bridge. At that point the community map of Mariner's Grove became fully differentiated. It centered on the bridge and its relationship to their community, Mariner's Road, Hazelton Boulevard, and Old Coast Road. The conspicuousness of the bridge in everyone's spatial representation of their neighborhood clearly reflected the long fight with the neighboring communities, a sense of betrayal and mistrust of the suburban government, an increasing concern that the community would deteriorate further, and a redoubled effort to defend the community against further encroachment. To be sure, the subjectively and socially constructed map was similar in form to one that any cartographer would produce. But special emphasis was given to a strongly felt symbol of the community—its boundaries and "the bridge." The community vowed that a fundamental breach of this kind would never occur again.

Our example of Mariner's Grove, because it is an extreme case, can be used to suggest some of the ways in which such a map might vary and some of the dimensions relevant for distinguishing among communities. First, the community—despite its commitment to battle the bridge—was what Janowitz (1952) has called a community of "limited liability." None of its residents worked in the community, many of the wealthier families sent their children away to private schools, and all the families could move without great hardship to another community if they chose. Despite the passion of the fight against the bridge, the fight—for many—boiled down to a defense of property values, not a struggle to preserve a way of life. In other communities people are more rooted in one specific place: their families have lived there for generations, they live and work in one place, their resources are too limited to move. Second, the community felt embattled: its major emphasis was on its perimeters, not its internal structure. This could be reflected on the agendas of its citizen association: every meeting was almost exclusively devoted to the bridge, its aftermath, and other possible encroachments.[6] Less embattled communities focus more on the internal structure of the community: relationships between people, groups, the quality of public institutions, recreational activities, social support. Third, Mariner's Grove had a limited and to some extent pasteboard history. It was created by a single, profit-making developer. Its name was a contrivance to attach prestige to the community (it implied, "Here will live those wealthy enough to own a boat"). The major event in its very short history was an attack, unsuccessfully defended against. In conspicuous contrast are communities with a richer and longer history. Finally, the community map is rich with symbolic representation of what Warren (1972) calls "verticality." The community, for all its wealth and influence, felt under the control of—even torn apart by—a powerful suburban government it could not control. Other communities feel in greater concert with government agencies or corporations and still feel independent of higher authorities and more free to run their own affairs ("horizontal relationships," in Warren's terms).

Thus, the map concept suggests at least four dimensions by which communities might be distinguished: limited versus extended liability; embattled versus secure; rooted in history versus new and without such roots; and vertical versus horizontal. At the end of this chapter we provide a brief analysis of several prominent families in Philadelphia and illustrate how several of these community dimensions intertwine with other aspects of the families' social environment to reinforce the family's paradigm.

THE ORGANIZATIONAL OBJECTIVE

Formal organizations—such as factories, professional groups, schools, voluntary associations, and hospitals—are the third component of the family's environment included in our cycle hypothesis. We are coming to recognize that families contribute, directly and indirectly, to the shaping of these organizations. Our cycle hypothesis argues that families whose lives are structured by paradigms of a particular kind select organizations of a particular character. The cycle hypothesis continues with the additional hypothesis that this specific or particular engagement serves, in a reciprocal way, to reinforce or stabilize the family's paradigm. At the end of this chapter we will illustrate this point by describing the important reciprocal relationship between certain distinguished Philadelphia families and the major social clubs of the city in which they are central and prestigious members. In the next chapter we describe a study of the organizational objectives of psychiatric hospitals. At that point we provide a more detailed account of our concept of organizational objectives and a more thorough account of the possible relationships between organizational objective and family paradigm. Indeed, taking this section of the book as a whole, the concept of organizational objective is more fully worked out and illustrated than are the concepts of kinship code and community map. Thus, this section can be briefer than the preceding ones. At this point in our argument, a sketch of the concept of organizational objective will be helpful in clarifying our general approach to characterizing the family's social environment and permits, in the next section, a discussion of the similarities between paradigm, on the one hand, and code, map, and objective, on the other.

In contrast to kindreds and communities, organizations ordinarily have a reasonably clear and relatively delimited *task*. In some organizations, such as automobile factories and coal mines, the task is very clear and straightforward. In others, the task may be less clear and more subject to dispute and interpretation. For example, the tasks of police departments, schools, and welfare agencies are far from clear. Some police departments, for example, focus their efforts on catching criminals, whereas others take on a variety of community assistance projects. Some schools focus narrowly on instructing students in basic skills; others regard their task as supporting broad areas of social and intellectual development in their pupils. Clearly, differences in perceived tasks—between one police department and another or one school and another—reflect, to some degree, differences in the values and experience of the people who run them. The concept of organizational objective argues that in almost any organization, the perceived task or goal of the organization is shaped by the values, needs, and experiences of its members. Most crucial, the organizational objective represents an *objectification* of these needs and values; objectification converts a personal preference into a mission or task which is thought to be objectively required by the situation.[7] Those with the greatest influence on shaping the organizational objective, of course, are the members of the elite who run the organization. Indeed (as we will illustrate in this and the next chapter), larger organizations often have competing subgroups with different conceptions of the task of the organization.

The term *organizational objective*[8] emphasizes, then, that an organization's definition of its own task reflects the ruling elite's conception of the directions and activities the organization should pursue. Although perhaps more difficult to recognize, these are social constructions — objectified through patterns of social behavior — that are similar in many respects to paradigms, codes, and maps. Let us cite a very simple example. Consider a law firm dedicated to representing clients in civil rights cases (although forced, like most such firms, to take some commercially oriented cases "to make a living"). The firm is run by three young partners whose passion for civil rights flourished in their college years. All three were disillusioned by their experience in law school. They recognized how much of their future profession was dominated by large corporations seeking to maximize their profits and avoid taxes. Determined nonetheless to meld their personal values and their new profession, the three founded their civil rights–oriented firm soon after passing their bar examination.

The firm quickly developed a city-wide reputation as clever and effective, and the case load of the three partners, and the three associates whom they hired in the firm's first year, swelled rapidly. The firm's income did not rise, however, and stresses began to arise. The three partners, along with two of the three associates, became increasingly convinced of the extraordinary and thoroughly objective need for civil rights representation in their city. They worked long hours and attempted to engage their staff — secretaries, clerks, and assistants — in a fever of morally committed action. The objective of the firm was experienced as a thoroughly rational response to a vividly perceived reality. The city was in desperate need of civil rights representation; the objective of the firm, then, was seen as the natural, logical, unquestionably required response to that need.

Not everyone in the firm saw it that way. One of the associates had a more jaundiced eye. He found company for his views in one clerk and two of the secretaries. They viewed the passions of the three partners (and the others in the firm who joined with them) at best as "adolescent and unrealistic" and at worst as efforts for publicity and to gather fame as "white knights." The dissidents resented the long hours and the frequent exhaustion of the payroll accounts. A more realistic and mature firm, the dissidents felt, would recognize the crucial role of corporate business and curry the favor necessary to obtain it.

In the next chapter empirical evidence suggests at least two specific dimensions by which the organizational objectives of psychiatric hospitals may be distinguished from one another (these dimensions might be quite applicable to other organizations as well). The first of these we call "belief in the moral order." Briefly, organizations who score high on this dimension emphasize the social or interpersonal aspects of the task they face. They believe that all members of the organization can make a fundamental contribution to the accomplishment of the task by virtue of their experience in relationships with others. Our civil rights–oriented law firm exemplified this to some extent. In part, the partners viewed their task as providing social equality, through the law, to disadvantaged people. This was seen as a mission, and it was thought that everyone in the firm had the capacity to perceive the central elements, the core injustice inherent in each client's position. At the same time, the firm was committed to achieving its ends strictly through the use of legal practice, which at times was highly technical and intricate. Thus, the best trained and most experienced lawyers had a special place in the firm—not just as the ruling elite but as a technical elite whose authority derived, in part, from their special command of the apersonal intricacies of legal practice. Thus, the firm's objective could be located as high on a second dimension (whose derivation is illustrated in the next chapter). We call this dimension "belief in the technical order" because organizations high on this dimension perceive their task to be substantially a technical one; thus, they accord a central role to the technicians among them, with other roles being clearly subordinate and supportive. As we will show, these two dimensions are orthogonal; thus, it is possible for an organization to be high on both, low on both, or high on one and low on the other.

Paradigm, Code, Map, and Objective: Central Correspondences

The cycle hypothesis was constructed to explain how the family paradigm remains stable over long periods of time and also what environmental changes may make the paradigm unsteady and the family vulnerable to crisis. The cycle hypothesis proposes that the nature of the environment itself plays a crucial role in both stabilization and destabilization of the paradigm. We have aimed at making the cycle hypothesis testable by specifying, in some detail, just what aspects of the environment are crucial for their impact on paradigm. The concepts of code, map, and objective were developed as epigrams or conceptual starting points for deriving specific dimensions; these dimensions, in turn, were conceptualized in ways that will help us measure crucial differences in the family environment. We have approached our analytic task by identifying for three types of environment—kin, community, and organization—a central social organizer which, like paradigm, represents a shared construction built up over time and which constitutes the core of the collectivity's conception of itself and its own social surround. From the perspective of theory construction, we believe the concept of paradigm in families is strengthened if we have shown that it has central and critical similarities to social organizers in other collectivities. The concept of paradigm takes on, thereby, a Janus-like strength: it looks "in" at the family by yielding a number of useful concepts for explaining patterns of interaction between its members and it looks "out" at the family's social environment and explains something of the reciprocal influence between that environment and the family. We can accomplish both a summary of this section of the chapter and a critical review of the central attributes of the paradigm concept by reviewing briefly the central correspondence between family paradigm and the codes, maps, and objectives that shape the family's world.

One central correspondence between our four social organizers is that they are all *objectified through social process.* They are constructed through a complex and intertwined sequence of shared behaviors and beliefs of most members of the collectivity (the exception being communities and organizations where only the ruling elite may truly believe in the immutable reality of the conception of the organization). The quality of objectivity of these constructions and the pervasiveness of the belief in them gives them great potency as organizers of norms, roles, interaction patterns, and problem definitions, and in the construction of evaluation criteria by which all action is judged and all disputes are adjudicated. We saw how the code in our Belgian family regulated behavior across four generations. Moreover, the regulated behavior itself became a reaffirmation of the code, strengthening the reality and objectivity with which it was experienced. Thus, the Nevada granddaughter, through fulfilling her obligation to her father by maintaining close ties with her Belgian aunts, made the heritage of the Belgian family a living experience for her own children. Indeed in the children's play, carried to its quintessence in the musical, we could see the social construction of a reality—in a new generation—carried out in microcosm. Our glimpses of Mariner's Grove and the civil rights law firm were more brief. Even here, however, a socially constructed conception of the objective need for action had a powerful influence on the behavior of individuals in the community and the law firm and regulated their dealings with outsiders.

A second similarity between code, map, and objective, on the one hand, and paradigm, on the other, is that all of these social constructions *epitomize the history of the collectivity they organize.* A family paradigm, it should be recalled, contains a significant residue of family history. The crisis to which it was initially a response is conserved in the fabric of the family's ritual life and its patterned use of time and space. The kinship code clearly epitomizes the history of the kindred in a different, though analogous, way. An idealized and highly selective version of the family's history was woven into our Belgian family's code during the first generation in our four-generation history. The central and idealized elements of this historical image remained through subsequent generations but became embroidered with new elements of history: the near-poverty of the first generation, the Great House, the terror and privation of World War II, and the trips over the pole. In Mariner's Grove, the community map was built around "the bridge," which came to be the central historical fact of community life. The organizational objective of the civil rights-oriented firm served also as a repository for the central cases — those won and those lost — in the firm's history. Indeed, the firm's image in the local legal world as well as its conception of itself were built around the crucial cases it had handled. The objective itself, in this firm and (we contend) in all organizations, determines what items are included on its ledger of productivity, and that ledger itself becomes a central element of the organizational objective. The ledger of productivity is the organization's own running account of its successful and unsuccessful efforts. As a ledger of productivity, the organization objective serves the same memorial function as paradigm, code, and map do.

Third, code, map, and objective — like paradigm — epitomize or *highlight particular social functions of the collectivities they organize.* The concept of paradigm emphasizes the intertwining of intimacy, dependency, and intricate coordination of lives that must go forward, on a daily basis, in a nuclear family. Insofar as the paradigm is an epigram both of the crisis which gave rise to it and the exemplary crisis construct which forms its nucleus (see Chapters 4 and 5), it expresses, simultaneously, the intense need of family members for one another and the delicate coordination which are required for the survival of an intimate group. Indeed, the concept of paradigm expresses a coordinate construction of reality that embraces not just narrow aspects of current social life but, as we have shown in Chapter 5, the broadest aspects of time and space. The intimate and detailed coordination of living required in nuclear families requires a consensus on the underlying character of the greatest possible range of the experienced world (it should be apparent, at this stage in our argument, that consensus does not refer to surface agreements on specific issues but to a more pervasive, ineffable consensus on the possibilities for agreement and disagreement).

As we go from paradigm to code to map to objective, the range and depth of the organizing social construction becomes narrower and shallower. In other words, the range of social and environmental events "explained" by the construct is reduced. This is because, in most cases, the kindred, community, and organization require far less intricate dovetailing and coordination of separate lives. Indeed, code, map, and objective highlight more specific functions of the collectivities they organize. For example, the kinship code highlights the lineage or inheritance aspects of extended families. This can be conceived quite literally in some societies where kinship codes overlap societal inheritance rules. In such societies, extended kinship networks are society's primary medium for transmitting property from one generation to the next. We argue that in contemporary society an analogous function is carried on by kindreds. Inheritance of wealth and property, to be sure, plays a less frequent and less explicit role in kinship ties. Nonetheless, kinship codes—by defining the obligations each generation has to the other—establish the type and intensity of continuity across generations. Although formal inheritance may not be a specific issue in many kindreds, these obligations still refer to specifiable resources: time, energy, levels of collaboration, and so on. For example, how much emotional and practical support can an aged uncle expect from his niece? How much intervention on his behalf can a grandson in search of a job expect from his grandfather?

Community maps draw our attention to a fundamental social objective of community structure: the coordination—between families and individuals—of daily routines as they are carried out in actual time, with finite resources, and (most important) in concrete and specific spatial locations. Families and communities both differ in the intricacy and complexity of the structure required to accomplish this form of coordination. Janowitz (1952), as we have noted earlier, has described some communities as "communities of limited liability"; this term emphasizes that, in some communities, individual members and families spend little time or effort. The community serves very few functions for its members. It may serve only as a bedroom. It may have no shopping facilities, libraries, or other services. As a consequence, families invest little of themselves in community life. Likewise, even in much more involving and well-developed communities there are families whose primary investment lies outside the community. The daily routines of these families are "cosmopolitan" in Merton's sense: they are dispersed over a very wide area, a broad range of communities and locales (see Merton, 1949). Cosmopolitan families may have little investment in any particular community; they do not need access to a detailed community map. However, in communities of greater "liability" and with locally oriented families, detailed maps are necessary social organizers of the daily routines of its component individuals, families, and establishments.

Finally, organizational objectives reflect the central role of productivity in organizations. They embrace two intertwined functions: the organization—as an entity—must produce a marketable service or set of goods, and individual workers must derive a satisfactory recompense for their involvement.

In sum, all four organizers focus on the construction of social reality but in apposition to different social functions: in families to intimacy, in kindreds to obligations across generations, in communities to spatial coordination, and in organizations to productivity.

The four types of social organizers we are considering also have in common their function to shape an *identity for the collectivity they organize*. Identity in a collectivity is the experience each member shares with the others of the character of their collectivity in contrast to others of the same type. The group's conception of itself is often complemented by the conception which nonmembers hold of it. Indeed, the matter of group identity is often a reciprocal process between the perceptions of insiders and of outsiders. Thus, families may identify themselves as close or splintered, competent or incompetent, in ways that are shaped by their own paradigms and reinforced by nonmembers' views of them. Likewise, kinship codes help to shape the conception a kindred has of itself: loyal or unfettered, successful or unsuccessful, historically rooted or without history. Finally, the organizational objective helps clarify for workers the kind of corporation in which they labor. As we will illustrate in the next chapter, for example, the organizational objective helps to shape a corporation's conception of itself as a technical machine where individuals are valued only for their purely technical contributions to the corporation's productivity or as an institution where human relations are valued and individual members are admired for a mixture of technical and personal attributes.

The capacity of social organizers to clarify differences between collectivities of the same type (for example, differences between one family and another or between one community and another) extends beyond its relationship to group identity. Indeed, as we have shown explicitly for family paradigms and have suggested for codes, maps, and objectives, the concept of a socially constructed organizer can be a useful point of departure for elaborating operationalized dimensions which can be used for fine-grained distinctions between collectivities as well as a basis for a comprehensive typology. In the preceding sections we suggested some of these dimensions.

DOES THE FAMILY REALLY CHOOSE ITS LINKS?

Our cycle hypothesis consists of six steps. For simplicity we arranged these neatly in a circle, which implies a very orderly sequence. In actuality, we expect these relationships are much less clear. In particular, we expect that during family-environment transactions families are initiating and shaping links and also, in subtle ways, choosing particular environments to which they become linked. At the same time those links and particular environments are influencing the family. Whether it is the family that has the major initiative, the environment, or both together, is — under ordinary circumstances — very difficult to discover. The issue is nonetheless important. Traditional sociological thought has accorded all the initiative to the social environment. The family has been considered a passive responder to its social milieu.[9]

What we will argue in this section is that in order to think clearly about the relative contributions of the family and of the environment to the family's position in the social world, we must conceive of natural or artificial (researcher designed and run) "experiments" in which it is possible to see more clearly the direction of influence: from family to environment, from environment to family, or in both directions simultaneously.

We can identify a great range of experiments of this kind in contemporary as well as historical contexts. The migration of families from one social setting to another is a common natural experiment that can provide us with clear insight into this issue. Particularly instructive and accessible are the great waves of migration from Europe to the United States during the last century. How were families structured, and how did they function, before they made the transatlantic crossing? What kinds of choices did they make after they arrived? The opportunities were great for choosing what kinds of links to establish in the New World, as well as what types of communities and organizations with which to be engaged. There was even an opportunity to fashion new links with kindred. To be sure, racial, religious, and economic forces put substantial constraints on these opportunities. Nonetheless, as a repeating natural experiment we can confidently expect to be richly informed by a closer study of migrating families.

The formation of a new community is also an interesting natural experiment. Consider again, for example, the utopian communities created in nineteenth-century America. A natural experiment of this kind has two phases. In the first phase, the early days, a small group of families bands together for religious and ideological reasons. New community structures are formed; the fundamental outline of a community map is drawn.[10] In this first phase of new community development we can observe how families position themselves relative to one another—that is, what kinds of links they form with one another. Whatever we can learn about these families before they joined the utopian community will help us understand the continuity between the preexisting family structure and the links they forge in the new community. We can then examine the role of the family's inherent structure in initiating and shaping the family's links with the community.

The second phase of this natural experiment is when the community is well established. What happens to a new family entering the community? Again, we can learn about the continuity between the family's past, before it entered the community, and its present. But now we can also observe a particularly important struggle. What happens if the family's fundamental view of itself and social reality clashes with the community's prevailing view? Nineteenth-century utopias are particularly interesting here because their values, concept of morality, and sense of social reality were so clear, so unanimously felt. Indeed, these concepts formed the undergirding principle around which community life was developed and maintained. Thus, we can—with greater confidence—make a judgment about the initial fit between the entering family and the existing community. In those cases where there is a misfit we can examine a community-family struggle of great importance. Can the press of community life—with its daily reminders of the community's underlying social conceptions—transform the family's own shared constructions of social reality?

We would hypothesize that the community cannot exert this force very effectively.[11] In fact, the family that is a clear misfit may have only two choices: to feel alienated and ultimately leave the community, or to subordinate itself to the community. Subordination, in this sense, is a process quite different from internal transformation. Subordination involves a surrender of two crucial aspects of family self-experience: its concept of its own history and its sense of bounded identity. If a misfit family subordinates itself to the larger community it will no longer feel itself to be an intact family. Each member will feel committed to the larger community but will have comparatively little loyalty to his family as a unit. Indeed, it would appear that the successful utopian communities recognized this process and abetted it in every way possible: their social planning was engineered to reduce people's loyalties to their families.[12]

A more artificial experiment will be described in the next chapter. For research purposes, we and our colleagues have formed a number of multiple family groups. Each group of six to fifteen families meets for several months on a weekly basis. Some social processes in the groups are analogous to those reported in natural communities. We have been able to learn about the families before they entered the group. In particular, we have had a chance to assess their problem-solving skills (and, presumably, their underlying constructs and paradigms) before their entry or at a very early phase of their work with the group. Insofar as the family's problem-solving style predicts its behavior in the multiple family group, we have another chance of looking at the family's role or its initiative in forging links within these artificial communities.

Another form of natural experiment gives us a chance to examine the role of the social environment in shaping family paradigm and process. We have argued in Chapter 3 that family crisis — however undesirable from a human point of view — does give us an excellent opportunity to examine two ways in which the social environment shapes families and their paradigms. First, it enables us to examine how the deterioration of family-environment bonds, or of the collectivities to which the family is linked, makes the family vulnerable to crisis. Second, it helps us examine the hypothesis that at a time of crisis and reorganization, the social environment has a critical role in fundamentally reshaping the family paradigm and those processes in family life which the paradigm organizes. For the latter case, family therapy is one of several possible observational settings which give us an excellent opportunity to understand the kinds of long-term changes and fundamental transformations the family can accomplish. Family therapists will argue, for example, that the kind of relationship they form with the family has, by itself, a healing or transforming effect. If this is true, then family crisis followed by family therapy is a splendid opportunity to observe the family's transformation of links initiated by a social collectivity (and its ambassador, the therapist) into permanent family structures.

Thus, we return to our initial question: does the family really choose its links and its collectivities? We now recognize that this is part of a broader question encompassed by the cycle hypothesis: the direction of influence between family and environment. In this section we have begun to specify some observational fields which can provide information — historical records and direct studies of migration, historical records of utopian communities, research experiments with multiple family groups, and careful studies of family crisis and family change in family therapy.

Family Paradigm, Links, and Environment:
A Concluding Example

The interplay among family paradigm, links, and types of environment is illustrated in Baltzell's study (1958) of "Philadelphia Gentlemen"—a select set of powerful, patrician families in Philadelphia. Baltzell carefully delineated the origins, development,and family-community relations of a selected group of old-line Philadelphia families. The city of Philadelphia has been at the center of politics and business since the earliest days of this country; in particular, it was the center of political thought and action during the revolution and became a national center for banking and commerce soon after the new American state was founded. At the time of the revolution, a number of families achieved distinction through the preeminent contribution of some of its most gifted men to American independence. As examples, consider the famous Wharton, Biddle, and Rush families. Among the Whartons, Thomas, Charles, and John were prominent Philadelphia merchants who protested the Stamp Act. Ten years later, Thomas Wharton took charge of the famous Philadelphia Committee of Correspondence, which organized Philadelphia's armed resistance to British authority, and during the war he occupied a position equivalent to governor of the state. Owen and Clement Biddle were also prominent merchants who opposed the Stamp Act, and Edward Biddle was a member of the Continental Congress at the time the Declaration of Independence was signed. Clement became a close friend of George Washington and was delegated to receive the swords of the Hessians whom Washington had defeated at Trenton after crossing the Delaware. In the Rush family, Benjamin achieved preeminence as a signer of the Declaration of Independence; later he was Washington's surgeon-general.

The deeds of these distinguished men have become woven into the history and self-consciousness of Philadelphia. Schoolchildren in Philadelphia today have some awareness of the central role of the Whartons, Biddles, and Rushes in their city's and their nation's history. Perhaps more vividly, the exploits of these men were woven into the history and experience of the three families themselves. The families achieved a distinction in historically conscious Philadelphia that directly paralleled—indeed, was sustained by—the extraordinary achievements of the family founders. Through a century and a half and four or five generations, these families have continued to produce men of great distinction. They also accumulated great wealth and—along with a very select set of other Philadelphia families—formed a prestigious and powerful upper class that has guided and shaped the city's history almost until the present day. In the early part of the nineteenth century Robert Wharton was elected mayor of Philadelphia fifteen times, and a half-century later Joseph Wharton founded the Bethlehem Iron Company and then the Wharton School at the University of Pennsylvania. In the twentieth century the Biddle and Rush families have continued to play dominant roles in the life of the city; for example, Benjamin Rush became the chairman of the board of the powerful and prestigious Insurance Company of North America.

The most intriguing aspect of Baltzell's study, and the one most germane to our perspective, is his analysis of the interplay between the character of the ties of these prominent families to the Philadelphia community and their conceptions of themselves. Just as at the time of the family founders, the central ties to the community are established through the gifted male members of the family. The women were traditionally less well educated and were relegated to managing the great houses and extraordinary social life of the prominent families. These ambassadorial ties, to use our term, of the prominent men had a clear architecture. The most conspicuous manifestation of these links was in the relationship between the men and the giant corporations they led. Not only did these men occupy the most central and prestigious positions in these corporations, but the corporations themselves had enormous impact on the growth of the city itself. Equally important was the carefully crafted and highly ritualized social life of the men and their families. Exclusive social clubs were central here. A particularly interesting example is the Fishing Company of the State in Schuylkill, founded in 1732, which was the oldest exclusive social club of its kind in the country. It was originally organized as a mock state; its members are still called "citizens" and its officers are the governor, the secretary of state, the sheriff, and the coroner. Its membership is limited to thirty. Now called the Fish House, it is, in effect, a cooking club where Philadelphia's most prestigious and influential men serve as chef's assistants. Of much more functional significance are the somewhat less exclusive but much more influential metropolitan clubs. In Philadelphia the most distinguished is the Philadelphia Club, whose first president was a Biddle (James, from 1845 to 1848). Indeed, the three lineages we have selected to examine have been prominent members since the club opened; in 1940 the membership roster listed thirty-five Biddles, twelve Whartons, and seven Rushes. While the old-line families constitute the backbone of the club and insure its continuity, the club admits a few members each year from other families because of their conspicuous success in business or law (rarely other professions). Baltzell argues that by this practice the club maintains control of critical events, appointments, and policies in Philadelphia's business world. The club provides a meeting ground for the men of lineage and the most talented and influential of the new arrivals on the Philadelphia business and professional scene. The balance of influence is always tilted toward the former. It is reasonable to argue that it is the central position of the old-line families in the restricted social clubs that repeatedly highlights, for each prominent family, the central importance of its lineage and serves to maintain its power in the community.

In our terms, the Whartons, Biddles, and Rushes are families with a keen sense that their primary resources derive from their own past: the powerful mixture of historical distinction (amplified manyfold by the special historical self-consciousness of the city in which they live) and accumulated wealth. Because the very kernels of the families' conception of their social environment lie within themselves, not the outer world, we would call these families "solipsistic" or "internal" (see Chapter 6). But these are also powerful, accomplished families who understand the underlying business and social structures of their city and know how to control these structures for their own ends; clearly they would be placed on the stable end of our coherence dimension. The solipsism and stable coherence of their organizing paradigms, as our terms express it, are maintained by the nature of their links to the social environment and the character of that social environment itself. Most conspicuous in Baltzell's analysis is the picture of ambassadorial links of great status and centrality. The families have been, for many generations, represented in the council of power by their most gifted men. These men stand not only at the center of the giant corporations they control but in the supra-corporate social organizations, particularly the highly influential metropolitan clubs. The history and social structure of these clubs confirm the special social meaning of the lineage itself and thus play a crucial role in transmitting the sense of historical destiny to the next generation of these families. In an important sense the families' ties to corporate directorships and their ties to the exclusive clubs provide complementary support to the families' conception of themselves in the world. The corporate directorships reaffirm the families' sense of power and control; the social clubs reinforce the importance of their historical roots.

8 | Exploring the Cycle Hypothesis

In the preceding chapter we stated the cycle hypothesis in its simplest terms. As we developed our argument, however, it became apparent that the hypothesis is not simple. The sequential relationships of the cycle are easy enough to describe—for example, the family's paradigm determines the types of environments it selects and the types of links the family fashions with those environments. However, our beginning analysis of "types of links" and "types of environments" shows that these components of the cycle hypothesis are not straightforward; instead, they require detailed specifications and a much finer-grained theoretical rendering. The same is true for the remaining steps on the cycle—the reciprocal effects of type of link and type of environment on the family. Although Chapter 7 gave this part of the cycle less explicit attention, further exploration of these steps in the cycle would undoubtedly reveal the need for a theoretical statement of equally fine and detailed structure. The more specific and detailed theoretical statements, generated by the cycle hypothesis, are intended to serve a specific function: they convert the generalities of the hypothesis into specific propositions that are more testable.

The objective of this chapter is to continue this work of specification. In particular, we show our first attempts to use the cycle hypothesis to generate specific empirical studies. These studies represent only a fraction of those required to explore the range and depth of the cycle hypothesis. Indeed, in this chapter we will be concerned with only two aspects of the cycle hypothesis. First, we will explore social organizers in an environmental setting. One aspect of the cycle hypothesis we considered in some detail in the previous chapter was an approach to characterizing "type of environment." We argued that the environment could be typed in ways that were similar, in many respects, to the way we had typed or categorized families: according to a regnant or central social organizer. In the previous chapter we considered briefly three forms of social collectivities in the environment: kin, communities, and organizations. We argued that kindreds are organized by a loyalty code, communities by a map, and organizations by an objective. In this chapter we will explore, in greater detail, the concept of organizational objective and present data which illustrate the application of this notion.

The second component of the cycle hypothesis examined in this chapter is the concept of family-environment *links*. We will examine links between the family and two different sorts of environments. First we will look at rapidly fashioned links, of a relatively brief duration, which families establish with a psychiatric hospital when one of their adolescent children is hospitalized. Second, we will examine more typical links, established over time and for a longer duration, between the family and its kin. In the previous chapter we considered three aspects of these links: their medium, architecture, and motivation. In the present chapter we will examine in some detail only the architecture of the links. We will explore the applicability — in these two studies — of our three architectural features: centrality, openness, and engagement. The hospital study gives us an additional opportunity. We were able to type families according to their paradigm before they had established their ties or links to the hospital community and, using the cycle hypothesis, generate predictions concerning the architecture of links the families would form. The predictive aspects of this allows us to explore the causal direction implied in step 3 of the cycle hypothesis: family construct *leads to* particular architectural characteristics of family-environment links.

The Organizational Objective

In Chapter 3 we sketched some of the basic principles which have guided the construction of our overall model. We began with the individual and pictured him as facing two dilemmas. The first was to develop a stable and coherent explanatory system to guide his action in a world that was usually ambiguous and often chaotic. The second was to reconcile his own explanatory system with those of others. We argued that if he failed in this reconciliation the stability and coherence of his own system would be challenged. This was particularly true in those instances where he accorded any other person — with a different explanatory system — the power of independent regard, that is, the power to examine and explain him and his own system. A basic premise of our model is that individuals meet these two dilemmas through a single strategy; they do not elaborate their own explanatory system but join forces with others to develop shared explanatory systems. Chapters 4 and 5 showed how this shared elaboration is carried forward in families.

Social collectivities differ, however, in the forces pressing toward this form of sharing. We have argued that the pressure is inescapable in families. Indeed, if an individual does not share, to a significant extent, in the elaboration and conservation of the family's explanatory system — its paradigm — he becomes, in a crucial experiential sense, an outsider. Indeed, as we have pointed out, central to the concept of paradigm is an all-encompassing view of reality which cannot sustain a counterview. In kin, community, and corporation the pressures are probably less severe and more variable. Some kindred, some communities, and some corporations probably require all members to share certain regnant and organizing constructions. In Etzioni's sense, these collectives require all ties between the individual and the collectivity to be normative. However, in other kinds of kindred, communities, and corporations, only a small number of individuals share common conceptions. The collectivity allows other kinds of ties: remunerative or coercive.[1] This is almost certainly true for complex organizations. Some members develop clear conceptions of the task of the organization — what is expected or required of it by the outside world and what are the most important procedures for accomplishing that task. This shared conception, when it is held by those who actually run the organization, is called the organizational objective. As we indicated in the previous chapter, the organizational objective is a shared construction of reality quite equivalent — in an epistemological sense — to paradigms in families (and to codes in kindreds and maps in communities). Like other social organizers it establishes certain norms within the collectivity. In organizations, individuals can be recruited to carry out the organizational objectives even though their own explanatory systems are never reconciled with the overall organizational objective. Consider, for example, a janitor who works for a fundamentalist mission. The leaders of the mission may share a passionate belief both in the perfidy of the secular world and in the Second Coming; this conviction fuels their efforts to convert as many nonbelievers as possible to their faith. Indeed the entire organization is shaped and maintained by a zealous shared conception of the world and its future. The janitor may know little and care less about this vision. His hard work carries forward the work of the organization, although if you ask him why he works so hard he would say, "It's my job." By that he means he is paid a fair wage so he gives, in a strictly remunerative way, a fair return effort in his work. Not only does the janitor tolerate well his differences with the ruling elite of the mission (surely, he has his own conception of the morality of the world and possibility of redemption or retribution), but the mission's elite ruling can tolerate his divergent views (if they know about them at all). The elite does not, however, accord the janitor the power of independent regard.

In the current study we examine the psychiatric hospital, a very special form of formal or complex organization. In a general sense, most psychiatric hospitals may be thought of as having the same organizational objective—to make mental patients well. However, closer inspection yields a finer picture. Different hospitals are organized around different objectives and conceptions, particularly conceptions of psychiatric illness. For example, some hospitals (to put the matter a bit too simply) conceive of the major mental illnesses as manifestations of neurobiologic disorder. This fundamental conception of the "reality" of mental disorder organizes a great deal of the hospital's structure and activities. It not only influences how patients are assessed and treated but it influences how the staff is organized: who are regarded as experts, who as subordinates, and how they should relate to one another. Other hospitals, by contrast, see mental disorders as reflecting disordered relationships between the patients and others in their social world. This conception leads to different treatment techniques and staff organization. The distinction between the biologically oriented view and the socially oriented one probably goes beyond the simple conception of mental disorder. Psychiatrists who have a primary interest in biologic diagnosis and treatment probably have a substantially different view of many aspects of human nature and development than those with a primarily social view. Thus, a shared construction explaining or assuming probable etiologies in mental disorder is likely to contain a rich and broad set of conceptions of human nature. For example, a biologically oriented perspective would view much of human behavior as constrained by an individual's genetic endowment and shaped by the unfolding development of his central nervous system. A socially oriented construction conceives behavior as a reflection of the patient's relationship with family, neighborhood, place of employment, and so on.

Our first study of organizational objective had two interrelated objectives. The first was an attempt to delineate the mechanism by which individuals in organizations—particularly psychiatric hospitals—might coordinate their constructions of the fundamental nature of psychiatric disturbance and consolidate them into an organizational objective. The second objective was to learn from these mechanisms abouth the breadth and depth of the organizational objectives. As we have already indicated, a shared conception of the nature of mental disorder includes a rich set of assumptions about human development and human nature itself. A picture of the range and depth of the organizational objective should also suggest ways in which objectives might differ — from one psychiatric hospital to the next — and, most important, the kinds of dimensions which might be pertinent for clarifying and highlighting those distinctions. Thus, we conceived of this study as a significant step toward filling in a piece of the overall cycle hypothesis, a clarification of the term "types of environment."

In Chapters 4 and 5 we outlined a mechanism by which families develop shared conceptions of the social and inanimate world. We focused on crises which threaten to splinter the family group. For the family as a collectivity, the potential loss of the group is a devastating prospect. This prospect engenders enormous interest in and potential allegiance to any principle which promises restoration. If the family's old system of relationships, as organized by its previous paradigm, cannot restore a semblance of group cohesion, then any promising kernel of a new paradigm may be eagerly absorbed. The family's reorganization around a new set of shared conceptions occurs as a fundamental part of a process of self-healing after a disorganizing crisis. To be sure, crisis may play a significant role in the development of some organizations. Moreover, the organization may — for many or (in rare cases) all of its members — be experienced very much like a family: its potential dissolution is felt as an enormous potential loss. Ordinarily, however, crisis, potential dissolution, and redemption play a much less crucial role in the functioning of organizations and the development of their objectives.

In psychiatric hospitals there are three broad classes of treatment techniques: somatotherapies (including drugs and electroshock), sociotherapies (which emphasize group therapy and, probably most important, the healing powers inherent in all forms of relationships in the social milieu of the psychiatric ward), and psychotherapies (particularly individual, insight-oriented therapy conducted by a well-trained professional). Although these techniques are not necessarily incompatible, psychiatric hospitals are often organized around one or the other of them. As in any other branch of medicine, psychiatry can make use of a growing body of scientific data to select the technical approaches which are preferred in both inpatient and outpatient settings. However, the scientific data currently available do not unambiguously support one of these approaches to the exclusion of the others.[2] Moreover, psychiatric hospitals and other mental health treatment facilities can be divided into those which are "mainline" — clearly in the core of the profession and controlled by a variety of outside influences, including the full force of accepted research findings — and those which are peripheral and develop conceptions, and consequent objectives, more or less on their own.

In psychiatric hospitals (and probably other organizations) we propose that organizational objectives arise, in part, through a series of internal processes reflecting the personal needs of both patients and professional staff. We hypothesize three distinct steps in the development of the organizational objective. (1) Individuals enter an organization (in our study of psychiatric hospitals we include both patients and staff) with certain long-standing personal needs and values. In part, the strength of their bond to the organization reflects the degree to which the structure and process of the hospital satisfy these needs. (2) However, a successful organization cannot devote many of its resources to the direct satisfaction of its members' personal needs. The negotiation between individual and organization, concerning fulfillment of needs, is conducted in a language of *technical preferences*. Individuals convey the nature of their personal needs through their advocacy of particular technical preferences. For example, to provide a simple case, a psychiatric nurse with a strong personal need to control the lives of others will be attracted to therapies in which patients must strictly obey regimens developed by a professional staff (the clearest example here is forms of somatotherapy). By contrast, a psychiatrist with doubts about his personal attractiveness and a consequent strong need to be accepted by social groups may find certain sociotherapies very rewarding. (3) Not all technical preferences, however, can be honored in any one institution. Usually only a subset becomes ascendant and serves as the core of the organization's objective. In truly democratic organizations (and these are rare, though interesting) the organizational objective is strongly influenced by the technical preferences (and the associated values and personal needs with which they inextricably intertwined) held by the majority of members. Most organizations, however, are managed by an elite. The technical preferences of the elite constitute the core of the organizational objective. Individuals in effective elites usually share the same technical preferences. (4) When an individual joins an organization he will place himself in the subgroup of individuals who hold the same technical preferences (and underlying values and needs) as he does. If this subgroup is different from and subordinate to the ruling elite he will follow one of three alternatives: (a) he will subordinate his own conviction to those of the power elite, drawing whatever sustenance he can from the "out-group" of which he is a member; (b) he will seek, in some way, to overturn the power elite; or (c) he will become alienated and withdraw to the margins of the hospital or leave altogether.

A STUDY OF TWO PSYCHIATRIC HOSPITALS

We devised a study to examine part of this hypothesis, focusing particularly on the links between personal needs and values on the one hand and technical preferences on the other.[3] We developed a questionnaire to be administered to staff and patients in two psychiatric hospitals, with questions designed to measure all three of these domains. We examined four interrelated hypotheses. First, we expected that there would be specific links between a preference for somato-, socio-, or psychotherapy on the one hand, and particular values and needs on the other. Second, we expected these links to be the same for patients and staff. We reasoned that the links between personal needs and technical preferences are not dependent on the kind of information and experience that comes with professional training; they might even be resistant to it. Rather, the strength of these relationships reflects the central importance of the needs and values themselves and is limited only by the individual's familiarity with the particular techniques. (We assume adequate familiarity in both staff and patients.) Third, and for the same reason, we predicted that the links would be the same in two very different hospitals. While it may be true that individuals in two very different hospitals would have different absolute levels of technical preferences, the specific relationships between those preferences and personal needs and values should be invariant. Fourth, the same general line of reasoning led us to predict that results should be highly replicable; if needs and values are associated with technical preference in a sample studied during one year, the same relationships should be obtained three years later in entirely new sample.

Sample. Table 8.1 shows the size of the initial sample and of the replication, three years later, in each of the two institutions. The first institution, the National Institute of Mental Health (NIMH), maintains an intramural research hospital of approximately sixty beds on the National Institutes of Health campus in Bethesda, Maryland. Patients are treated free of charge and, in return, they participate in a variety of research procedures. Physicians involved in direct care of patients are almost entirely men with research skills and were serving at NIMH at the time of the study in lieu of military obligations. The second hospital, the Psychiatric Institute (PI), is a private psychiatric hospital offering inpatient and outpatient services. (All patient subjects in this study were inpatients.) The

TABLE 8.1   RESPONDERS AND NONRESPONDERS IN INITIAL AND REPLICATION (THREE YEARS LATER) SAMPLES

	Initial			Replication		
	Re-sponders	Nonre-sponders	Total	Re-sponders	Nonre-sponders	Total
	National Institute of Mental Health					
Physicians	21	2	23	30	2	32
Nurses	20	8	28	36	6	42
Patients	22	18	30	26	5	31
Total	63	28	91	92	13	105
	(69%)			(88%)		
	Psychiatric Institute					
Physicians	6	0	6	28	9	37
Nurses	52	0	52	48	34	82
Patients	70	–	–	38	37	75
Total	128	–	–	114	80	194
				(59%)		

fees of many of the patients are covered in their entirety by an unusually comprehensive mental health insurance policy available to federal and other workers in the District of Columbia area. Physicians are almost all American-trained and drawn from leading academic centers around the country. Patients at NIMH range in age from mid-adolescent to old. At the time of both the initial and the replication studies, NIMH adolescents showed primarily non-psychotic adjustment reactions, and among the adults approximately two-thirds were depressed (bipolar and unipolar) and one-third were schizophrenic. The patients at PI were in the same age range (children were excluded from the sample); adult diagnoses tended to include more nonpsychotic conditions and some organic psychoses. Care was taken to avoid including any subject more than once in the study. For the PI sample, hospital records did not permit a precise identification of the initial nonresponders, although estimates are that the number was extremely small. Since the number of nonresponders for the whole study, is fairly substantial, we tried to collect data on both the responder and nonresponder groups in order to estimate sampling biases. For responders and nonresponders, information was available for age, sex, marital status, and length of time in the institution prior to presentation of the questionnaire. Sixteen separate comparisons between responders and nonresponders were made (four variables for PI staff, PI patients, NIMH staff, and NIMH patients); of these only two were statistically significant, a finding that could be attributable to chance alone.

Questionnaire. NEEDS. Our basic strategy was to select scales that assessed needs and personality attributes that past findings indicate are highly relevant to the outlook and behavior of psychiatric staff and patients. The most specific was Whitehorn and Betz's A-B Scale (see Whitehorn and Betz, 1960, and Betz, 1962). On the surface, this scale seems only to assess the respondent's preferences for particular career choices (social and helping occupations as distinct from logical and technical occupations). However, a large volume of data suggests that high-scoring psychiatrists are more receptive to peripheral sensory stimuli, more inclined to use intuition, and more personally involved with patients,[4] and, as a consequence, they appear to be more effective with seriously disturbed (particularly schizophrenic) patients (see Betz, 1962). We also chose the Machiavellian and Fundamental Interpersonal Relations Orientation (FIRO) scales because they have been extremely successful in predicting behavior of individuals in group settings. The Machiavellian Scale assesses the respondent's view of human nature (see Christie and Geis, 1970). A high scorer is skeptical about the motivations of others and as a consequence insulates himself from others' feelings and, with cool detachment, pursues his affairs according to his own self-interest. We reasoned that this fundamental view of human nature would play a large part in elaborating a value orientation about appropriate behavior of staff and patients in a psychiatric hospital and in the selection of particular therapeutic techniques. The FIRO Scale has six subscales that measure an individual's needs for social control, for inclusion in groups, and for personal affection (see Schutz, 1966). These needs, too, we thought might contribute to the kinds of objectives formulated by an individual in a psychiatric hospital.

VALUES. We selected three scales assessing values highly pertinent to an individual's conception of the goal of a psychiatric hospital. Each scale measures the kinds of behavior—in staff or patients—that the respondent esteems. The first was Almond's Social Openness and Ward Involvement Scale, SOWI (see Almond, Kenniston, and Boltax, 1968); it measures the respondent's valuation of active social interaction with such items as, "A patient should prefer talking with any other patient over reading a book" (strongly agree, agree, mildly agree, mildly disagree, strongly disagree); "A patient should like to go to lots of hospital activities."

The second scale was Levinson's Nurturance Scale (see Levinson and Gallagher, 1964). This scale measures the respondent's valuation of caring and nurturant behavior on the part of hospital and staff with such items as, "Doctors should take a deep personal interest in patients."

The third scale was Levinson's Benign Autocracy Scale (see Levinson and Gallagher, 1964), which measured the respondent's valuation of authoritarian behavior in staff and self-control in patients with items such as, "The main job of attendants and nurses is to see that patients stay in line"; "When a person has a problem or worry, it is best for him not to think about it, but to keep busy with more cheerful things."

TECHNICAL PREFERENCES. We used three scales developed by Strauss to measure each subject's preferences for particular technical activity (see Strauss, Schatzman, and Bucher, 1964). Since these scales correlate highly with more direct evidence of technical preferences and activity, we regard them as suitable measures of technical preference. As described above, these three scales measure preferences for psychotherapy (emphasizing intensive, insight-oriented treatment), sociotherapy (emphasizing group and milieu therapy), and somatotherapy (emphasizing drug therapy and organic causes of mental illness).

Scoring and analysis. All scoring was done by computer. For each subject, fourteen scale scores were derived, using the procedures described by the originators of the several scales already cited. These fourteen scale scores were subjected to principal components factor analysis and varimax rotation. Separate analyses were done on pairs of subsamples created first by dividing all subjects into those tested initially and those in the replication; then by dividing those in NIMH and those in PI; and, finally, by dividing staff and patients. Comparison of the factor structure between the two members of each pair was accomplished by obtaining factor scores with the use of the factor matrix from each subsample on the larger of the two subsamples. Thus, the factor matrix from the initial and replication analyses was used to obtain two matrices of factor scores for the replication subjects. These two matrices of factor scores were intercorrelated. This method has been described by Pinneau and Newhouse (1964), Ryder (1966), and Reiss (1976). Complete factor stability is indicated by correlations of ± 1.000 between corresponding factors and correlations of 0.000 between any other factors. No techniques have been developed for assessing the statistical significance of these correlations. They are best regarded as a quasi-objective method for assessing the similarity of two different factor matrices. The magnitude — and not the sign —

of these coefficients are crucial for interpretation. The sign merely reflects the sign of the loadings.

Results. Tables 8.2, 8.3, and 8.4 present the results of factor analyses for our three pairs of subsamples: initial and replication; NIMH and PI; staff and patients. As the footnotes to each of these tables indicate, the correlations on which the factor analyses were based contained a substantial proportion that were statistically significant at or beyond the .05 level. In all the analyses, the first three factors accounted for a total of about 50 percent of the variance. A fourth factor, not shown in the tables, had a loading only from our empathy scale and accounted for less than 10 percent of the variance. Further factors were derived, but they are not shown in the tables because they were unreliable and each accounted for only a very small portion of the total variance. The factor matrices are displayed to facilitate comparison within each pair of subsamples; thus, for example, factor I from the initial sample and factor I from the replication are displayed side by side, although they were drawn from two separate factor matrices. Also to facilitate comparison, some factor vectors were multiplied by −1 for tabular presentation so that the defining (high loading) variables would have a positive sign. The factors are numbered in order of declining eigenvalues in the principal components matrix except for the patient and NIMH matrices, where factors II and III were interchanged. This was done in order to display them next to the comparable factor (as defined by the pattern of loadings) in the staff and PI matrices, respectively.

Inspection of the tables shows that our need-value-technique hypothesis is partially confirmed. Factor III most closely conforms to the hypothesis. In four of the six matrices, it has high loadings from at least one personal need, one value, and one technical preference; in the other two matrices, it has high loadings from need and value variables. Factor II conforms less closely to expectations; in all six matrices it has loadings from technical and value variables, but not from personal need variables. Factor I does not correspond at all to predictions; in all six matrices it loads only on need variables.

Tables 8.5, 8.6, and 8.7, which present the estimate of similarity between pairs of factors, indicate a very impressive reliability of the factors. What this reflects, of course, is a remarkable similarity — within each pair of subsamples — between the underlying correlations. Indeed, visual inspection of these intercorrelation matrices reveals that comparable correlations (for example, between SOWI and sociotherapy in the matrix from the initial sample

TABLE 8.2 FACTOR ANALYSIS OF FOURTEEN SCALE SCORES FOR INITIAL (N = 191) AND REPLICATION (THREE YEARS LATER) (N = 206) SAMPLES

	Factor I, personal affiliation		Factor II, belief in technical order		Factor III, belief in moral order	
	Initial	Replication	Initial	Replication	Initial	Replication
Variance accounted for, %	20	21	14	15	15	13
Technical preferences						
Somatotherapy	.01	.05	**.58**	.35	.14	.33
Psychotherapy	.01	.14	**.66**	**.67**	−.06	.02
Sociotherapy	.16	.29	**−.58**	**−.75**	**.45**	.20
Values						
Social openness and ward involvement	.23	.28	−.23	−.32	**.61**	**.55**
Benign autocracy	−.02	−.15	**.79**	**.83**	−.15	−.05
Nurturance	.11	.21	.17	.07	**.83**	**.69**
Personality						
Machiavellianism	−.13	−.37	.16	.18	**−.73**	**−.56**
Empathy[a]	−.12	−.03	−.10	−.02	−.02	.23
Expressed inclusion	**.72**	**.77**	−.13	.12	.09	.05
Wanted inclusion	**.84**	**.85**	−.03	−.07	.07	−.11
Expressed control	.30	.23	−.04	−.28	−.38	**−.58**
Wanted control	.05	.22	.33	.07	−.30	−.27
Expressed affection	**.83**	**.70**	−.08	−.24	.00	.06
Wanted affection	**.82**	**.80**	−.13	−.07	.14	.15

Note: Corresponding factors from the two samples are shown next to one another, and loadings greater than .40 are in boldface. In the original correlation matrices from which these factor matrices were derived, 39 of the 84 initial correlations and 41 of the 84 replication correlations were significant at or beyond the .05 level.

a. Whitehorn and Betz A-B Scale.

TABLE 8.3   FACTOR ANALYSIS OF FOURTEEN SCALES, COMBINING INITIAL AND REPLICATION DATA FOR THE NATIONAL INSTITUTE OF MENTAL HEALTH (N = 155) AND THE PSYCHIATRIC INSTITUTE (N = 242)

	Factor I, personal affiliation		Factor II, belief in technical order		Factor III, belief in moral order	
	NIMH	PI	NIMH	PI	NIMH	PI
Variance accounted for, %	21	20	14	15	14	15
Technical preferences						
Somatotherapy	.04	.25	.27	**.57**	**.44**	.18
Psychotherapy	.19	−.13	**.53**	**.73**	−.07	.03
Sociotherapy	.25	.07	**−.80**	**−.51**	−.03	**.51**
Values						
Social openness and ward involvement	.31	.02	**−.44**	−.21	.39	**.72**
Benign autocracy	−.03	−.04	**.80**	**.80**	.08	−.15
Nurturance	.30	.20	−.04	.13	**.68**	**.78**
Personality						
Machiavellianism	−.23	−.28	.24	.14	**−.54**	**−.68**
Empathy	−.16	.07	.00	−.03	.36	−.08
Expressed inclusion	**.71**	**.73**	.01	.22	−.09	.19
Wanted inclusion	**.85**	**.84**	−.05	.00	−.15	.06
Expressed control	.28	.21	−.19	−.05	**−.64**	−.30
Wanted control	.19	.02	.25	.30	**−.54**	−.02
Expressed affection	**.74**	**.81**	−.06	−.17	−.01	.00
Wanted affection	**.82**	**.84**	.02	−.15	.16	.09

Note: In the original correlation matrices from which these factor matrices were derived, 35 of the 84 NIMH correlations and 40 of the 84 PI correlations were significant at or beyond the .05 level.

TABLE 8.4 FACTOR ANALYSIS OF FOURTEEN SCALES FOR STAFF (N = 241) AND PATIENTS (N = 156)

	Factor I, personal affiliation		Factor II, belief in technical order		Factor III, belief in moral order	
	Staff	Patients	Staff	Patients	Staff	Patients
Variance accounted for, %	21	19	13	12	14	16
Technical preferences						
Somatotherapy	.10	−.03	.44	.70	.00	.09
Psychotherapy	.11	−.02	.57	.61	.13	.11
Sociotherapy	.26	.10	−.70	−.19	.33	.56
Values						
Social openness and ward involvement	.11	.31	−.20	.27	.69	.59
Benign autocracy	−.16	.05	.83	.64	.03	−.45
Nurturance	.07	.14	.25	.31	.63	.74
Personality						
Machiavellianism	−.15	−.22	.16	−.08	−.65	−.70
Empathy	.08	−.26	.02	−.17	−.03	−.28
Expressed inclusion	.75	.75	.13	.28	.03	.05
Wanted inclusion	.83	.85	−.13	.05	.00	.17
Expressed control	.41	.14	−.32	.15	−.46	−.37
Wanted control	.23	.01	−.12	.24	−.21	−.08
Expressed affection	.76	.79	−.15	−.13	.20	−.08
Wanted affection	.81	.78	.01	−.23	.25	.25

Note: In the original correlation matrices from which these factor matrices were derived, 40 of the 84 staff and 31 of the 84 patient correlations were significant at or beyond the .05 level.

TABLE 8.5   CORRELATION OF FACTOR SCORES AS DERIVED FROM FACTORS, I, II, AND III, USING REPLICATION SAMPLE ($N = 206$)

	Replication factors		
Initial factors	I	II	III
I	.99	.15	−.03
II	−.10	−.95	.05
III	.22	−.15	−.95

TABLE 8.6   CORRELATION OF FACTOR SCORES AS DERIVED FROM NIMH AND PI FACTOR MATRICES, USING PI SUBJECTS ($N = 242$)

	PI matrix		
NIMH matrix	I	II	III
I	.97	−.14	.08
II	.02	−.91	−.33
III	.06	.09	−.79

TABLE 8.7   CORRELATION OF FACTOR SCORES AS DERIVED FROM STAFF AND PATIENT MATRICES, USING STAFF SUBJECTS ($N = 241$)

	Staff matrix		
Patient matrix	I	II	III
I	.97	−.04	.03
II	−.04	.82	.09
III	−.15	.19	−.90

and the same two variables in the matrix from the replication sample) rarely differ by as much as ±.20. Thus, the fundamental correlations—on which the factor matrices are based—are highly replicable across time, institution, and from staff to patients.

Interpretation of factors. The patterns of loading on factors II and III conform most closely to our predictions and are therefore easier to interpret. Factor II, in our six subsamples, seems regularly to have high loadings from somatotherapy, psychotherapy, and benign autocracy. In some of the subsamples there is a negative loading from sociotherapy. What do the first three variables have in common? Somatotherapy and psychotherapy are treatments usually given by clinical experts on the basis of specific, technical knowledge. Drugs are always prescribed by physicians. These physicians may not know the precise mechanism of action of the drug nor fully understand the biologic basis of the illness they are treating. Nonetheless, they must have a good working knowledge of technical issues such as indications and contraindications, dose-response relationships, side effects, and drug combinations. Likewise, psychotherapy is almost always administered by a specially trained technical expert (a physician, a psychologist, or a specially trained social worker). Again, the therapy rests on particular technical knowledge: transference and countertransference, psychic conflict, termination problems. In sum, both therapies require a trained and certified healer—someone who is singled out and granted special status within a healing institution. It is understandable that a preference for these techniques would fit with a valuation of benign autocracy. In effect, nonhealers must fall into line behind the healers, follow their recommendations, and defer to them and their treatment plans.

A very different complex of variables characterizes factor III. Here sociotherapy loads positively on all subsamples, although the magnitude of the loading is less than the technical preference loadings on factor II. Also, we see positive loadings for nurturance and negative loadings for Machiavellianism and control variables. In their initial conception of sociotherapy as an ideology, Strauss, Schatzman, and Bucher (1964) emphasized its relatively nontechnical nature. (To be sure, sociotherapy is technical, in the same general and approximate sense in which psychotherapy and somatotherapy are technical. We are here attempting to make a finer distinction between the "highly technical" techniques and the "less technical" techniques. Organizational theorists have attempted the same kind of distinction between occupational activities, referring to the former as "professionalized" and the latter as "nonprofessionalized"—see Wilensky, 1964, and Hall, 1968.) The pure sociotherapist believes healing can come from many sources—physicians, nurses, and other patients. Social openness among members of the ward community is clearly required to achieve the open social system required by the sociotherapist. The nurturance, negative Machiavellian, and negative control scores add another facet: the sociotherapist has confidence in the fundamental goodness and genuineness of others; their importance to the success of the social community requires encouragement of their autonomy rather than control. The valuation of nurturance can be understood as the glue that bonds these several elements. Nurturance is the extent to which the responder feels the hospital is gratifying and the people in it value one another personally. In sum, an individual scoring high on this dimension perceives the personal importance individuals can have for one another; mental illness arises when these relationships go astray; and the cure resides in activating the latent healing power inherent in any positive relationship between two individuals. This set of attitudes is entirely harmonious with the sociotherapists' conception of mental illness: the disorder resides in disfigured and ungratifying relationships, and is not a fundamental property of the individual patient.

Factor II, then, seems to stress a technical (or "professionalized") conception of mental illness: mental illness is a product of a disordered mechanism in the individual and is curable by a trained and certified technical expert; social structure and interaction in the treating institution must accord prestige, deference, and resources to the certified healers. It is not important whether patients and staff have personal significance; what matters is the technical relationship of one to another. To somewhat overstate the matter, for purposes of contrast, factor III stresses the human relations aspect of mental illness. A relatively undifferentiated social structure, it is believed, encourages the healing properties of all relationships; individuals have personal significance to one another.

These distinctions between social structure, quality of relationship, and technical development were first made, to our knowledge, by Robert Redfield (1953). He contrasted "two distinguishable ways by which the activities of men are coordinated." One he called the *technical order*: "The bonds that coordinate the activities in the technical order do not rest on [shared] convictions of the good life; they are not characterized by a foundation in human sentiments; they can exist even without the knowledge of those bound together that they are bound together. The technical order is that order which results from mutual usefulness . . . In the technical order men are bound by things, or are themselves things. They are organized by necessity or expediency." In contrast, the *moral order* is "always based on what is peculiarly human — sentiments, morality, conscience — and in the first place arises in the groups where people are intimately associated with one another . . . 'Moral order' includes the binding sentiments of rightness that attend religion, the social solidarity that accompanies religious ritual, the sense of religious seriousness and obligation that strengthens men, and the effects of belief in invisible beings that embody goodness." Thus, we may borrow Redfield's terms to name two factors: factor II becomes belief in the technical order; factor III becomes belief in the moral order.

What of factor I? It is more difficult to interpret from an institutional perspective because it lacks reliable loadings on the technical preference scales. We suggest that this factor reflects a dimension of *acknowledged*, rather than *externalized*, personal need. This is a contrast to factors II and III, which, because they combine needs, values, and technical preferences, are dimensions defining individual organizational objectives, that is, the externalization of personal needs through choice of techniques. We base this interpretation on contrasting the personal need scales that correlated highly with technical preferences (Machiavellianism and control) with those that did not (affection, inclusion, and empathy). As it turns out, there is a very clear difference between these two groups of scales. Affection, inclusion, and empathy all ask the responder directly about his own likes and dislikes. In other words, they assess what he himself recognizes as his own needs and interests. In contrast, items on the Machiavellian Scale purport to question the responder's view of reality outside himself: "The best way to handle people is to tell them what they want to hear"; "It is safest to assume that all people have a vicious streak and it will come out when they are given a chance."

The control scale lies somewhere in between the two groups. It is similar to the Machiavellian Scale in that it does not directly query the individual about his inner feelings. More ambiguously, it questions him about his usual practices. It is quite possible to read these questions, however, as queries about what the realities in the outside world require of the responder, rather than what he himself needs or likes to do, for example, "I try to take charge of things when I'm with people" (*usually, often,* sometimes, occasionally, rarely, never); "I let other people strongly influence my actions" (*most people, many people, some people, a few people,* one or two people, nobody). Acceptance of these items is indicated by answering positively any of the italicized alternatives; acceptance could be viewed by the responder as strategic under certain circumstances, that is, a rational response to outside reality. This interpretation seems much less likely for affection and inclusion items such as, "I like people to include me in their activities" (*usually, often,* sometimes, occasionally, rarely, never); "I like people to act close and personal with me" (*usually, often,* sometimes, occasionally, rarely, never). On the face of it, the responder must conclude that he is being asked about his own needs, independent of external reality.

In our introductory synopsis of the theory of organizational objectives, we said that personal needs must be *externalized* before they are included in organizational objectives. A voluminous literature on externalization suggests that personal needs have, fundamentally, two different fates. Some needs are tolerable, acceptable, or even prized by the individual. Thus, he can recognize them, accept them as his own, and act directly to fulfill them. Other needs, for a variety of reasons, are not tolerable. Often these needs are externalized: the individual sees the outside world as requiring him to perform in certain ways. In this way, he disavows the personal origin of these needs. It is the second group of disavowed needs that are more likely to influence and combine with values and technical preference and much less likely to be determinable by direct questions such as those on the affection and inclusion scales. In retrospect, we suspect that our need-value-technique hypothesis would have been better tested by an indirect assessment of personal needs. Had we done so, it is plausible to argue that all our principal factors would have shown a stronger relationship between needs and values on one hand, and technical preferences on the other.

Personal and organizational dimensions. Our results delineate personal or individual dimensions relating needs, values, and technical preferences. They are an indication of how individuals externalize personal needs in the formation of technical preferences. In a more speculative vein, these data can be used to specify dimensions of the organizational objective as well. In extending our results in this direction we approach our main target: the characterization of organizations — through a study of their objectives — and their potential relationship to families of particular kinds, as defined by the nature of their paradigms. In extending these dimensions to the organization as a whole, we assume that the organization is ruled by a single power elite and that each member of that elite occupies the same position on each of the two dimensions of technical order and moral order (for example, all members of the elite might be high on the first and low on the second). Since these two dimensions are orthogonal, it is possible to have institutions shaped by an elite (or a majority with a particular objective, in a democratic institution) of one of four possible kinds: high on both dimensions; low on both; high on technical and low on moral; and high on moral and low on technical. Let us examine what institutions shaped by these four different combinations might look like. Table 8.8 illustrates these possibilities.

LOW ON BOTH BELIEF IN MORAL ORDER AND BELIEF IN TECHNICAL ORDER. In such a hospital the activities of patients and staff are coordinated neither by a belief that people are of technical use to one another nor a belief that each has a personal meaning for the other. We would expect such an institution to be dominated by a sense of technical confusion and helplessness as well as a widespread social alienation between most individuals, within the staff

TABLE 8.8   SCHEMATIC REPRESENTATION OF ORGANIZATIONAL OBJECTIVES AND THEIR HYPOTHESIZED IMPACT ON PSYCHIATRIC HOSPITALS

Belief in the moral order	Belief in the technical order	
	Low	High
High	1. Therapeutic community: Synanon, Alcoholics Anonymous 2. Dedifferentiation of formal authority and task specialization; heavy emphasis on inter-personal solidarity	1. "Contemporary mental health centers" 2. Participant instruction, with upward mobility of patients and staff; subgroup definition and distinction by experience rather than formal, professional discipline
Low	1. Custodial or disintegrating institutions 2. Widespread alienation between individuals and staff subgroups; organizational function maintained only through strong, arbitrary central authority	1. Medical hospitals and medically oriented psychiatric hospitals 2. Formal authority structure, with delegation of subtasks to technically specialized sub-groups that function independently of each other.

Note: This table shows the possible combinations of the two fundamental dimensions of organizational objective and the hypothesized impact such objectives might have on the character of the psychiatric hospital. These speculations are based on the assumption that the hospital has only one distinct, regnant group whose shared objective dominates the life of the hospital without serious competition from other subgroups. Each cell contains (1) the type of treatment institution and (2) its social structure.

and patient groups as well as between staff and patients. Only a strong, often arbitrary central authority can maintain a working organization. Such an ambience might characterize a hospital in the process of agonal dissolution. Some custodial care hospitals may exemplify this class.

HIGH ON BELIEF IN MORAL ORDER; LOW ON BELIEF IN TECHNICAL ORDER. These hospitals emphasize the healing potential in all individuals and relative undifferentiation of roles. For example, the functions of doctors, nurses, social workers, and experienced patients are very blurred. There is a focus on maintaining strong interpersonal solidarity. There is no strong need for special technical knowledge or even formal knowledge of theoretical models. The purest conception of the therapeutic community exemplifies this class. Alcoholics Anonymous and Synanon (in its earliest days) may also be examples. As Perrow's work (1967) suggests, we would expect relatively little specialization of function among subgroups within the hospital or treatment community. Moreover, since there is no strong tradition of authority nor a recognition of an objective technical standard, disputes within the organization would be resolved more by negotiation than by directives.

HIGH ON BELIEF IN TECHNICAL ORDER; LOW ON BELIEF IN MORAL ORDER. Most medical hospitals exemplify this class; so do psychiatric hospitals that model themselves after medical hospitals. The critical feature here is that the hospital is carefully organized around a technically complex model of mental illness. This model has distinct treatment implications; only those individuals with sufficient knowledge to understand and apply the model can be certified to administer the treatment. In practice, this model can be psychologic, biologic, or a mixture of both. In theory, it could also be a sociologic model, but in practice this is less frequent. Some of the psychotherapeutically purist hospitals of the 1950s and early 1960s exemplify this class. Disturbed patients were admitted in order to receive psychotherapy for fifty minutes a day at most. Other activities were auxiliary or supportive to this *fundamentum* of the hospital. Biologic hospitals corresponding to the psychotherapeutically purist ones are difficult to find. It is not sufficient to locate hospitals where organic therapies are the major modality. Often these turn out to be custodial hospitals (either the long-term state hospital for the indigent or the short-term proprietary institution for the wealthy). In order to qualify for this category, a biologic hospital would have to be led by a power elite that genuinely believes in the biologic origins of mental illness and conceives of its treatment modalities as specifically related to this concept. Using Perrow's analysis of organizations of this type, we may posit the outlines of the hospital's structure. Since the problem or task is defined in relatively clear, organized, and technical terms, it is possible to create subgroups within the staff, each of which has a particular technical function to perform. In psychotherapeutically pure hospitals, the psychiatrists see the patient for psychotherapy, the social workers see the relatives for ancillary support, the psychologists do diagnostic testing, and the nurses take care of the patient for the twenty-three hours a day when there is no psychotherapy. The senior psychiatrists set the great therapeutic machine into operation and guide it along, but the subgroups of technical subspecialists can function with relative independence of one another.

HIGH ON BOTH BELIEF IN MORAL ORDER AND BELIEF IN TECHNICAL ORDER. The fundamental theoretical challenge here is to conceptualize a treatment program in which there are both technical experts (a fundamental component of belief in the technical order) and a pervasive concept of healing personal relationships among all individuals. In other words, the treatment has to be understood as arising from the healing power of all individuals, or from the healing power residing in human relationships, and yet within those relationships there must be some individuals who are technically expert. This paradoxical situation can be resolved by the concept of the technical expert as participant-instructor. The central concept here is that the patient must enter into an intense and meaningful relationship with a therapist (technical expert). The relationship between the participants, therapist and patient, is genuine and may be based on genuine feelings and the personal importance of the one for the other. The cure does indeed reside in the relationship and depends absolutely on its genuineness. But this is not enough; for the cure to be permanent, the patient (the nonexpert) must understand, in technical terms, what has happened to him in the flux of the curative relationship. The technical expert must use his technical knowledge to show the patient what is happening to both of them in the course of their relationship. Some forms of psychoanalysis and individual and group psychotherapy are conducted along these lines, and the hospitals in which these therapies are dominant may also reflect this thesis. It is common for the therapists to have been, at one time in their training, patients in the same form of therapy that they administer. Thus, psychoanalysts will have been psychoanalyzed themselves and group therapists will have been members of therapy-type groups; the participant-instructor was himself once a participant-student. Moreover, a hospital high on technical and moral order is likely to insist that he periodically reinvolve himself as a participant-student (further psychoanalysis, individual supervision, T-groups, study groups, and so on). Both dimensions help to shape the definition of "cure." Belief in the moral order prompts the view that a partial cure is achieved through full and uninhibited participation in the social life of the hospital or therapeutic community. Belief in the technical order implies that this is not enough. A permanent cure can only be obtained by the technical understanding, by both the healer and the patient, of what each has been through as a participant. Often this does not indicate just the fact of recognition but also the capacity to understand; the patient must undergo a fundamental change in the capacity of his faculties to recognize the impact on him of his involvement with others.

The sociologic literature does not contain any formal analyses of organizations shaped by objectives of this character. We can speculate, however, that upward mobility is a fundamental feature of both structure and process. The patient himself is upwardly mobile in the system. He enters dependent and bewildered, but a substantial quantity of technical knowledge is given to him in the treatment process. Capable patients, at the end of their tenure, function as junior staff members, actively assisting in the care of new patients who, as they themselves had been on first arrival, enter as bewildered and powerless in dependency. Staff, likewise, is constantly mobile, usually upwardly. Individuals receive prestigious and powerful appointments according to their capacity to learn through participation. Although subgroups may still specialize in certain restricted technical functions, their membership is not defined exclusively by professional background outside the organization (for example, social workers and psychologists are not necessarily segregated into disciplinary subgroups). The most prestigious and technically complex tasks are handled by individuals who have been most adept at learning through participation.

Organizational Objective and Family Paradigm

We are now in a position to complete the last step in this line of argument. Our description of dimensions of the organizational objective enables us to relate these dimensions to comparable dimensions describing the family paradigm. The reader may have already anticipated the connections we are about to propose: the dimension of technical order bears some intriguing similarities to the dimensions of coherence and configuration. Likewise, the dimension of moral order seems related to the dimensions of integration and coordination.

Technical order and coherence/configuration. We are proposing that on the organizational level the dimension of belief in the technical order bears important similarities to family organization—the fundamental nature of family assumptions delineated by the dimension of coherence, and the nature of family's shared experience delineated by the dimension of configuration. The dimension of technical order emphasizes, first and foremost, that experience is added to build up a complex and enlarging model of mental illness. Organizational members high on this dimension organize their understanding of mental illness around a *mechanism:* a picture of mental illnesses that has components in specifiable relationship to one another (for example, the relationship of dopaminergic synaptic transmission to the functioning of the hypothalamus and pituitary in depressive disorders, or the relationship between drives and superego organization in obsessive compulsive neuroses). Members' specific conceptions of mental disorder are organized around the even deeper conviction that specific and universally true principles of mental functioning—disordered and normal—can be built up through the experience of professional training and ongoing research. The structure of psychiatric hospitals organized by the technical order may be understood to follow from the conviction that treatment of mental disorder must be directed at faults in the mechanism.

Likewise, families high on coherence and configuration (our model proposes that these are invariably correlated) are organized by a conception that outer reality can be understood by the ordered accumulation and interpretation of experience. Underlying patterns can be discovered that are stable and universal. This is true for laboratory puzzles where such families are convinced, even before they begin work, that the task has a single solution. This is equally true in the family's conception of its social environment: the family defines underlying mechanisms in the other families it comes to know and it can grasp subtle cues presumably in the service of maintaining accurate preceptions of an environment it views as orderly rather than dangerous or capricious. Chapter 2 reviewed findings supporting these conceptions of high coherence, high configuration families. Indeed, a fundamental corollary of this veiwpoint of the family, with respect to its environment, is that through shrewd observation and long experience the family can become an *expert*. Indeed, expertise—in the sense we are defining it here—is as much valued in high coherence, high configuration families as it is in an organization governed by the technical order.

Moral order and integration/coordination. The organizing conception, in organizations high on moral order, is the fundamental interdependence of all individuals. People have a primary value to one another and mental disorder is viewed as a breakdown in these sustaining relationships. To be sure, this is a model similar in some respects to those developed by the technical order. But the similarities are superficial. The conception that individuals are important to one another is an emotionally enriched belief, an abiding sense of the significance people have for one another. The central features of this "model" are not amenable to confirmation or disconfirmation by shrewd observation or careful research.

Likewise, the belief in the fundamental interdependence of family members lies at the core of the paradigm and constructs of the family high in integration/coordination. The central element of this family's paradigm is the recognition that one can take the perspective of the other. This elementary grasp of the continuing possibility of the world as another sees it sustains a fundamental family assumption which can be stated, "We are all in this world together." The most significant derivative of this fundamental position is that the perception and action of one member necessarily has enormous implications for the others. An abiding conviction in the interdependence of family members is represented in every aspect of the family's life. It would come as no surprise to a family of this kind that psychiatric distress and disorder is an unavoidable consequence of disordered relationships. Every aspect of their life reflects their conviction of the central importance each has for the other: their shared pacing and joint explorations in laboratory problem-solving tasks; their careful acknowledgment of each other's views as they develop conceptions of other families; their congruence of views of new social settings; and (as we have hypothesized) the careful synchrony of their daily lives.

In outlining our model of crisis and family paradigm we delineated a third family dimension, reference, with a corresponding dimension describing shared family experience, closure. In this first study of organizations, we did not delineate a dimension which seems to correspond to reference/closure on the family level.

We may now return to the cycle hypothesis. We have taken a small step toward specifying what we mean by "types of environment." Belief in the technical order and belief in the moral order are dimensions for describing a very specialized form of an organizational environment, the psychiatric hospital. We have also shown that these two dimensions bear significant formal similarities to two dimensions describing the family paradigm and its associated shared experiences. How can this be fit into the cycle hypothesis? A review of Figure 7.1 will help advance our argument. The portion of the cycle most pertinent to our current discussion is steps 4 and 6, the family's selection of a specific environment and the influence of that environment on the family. We will want to consider these steps as they relate to the relatively limited case of family-hospital transactions and the more general case of family-corporation transactions.

With respect to step 4 and hospitals, there are two mechanisms by which a family may actively choose a hospital for the quality of its social environment. We would hypothesize that, other factors being equal, a family might choose a hospital whose organizational objective matches, in some measure, its paradigm. The first mechanism involves the processing of advance information about the hospital. In nonemergency situations, particularly in large metropolitan areas, the family may get some advance information about several hospitals or they may turn to particular individuals for advice. In either case, it is conceivable that a family—without, in all cases, being fully aware of what it is doing—might select an institution which it believes to have the same outlook at it does. In other words, the family scans the information or advice it receives about potential hospitals for evidence of the hospital's organizational objective. We would hypothesize that high coordination families would be attracted to hospitals high on moral order and that high configuration families would be attracted to hospitals high on the technical order. A second mechanism by which families may select a particular environment is trial and error. It is not uncommon for families of adolescents to withdraw their child once he has been admitted. Occasionally this is done directly, although equally often families withdraw their child by subtly undermining the treatment program, or the child—serving as the family's ambassador—may engineer the withdrawal by blocking treatment in a variety of ways. In any case, the family is then left with a serious problem and a second hospitalization may ensue. Again, we hypothesize that by a process of successive approximations many families will find a hospital whose objectives match its own paradigm and shared constructs.

Once a family is engaged in a treatment program in a hospital whose organizational objectives match its own paradigm, there is significant mutual reinforcement of family and hospital. From the perspective of the family, its basic, shared constructions and underlying paradigm are reinforced by its engagement with an organization which construes the social world in similar terms. An interesting dilemma arises when the family and the hospital are not well-matched. As we indicated above, one major option is for the family, using a variety of direct and indirect methods, to withdraw altogether and find another hospital or make do without any hospital. However, there are other options. First, the family itself may change. This may be particularly true for pyschiatric hospitals.

At the time a child is admitted to a pyschiatric hospital, the whole family itself is in turmoil. Many have reached such a level of crisis and disorganization that there is a weakening of its grasp and structuring of the social world and a gaping openness to the influence of outsiders.[5] Significant change in the constructions of a family is possible as a consequence of its engagement with inpatient treatment programs. Indeed, the family-hospital transactions leading to change of this sort constitute an important model system for studying the relationship between family crisis, openness, and change more generally. A second possibility is that the family (probably one that is not in the midst of a disorganizing crisis) will try to change the hospital. Recent studies of Harbin and his associates (1978) document efforts of this kind, which may sometimes achieve partial success. A third possibility is the loss of a family member, usually the one who is hospitalized twenty-four hours a day. There are times when the admitted member of a family becomes engaged in the hospital community and comes fully to subscribe to the perspectives and values undergirding its organizational objectives (see Almond, Kenniston, and Boltax, 1969, for a careful, longitudinal study of this process). The individual may be caught by conflicting constructions of reality—the hospital on the one hand and the family on the other. Families can occasionally sense this coming. They will undermine the treatment program in some way to protect their integrity as a group. If families do not do this they may lose the hospitalized member, who remains a member of the hospital community through being treated as an outpatient, maintaining friendship ties with other families and peers, and making a significant alteration in his own life course. The discharged patient may return home for greater or lesser periods of time, but he is now a boarder held to his family by a mixture of remunerative or coercive ties; he is no longer a subscriber to the family's fundamental construction of social reality.

The extension of this reasoning to other, more typical family-organization transactions must be very speculative indeed. Nonetheless, we suspect that organizations such as schools and large places of employment, and other organizations such as churches and recreational clubs, are likewise governed by organizational objectives. The dimensions of technical order and moral order may not be adequate to describe the differences among these objectives, but we would expect that dimensions could be defined which characterized the ruling elite in these corporations. In more complex organizations there may be stable subgroups with their own organizational objective, that is, their own conception of what the subgroup should accomplish and their own concept of what allegiance is appropriate between that subgroup and the larger organization. For example, Gouldner (1965) studied the social organization of a gypsum mine before and after a wildcat strike. He was able to show that before the strike, managers and workers in a local mine developed a shared conception of the work group. Their perspective deemphasized conventional management-employee relations; instead, the local mine was seen as a component of the community in which it was located. Friendships between management and labor—friendships which developed in the community—continued on the job; workers could take company tools home for their own personal use; management allowed workers to establish their own pace of work. This was at sharp variance with the more conventional objectives of the mine's home office in another city: that conception revolved around impersonal standards of productivity and efficiency. The clash between the two ultimately led to a wildcat strike. It is tempting to speculate that the local mining crew—management and labor—was organized around objectives high on the moral order; the home office's objective was high on the technical order.

In any event, we would suggest that in the everyday world the family is faced with corporate collectivities of many stripes and, further, has the opportunity and initative to select among them, to a limited extent. Where a family has been successful in linking up to a corporation whose overriding objectives are similar to the family's (in the sense we have illustrated for families and psychiatric hospitals), its own constructions and paradigm will be reinforced. Where conflict exists, the outcomes that we have illustrated for families in conflict with hospitals, may exist.

Short-Term Links between the Family and the Environment

In the previous section we tried to clarify two steps of the cycle hypothesis: step 4, in which the family selects environments of particular character, and step 6, where those environments, acting reflexively, support the attributes of the family that led the family to select the environments in the first place. We tried to clarify these steps by illustrating, with an actual study, what we mean by the notion "type of environment." We used a more specific example of this concept—organizational objective—to fill out, in more detail, one section of the cycle hypothesis. In the next two sections we attempt to fill out three remaining portions of the cycle hypothesis: step 2, the relationship of the form of the family's ordinary constructs (and, less directly, paradigm) to the family's style of interaction with the environment; step 3, the relationship of these interaction patterns to the formation of links with the environment of a specific character; and step 5, the reflexive influence of these links on the family constructs and paradigms which initiated them in the first place.

In this section we will focus on short-term links as they develop over a period of one to three months. We will have a chance to look closely at the relationship between family paradigm and construct on the one hand and specific interaction patterns on the other and observe how the latter may be transformed into experiential links between the family and a particular social community. In the next section we will examine longer-term links, particularly between the family and its kin. The second section will also allow us to examine results from a large nonclinical sample of families for the first time. Most of the empirical findings in this book so far have been drawn from clinical samples of families who were recruited into the study by virtue of their participation in some form of psychiatric treatment program.

A STUDY OF SHORT-TERM FAMILY-ENVIRONMENT LINKS

Our first study of short-term links between the family and its environment examined the relationships between the family and a family-oriented psychiatric inpatient program.[6] The program actively involved the parents, and in some cases the siblings, as well as the identified adolescent patient. The treatment program explicitly required all families to attend three group meetings a week. This requirement implicitly engaged families in more subtle, but equally important, ties to the treatment program. The group meetings allowed families to meet the staff, other families, and other patients. For each family the inpatient program was a genuine social community. However, from clinical observations, we knew that families differed a great deal in the quality of their transactions and ties with that community. For example, some families became actively and conspicuously engaged in the life of the ward: they interacted freely with many staff members and other families, they seemed to be well-known and well-liked by everyone, and they quickly and effectively engaged themselves in the actual work of the treatment program. Other families hovered at the periphery: their attendance at the required meetings was spotty, they formed no relationships with anyone in the community, and they were ready to drop out of the program at any time. In this study we attempted to see if the cycle hypothesis could predict and then make sense of these between-family differences.

The psychiatric setting offers significant advantages for examining the cycle hypothesis. In the first place, the entire family becomes engaged — in one way or another — in this special form of social community. Therefore, we did not have to be concerned with trying to monitor overt or covert ambassadorial functions served by just a single member (see Chapter 6). The study of ambassadorial links is complex and often requires high levels of inference. For example, one must distinguish, in observing the family ambassador (and presumably any ambassador), which of his transactions with the outside social community are properly regarded as representing his family and which are representing only himself. In the family-oriented psychiatric inpatient setting we get a relatively rare opportunity to observe directly the transactions of the entire family unit with the community. In addition, psychiatric hospitals are particularly open to observation of social processes. Self-study and self-observation are no strangers to the modern psychiatric service; a research-oriented inspection of its social process does not seem foreign or particularly threatening. Another advantage is the relative simplicity of the inpatient community itself: (1) it is located in one circumscribed place; (2) a great majority of significant social interaction goes on in public spaces where it can be directly observed; and (3) the social structure of the inpatient ward—despite its subtlety and complexity—is simpler than other kinds of organizations. In many cases—and this was true of the inpatient service we studied—we can be confident that a single organizational objective structures the social system and guides its operation.

The study of families with psychiatric patients and of a psychiatric setting has an obvious disadvantage: it is a very special situation in which family crises may be more overt, the family's adaptive capacity less secure, and the organization particularly specialized and perhaps stigmatized in the public view. However, it is important to emphasize that the *direct* observation of family-environment transactions will invariably require selecting a relatively small number of families in particular settings. No single study will be able to embrace a truly representative set of families and organizations. One can only hope to build up information about a variety of families and organizations over time; because of its special openness to direct observation, the psychiatric hospital is a perfectly reasonable place to begin.

Ironically, despite the relative openness and simplicity of the inpatient ward, there remain significant difficulties in directly observing the nature the family's link to it. From clinical observations we know that families express the nature of their ties to the ward community in a great range of fleeting contacts: phone calls to the staff, visits to patients, conversations with other families inside and outside the ward setting, complaints written to the hospital director, presents given to the staff, paying (or not paying) hospital bills. No study can keep track of all these behaviors and the countless others by which any particular family expresses its connectedness or separateness from the ward community. We needed an observational setting even simpler than the entire ward community but one in which the family's overall ties to the ward community might be reflected. The ideal solution to this dilemma was the multiple family group.

On the ward that we studied, a group consisting of all patients and their families was held for sixty minutes weekly. The major explicit objective of the meeting was to involve families in specific planning of activities and programs such as sports nights or picnics; the implicit objective here was to encourage families to engage in meaningful activities together, experience a sense of mastery, and get some perceptions of their efforts from the staff and other families. Though these objectives were at least partially met, the meeting became a microcosm of the entire span of ward social life. The conflicts, alliances, and transactions between one family and another or between family and staff, patterns which were apparent in the everyday life of the ward, also emerged in the multiple family group.

Because of the relative simplicity and accessibility of the multiple family group, we could develop relatively straightforward measures of the quality or architecture of the family's links to it. All our measurements came from two sources. A silent observer in the group meeting recorded all seating positions of each group member and who in the group spoke to whom. The remaining data came from a sociometry questionnaire and a questionnaire directly assessing the family's experience of cohesiveness and engagement with the larger social group. As described in Chapter 7, our initial interest was in three aspects of the link's architecture: status, boundary openness, and cohesion.

STATUS. We have defined status as the family's centrality in a social setting. It is an amalgam of several simpler concepts, chiefly influence and prestige. In the multiple family group, the staff functioned more as co-participants than as authoritarian leaders. They did not make concerted efforts to control the flow of discussion. Thus, the amount of talking any family did reflected its capacity to insert itself into the flow of interaction. To talk in a multiple family group is to command a central resource of the group: its time. Families who talk a lot invariably are talked to almost as frequently (the correlation between number of statements made by a family and number made to a family is usually over .90). Thus, talking clearly attracts a good deal of attention.[7] This is reflected in choices members of the multiple family group made when filling out their sociometry questionnaire each month. They were asked four simple questions: "List below the four individuals in the Tuesday evening large family group whom you MOST LIKE; . . . you LEAST LIKE; . . . you KNOW THE BEST; . . . you KNOW THE LEAST." If any individual is chosen frequently on any of the first three he is clearly a conspicuous member of the group. We discovered that being chosen on the last item — know the least — also indexed a more subtle form of conspicuousness. When a member picks another as the person he knows the least, he seems to be saying, "This is someone I don't know very well but would like to." In all the multiple family groups we have studied, there is a significant and positive correlation between the amount of talking a family does and the frequency with which their members are selected for any or all of these sociometric choices.

BOUNDARY OPENNESS. In Chapter 7 we offered a broad definition of boundary openness which focused on the freedom with which a family allowed people and information to enter into its midst and shape its development. In the current study we explore a more restricted aspect of this concept. We examined indicators of the family's readiness to form sustained relationships with others. Families with closed boundaries tend to cling to one another in a novel social situation. We observed the frequency with which individuals chose other members of their own families on the sociometry questionnaires. Here, in contrast to the sociometric measurement of status, all four categories of choice should not be considered equivalent. For example, if members in a family choose each other as "know the least" they are probably being sarcastic. If they frequently or exclusively choose one another as "most like" or "know the best," they probably are showing evidence of a relatively closed family boundary. If they choose one another as "least like" very often or exclusively, the family probably has a relatively closed boundary constructed around a good deal of hostility, which members may or may not be acknowledging to one another (sociometry is done in private and never disclosed to others). A long series of studies of natural groups supports the notion that sociometry may be used to identify bounded subgroups within a larger social system.[8] Seating patterns can supplement information about subgroup boundaries. Previous studies suggest that, when people are free to choose their own seats, proximity of one individual to another may indicate an attraction between the two or readiness for developing a relationship.[9] In our large family group some proximal seating locations may reflect established relationships, whereas others may be purely coincidental. However, if a family group tends to sit together rather than disperse, and if the pattern persists over most of the meetings the family attends, we feel justified in assuming that this reflects a continuing strong bond within the family and relatively weak bonds with the rest of the group—that is closed boundaries.

COHESION. We have defined cohesion as the investment and commitment the family feels toward the social environment. We developed two measures of this aspect of the family's link. The first was a questionnaire—adapted from Yalom's studies (1966) of therapy groups—given monthly; this was designed to assess directly the family's feelings about the multiple family group. The questionnaire contained items such as: "If most families in your group decided to dissolve the group by leaving, would you like an opportunity to dissuade them?" and "To what degree do you feel you are included, as a family, by the group in the group's activities?" A third example is, "I expect my family's problems to be helped by family group therapy." A recent study has shown that the *number* of items a respondent answers to this self-administered questionnaire may be a more valid indicator of his engagement in the group than the *content* of his answers (see Koran and Costell, 1973). A second measure of cohesion was simply attendence at the large multiple family group meeting. The identified patients were under considerable pressure from the staff to attend. Thus, attendance patterns by the parents were the most crucial data here; the index most sensitive to variation of parental attendance was a simple frequency measure: percentage of total meetings attended by at least one parent.

Predictions. Our basic task in assessing the cycle hypothesis is to use it, in concert with our concepts about family paradigms and shared constructs, to generate specific hypotheses or predictions. As we will detail below, the predictions in this study involved more than establishing hypotheses prior to collecting our data. They were predictions in the more literal sense of the term: we measured a family's paradigm as soon after its entry into the treatment program as we could and used these measures to predict the kind of links the family would form with that program, as evidenced by its relationships with the multiple family group. We could use the basic model in two ways to fashion our predictions. The first would be to take two or three of the main dimensions of paradigm and construct (for example, coordination, configuration, and closure) and derive specific predictions about the kinds of links families who are high or low on these dimensions will fashion with the inpatient community. We might predict, for instance, that families high in configuration will develop links high in status. This strategy would certainly be the most continuous with the way our model was set forth in Chapters 4 and 5. A second approach is to derive predictions from our conceptualization of family types. For example, we might contrast four groups of families to their position on the coordination and configuration dimensions: high-high (environment-sensitive); high-low (consensus-sensitive); low-high (achievement-sensitive); and low-low (distance-sensitive). We chose the second strategy—a very close relative, actually, of the first—because it seemed both easier and more sure-footed in a first test of the cycle hypothesis. It was easier to imagine how a particular family, with a profile of individual scores, would react in a new setting than to imagine how a single dimension of shared construing could influence the character of family-community link.

Whether we use family types or dimensions, the model—as illustrated in Figure 7.1 and described in Chapter 7—is too simple by itself to generate plausible hypotheses. A major fault lies between steps 2 and 3, "interaction patterns with the social environment." The model implies that these patterns are strictly a consequence of the family's paradigm and ordinary constructs. However, on intuitive, logical, and empirical grounds it is safe to argue that these patterns must be jointly determined by the family and the social environment with which it interacts. Thus, in fashioning our predictions for our four family types we will include what we regard as salient aspects of the ward as we know it from clinical observations of its processes. In particular, we note the high level of social interaction among almost all members resulting from the ward's emphasis on sociotherapy. Although we did not measure it specifically, the inpatient service would probably score high on belief in the moral order. The authority structure of the ward as well as an interest in medical diagnosis and somatotherapy indicate that it would score somewhat high on the technical order as well, although this is less clear.

ENVIRONMENT-SENSITIVE FAMILIES. Families who are high on both the coherence and the integration dimensions, environment-sensitive families, have shared constructs showing high configuration and coordination. As a group, then, they experience themselves in the same universe, a universe they have confidence they can understand and master. According to the cycle hypothesis, they should view the new world of the psychiatric hospital in the same way. Environment-sensitive families should effectively explore this new social world together; they should be able to understand quickly the social structure of the community and to make conspicuous contributions to it as well as effectively express their own needs. They should score high on measures of status within the community. Moreover, they are oriented outward; they are collectively preoccupied with the outer world. This fundamental orientation is shaped by their empiricist position on the reference dimension of the paradigm. Their boundaries should be porous, open, and flexible. Finally, their quick grasp of the ins and outs of the community, their consequent success in managing their relations within it, and the notice they receive from others should maintain a high level of morale and a subjective feeling of mastery. Thus, we predict they should also score high on measures of cohesion.

ACHIEVEMENT-SENSITIVE FAMILIES. Families high on the coherence dimension of paradigm, achievement-sensitives, have constructs which, like those of environment-sensitives, show high configuration. However, they are low on the integration dimension and their constructs show little coordination. In some new and unfamiliar settings we might expect members in these families to branch out on their own; there would be a strong tendency for each member to form his own relationships, make his own observations, and gradually build his own social world. However, some aspects of this pattern are likely to be blocked when a family of this kind interacts with a community that is itself highly integrated, as we believe the ward we studied to be. The community plans so many of its activities together and gives such high priority to its own integration that it is likely to resist being divided up, as achievement-sensitive families would ordinarily be inclined to do. If members are to achieve their separate worlds in the ward community, they may run into one another's interests. The family must coexist in the same multiple family group, deal with the same psychiatrist, and, while it is on the ward, be in the same confined space. Competition may develop between members. Competition may not be the primary aim in such families, but, it is reasonable to argue, it results from the conflict between members' preferred modes of transacting with the environment and the type of environment with which they are interacting. It is difficult to predict in advance precisely what the impact of this secondarily induced competition might be on the three aspects of links we are studying. It is plausible to assume, however, that cohesion will be relatively immune from it. Cohesion, we have argued, reflects the family's sense of investment in and commitment to the ward community. Environment-sensitive families should score high on this dimension as a consequence of the family's growing mastery and confidence in the ward setting; they probably feel, "Our family is doing pretty well in this place." In contrast, individuals in achievement-sensitive families are likely to experience a personal optimism and investment — "This is the kind of place I think I can handle." As a consequence, their scores on the questionnaire and attendance measures of cohesion should be reasonably high. Their competitiveness, however, should intrude in the two other aspects of linkage we examine. First, their competitiveness will interfere with attainment of status or centrality. Just as one member is beginning to achieve some recognition in the eyes of the community, another member will undercut it. The net effect will be relatively low scores on status. Similarly, the high level of competitiveness will force the members to pay a great deal of attention to one another. The competition will be absorbing and distracting. The result will be that family members are less open to experience and relationships from the outside. The net effect should be low scores on measures of boundary openness.

CONSENSUS-SENSITIVE FAMILIES. Families who are high on the integration dimension but low on the coherence dimension, consensus-sensitives, experience their world as in constant flux and movement, controlled by forces beyond their control and understanding. Nonetheless, they are bound together by an abiding belief that they, as a group, face the same fate in an unpredictable world. Indeed, in Chapter 1 we suggested that these families may derive their sense of order and predictability from their own interaction and patterns. When a family of this type enters an entirely unknown social world such as an inpatient service, we would predict that it would be especially frightened and mistrustful. It might hover on the periphery of the community, relatively unnoticed by others, and hence show low scores on measures of status. Since it is preoccupied with self-protection, we would expect it to develop firm boundaries and not be accessible to new relationships, thus achieving low scores on measures of boundary openness. Finally, consensus-sensitives' fear of a social world they regard as uncontrollable ought to lead to low morale and subjective feelings of estrangement. We expect low scores on cohesion.

DISTANCE-SENSITIVE FAMILIES. A distance-sensitive family, low on both the coherence and integration dimensions, not only experiences the world outside itself as unknowable and uncontrollable, but family members feel themselves to be isolated individuals alone in a chaotic sea. Unlike the consensus-sensitives, they cannot derive a sense of order from a belief that the family is a stable, dependable, and bounded group. We expect them to take the same stance toward the ward community. The family will disperse. Each member will function independently from the others in his family. The family boundary will be open, but for a different reason than for environment-sensitives. In the latter case, the family is collectively open and alive to the new possibilities in a novel social situation. In distance-sensitive families members simply have no strong connection to each other. In the laboratory these families do poorly on problems. We provided evidence in Chapter 2 that this poor performance is unrelated to their cognitive skills or intelligence; rather, it seems to be socially determined. The family conceives of itself as a failing and dispersing group. We predict that these families will feel as hopeless and helpless on the ward as they do in the laboratory. They will grasp little of the ward's structure and, failing to distinguish themselves in the eyes of others in any way, will never achieve high status. Moreover, they will feel pessimistic and remote and will score low on measures of cohesion. Their low scores will reflect a somewhat different subjective state than similarly low scores in the consensus-sensitive families. In the latter, low scores reflect each member's feeling of being huddled with his family against a threatening social world. In the distance-sensitive families, each member feels a solitary helplessness and pessimism.

Table 8.9 summarizes the predictions for each of our four groups of families.

Subjects. The subjects were the same as those used for the ward and family perception studies described in Chapter 2. All families of patients who were admitted during a two-year period were eligible to participate if they met the following criteria: there must be two parents in the home; if the child was not a biological offspring, then the step- or adopting parents must have been in the home for a minimum of five years; all members must be fluent in English; and no member should have had medical problems which would hinder sight, hearing, or mobility. Thirty-seven of the eligible seventy

TABLE 8.9   PREDICTIONS OF THE LINKS BETWEEN EACH OF THE FOUR TYPES OF FAMILIES AND THE MULTIPLE FAMILY GROUP

Type of Family	Architecture of the Links		
	Status	Boundary openness	Cohesion
Environment-sensitive	High	High	High
Consensus-sensitive	Low	Low	Low
Achievement-sensitive	Low	Low	High
Distance-sensitive	Low	High	Low

families chose to participate. Of this number, two were dropped from the sample because their education and social class were far below the other families'; a variety of technical problems prevented us from analyzing data for three others, which left a final sample of thirty-two.

Classification of families. We used the card sorting procedure, as described in Chapter 2, to classify the families into four groups (environment-sensitive, achievement-sensitive, and so on). Each family was asked to sort a group of cards while each member was isolated in a booth but had telephone contact with other members. In the first phase of the task the members could not talk to one another and thus had to work alone; in the second phase they could talk together and thus could work together if they chose; in the third phase of the task they again worked without talking. Configuration was measured by improvement in the quality of the sort from the initial to the second phase and by improvement from the initial to the final phase. Coordination was measured by similarity of the individual members' sorts on the second and third phases of the task.

The distribution of our thirty-two families is shown in Figure 8.1. Note that our eight consensus-sensitive families have lower coordination scores than our seven environment-sensitive families. We will return later to that anomaly of the distribution. The four groups of families, as classified by the card sorting task, were approximately equal with respect to father's and mother's age; the intelligence of father, mother, child, and the total family (mean of three individuals), as measured by the Shipley-Hartford scale; mother's and father's education; and distribution among Catholicism, Judaism, and Protestantism. From a clinical perspective, some of the patients in the consensus-sensitive group may have had a more serious disturbance: two of the eight were diagnosed as schizophrenic and four of the eight had been hospitalized previously.

Summary of methods. As soon as the family entered the treatment program they joined the multiple family group. Variables assessing their links to this group were computed from the first meeting to the last meeting they attended. The card sort was administered at another institution. We were concerned that a family's attitude might be shaped quickly by its experience in the first few days or even hours in the program; had the testing occurred at the hospital site, this attitude might have heavily influenced the family's performance. We hoped that testing at another site might be perceived as more neutral by the families; thus we hoped to gain a better picture of their usual patterns. However, testing at another

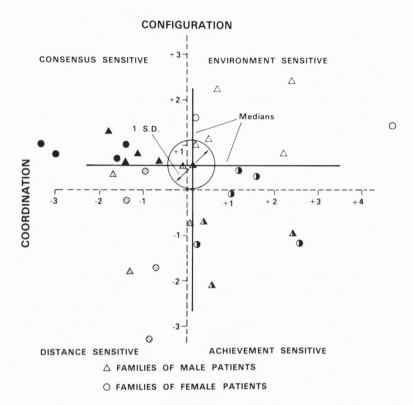

Figure 8.1.　*The distribution of thirty-two families in the sample into four major family groups*

site often led to delays. The median week of testing was 5; the median length of stay in the program was 19.5 weeks.

Our critical dependent variables were measured by a mixture of questionnaire and direct observation methods. All direct observation coding was carefully checked for reliability, which was quite high. For each variable the score for each family, on all dependent variables, was a mean of the scores for individual sessions.

These individual session scores were the rank percentile — that is, the family's rank position on any score divided by the number of families present at the session. This score simultaneously corrects for variation in overall score levels from session to session (for example, some sessions are very talkative ones; others nearly silent) and for variation in the number of families attending sessions.

STATUS. Two measures were used here: the total number of statements per session made by the family, and the frequency with which the family was chosen on any of the four categories of the sociometry questionnaire (given monthly to all families in the multiple family group, whether or not they participated in the study).

OPENNESS OF BOUNDARY. The two measures here were: the mean distance each family sat from the others in each session (averaged across all sessions), and the frequency with which family members chose others in the family as best known, most liked, or least liked.

COHESION. The two measures here were: a cohesiveness questionnaire, and the percentage of sessions attended by at least one parent. The former had two scores: a cohesiveness score based on the substantive response of the subject to each item, and a simpler score for the number of items actually answered rather than left blank (whatever the substance of the answer was).

Results. STATUS. Table 8.10 shows the findings for sociometry,

TABLE 8.10   RELATIVE FREQUENCY OF BEING CHOSEN ON SOCIOMETRY IN ALL CATEGORIES OF CHOICE (MOST LIKE, LEAST LIKE, MOST KNOW, LEAST KNOW). THE SCORES SHOWN ARE PARENTAL RANK PERCENTILES AGGREGATED ACROSS SESSIONS BY A MEAN WEIGHTED FOR NUMBER OF FAMILY MEMBERS PRESENT AT THE SESSION. (*Prediction*: Environment-sensitive high.)

Review of family types

	Configuration	
Coordination	**Low**	**High**
High	Consensus-sensitive	Environment-sensitive
Low	Distance sensitive	Achievement-sensitive

Sociometry data

	Configuration		
Coordination	**Low**	**High**	
High	.59	.62	$F_{coor} = 4.84 \ (p = .039)$
Low	.55	.50	

Analysis within roles across groups: Analysis of fathers' scores and mothers' scores separately replicated that of the family scores shown above. For fathers, $F_{coor} = 5.79$ ($p = .025$), and for mothers, $F_{coor} = 3.47$ ($p = .08$). Children showed a trend in the same direction but there was no significant main or interaction effects.

Note: The ANOVAs reported in this table as well as those reported in Tables 8.11-8.15 were three-way ANOVAs with sex of patient as the third independent variable. Analysis by sex has been omitted from the tables for simplicity. In these five analyses there were no main effects due to sex and only three interactions involving sex.

the across-session weighted mean rank percentiles for the number of times a family, the parents, or the patient were chosen by non-family members. All four categories of sociometric choice have been summed: most like, least like, know best, and know least. The "family" analysis uses family means which were ranked—within each session—with respect to other family means. This analysis, not shown in the table, yielded a small coordination effect (F = 3.00; p = .097). The "parental" analysis uses parental means ranked with respect to other parental means. Father, mother, and child analyses use the appropriate individual scores. We predicted that only environment-sensitive families would show high scores on this variable. As Table 8.10 shows, both environment-sensitive and consensus-sensitive parents achieved high scores (these two groups comprise families high in coordination). The difference between the families is attributable to very significant differences between fathers from high and low coordination families and somewhat less clear-cut differences, in the same direction, between mothers. Type of family does not clearly predict the number of sociometric choices received by children.

The findings in Table 8.11 for number of speech units initiated, show a similar picture. Again, the highly coordinated parents have higher scores. However, when examined separately, neither fathers' nor mothers' scores show differences across the four types of families, which suggests that only when they are added together can a clear-cut difference be observed. (These findings for individuals are not shown in Table 8.11.) There is a possibility that the staff—particularly the multiple family group leader (who did the vast majority of total staff talking)—could encourage quieter families to speak. Might the findings in the table be attributable to the intervention of staff? In the multiple family group a very

TABLE 8.11 RELATIVE FREQUENCY OF SPEECH INITIATION. THE TABLE SHOWS PARENTAL MEANS ONLY. THE SCORES SHOWN ARE RANK PERCENTILES AGGREGATED ACROSS SESSIONS BY A WEIGHTED MEAN. (*Prediction*: Environment-sensitive high.)

	Configuration		
Coordination	Low	High	
High	.61	.59	F_{coor} = 3.49 (p = .074)
Low	.47	.53	

Analysis within roles across groups: Separate analyses of fathers', mothers', and children's scores did not show any significant across-group differences.

reliable way to get someone to speak is to talk to him. Analysis of speech sequences in many sessions shows that the person most likely to initiate a speech at any given moment is the person addressed by the most recent previous speech. Thus, a simple way for staff to encourage more speaking in a particular family is to talk more to that family. However, analysis of speech to and from staff shows virtually no differences for the four family types.

In sum, parents in high coordination families received more sociometric choices and talked more than those in low coordination families. We infer that they have achieved higher status in the group. This finding conforms to predictions, except that consensus-sensitive families achieve high rather than low scores. Further, family type predicts only parents' scores, not children's. We will discuss these two unanticipated findings later.

OPENNESS OF BOUNDARIES. Table 8.12 shows the relative frequency with which family members picked each other as most-liked members of the group. All five analyses show consensus- and achievement-sensitive families with higher scores than environment- and distance-sensitive families. This is statistically significant beyond the 0.1 level in four of the analyses, as shown by the *F* value for interaction of coordination and configuration. This pattern is more significant for families of male patients, as indicated by the *F* levels for the coordination × configuration × sex.

Table 8.13 shows the relative frequency with which family

TABLE 8.12 RELATIVE FREQUENCY OF WITHIN-FAMILY CHOICE OF SOCIOMETRY, MOST LIKE. THE SCORES SHOWN ARE RANK PERCENTILES FOR THE FAMILY MEANS AGGREGATED ACROSS ALL SESSIONS BY A WEIGHTED MEAN. (*Prediction*: Since this index is inversely proportional to boundary openness, environment-sensitive and distance-sensitive families are expected to be low.)

Coordination	Configuration	
	Low	High
High	.65	.50	$F_{coor \times conf} = 3.08$ ($p = .09$)
Low	.56	.69	

Analysis within roles across groups: Analysis for parents, fathers and mothers separately replicated the findings for the family-level analysis shown above. For parents, $F_{coor \times conf} = 3.79$ ($p = .064$); for fathers, $F_{coor \times conf} = 3.30$ ($p = .08$); for mothers, $F_{coor \times conf} = 8.39$ ($p = .008$). For children the finding was replicated for boys only, $F_{coor \times conf \times sex} = 4.81$ ($p = .039$).

TABLE 8.13 INTRAFAMILY CHOICES, LEAST LIKE, ON SOCIOMETRY. ACROSS-SESSION MEAN OF PERCENTAGES OF TOTAL SOCIOMETRY CHOICES WHICH WERE INTRAFAMILY, LEAST LIKE. (*Prediction*: Since this index is inversely proportional to boundary openness, environment-sensitive and distance-sensitive families are expected to be low.)

Coordination	Configuration				
	Low		High		
Families					
High	0	.07	0	0	$P = .26$
	.07	.07	0	0	$k = 6$
	0	.28	0	0	$n = 8$
	.05	.04	0	0	$p = .005$
Low	0	0	0	0	
	0	0	0	.10	
	0	.08	0	0	
	0	0	0		
Parents					
High	0	0	0	0	$P = .23$
	.05	.03	0	0	$k = 5$
	0	.17	0	0	$n = 8$
	.08	.03	0		$p = .02$
Low	0	0	0	0	
	0	0	0	.13	
	0	.18	0	0	
	0	0	0		
Fathers					
High	0	0	0	0	
	0	0	0	0	
	0	.17	0	0	
	0	.05	0		$p = $ n.s.
Low	0	0	0	0	
	0	0	0	.17	
	0	0	0	0	
	0	0	0		
Mothers					
High	0	0	0	0	$P = .20$
	.08	.07	0	0	$k = 4$
	0	.18	0	0	$n = 8$
	.17	0	0	0	$p = .056$
Low	0	0	0	0	
	0	0	0	.08	
	0	.17	0	0	
	0		0	0	

TABLE 8.13, *continued*

Coordination	Configuration				
	Low		High		
Children					
High	0	.17	0	0	$P = .20$
	.10	.17	0	0	$k = 5$
	0	.50	0	0	$n = 8$
	0	.08	0		$p = .01$
Low	0	0	0	0	
	0	0	0	.05	
	0	0	0	0	
	0	0	0		

members picked others in their own family as least liked. The table shows the proportion of total choices made by the family that were in this category. For example, .08 means that 8 percent of the family's total sociometric choices of anyone, on any of the four questions, consisted of choices of a member in the same family as "least like." As the table shows, only eight families gave the intrafamily, least-like choices at all. Of these, a heavy concentration were in the consensus-sensitive group, particularly for mothers and children. The binomial theorem was used to assess the statistical significance of this finding, where P = number of families (or parents or particular individual) showing any intrafamily, least-like choices divided by the total number of families; k = number of consensus-sensitive families showing those choices and n = the number of consensus-sensitive families. Thus, the binomial probabilities in the table should be interpreted as the probability that as many as k consensus-families would show intrafamily, least-like choices by chance alone.

Finally, Table 8.14 shows that the pattern of findings for within-family choices on the sociometry is repeated for a very different kind of measure, intrafamily seating distance. Here the consensus-sensitives and achievement-sensitives are lower than the other two. Small distances imply closed boundary, just as frequent within-family sociometric choices do. Hence, this finding — numerically the opposite of the findings in Tables 8.12 and 8.13 — is, is fact, a replication. The finding, however, is only at the .099 level. Intrafamily distance scores, as computed here, have no strict analog for individuals. However, we computed an intraparent distance score, which showed virtually no difference across the four groups; this suggests that the seating distance between the child and

TABLE 8.14 INTRAFAMILY SEATING DISTANCE. THE SCORES SHOWN ARE
RANK PERCENTILES AGGREGATED ACROSS ALL SESSIONS BY A
WEIGHTED MEAN. (*Prediction*: Environment-sensitive and
distance-sensitive high.)

Coordination	Configuration		
	Low	High	
High	.55	.60	$F_{coor \times conf} = 2.94 \, (p = .099)$
Low	.64	.51	

his parents was a major contributor to the between-family
differences on the intrafamily distance score.

In sum, within-family sociometric choices and seating data suggest that boundaries are closed in achievement- and consensus-
sensitive families and open in environment- and distance-sensitives;
this conforms to predictions.

COHESION WITH THE GROUP. For this variable we had predicted
that high configuration families — environment-sensitive and
achievement-sensitive — would be high. Tables 8.15 and 8.16 show
the results actually obtained.

Table 8.15 presents data on the number of items answered on the
cohesiveness questionnaire. This is shown in absolute scores
averaged across all questionnaires submitted by the family. The
table shows that high coordination families tended to do better
than low coordination families; this finding appears entirely attributable to differences in the children's responses:

$$F_{coor} = 5.26 \quad (p = .032).$$

Children in distance-sensitive families have particularly low scores.
They filled out, on the average, fewer than half of the total items on
each cohesiveness questionnaire they submitted. It is of interest
that a very similar pattern of findings was obtained for the
sociometric questionnaires. Children in distance-sensitive families — and to a lesser extent their mothers — made fewer sociometric
choices than those in other groups.

Table 8.16 presents data on attendance. The distance-sensitive
families again show the lowest scores. Environment-sensitive
families of female patients also have low scores. We examined the
scores of each family in this group. All were high except for one
set of parents who never attended the group at all. A careful review
of charts and notes revealed that this family had a young child for
whom no childcare arrangements could be made. Clinical records
were quite explicit in indicating this to be an insurmountable prac-

TABLE 8.15   COHESIVENESS QUESTIONAIRE, NUMBER OF ITEMS ANSWERED. THE SCORES SHOWN ARE FAMILY MEAN RAW VALUES SUMMED ACROSS ALL SESSIONS BY A WEIGHTED MEAN. (*Prediction*: Environment-sensitive and achievement-sensitive high.)

	Configuration		
Coordination	Low	High	
High	16.2	16.4	$F_{coor} = 3.47\,(p = .076)$
Low	12.1	15.1	

TABLE 8.16   ATTENDANCE, PERCENTAGE OF MEETINGS ATTENDED BY AT LEAST ONE PARENT. THE SCORES SHOWN ARE AGGREGATED ACROSS SESSIONS BY A MEAN. (*Prediction:* Environment-sensitive and achievement-sensitive high.)

	Configuration		
Coordination	Low	High	
High	.94	.82	$F_{coor \times conf} = 10.79\,(p = .003)$
Low	.76	.92	

tical obstacle for attendance by a family otherwise engaged in the treatment program. We then looked at all other families with relatively poor attendance records. In all of these cases low motivation or family disorganization, rather than identifiable practical difficulties, was clearly a reason for poor attendance. Thus, a post hoc reanalysis of attendance, deleting the one environment-sensitive family, seemed justifiable. The mean attendance percentage for the environment-sensitive group became .90 with significant effects on analysis of variance:

$$F_{coor} = 2.95 \quad (p < .10).$$
$$F_{coor \times conf} = 4.70 \quad (p < .05).$$

For the profile analyses to follow, the deleted family is reincluded in the analyses.

We also examined the content of the family members' response to the questionnaire. The parents in achievement- and environment-sensitive families had higher scores than the others. Although this trend did not reach statistical significance, its direction conformed to predictions. In sum, it appears that the distance-sensitive families are consistently low on these measures of cohesion with the group.

Having examined the dependent variables one at a time, we may ask whether the entire set of variables taken together helps to distinguish our four groups of families. In particular, we can ask whether the profile or pattern of scores distinguished the four groups. For the six variables suitable for further analyses of variance we performed a profile analysis using a coordination x configuration x process variable measure design with repeated measures on the process variables. We used the most discriminating scores from each of the six variables: sociometric choices of parents, parental speech initiation, parents' within-family choices of most like, intrafamily seating distance, children's number of cohesiveness items answered, and parental attendance. For all six variables, significant F values were obtained for the following effects:

$$F_{coor} = 6.1 \quad (df = 1,26; p < .05).$$
$$F_{coor \times conf} = 3.8 \quad (df = 1,26; p < .10).$$

In this analysis, profile differences are suggested by these trends:

$$F_{coor \times process\ var} = 2.6 \quad (df = 1,26; p < .10).$$
$$F_{coor \times conf \times process\ var} = 3.12 \quad (df = 1,26; p < .10).$$

A more adequate test of profile differences requires analyses including only those variables without conceptual or statistical interrelationships. This may be done with triplets of variables, one from each of the three domains (status, boundaries, cohesion). For example, we can form two triplets by dividing the variables into those collected by direct, weekly observation of behavior (speech initiation, seating, and attendance) and those derived from the monthly questionnaires (being chosen on sociometry, within-family choices, and number of items answered on the cohesiveness questionnaire). The first of these two analyses yields a significant profile effect:

$$F_{conf \times coor \times process\ var} = 7.1 \quad (df = 1,26; p < .05).$$

The same is true for the second analysis of questionnaire responses:

$$F_{coor \times process\ var} = 7.1 \quad (df = 1,26; p < .05).$$

THE RELATIONSHIP BETWEEN PREDICTIONS AND OUTCOME

For two of our groups of families, the actual findings followed quite closely from predictions. Environment-sensitive families achieved high status, maintained open boundaries, and showed evidence of engagement and cohesion with the large group. Their behavior, in accord with our model, suggests optimism, a sense of mastery, and a capacity to understand new situations through open cooperation among members. Likewise, distance-sensitive families showed—as expected—low status, open boundaries, and little cohesion with the larger group. This also seems consistent with their laboratory performance, which suggested isolation between members, a deteriorating grasp of the problem situation, and a persistent pessimism. Achievement-sensitive families also showed findings consistent with predictions. We expected that members of individualistic families would compete with one another in the ward situation, particularly for status positions; we expected that as a result the family would not achieve high status. This expectation was confirmed. Achievement-sensitive families' competition may interfere with gaining status but does not impair their overall sense of understanding or controlling their environment. Hence, we predicted a high level of experienced cohesion with the group; this was found to some degree. We expected somewhat closed boundaries because family members would be relatively preoccupied with competitive issues among themselves and less free to form relationships with others. While findings confirmed this prediction, there was one surprise: members of achievement-sensitive families often selected each other on sociometry as most liked and rarely picked one another as least liked.

The most surprising findings were for consensus-sensitive families. We had pictured these families as frightened of or easily alienated from new environments. We expected them to remain withdrawn from the group and inconspicuous to other families; this should have shown up in low status and cohesion scores. We found just the reverse. One approach to explaining this surprising finding starts with the observation that although consensus-sensitive families all achieve relatively high coordination scores on the card sort (by definition), their scores are lower than those of environment-sensitive families (see Figure 8.1). We asked what the results for status might be if our sample had contained a more "purified" subsample of consensus-sensitive families, that is, those with very high coordination scores. Our data permit us to extrapolate from our current findings by correlating coordination with the status variables for the consensus-sensitive families as a separate group and to contrast these correlations with the environment-sensitive families. It must be emphasized that these groups are very small, containing eight and seven families respectively; thus, the analysis is presented for heuristic purposes only. Table 8.17 shows the results of this analysis: in every case, the correlations are negative for the consensus-sensitive group and positive for the environment-sensitive group. This suggests that if our sample had contained "pure" consensus-sensitive families (with very high coordination), they would have achieved very low status

TABLE 8.17   CONTRAST BETWEEN ENVIRONMENT AND CONSENSUS-SENSITIVE FAMILIES ON
THE RELATIONSHIP OF COORDINATION AND STATUS. STATISTIC SHOWN IS THE
PRODUCT-MOMENT CORRELATION, COMPUTED SEPARATELY FOR EACH
GROUP, BETWEEN COORDINATION AND FOUR INDICATORS OF STATUS. ALSO
SHOWN ARE z_r SCORES FOR ESTIMATING THE SIGNIFICANCE OF THE DIF-
FERENCE BETWEEN THE CORRELATIONS.

Status variable	Family type	r	z_r	z_r difference btwn. two groups	Signif. level (two-tailed)
Speech initiation, family	Environment-sensitive	.61	.71	1.78	< .05
	Consensus-sensitive	− .79	− 1.07		
Speech initiation, parental	Environment-sensitive	.44	.41	1.28	< .10
	Consensus-sensitive	− .67	− .81		
Chosen by others (sociometry), family	Environment-sensitive	.19	.19	.75	n.s.
	Consensus-sensitive	− .51	− .56		
Chosen by others (sociometry), parental	Environment-sensitive	.36	.38	.95	n.s.
	Consensus-sensitive	− .52	− .58		

scores, as predicted. Figure 8.2 displays the point graphically. It shows values for two of the status variables which the regression equation estimates for a consensus-sensitive group of families whose coordination scores are equal to those high scores obtained by the environment-sensitive group. We performed the same within-group correlations between coordination and the cohesion variables. Most of the coefficients approached zero; hence this approach does not explain the surprisingly high cohesion scores in the consensus-sensitive group. It is possible that in the consensus-sensitive group high cohesion may be a secondary result of achieving high status. However, within this group of families, correlations between status variables and cohesion variables approach zero.

Why is coordination negatively correlated with status in the

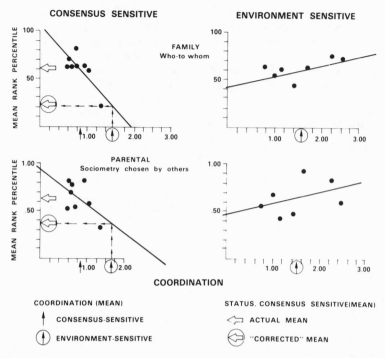

Figure 8.2. *The relationship between coordination and status in consensus-sensitive and environment-sensitive groups*

consensus-sensitive group and positively correlated in the environment-sensitive group? Our initial concept of consensus-sensitive families provides a partial explanation. We have argued that coordination in a consensus-sensitive family functions to protect the family from an outside world it perceives as hostile. Thus, very high levels of coordination in a consensus-sensitive family would suggest greater feelings of danger and a greater need to withdraw. In Chapter 2 the automated teletype experiment demonstrated a similar mechanism in the laboratory. In this experiment, the consensus-sensitive—but not environment-sensitive—family improved its problem-solving effectiveness as coordination between its members was reduced. In other words, as the family's coordination is reduced, its capacity to deal effectively with an externally given problem increases. We may be seeing the same phenomenon in the multiple family group. Consensus-sensitive families with relatively reduced coordination are more effective in claiming group resources (for example, the time to speak often) and attracting group attention than are the more highly coordinated consensus-sensitive families—hence the negative correlations between coordination and status measures in this group. By contrast, coordination in environment-sensitive families—according to our initial concept—reflects true cooperation aimed at effective problem solving; higher levels ought to, and do, lead to more status.

Our current findings suggest an important addition to our view of consensus-sensitive families: the danger they most fear may not come from without but from unacknowledged negative feelings within the family itself. Recall that these are virtually the only families to select one another, on sociometry, as least liked. Since members know that others in their family will never see the sociometric questionnaires they fill out, sociometry may give them a chance to express hidden feelings which are never openly shared with other family members. It is possible that consensus-sensitive families, with particularly high levels of coordination, are especially unable to tolerate and acknowledge negative feelings. They project these feelings onto the outer world from which they then withdraw. An indicator of this withdrawal may be the relatively low status they achieve (in contrast to the less coordinated consensus-sensitive families).

One further point, concerning the match between predictions and outcome, is important. Our model was conceived as an aid to predicting the quality of the engagement of the whole family in a milieu therapy program. Our results showed that for several dependent variables the predictions were significant only for parents. The clearest example is the two status variables: being chosen by sociometry and initiating speech. A child's status in the multiple family group is not predictable from our classification of his family. This may be due to his much greater opportunity to interact as an individual apart from his family with staff, other patients, and even a few other families. He can establish his own status based on many of his own attributes, and in response to many group processes, which are not connected to his family. The boundary variables show a more consistent influence of family type on all members of the family. Within-family sociometric choices of "like most" conform to predictions for mothers (very clearly), for fathers (trend), and for boys. Within-family choices of "like least" conform to predictions for mothers and children; the seating measure probably reflects, at least in part, behavior of both children and parents. The cohesion measures show a striking split: the family classification predicts attendance patterns for parents and the degree of completion of questionnaire for the children. It is possible that the multiple family group we studied—or the inpatient service which sponsored it—had developed covert norms concerning what forms of resistance or uncooperativeness were tolerable. The covert norms might be quite age-specific. Poor attendance might have been tolerable for adults because they are perceived as more peripheral members of the overall community. However, failure to complete the questionnaire might be seen as very gauche for those parents who do attend but tolerable misbehavior for "acting out" adolescents.

Long-Term Links between the Family and the Environment

Our main concern in this chapter has been to clarify the simple cycle hypothesis in order to derive from it propositions that are clear enough for empirical testing. In the first section of this chapter we focused on steps 4 and 6 of the cycle hypothesis: the reciprocal influence beween type of environment and family paradigm. In particular, we clarified our scheme for typifying social environments through delineating the social organizers which shape and maintain them. Our concern in the first section was a relatively narrow one: to define how social organizers in a very special form of organization, the psychiatric hospital, might develop and then exert their influence. We presented data which supported certain aspects of these more specific hypotheses: the relationships between personal needs and technical preferences. We argued that organizational objectives of psychiatric hospitals consist of technical preferences of the ruling elite, technical preferences which are rooted in the personal needs and values of that elite. The data in this section helped to clarify the dimensions which might distinguish organizational objectives of psychiatric hospitals and perhaps other kinds of corporate social environments. We specified two: belief in the technical order and belief in the moral order. We speculated that the former might reciprocally influence and be influenced by configuration/coherence and that latter would be reciprocally related to coordination/integration.

In the second section we looked at another aspect of the cycle hypothesis, what we have called family-environment links. In Chapter 7 we had already begun to specify in what ways family-environment links could differ from one another. We outlined three different modes of analysis: examination of the medium of the link (does the family establish an ambassador or does it engage the environment as a coherent group?); the motivation of the link (is the family coerced, is it paid in some form of currency, or is it involved out of its own sense of commitment?); and the architecture of the link (the family's status or centrality; its openness and the intensity of its engagement). The second section of this chapter examined only the last of these three, the architecture of the links. We sought to derive from the cycle hypothesis specific predictions linking type of family paradigm and specific architecture of the family-environment link. The specific empirical test was again a narrow one: the short-term links a family makes with a psychiatric hospital.

In this section we seek, in several ways, to broaden our examination of the relationship between family paradigm and the architecture of family-environment links. First, we employ a nonclinical sample of families; this sample is probably more representative than the families of psychiatric patients we have employed at many other points in this book. Second, we will examine three dimensions of paradigm—configuration (coherence), coordination (integration), and closure (reference)—and their relationship to family-environment links. Most important, we will examine longer-term links between the family and its social environment. We are interested, in particular, in the links between the family and its kin and friends. Our first findings—which we summarize here—pertain primarily to kin.

A Study of Families' Ties to their Kin

We are, in effect, extending a tradition of research begun by Elizabeth Bott almost twenty-five years ago (see Bott, 1957). We are proposing to examine the relationship between internal family process and the family's network of relationships with people outside the family. However, our specific concerns are quite different from those of Bott and the long line of investigators who have followed her. First, we are not interested simply in the effects of the network on family process. Rather, our cycle hypothesis alerts us to a more reciprocal influence between family and network. Furthermore, it adds, quite specifically, the notion that properties intrinsic to the family can shape the character of its network relations. In addition, we are interested in aspects of family process—its paradigm, shared constructions, and the problem-solving patterns under their control—which no previous investigator has thought relevant to network relations. Nonetheless, in our own investigation of the relationship between internal family process and the family's ties to its network it will be useful to use traditional measures of the family's network or relatively modest elaborations of these. By doing so, we will be able to relate our findings to a relatively rich tradition of previous research in this area. In order to use these traditional measures it will be necessary to show how they relate to our three major linkage variables: status or centrality; openness; and engagement or cohesion.

The most traditional and frequently used measure of a family's (or an individual's) network is its *size*. We can ask each member of the family to list those individuals who are important to him in any way.[10] He can list kin and nonkin, but he should exclude members of his immediate family. Network size, then, is simply the number of people so listed. This number is similar to the sociometry measure we used in the previous section to define openness of family boundary. In other words, the size of a family's network gives some indication of its openness to relationships with others and more important, we postulate, to a wide range of experience, viewpoints, stimulation, and information from outside the family. We can thus recognize in the traditional variable of network size our own architectural variable of openness.

The second highly traditional measure of network is *degree*.[11] Degree measures the interconnection between the individuals in the family's network. We ask each family member to consider the list of people he has selected as important to him and tell us which of these people know one another. Degree is computed by dividing two times the number of connections, as indicated by each member, by the total number of different individuals listed. In effect, degree is the average number of other people known by each individual in the network. Traditionally, degree is seen more as a measure of the relationships between the members of the family's network and not a measure of the family's link to that network. However, Figure 8.3 makes clear that degree is a very good index of the latter. When degree is low the family is tied to its network by a series of single, direct strands. In effect, the family in low degree networks occupies a central position. When degree is very high, the target family is just a component of a richly cross-joined large group; it occupies a much less central position. Indeed, it was the substance of Bott's work that highly cross-joined networks exerted profound control over its component families, whereas families in poorly cross-joined networks had much more autonomy in fashioning their own lives. Thus, we can recognize in the traditional measure of degree our own concerns with centrality. In our hospital study centrality and status were closely linked. We cannot here claim that low degree necessarily implies that the family has more status in its kin or friendship network, but it is highly plausible that the family with a low degree network has more autonomy and room for initiative.

We used these two traditional measures of size and degree to fashion a third index, which we called *shared connection*. It was an attempt, on the one hand, to stick close to the traditional network measures, and on the other, to represent our own interest in exploring the intensity of engagement by the family in its network. The

NETWORK SIZE: NUMBER OF SIGNIFICANT INDIVIDUALS
OUTSIDE THE NUCLEAR FAMILY

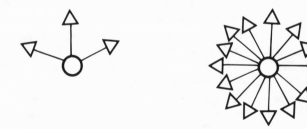

LOW: 3   HIGH: 14

DEGREE OF CONNECTION: EMBEDDEDNESS IN
A SYSTEM OF EXTRA-FAMILY RELATIONSHIPS

2 x NO. CONNECTIONS/NO. NAMES

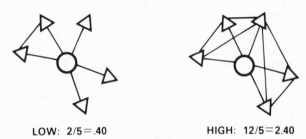

LOW: 2/5=.40   HIGH: 12/5=2.40

SHARED PERCEPTION OF CONNECTION: FAMILY MEMBERS'
JOINT EMBEDDEDNESS IN A SYSTEM OF
EXTRA-FAMILY RELATIONSHIPS

NO. COMMON CONNECTIONS/NO. TOTAL CONNECTIONS

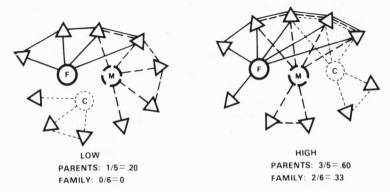

LOW   HIGH
PARENTS: 1/5=.20   PARENTS: 3/5=.60
FAMILY: 0/6=0   FAMILY: 2/6=.33

Figure 8.3. *Illustrations of network indices*

measure is computed by counting the number of specific linkages between people in the network, reported in common by the family, and dividing by the total number of linkages the family reports. This index, then, is a measure of the extent to which the family is jointly invested in the same network groupings. A high score implies that the whole family is engaged in the same richly cross-joined network. In this sense, it reflects the family's heavy investment in being a component of a larger, coherent group (or perhaps several of these groups). This measure bears only some resemblance to the measures of engagement or cohesion we used in the hospital study. The latter emphasized variation in the involvement each individual felt in the ward community. Shared connection, on the other hand, reflects variation in the shared involvement in the most communal aspects of the overall network.

As in our study of short-term links between the family and the psychiatric hospital, we want to clarify our cycle hypothesis in order to develop specific predictions about the relationship between family paradigm, on the one hand, and network size, degree, and shared connection, on the other. We face several new problems in fashioning these predictions. First, we seek to employ three dimensions of paradigm, instead of the two used in the hospital study. We are adding closure/reference to configuration/coherence and coordination/integration. In the hospital study we had only two dimensions, and thus only four types of families. Three dimensions yield eight types of families, which makes predictions, using types, very unwieldy. Thus, in this study our predictions were developed to relate the three dimensions to size, degree, and shared connection.

A second problem is that networks are collectivities quite unlike psychiatric wards. Perhaps the central difference is that they are not closed, bounded groups; indeed they are open and unbounded. Except for those of very high degree, networks are not even collectivities in the true sense of the word: there is no consensus among members as to who is part of the collectivity and who is not. There is, in effect, a different network for each individual who is asked to describe the people important to him. The impact of family paradigm on network relationships is likely, therefore, to be different than on relations to a relatively closed community such as a psychiatric ward. For example, we predicted (accurately, as it turned out) that achievement-sensitive families would not achieve high status in the community. Our prediction was based on a view that in these families members would compete with one another and thereby undercut one another's attempts to establish status. We saw competition in achievement-sensitive families as a product of both the separateness of members inherent to the family and the closedness of the community which would not tolerate being divided. Networks, however, are much more susceptible to division; it is quite possible for each member to fashion his own relationships with an exclusive group of others. Overlap between the networks of family members can be quite small or entirely absent. We will take this central difference between closed communities and open networks into account in making our predictions.

A third problem in making predictions is that we are studying networks composed of kin and nonkin. On the one hand, it seems quite plausible that relationships between paradigm and network might take one form for kin and quite another for nonkin. There is nothing in the cycle hypothesis, as so far stated, which clarifies exactly what these differences might be. It seems conservative to make general predictions relating paradigm and network, neglecting the distinction between kin and nonkin.

Finally, our findings from the hospital study alert us to the possibility that paradigm dimensions may be related to the architecture of family-environment links only for *specific role players*. For example, coordination seems closely related to status only for parents. Despite our awareness that this specificity might be required for fully comprehensive predictions to be generated we chose to neglect role in our first attempts here. In other words, predictions focus on the relationship between family paradigm and the architecture of the family-network link for the family considered as a whole.

Using the cycle hypothesis we derived the following predictions:

1. Configuration should be negatively related to degree. We have argued that degree is really a measure of centrality; low degree networks are likely to afford the family a good deal of initiative and autonomy. Thus, it seems reasonable that high configuration families would choose or structure networks that would allow them the range and initiative central to their conceptions of themselves in the social world; at the same time low degree networks should sustain the sense of autonomy and control inherent in high configuration families.

2. Coordination should be related to shared connection. If shared connection were just a simple measure of engagement then it too should be related more to configuration than coordination; indeed, in the hospital study we predicted (with some accuracy) that engagement in the ward community would be related to configuration. However, shared connection is a measure of *shared* engagement in a richly cross-joined network. It reflects the shared involvement of the family in a portion of the network that is most likely to

be homogeneous, bounded, and coherent. To put it another way, members in families high on shared connection are jointly engaged in a social world that is itself highly connected. This type of family-environment link would, quite reasonably, be most characteristic of high coordination families.

3. Closure should be related to network size. We have already argued that the size of the network expresses the family's openness to a variety of outside experiences and perspectives. This openness is the central feature of closure and thus the connection we are proposing seems quite plausible.

Subjects.[12] Subjects were eighty-two family triads (father, mother, high school-age child) recruited through suburban Washington, D.C., Parent-Teacher-Student Associations. The sample was predominantly white and middle- to upper-middle class. Families that were "reconstituted" by remarriage following divorce or death were included in the study if the child and parents participating had been living together as a family unit for at least five years.

The Hollingshead-Redlich Two-Factor Index of Social Position (see Myers and Bean, 1968), based on father's occupation and education, classified 66 percent of the sample in Class II (managerial personnel and minor professionals), and 19 percent, 11 percent, and 4 percent in Classes I (executives and major professionals), III (administrative personnel and semiprofessionals), and IV (skilled workers), respectively. Total parental annual incomes ranged from $20,000 to $100,000, with a mean of $42,600. Length of present marriage for parents ranged from 5 to 35 years, with a mean of 21.7 years. Parental age ranged from 37 to 64, with a mean of 48.0 years. The number of families with sons as participants was 29 and with daughters was 53.

Procedure. As in previous studies, we assessed the character of the family's paradigm in our card sorting procedure. This procedure was somewhat modified from its previous use. First, we added another card to bring the total to sixteen in each phase of the task. A perfect pattern sort yielded four groups of four cards each (rather than three groups of five cards each, as in the previous procedure). The same was true for the ideal length system (the cards contained sequences of only four different lengths, rather than the eight or more different lengths in the older procedure).[13] Second, we eliminated the final individual sort in order to shorten the procedure and because the three major dimensions have been clearly represented by variables drawn from the initial and family phases of the card sort. Third, we used somewhat different measures to index the three basic dimensions. Configuration was measured using the pattern sort score of the initial and family phases of the task. Coordination was measured by using (1) the similarity of sorts in the family phase (as before), and (2) the standard deviation of trial times in this phase divided by the absolute length of the average trial time (a somewhat new index). The latter is similar to a measure used in one of the studies in Chapter 2 when the card sort was used as a dependent variable; the new measure seemed to us to reflect, quite precisely, the level at which family members integrated their problem-solving activities with one another, an important aspect of coordination. Closure was measured by three different problem-solving behaviors. The first was radicalism, the changes in card arrangements from trial to trial in the family phase. An early closure family will not alter its card placements once it establishes a system in the early trials. A similar measure was the trial number after which two of the three family members made no further changes in their sorts; again early closure families will not change their sorts after the first one or two trials. These same families will also hurry through most of the trials subsequent to the first one or two. Thus, their overall trial time will be relatively short. Thus, the average trial time is also an index of closure.

In order to verify that these seven variables do measure three distinct underlying variables, we included them, along with parental education and income and family mean abstract and verbal intelligence (as measured by the Shipley-Hartford), in a principal components factor analysis. Three of the first five factors extracted had very high loadings on just the variables we would predict: (1) factor I, clearly the *closure factor,* had very high loadings on trial for last change, radicalism, and trial time; (2) factor III, the *configuration factor,* had high loadings only for the pattern sort scores; and (3) factor IV, the *coordination factor,* had high loadings for sort similarity and trial time standard deviation. The intelligence, income, and education variables loaded only on the remaining two factors. Table 8.18 summarizes the findings. We replicated this factor analysis on an entirely different sample of nonclinical families, recruited in a way similar to the present sample. An identical factor structure emerged suggesting great stability of the factor matrix. Because of this stability we felt justified in using factor scores derived from factors 1, 3, and 4 to measure closure, configuration, and coordination, respectively. These three dimensions were independent of the family's intelligence, education, and income (as one might suspect from Table 8.18), as well as number of children in the family, sex and birth order of the child tested, parental age, years of parental marriage, and the Hollingshead-Redlich two-factor index of social class. The three

TABLE 8.18 FACTOR LOADINGS FROM PRINCIPAL COMPONENTS ANALYSIS (WITH VARIMAX ROTATION) OF FAMILY PROBLEM-SOLVING DATA

	Factor				
	I	II	III	IV	V
Variable	Closure	Intelligence	Configuration	Coordination	Income
EDUCATION Parents' education (mean years)	−.06	**.75**	.10	−.21	.19
INCOME Parental salary	−.10	.12	−.04	−.08	**.97**
VERBAL INTELLIGENCE Shipley-Hartford	−.06	**.83**	.17	−.06	−.03
ABSTRACT INTELLIGENCE Shipley-Hartford	−.19	**.78**	−.16	.07	.03
INITIAL PROBLEM SOLVING Mean initial phase problem-solving	0	.04	**.91**	−.09	−.02
FAMILY PROBLEM SOLVING Mean family phase problem-solving	.35	.09	**.77**	.07	−.03
SORT SIMILARITY Family phase sort similarity	−.20	−.04	−.02	**.83**	−.02
TRIAL TIME, STANDARD DEVIATION Corrected	−.06	.11	0	**−.83**[a]	.07
LAST TRIAL CHANGE	**.85**	−.16	.12	−.07	−.16
RADICALISM	**.82**	−.08	−.02	−.27	.01
FAMILY PHASE TRIAL TIME	**.67**	−.11	.33	.20	0

Note: the first five principal components (all having eigenvalues ≥ .88 and collectively accounting for 74.8 percent of the variance) were rotated according to varimax criteria. In the original correlation matrix 19 of 55 correlations (35 percent) were significant at or beyond the .05 level. Factor loadings greater than .60 are shown in boldface.

a. The sign of the TRIAL TIME, STANDARD DEVIATION loading is the reverse of that for SORT SIMILARITY on the coordination factor, since a small trial time standard deviation signifies high coordination.

variables of configuration, coordination, and closure—as measured by their respective factor scores—could then be used in a straightforward three-way ANOVA design. We could be reasonably confident that our three independent variables were not contaminated by the social class and family variables listed above which might independently influence ties of the family to kin or nonkin networks.

Network inventory. This was a self-administered inventory; each family member completed it alone. First, each member defined the composition of the network by listing all individuals outside the nuclear family that he or she thought important in some way. Two major categories of individuals were requested: a maximum of twelve relatives living outside the nuclear family's household, and a maximum of eighteen friends or other significant individuals (neighbors, co-workers, and so on). We refer to the former as the kinship or extended family network, and to the latter as the friendship network. The respondent then answered a series of questions on functional and contextual aspects of each relationship, for example, the form and frequency of both direct and indirect content, feelings about the relationship, and the quality and amount of help exchanged. Last, the respondent indicated who among the individuals listed knew one another; each pair of individuals reported as knowing one another we called a connection. The information on connection, as well as the number of individuals listed, formed the basis for examining the three structural network descriptors: size, degree, and shared connection.

The indices were computed on various levels: family, parental, and individual (father, mother, and child separately). Shared connection was computed only on the family and parental levels, since it is by definition a group or dyadic score. Individual-level indices were computed as described above. For family- and parental-level variants, we first constructed combined lists of discrete names and connections by consolidating the lists of all three members (family level) or of the parents (parental level), and deleting any duplicates. Then the formulas described above were applied. All indices were also computed for the kinship and friendship networks separately, as well as for the total network that results from their combination.

Results. Since our original notions concerning predicted associations between characteristics of family paradigms and network structure referred to the total network including both kin and friends, we first examined relationships between problem-solving dimensions and structural indices computed for this combined network. Strong relationships were found for each of the three dimensions, but subsequent analyses separating kin and friend subgroup clarified that most of the findings for the total network were attributable solely to kin. There were fewer findings for friends and, furthermore, these were individual-level findings for separate role members, rather than for the parental or family units. Further inspection of the data on friends showed, on the average, extremely little overlap among family members in specific friends listed, a surprising circumstance in itself, but one that plausibly accounts for the inability of family- or parental-level structural descriptors of the friendship network to discriminate meaningfully among the families studied.

In this description of results obtained, then, we emphasize the kinship network and, within that, family- and parental-level indices, since these come closest to tapping dominant characteristics of an entire family group. Relationships between family problem-solving dimensions and indices of kinship network structure were analyzed using multivariate and univariate analyses of variance (MANOVA and ANOVA respectively); independent variables were the three problem-solving dimensions (scores on each dimension were divided at the median to describe low and high levels), and dependent variables were the three network indices. Two separate MANOVAs were performed: one for family-level and one for parental-level indices.[14] In order to avoid possible overinterpretation of isolated effects, then, we emphasized, as primary findings, those ANOVA effects producing a MANOVA effect with a significance level of less than .10. None of the interaction effects in either of the MANOVAs reached this criterion, so only main effects from the MANOVAs and ANOVAs appear in the summary of results that is presented in Table 8.19.

Also included in the table are results of analyses of individual-level indices corresponding to statistically significant family- and parental-level effects. These were only computable for size and degree (shared connection is by definition a group or dyadic level score) and were examined for the purpose of determining whether a family- or parental-level effect might be due to only one role member, and thus not truly a reflection of a family or parental unit. In making this judgment, we did not require all individual role member effects to be uniformly statistically significant, since this would be extremely unlikely to occur. It seemed enough to know only if each role member contributed to a higher-level effect in a similar way by examining directions of mean differences. The relative strengths of various role members' contributions may be of interest in themselves, but are not crucial for the characterization of an effect on the family- or parental-level as a reflection of a group rather than solely an individual process.

As Table 8.19 indicates, several strong relationships between problem-solving and network structure were found, although particularly in the case of shared connection, they were more complex than our original predictions in that the patterns of association changed depending upon the level of measurement. Of the three network indices, shared connection is by far the most difficult to interpret; thus it became necessary to consider ancillary findings on variables not included in the MANOVAs as an aid in interpretation of the primary findings. These ancillary findings are, for the most part, effects on individual role members' friendship networks, as we report every significant main effect of this kind obtained. As a final step in interpretation, we examined the findings in light of two additional variables that could be expected to influence network structure: previous geographic mobility of the nuclear family, and geographic accessibility of kinsmen.

We describe first, however, the central findings that are presented in Table 8.19; we consider each problem-solving dimension in turn.

CONFIGURATION. High configuration, the sense of potential

TABLE 8.19 SUMMARY OF ANALYSES OF KINSHIP NETWORK STRUCTURE ($N = 82$ FAMILIES)

Source of Variation	MANOVA F(3,72)	ANOVA F(1,74)		
		Size	Degree	Shared connection
		Family Level		
Configuration	2.43[a]	< 1	< 1	6.26[b]
				$\overline{X}_H = .05$
				$\overline{X}_L = .09$
Coordination	4.42[c]	< 1	8.22[d] (i)	5.91[b]
			$\overline{X}_H = 7.7$	$\overline{X}_H = .09$
			$\overline{X}_L = 6.4$	$\overline{X}_L = .05$
Closure	3.10[b]	7.71[b] (ii)	< 1	2.19
		$\overline{X}_D = 17.5$		
		$\overline{X}_E = 15.2$		
		Parental Level		
Configuration	< 1	< 1	< 1	1.72
Coordination	3.48[b]	< 1	6.96[c] (i)	1.11
			$\overline{X}_H = 7.0$	
			$\overline{X}_L = 5.7$	
Closure	3.89[c]	9.28[d] (ii)	< 1	5.32[b]
		$\overline{X}_D = 14.4$		$\overline{X}_D = .14$
		$\overline{X}_E = 12.3$		$\overline{X}_E = .24$

TABLE 8.19, *continued*

Individual-level effects corresponding to (i) and (ii) above

Father	Mother	Child
	(i) *Coordination F(1,74) on degree*	
1.99	*4.45*[b]	*7.50*[c]
$\overline{X}_H = 5.1$	$\overline{X}_H = 5.9$	$\overline{X}_H = 5.3$
$\overline{X}_L = 4.2$	$\overline{X}_L = 4.7$	$\overline{X}_L = 4.1$
	(ii) *Closure F(1,74) on size*	
1.07	*1.95*	*3.45*
$\overline{X}_D = 9.6$	$\overline{X}_D = 10.4$	$\overline{X}_D = 10.0$
$\overline{X}_E = 9.1$	$\overline{X}_E = 9.8$	$\overline{X}_E = 9.1$

Note: $\overline{X}$ = group mean for variable yielding significant effect; for configuration and coordination, subscripts H and L refer to high and low respectively; for closure, subscripts D and E refer to delayed and early respectively.
   a. $p < .07$.
   b. $p < .05$.
   c. $p < .01$.
   d. $p < .005$.

mastery over the social environment, was predicted to be associated with low degree of network interconnection. Instead, however, it is associated — on the family level — with low shared connection, that is, with a relative independence of family members from one another in their network involvements. Since this effect disappears on the parental level it is clear that the family-level effect is not due to interparental differences of opinion or perception; it must then be due to child-parent differences. It indicates that children in high configuration families are relatively independent of their parents in their ties to extended family. They may well have an investment in extended family as a whole that is no different from their parents' investment, but the specific network groupings in which they are involved differ from those of their parents to a greater extent than is the case in low configuration families.

This unanticipated finding required a rethinking of how configuration may manifest itself in network relationships — particularly extended family relationships. Our general prediction that high configuration should be associated with low degree of network interconnection was not borne out for the extended family network. Three individual-level findings on friendship networks, however, provide an additional examination of the predicted relationship and point to a more complex, yet plausible, state of affairs than we were able to predict at the outset. First, in fathers' (but not mothers') individual friendship networks, configuration is associated with degree in the predicted negative direction ($F(1,74) = 5.22$, $p < .03$), thus providing partial confirmation of our original, albeit less specific, prediction. For children, however, the opposite effect was found. Children in high configuration families have friendship networks with higher degree ($F(1,74) = 5.51$, $p < .02$). They also have an unanticipated network of larger size ($F(1,74) = 7.60$, $p < .007$) than children in low configuration families.

The latter findings can be used to interpret the unanticipated family-level effect on shared connection in the kinship network in a way that is consistent with our notion of configuration as representing effectiveness in dealing with complexity in the social environment. We suggest that investment in a large and highly connected peer group represents a level of interpersonal effectiveness for adolescents that it may not represent for adults, since many adolescents' peer groups are by definition homogeneous by virtue of being primarily school- and neighborhood-based. According to that view, children in high configuration families manifest a relatively high level of effectiveness in dealing with social relationships in two ways: by relatively autonomous interaction with extended family, and by age-appropriate investment in peer group relations.

In sum, our prediction linking high configuration with low degree was not obtained. However, a set of unanticipated findings of equal interest emerged. In high configuration families, adolescents have relationships with their kin which are different from their parents'; further, they are members of large, connected peer networks. Both of these findings might plausibly be regarded as signs of vigorous development of social skills in these adolescents. In addition, fathers do have the autonomous, and perhaps central, role in friendship networks, as indicated by the finding of low degree for them. At least for fathers and children, then, high configuration families seem to contain individuals with the kind of social autonomy and mastery we had anticipated for the whole family. It is not clear why mothers do not enter this picture.

COORDINATION. As predicted, coordination—uniformity of outlook and values within a nuclear family—is positively associated with shared connection. This finding, however, holds only on the family level, not on the parental level. Again, child-parent differences are responsible for variation in shared connection;

children in high coordination families are especially tuned-into their parents (or vice versa) regarding the specific groupings in extended family with which they are invested. In contrast, however, to the analogous association between shared connection and configuration, the association of shared connection with coordination seems not to have implications for children's relationships with friends; we found no significant effects of coordination on either size or degree of children's individually reported friendship networks (for both, $F < 1$).

An unanticipated additional finding is the positive association of coordination with degree—both on family and parental levels. (As can be seen in Table 8.19, all family role members contributed to these effects—most particularly mothers and children.) High coordination families manifest the most close-knit extended family networks. That this is not simply a reflection of the coordination effect on shared connection (or alternatively, that the effect on shared connection is not simply a reflection of the effect on degree) is supported by the two variables' low and nonsignificant correlation ($r = .18$; $p = $ n.s.). Further, when each of the two variables (computed on the family-level) is covaried from the ANOVA on the other, both significant coordination effects remain; the probabilities of chance outcome diminish only slightly—to .01 for degree and to .04 for shared connection.

The two findings, then, must be considered to be independent of one another. In addition to being positively related to child-parent congruence in network involvements, coordination is also positively related to the degree of interconnection among significant members of extended family. Since a closeknit network is most likely to have relative uniformity of values and norms within its bounds, the latter finding indicates that the level of coordination in a nuclear family runs parallel to the level of coordination of prevailing attitudes and values we may presume among significant members of the extended family. This finding that a closeknit network is associated with intrafamily unity may seem, on the surface, contrary to Bott's observation (1957) that network connectedness is associated with a certain kind of family intrafamily disunity—segregated rather than joint marital role relationships. However, coordination, as we define it, need not be manifested in the marital behaviors used to define variation in role segregation (the level of interchangeability of household tasks, joint versus separate leisure-time pursuits). The concept of high coordination implies a fundamental sharing of outlook and beliefs that should translate into cooperation and collaboration regarding important family issues, but not necessarily into similarity of everyday instrumental behaviors of constant companionship.[15]

CLOSURE. Delayed closure—openness to environmental experience—is, as predicted, positively associated with network size on both family and parental levels. It is also associated with low shared connection, but only on the parental level. Although the shared connection effect was unanticipated, both effects can be interpreted as reflections of the same underlying process. It is important to note a significant negative correlation between size and shared connection ($r = -.31$; $p = .01$).

Parents in delayed closure families are shown by their relatively low shared connection scores to be relatively independent of one another in their network involvements. A comparison of the strong effect on parental-level size with the much weaker effects for fathers and mothers separately (see Table 8.19) indicates that the parental-level size finding reflects this independence also. Since two identical names are counted as only one when computing the dyadic or group-level size index, it follows that a large combined network in the absence of similarly large separate networks indicates that the separate networks contain few of the same individuals. Thus, although the individual-level findings in Table 8.20 show that both fathers and mothers in delayed closure families have slightly larger individual networks than those in early closure families, this is not the primary way each parent in delayed closure families contributes to a large joint network. The key is that each parent is invested in somewhat different relationships, a circumstance that—all other things being relatively equal (for example, size of individual networks)—maximizes the chance that the total set of sources of environmental input to the parental unit will be large and varied.

The closure findings, however, do not concern parents only. Although the closure effect on family-level size is not as large as that on the parental-level, the former should not be construed as a simple byproduct of the latter. As Table 8.19 shows, children in delayed closure families show larger individual kinship networks than children in early closure families; although this effect only approaches statistical significance ($p < .07$), it doubtless contributes to the closure effect on family-level size and suggests that variation in closure affects the extent to which the entire nuclear family is invested in and has access to a range of sources of input from the environment. A consideration of all the findings for closure in combination, then, suggests an interpretation more complex than predicted yet consistent with our notions of what variation in closure represents: the relative independence of parents from one another in delayed closure families, by allowing a large number of external relationships to impinge on the family, opens the entire nuclear family group to a breadth of experience with extended family.

It is legitimate to question, however, whether the parental-level findings for closure really reflect adaptive breadth of experience, as we suggest, or rather a presumably less adaptive interparental split—a rigid isolation of each parent from the other's social relationships. Within extended family, the most likely location of such a split, if it existed, would be in the area of in-law relationships, so we checked whether the low interparental shared connection in delayed closure families might result from each parent's exclusive investment in his or her own origin family. We found no evidence to support this alternate interpretation; the proportion of in-laws listed by either or both parents (averaging 35 percent for the entire sample) does not discriminate delayed from early closure families (for all, $F < 1$).

Family mobility, geographic accessibility of kin, and number of kin. To what extent are the findings so far presented independent of other variables that could influence network structure? The two most obvious of these are social status and family's place of residence, and they can be ruled out in the present study—the former by virtue of its lack of association to problem solving, and the latter by virtue of its being held constant (all of the families lived within a five-to-ten-mile radius in Montgomery County, Maryland, within approximately ten to twenty miles of center-city Washington, D.C.).

Three additional variables, however, may be seen as particularly pertinent to networks of extended family: (1) the extent to which the nuclear family has moved from place to place over the years; (2) the geographic accessibility of kinship members to the nuclear family and to one another; and (3) the total number of kinsmen. All three of these variables are appropriate to consider in connection with those findings indicating differences between parents' and children's network involvements. For example, could those findings have resulted simply from children's limited direct knowledge of certain kinsmen who remain important to parents despite several years of geographic separation? The issue of the geographic accessibility of kinsmen is also important for interpretation of findings on degree of interconnection of the extended family network. For example, is simple proximity of extended family members to one another the prime determinant of whether or not they know one another? The issue of number of kinsmen is important in the interpretation of all our findings. A family with many relatives may, independent of its particular paradigm, select more relatives as important (scoring higher on size), report a greater percentage of connections between relatives (scoring higher on degree), and jointly select more of these connected relatives (scoring higher on shared connection).

We assessed the possible influence of these three variables on the findings reported above by means of analyses of covariance. An index of *geographic mobility* was constructed by combining information from parental reports regarding the number of years they had lived in the Washington metropolitan area, the number of moves within the area, the number of communities lived in before coming to the area, and the distance of last community lived from Washington. *Geographic accessibility of kinsmen* to the target family and to one another was assessed by computing the proportion of kinsmen in the selected network who lived within the Washington metropolitan area (including suburban Maryland and Virginia); this is a small enough area, relatively speaking, to allow for the formation and maintenance of relationships without geographic constraints. *Total number of kinsmen* was measured by asking each parent to enumerate the total number of their parents' and their own brothers and sisters (including half- and step-siblings).[16]

With these three measures as covariates, the ANOVAs represented in Table 8.19 were performed again, and none of the significant effects were diminished. Thus, the findings reported here cannot be construed as resulting from constraints placed on either the nuclear or the extended family by factors related to geographic mobility, proximity, or number of kinsmen.

Matching the Cycle Hypothesis and the Findings

Table 8.20 summarizes the overall fit between our most important predictions—generated from the cycle hypothesis—and the findings in the hospital and network studies. It is important to emphasize that this summary is highly schematic. The specific constraints and assumptions that governed the derivation of specific propositions from the cycle hypothesis and the detailed qualifications of these propositions required by the data have been described in some detail in this chapter. Nonetheless, this table provides an impressive overview. Out of twenty-one predictions generated by the cycle hypothesis, sixteen were confirmed. Of the five failures to confirm predictions, only one offers a significant challenge to the model; the remainder can be reconciled—without substantial difficulty—to the basic concepts of the model.

Despite this initial success, the cycle hypothesis remains—at best—a plausible approach to organizing the investigation of family-environment transactions. The two studies we have reported do not even scratch the surface of implications inherent in the model. First, the specific causal sequences proposed in the model have barely been addressed in the two studies reported. The hospital study, by virtue of its longitudinal design, provided some evidence that family paradigm can influence short-term family-environment links. The network study provided no direct evidence of causal direction of the proposed reciprocal effects. Clearly, longitudinal studies of a much finer grain are required here. Second, we have only examined one of several aspects of family-environment links. We have not looked at motivational aspects of the links, nor have we even broached the very tricky question of ambassadorial links. Finally, our study on the relationship between personal needs and technical preferences gives only indirect support to our concept of social organizers in general and organizational objectives in psychiatric hospitals in particular. It is our first entry into the problem of understanding and specifying types of social environments. Only when this task is complete can a first approach

TABLE 8.20 A SUMMARY COMPARISON OF PREDICTIONS DERIVED FROM THE CYCLE HYPOTHESIS AND ACTUAL FINDINGS. THE TABLE INDICATES, FOR OUR STUDY OF SHORT-TERM LINKS, THE PREDICTIONS MADE FOR EACH OF FOUR TYPES OF FAMILIES AND, FOR OUR STUDY OF LONG-TERM KINSHIP LINKS, THE PREDICTIONS MADE FOR FAMILIES SCORING HIGH ON EACH OF OUR THREE FUNDAMENTAL DIMENSIONS. AN ASTERISK INDICATES THOSE INSTANCES WHERE PREDICTIONS WERE NOT CONFIRMED; THE ACTUAL FINDING IS DESCRIBED IN PARENTHESES. FOOTNOTES SUMMARIZE THE DISCREPANCY BETWEEN PREDICTIONS AND FINDINGS AND OUR INTERPRETATION OF THOSE DISCREPANCIES. TOTAL NUMBER OF PREDICTIONS: 21. NUMBER OF PREDICTIONS CONFIRMED: 16.

Short-term links between family and hospital

Dependent variable	Family Type			
	Environment-sensitive	Consensus-sensitive	Achievement-sensitive	Distance-sensitive
Status[a] (Speech initiation and chosen on sociometry)	High	Low* (High)[b]	Low	Low
Openness (Not choosing own family on sociometry and seating dispersal)	High	Low	Low	High
Cohesion (Attendance[c] and cohesiveness questionnaire items answered[d])	High	Low* (High)[e]	High	Low

TABLE 8.20, *continued*

	Long-term links between family and kindred		
	Family paradigm variable (Predictions for high-scoring families)		
Network	Configuration	Coordination	Closure
Degree (Shares centrality characteristics with status)	High* (No effect)[f]	No effect* (High)[g]	No effect
Size (Similar to openness)	No effect	No effect	High
Shared connection (A form of shared cohesion)	No effect* (Low)[h]	High	No effect

a. Status predictions confirmed for parents only.

b. This failure of prediction may be partially or entirely explained by the relatively low levels of coordination in this sample of consensus-sensitive families.

c. Attendance predictions confirmed for parents only.

d. Cohesiveness questionnaire, items answered, predictions confirmed for children only.

e. A genuinely surprising finding which cannot readily be explained in the post hoc analyses or by our model as elaborated so far.

f. Although this prediction was not confirmed, the unpredicted findings of low shared configuration, low network degree for father, and high network size and degree for children support our general concept of autonomous links for high configuration families.

g. Although this finding was not predicted by our model, it does not significantly challenge it either.

h. This finding, as indicated in note f above, is consistent with our overall model, even though it was not specifically predicted by it.

be made to that aspect of the cycle hypothesis which proposes reciprocal relationships between family paradigm and type of social environment.

What the data strongly suggest so far is that there is an important relationship between the process of shared construing in a family and the types of links it forges with its social environment. Thus, these data should serve to draw attention to concepts about construction processes in families as a powerful tool for understanding family-environment transactions. The findings permit us to assert with greater confidence that the family's construction of social reality simultaneously determines the experience of family membership for each of its individuals and the interactional styles and strategies by which families relate to their social world.

Conclusion
A Second Look at Shared
Constructs

The main objective of this book has been to develop a theory of family process focusing on the transaction of the family with its social world. The theory centers on a concept borrowed from the philosophical analysis of scientific process, the concept of paradigm. We have shown how the concept grew out of a series of laboratory observations of family process. Given the plausibility of the central concept, we have tried to indicate how paradigms arise, develop, and change within families and how they function to regulate the family's relationships with its social community. How successful have we been?

The most straightforward approach to answering this question is to examine the fit between our data, on the one hand, and the concept of paradigm and the fabric of ideas into which it has been woven, on the other hand. We have already attended to this task at several points in the book. For example, in Chapters 2 and 8 we presented tabular summaries of the fit between the data and the expectations drawn from our central ideas (see Tables 2.11 and 8.20). On the surface, the tables are comforting enough (depending, of course, on the level of surcease sought by the reader). However, whatever their probative value, these tables work better as descriptions of our analytic strategies. As descriptions they serve two related functions—functions more dynamic and incomplete than service as empirical "proof." The first function is to clarify the partial realization of useful strategies for exploring our basic ideas about family paradigms; the second function is to illustrate where our strategies are running into difficulty. Let us review examples of each of these.

A critical component of our notions about family paradigm is the cycle hypothesis, summarized in Figure 7.1. Two components of the hypothesis are the notions of ordinary construct and family-environment links. Both of these notions—which Chapter 7 transforms into more useful sets of variables—are quite specifically connected, by theory, to the family paradigm. The burden of Chapters 3 through 6, from one perspective, was to accomplish a similar transformation of the notion of family paradigm—that is, convert it into a usable set of variables. A critical realization of our theory, then, was the development of measures of the variables derived from these three related concepts: ordinary constructs, family-environment links, and paradigms. Tables 2.11 and 8.20 are highly condensed summaries of our efforts to develop this strategy. Table 2.11, for example, summarizes two studies: one on the family's perceptions of the ward community, and the other on the family's perceptions of other families. It is a record, then, of our efforts to study the family's experience of its social world—its attitudes, observations, fantasies, explanatory notions. This congeries we have termed the family's ordinary construct. Table 2.11 can serve as an epigrammatic illustration of how we have gone about realizing the concept of ordinary construct through the development of objective methods. Precisely the same function is served by the top half of Table 8.20. Here we summarize direct observations of family behavior toward a social community in which it very temporarily resides, the psychiatric ward. Because these behaviors (in contrast to the feelings which go with them) are joint products of the family and its social world, we are justified in viewing this behavior as reflecting family-environment links. The top half of Table 8.20, then, is also an epigrammatic illustration of how we have gone about realizing a different part of the theory represented in Figure 7.1, our notion of specific links.

The bottom half of Table 8.20 sustains a different type of description—a clarification of the limits or ambiguities of our strategies for realizing theory. A summary of links between the family and its kin, is presented. However, the raw data are not drawn from our observations of actual family behavior; rather, they are taken from reports from our families about their behavior, feelings, and knowledge about their kin. If we regard our families as accurate self-observers, the data are pertinent to the notion of link; if the families are reporting purely subjective constructions of kinship and friendship ties, we are closer to measuring an ordinary construct. In Chapter 8 we chose to regard the family as an accurate self-reporter, but this choice reflected expedience as much as prudence. It is very costly and time-consuming (perhaps prohibitively so) to directly observe a family's relationship with its kin. Choosing expediency does not solve our problem; it forces us to live with a strategic ambiguity.

This little example—using our two summary tables—could be repeated for many of our attempts to reconcile data and theory throughout the book. It illustrates that empirical support for our overall model depends on the realization of specific strategies to test it. Beyond that, these tables, and our discussion, illustrate something even more fundamental about the assessment of broad-ranging theoretical constructions. A reader will apply himself to the relative trivia—such as distinguishing ordinary constructs from family-environment links and the appropriate strategies for exploring each—only if he is sufficiently intrigued with the fabric of ideas in which these concepts are embedded. In sum, the empirical status of a model—including the painstaking examination of the strategies devised to assess that status—will be closely evaluated, we believe, only if scholars find the model intriguing to begin with.

But what makes a model intriguing? Posing this question at the end of a book on family paradigms is, of course, ironic. Although it seems indelicate even to raise the point, are social scientists like families? Do crises engender deteriorations among work groups within social science, and is group integrity restored through theoretical perspectives which guide the fundamental lines of collaborative work within the restructed group? This is, of course, one of the several lines in Kuhn's original analysis, although his interest in the social rather than intellectual relationships between scientists is, we believe, largely implicit in his work. Moreover, this question—complex and unwieldy as it is—cannot be pursued here without becoming a serious distraction. Nonetheless, raising the question gives emphasis to the central idea of this concluding chapter: we believe scholars examine the empirical status of a model only after they make a set of other decisions—some implicit and others explicit—about whether the model is interesting enough to be worth the bother.

We suggest that these evaluations, evaluations rendered before assessing the empirical status of the model, rest on the scholar's sense of the opportunities for his own dialogue with the new model. An inquisitive and intellectually autonomous scholar will become interested in a model if he feels he can talk to it and struggle with it and that somehow both he and the model will benefit from the encounter. We feel that there are three interpenetrating phases in the evolution of such a struggle. First, the scholar must find something both familiar and plausible in the new model. He will not go further if the model is entirely foreign nor if its assertions, on their face, seem improbable. Second, he must recognize limited imperfections. A model that is perceived as complete, as fully worked through, offers no space for the scholar to insert his own analyses.

However, these imperfections must be limited; reworking them must not threaten the entire structure. The fundamental structure of the model must appear strong enough to sustain many inroads, reworkings, and revisions of subsidiary or component concepts. Perhaps most important, a scholar must have a sense of the expansile quality of the model — its potential to lead in many directions by explaining an increasingly larger array of observations or by revealing increasingly fascinating details of familiar processes. Most important, the scholar must have a sense that his own participation in the model, through reworking of its imperfections, serves this expansion. In this limited sense, the social scientist is in the position of the potential convert to the four-brother cosmology about which we mused in Chapter 3. The four-brother cosmology appeared attractive to the potential convert, in part, because the convert could recognize in the cosmology an opportunity of his own to expand and deepen it.

The social scientist, however, is more than a potential convert to a new religion. He will not willingly be seduced by a model on intellectual grounds alone. Throughout his initial survey of the model he will want some assurances that it is verifiable (however imprecise even the best of such assurances might be). The specific methods and data presented in this book are meant to provide this somewhat secondary and peripheral assurance. Our description of methods and data constitutes a message to scholars: if just one investigator and a handful of his colleagues can devise this many methods and strategies for verifying the basic model (however imperfect they are), think of how many better methods and strategies could be devised if a larger group of scholars explored these ideas. Specific methods and findings, at this point in the presentation and development of the model, serve not, primarily, to verify the model, but rather to legitimize and strengthen the interest of other scholars in reworking and developing the model further.

We come now to a second point of irony. We have argued that scholars will become intrigued with a new model only if they perceive imperfections which allow them to develop the model to points they regard as central and significant. A model's author is least able to evaluate this potential in his own work. We believe, however, that there is just one piece of work that may increase the probability of engaging scholars in a productive struggle with our model. A brief reconsideration of some of the major concepts in the model may enhance its plausibility and perhaps broaden its familiarity, particularly now that both the model and the strategies devised to examine it have been described in detail. Three concepts are central to the model, central in the sense that if scholars find these ideas plausible they may be encouraged to continue their reconnaissance of this model to the point of struggle. First, the family's shared conception of the world in which it lives plays a central regulatory role in family life. Second, crisis plays a mutative and generative role in family life; in particular, it initiates change and development in the family's shared concepts of its world. Third, intimate social groups conserve their shared conceptions of the outside world not through individual memory—the agency familiar to psychologists—but through regular patterns of their own interaction behavior. Of these three ideas, the most important is our notion about the central role of the family's shared construction of this world in governing its action and transaction with that world. It is this central concept to which we want to return in this brief, concluding chapter.

We have argued at several points in this book that the transactions of individuals in a family with the outside world are coordinated by a shared conception—held by all of them—of the fundamental nature or structure of that world. Three problematic aspects of this hypothesis need attention. The first is the notion of sharing. Do all members of a family really agree on these constructs, or may one or two members rule the roost with others going along out of fear or indifference and concealing their differences from public scrutiny? The second problematic aspect is the notion of construct. Despite our attempts to clarify the strong emotional components of this hypothesized structure in families, the term—in the end—implies something explicit and rational. The third major problem is that the core hypothesis emphasizes the world outside the family. One might have thought it was the family's conception of itself that mattered, not the outside world. Most people's views of the outside world, it might be argued, are more or less the same—except for a few delusional or badly isolated people. If the concept of shared construct is valid at all, it ought to be applied to the family's own concept of itself—not to the outside world. It is certainly this self-concept that varies greatly from family to family and accounts for differences between them. We will discuss each problematic aspect in turn.

First, to what extent is a family's construction of its world genuinely shared by all its members?[1] (We leave aside the thorny issue, for the moment, of which individuals may actually be called members of the "family.") So far, we have left the notion of sharing largely undefined and unexplored; on the other hand, a comprehensive and systematic exploration and development of this idea goes beyond the intent of this concluding chapter. Considering this chapter as a way-station for further development of our model by us and, we hope, others, we wish to emphasize two aspects of our evolving concept of this sharing process in families.

As we conceive it, the process of sharing is different from simple agreement or consensus. Agreement or consensus implies an explicit and self-aware process of reconciling actual or potential divergent points of view. Indeed, the presence of disagreement or dissensus in family life—viewed in terms of self-aware reconciliation—does not necessarily imply the absence of sharing as we conceive it. Conflict in family life can underscore fundamental conceptions which stimulate the conflict and define the permissible modes by which it may be resolved. For example, a couple fights bitterly over whose responsibility it is to clean up the children's toys from the sidewalk in front of the street. Each accuses the other of jeopardizing the family's relationships with neighbors who may trip over the toys. The argument may be bitter and long, but it reveals a shared preoccupation—of both marital partners—with the importance of not antagonizing the neighbors. To be sure, conflict may also imply a fracture in the underlying shared conceptions we have claimed guide much of family life. But we require more than serious and sustained conflict in the family to make such a determination. We have argued that it is a fundamental shift in the focus of experience of family members that betrays such a fracture: the family becoming more preoccupied with itself. In Chapter 4 we detailed several stages of family crisis: the emergence of rules, the emergence of the explicit family, and rebellion. These three can be considered to be styles of relationships among all members of a family (not just within any particular dyad). We have argued that a failure or a loosening of this fundamental sharing in families—as we conceive the sharing of constructs or concepts—is conveyed by an emergence of these stages, not by simple conflict. Moreover, we are hypothesizing that the sharing process does not simply dissolve, does not simply pass into a state of nonsharing or dissolution. A more important route of dissolution is one of *projection*.[2] What was once shared by members of a family is now disowned and felt as external to the self. Indeed, we have argued that this projection process is fundamental in the family's capacity to heal itself by opening itself to outside influences and making radical changes together in the fundamental conceptions which regulate family members' common life. To return to our couple fighting over the toys, we can learn very little, just from observing their fight, about the stability and depth of their shared conception of their social world and their place in it. The substance of their argument gives us a hint of the content of their shared construction. The depth and stability of the sharing must be gauged by a more comprehensive survey of the mode of interaction among all members of their immediate family.

A second critical feature of our concept of sharing marks it off from simple agreement or consensus. As we have already said, the latter concept implies a self-aware process or reconciliation. Sharing processes as we conceive them are not self-aware. As we understand it, the self as a bounded and discrete experiential territory is often partially, and sometimes totally, dissolved in the flux of family affairs.[3] In Chapter 6 we emphasized this point by using Turner's concept about ritual. A central impact of ritual on family life is that it temporarily dissolves each member's sense of selfhood. At certain climactic moments of family ritual, a great range of memory and experience by which each member defines himself as distinct from others and, most important, as distinct from his family are washed away. Recall our example of the young woman professor who, at Christmas, reenacts the role of Santa Claus; with the ritual, she dissolves—for a moment—the extraordinary range of skills, meanings, and experiences by which she defines herself in her ordinary world. Sharing in family life involves this form of fusion—the episodic dissolution of the boundaries of self in subordination to a dominant, organizing conception of the natural and social world. As an active process controlling thought and behavior, sharing is not continuous but rather episodic, even in the most durable and consistent of families. Individuals can—with greater or less freedom (depending on many variables)—enter and leave their experiential families and the sharing process which binds it. When they enter, when their behavior becomes dominated by a common construction, they do not retain a full sense of bounded self. Sharing, as we conceive it, requires some surrender of these boundaries. Another mode by which members reconstitute an individual, bounded self—distinct from the family—is at times of family crisis. We have alluded to this process earlier in this chapter and described it more fully in Chapter 4. In the midst of severe crisis, members *project* aspects of their family—in which they formally felt engaged as full participants—onto other members. Members engage in this mutual projection because they wish to disown or divest themselves of terrifying aspects of the family crisis. The resulting individual selves, newly demarcated by the process of mutual projection tend to become impoverished in some major way. Recall for example the Michaels family, described in Chapter 4. They constructed a series of explicit rules controlling the children's access to life outside the home in response to the unexpected death of the father. Each member of the family became impoverished in the process; each had limited access to his own feelings and to those of others. Family members' sense of meaningful commitment to school or work declined.

The scientific connotation of the term "conception" or "construct" is the second problematic aspect of the notion of shared conceptions. Despite the efforts of previous chapters many readers may still feel our discussion of shared conceptions or constructs belongs more properly in a discourse about science than in an essay on families. Families, after all, are seething cauldrons of feelings. They are not scientific teams jointly exploring their social environment, calmly sifting through their observations, and then elaborating and testing "constructs." To be sure, as we have just phrased it, this anticipated difficulty on the part of some readers is a burlesque, not a summary, of our model. Nonetheless, a position of that kind might quite understandably undergird a view that our model has put the wrong concepts at its core. To be sure (the argument might run), a family's subjective views of its social world may play some role in its behavior toward that world. But surely a large part of the construing process, dealt with so far in this book, is epiphenomenal. At its core each family struggles with nearly overpowering incestuous impulses, or intense rivalries, or enduring power struggles. Surely (the reader may say), concepts coming closer to this affect-laden center of family life should have a more central role in our model.

It is our general view that theories built around impulse, affect, and power have fared badly. While they may be helpful in giving a general perspective and providing explanatory frameworks for behavior, they tend to be much weaker in predicting specific behavior of specific individuals or groups and, more important for our purposes, in explaining how these specific differences between individuals or groups came about.

Although one could cite many examples, certain trends in the development of psychoanalysis are particularly instructive. Psychoanalysis first emerged as theory based on hidden though highly determinative affects and impulses. Indeed, *Studies on Hysteria*—Freud's first published book-length monograph on psychoanalysis—can be read as something of a magic book on hidden affect. Before treatment, hidden impulse and affect shaped the entire neurosis of the patients described. Once brought out of hiding, these affects lost their force and the neurosis dissolved, as if by magic. No one was more dissatisfied with formulations of this kind than Freud himself, and in the mid-1920s he began to rework the entire theoretical foundations of psychoanalysis. Now, in the new structural theory, behavior was seen as determined by three agencies (operating in various degrees of conflict and cooperation):

the ego, the superego, and the id. It would be unfair to say that affect and impulse were demoted in this reworking. Freud, however, was deeply dissatisfied with the explanatory power of a theory built on hidden impulses and other affect-laden states. Importantly, other concepts—in which affect and impulse were embedded—came to the fore. In our view, the most useful of all of these was the concept of transference. In psychoanalysis, transference—as a concept both about the patient's symbolic communication to the analyst and about his resistance to such communication—has been extraordinarily useful for providing highly detailed predictions and explanations of differences in behavior of patients. The concept of transference was clearly demarcated in *Studies on Hysteria,* but it was only after the development of the structural theory that its full power to predict and explain differences in the behavior of different individuals was realized. At its core, transference is a highly structured—and often very detailed—picture that the patient has of his analyst. It is maintained over time by structures within the patient (more particularly, within the ego and superego) which are themselves highly abstracted residues of specific patterns of the patient's experience in the past.[4]

In Chapter 2 we acknowledged our debt to the concept of transference in developing our own notions about shared constructs. Bringing the concept of transference to the fore once again will, perhaps, make the connotations we intend in the term construct more accessible. First, the term "transference" has two advantages over "shared construct." One, it clearly implies the influence of the past—feelings and attitudes about an important figure in the past are transferred to the analyst. Two, the concept of a transfer of this kind seems inextricably linked to the notion of irrationality; that is, if a person transfers feelings about a person in the past to a person in the present we suspect him of committing an irrational act unless proven otherwise. Thus, the role of the past and the role of irrationality are woven into the term transference in ways that they are not woven into the term shared construct. Transference, then, is quite clearly not a term suitable for discourse on science but it is, self-evidently, more appropriate for discourse on human experience. It was, of course, not adequate for our purposes. Its connotations root it too securely in concepts about individuals and not groups, and in discourse on patients rather than people. In our usage, shared construct is tied more securely to groups and has no necessary clinical implications—that is, families who develop constructs are not axiomatically regarded as ill.[5] However, the connotations we intend for the term shared construct are rooted in two very specific intellectual traditions. As we have previously described, the first of these is Kuhn's analysis. We were attracted by his notion of the role of constructs in returning a group from a state of crisis to a state of productive routine. The second tradition, that of Berger and Luckmann, emphasizes the subjective (if not creative) core of social constructions. We are counting on these traditions to provide a connotative frame for our concept of shared construct, a frame which softens the more intellectual and dry associations a reader might, quite rightly, connect to the term.

Bringing the psychoanalytic concept of transference to the fore once again illustrates a more fundamental point about the notion of shared construct. Like transference, the notion of shared construct does not strip affect or impulse from our model. It imbeds these terms in a more highly and specifically structured conception. We have tried, at several points in this book, to provide examples of this point. For example, early in the book we presented case vignettes illustrating the strong emotional components of the family's shared view of a particular social environment. Recall for example, the Raab family. This pessimistic family had four children, two of whom has been psychiatrically hospitalized. Their shared construct of our laboratory was filled with searing terror. The same pervasiveness of emotionality—though more muted—is present in the shared constructs of the O'Hara family, described toward the end of the book (in Chapter 6). Recall that this family's greeting ritual: father and the three grown sons would briefly arm-wrestle. We argued that this ritual conserved the family's sense of toughness and excluded a fear that the suicidal depression on mother's side of the family would crop up once again.

Thus, the concept of shared construct does not ignore the family as a seething cauldron of impulse and affect. But terror, pride, anger, and love—which, in our model, are woven into the concept of shared construct—are universals. They are both undifferentiated and undifferentiating because, as raw and unadorned motives of human action, they fail to account for why specific families behave in specific ways. A shared construct—like transference—weaves these nonspecific affective elements into a more organized conception which is meant to account for action. The concept of transference specifies that *this* patient acts in *this* way because he is convinced that his analyst is (without a doubt) *this* kind of a person. In precisely the same terms, a shared construct specifies that *this* family behaves in *this* way because, collectively, it is convinced that its social environment is (without a doubt) just *this* kind of a world.

A comparison of shared constructs with transference addresses the third and final point about our notion of shared constructs: our emphasis on the family's construction of its world rather than of itself. The concept of transference too gives primacy to the patient's view of the analyst—not of himself. The patient, for example, says to himself, "My analyst is critical and condescending. I have to be on my guard with him." The patient's view of the analyst forms a sturdy basis for action by the patient—a systematic suppression of sensitive or embarrassing materials from his talk to his analyst. If he were to say to himself, putting the emphasis on himself, "I am rather sensitive to criticism and condescension," his behavior would be less certain. Indeed, any number of behaviors might be tried, each without much conviction. In psychoanalysis—which is aimed at making fundamental changes in a patient's patterns of behavior—a patient's shift from a conviction in his image of his analyst to a more reflective conception of himself is a potential sign of progress, because the patient may simultaneously stop his usual patterns of action and consider new options.[6] However, our own model of the family is directed at explaining action—particularly the family's transaction with its social environment. A family's shared conviction in a particular view of its social reality constitutes a basis for action. If a family comes to be preoccupied with a conception of itself, its action is less determined and sustained and more in flux. Consider again the couple who fought over toys on the sidewalk. An underlying shared construct—accounting for their fight—might be, "People in this neighborhood get very angry at children's toys on the sidewalk," and, beyond that, "People in this neighborhood are strict and exacting." If their shared construction was directed at themselves it might read, "We are very sensitive to the opinion of others." This self-conception, in and of itself, is a very uncertain basis for action. It, at the very least, begs a companion conception which addresses this question: "How (in fact) does this neighborhood in which we live deal with families (such as ourselves) who are sensitive to criticism?" In other words, for a self-concept to be the basis of action it must, at the very least, be subordinate to a concept, felt as reality, of the outside world.

Notes

1. The Family's Construction of the Laboratory

1. A good description of the Würzburg school can be found in Boring, (1950).

2. Miller, 1967, has provided an engaging summary of his work in this area. See also Chomsky and Miller, 1958, and Chomsky, 1957.

3. Kraepelin's concepts and their place in the historical evolution of concepts about schizophrenia are concisely summarized in Ackerknect, 1968.

4. See, for example, Cohen, Senf, and Huston, 1956; Snyder, Rosenthal, and Taylor, 1961; and Payne, Caird, and Laverty, 1964.

5. The pathbreaking and original formulations in this field were by Shannon and Weaver, 1949. A decade summary of the application of these concepts to psychology can be found in Attneave, 1959.

6. In retrospect, information theory—like many developments in the behavioral sciences—was oversold. Initially, it seemed to provide the mathematical tools which would simultaneously unlock the mysteries of human perception and cognition on the one hand, and human communication on the other. It now seems as if it did neither. Today, the most promising approach to understanding human communication—particularly its social aspects—takes a decidedly nonmathematical tack. This field—sociolinguistics—is highly descriptive in its approach. It seeks to explore the social use of language by studying critical, arresting, or representative samples of speech and exploring how speech serves both to express and modify social function. The basic method is scrupulously detailed description and inventive interpretation. Some of the philosophical or analytic underpinings of this work may be found in Searle, 1969, and Halliday, 1973. Recent collections of a range of empirical studies may be found in Turner, 1974; Sudnow, 1972; Bauman and Sherzer, 1974; and Schenkein, 1978.

7. See Lidz, 1958; Lidz et al, 1963; Rosman et al, 1964; and Wild et al., 1965.

8. See Wynne and Singer, 1963, 1965; and Singer and Wynne, 1965.

9. Case examples are used throughout this book. We have altered data

to conceal, as much as possible, the identity of the individuals and families involved. These alterations include names, of course, but also other possibly identifying details.

10. Throughout our work, using many different procedures, we have often isolated family members in booths. This gives us greater control over their communication with one another. First of all, it prevents them from using nonverbal means of communicating (these are devilishly hard to measure). Second, it reduces the likelihood they will talk to one another unless specifically instructed to do so or given an obvious means such as a telephone. Most families rapidly accustom themselves to this arrangement. Although it is obviously artificial, it does not appear to inhibit significantly family members' interaction with one another.

11. We have described in detail elsewhere an algebraic system for canonically drawing inferences from any set of sequences a subject selects (checks) on the initial and final inventory (see Reiss, 1967b). As we will indicate later, this scoring system permits us to quantify the precision and comprehensiveness of the subject's underlying concept of what pattern is right and which are wrong. It also permits the subject to be classified, according to his selection, into one of several nominal categories.

12. The methods of analyses, results, and interpretations described in this section are covered in greater detail in a series of journal articles (see Reiss, 1967a, 1967b, 1968a, 1968b, 1971a). In order to improve the readability of this section we have simplified the names of some of the dependent variables.

13. Strict criteria—the details of which were described in previous publications—were used to assess similarity between hypotheses. The judgment of similarity is necessary for the simple copying score as well as for the change risk score to be described below.

14. The criterion for similarity here was broader than for the influence or risk measure: see Reiss, 1967b.

15. It should be emphasized that with such a tiny sample, the use of factor analysis serves—even more than usual—heuristic purposes only. It should be regarded as strictly a descriptive statistic epitomizing the intercorrelations among the twelve variables we selected for this analysis (see Reiss, 1971a).

16. Two variables don't quite fall into this pattern. Person selection loads high in factor I. We have to stretch things a bit to say this score takes into account a relevant stimulus field, three possible receivers for the subject messages, and then the subject's subjective experience that only one or two are suitable. Even stretching won't account for risking change, which does involve an assessment of the stimulus situation facing the subject (the nature of the previous hypothesis and whether it was right or wrong) and his experience of it (compelling or not compelling enough to imitate).

17. It is important to emphasize that the perception of the laboratory as safe is just as subjective as the perception that it is dangerous. A *perception* of safety is based on a *feeling* of trust. Even an hour or two's experience does not rationally prove the safety of the situation. For example, a family must still feel trust that the tester will not misuse the data he has collected

from them, even if the tester's behavior during the laboratory session has been exemplary.

18. We are certainly not the first to apply a concept of this kind to families. Hess and Handel (1959), as we point out in more detail below, talked of the family's function in defining and shaping its members' conception of the variety and intensity of experience of the world. In a more general and systematic treatise, Berger and Luckmann (1966) propose that an intimate group develops its own conception of reality as a derivative of the patterned and habitualized interaction patterns among themselves. We will not go into their subtle, elegant thesis here; it plays a more crucial role later in our argument. We pause only to acknowledge its role in shaping our early concepts.

19. Analogous to a family high on factors I and II; members amplify the outer world for one another.

20. Analogous to the family low on factors I and II where members are isolated from one another.

21. Analogous to the family high on factor I and low on factor II where the family process itself is amplified.

22. An expansion of the concept of environment responsiveness.

23. An expansion of within-family responsiveness.

24. The name of this dimension should more accurately be "delayed closure" or "premature closure," since it refers to families who keep open to new information and experience in contrast to those who reach closure very early. We could not resist the pressures of alliteration.

2. Family Problem Solving and Shared Construing

1. Earlier studies in this area, which influenced our work at the time it was designed, were those by Fisher et al., 1959; Lerner, 1965; and Morris and Wynne, 1965. However, many additional studies in this area have been completed in the last decade and a half. Two useful reviews are Jacob, 1975, and Broderick and Pulliam-Krager, 1979.

2. Further details of the sample, methods, findings, and interpretations in this study may be found in Reiss, 1971c.

3. Of course, spontaneous change unrelated to the family in either direction is possible. Much of the data to be presented later supports the concept that the change score does measure the family's contribution.

4. A very liberal confidence level of .20 is used here because the analysis is an exploratory one on an extremely small sample ($n = 16$).

5. We have used a psychiatric sample in the studies reported so far in this book. We have had a growing sense that the phenomenon we have observed in families of psychiatric patients has equal importance for samples of nonclinical families. Thus, our major efforts in more recent years have involved the study of much larger samples of nonclinical families. Some results of this work are reported in Chapter 8.

6. A more detailed description of the study reported in this section may be found in Costell et al., in press.

7. Those who show primarily early closure would go in cell 8 of Table 1.12; those with delayed closure in cell 6. Further study might lead us to

restrict the term "achievement-sensitive" to just one of these two subtypes; the issue is moot in this study since we did not study closure.

8. As measured by the raw scores of the Shipley-Hartford test.

9. A more detailed description of this study may be found in Reiss et al., in press.

10. This procedure was adapted from Kelly's Role Rep Test (see Kelly, 1955).

11. Of course families differed in how they applied this criterion. Usually, however, there was little dispute and almost all families concentrated on weeding out those families who were virtually unknown to them.

12. It is important to recall that indices 1 and 2 are computationally independent, so that high scores on 1 do not necessarily imply low scores on 2.

13. Theoretical and empirical work in family development is now appearing frequently in the literature. Three somewhat different theoretical perspectives are articulated by Hill and Rogers, 1964; Duvall, 1971; and Steinglass, 1978.

14. See Kety et al., 1968, 1975; Rosenthal et al., 1968; Wender et al., 1968, 1974, 1977.

15. A review of Rotter's work, as well as subsequent findings by others, can be found in Lefcourt, 1976. See Gardner et al., 1959, 1960, for the work of Gardner's group.

16. Details of this experiment are reported elsewhere (see Reiss and Salzman, 1973).

17. Details of the methods, findings, and interpretations in this study are reported elsewhere (see Reiss and Sherriff, 1970, and Reiss, 1971d).

3. The Role of the Family in Organizing Experience

1. See A. Freud, 1946. Hartman and Gardner have argued that cognitive controls and defensive mechanisms may actually be two functional aspects of the same psychological structures: cognitive controls are the adaptive aspect, fitting the individual to his environment, whereas defensive mechanisms are directed at management of conflict within the psychic apparatus.

2. Some readers may regard the present discussion—particularly as it concerns the continuity of elaborated and elementary controls—somewhat far afield. Nonetheless, it does set the stage for crucial parts of our argument later in this book. For example, in Chapters 5 and 6 we will expand our ideas about shared construing in families. Particularly in Chapter 6 we will argue that the family develops shared notions not only of its social world but of its inanimate world as well. Our exposition in those chapters is admittedly, if not intentionally, incomplete. We leave room for, but do not systematically work out, ideas that the family shapes a conception of reality which includes very detailed assumptions about and preferences for elementary stimuli and their relationship. Indeed, in the sense in which we are discussing them here, the family plays a singular role—we are prepared to argue—in the elaboration of both elementary and elaborated controls. In Chapter 6 we ascribe to family interaction patterns (that is, the detailed

patterns of family behavior) an information-regulating function quite analogous to some of the elementary controls we describe briefly in this chapter.

3. Berger and Luckmann (1966) delineated the central importance of face-to-face encounters in the social construction of reality. Our argument, from this point forward, owes a great deal to their analysis.

4. In fact, we can define a face-to-face encounter as one which requires this accord. Experientially, this accord is impossible where two (or more) individuals perceive each other entirely through the filter of pre-existing constructs, or stereotypes.

5. Once again, the concept of objectification—as applied to socially constructed reality—is most clearly stated by Berger and Luckmann (1966).

6. This picture of the Puritan family is derived primarily from the work of Demos (1970) and Flaherty (1967).

7. Analyses by a number of scholars, supporting a view of the contemporary family as resilient and active, may be found in Reiss and Hoffman (1979). Bane (1976) provides interesting demographic data, which complement the somewhat more qualitative analyses in Reiss and Hoffman, to support the general thesis that the contemporary family is an active and resilient social group.

8. This is an area of great interest to contemporary scholars. Particularly interesting syntheses may be found in Ariès (1962, 1977), Laslett (1973), and Shorter (1975). These syntheses, which argue that the family has become more private, more shaped by the needs of its members rather than driven by forces external to it, have not been without their methodologic and substantive critics; on Shorter's work see, for example, Vann, 1976.

9. Two interesting case studies can serve as examples of a large literature here. Ishwaran (1977) observed the crucial role of the family in the maintenance of Dutch ethnicity in a Dutch-Canadian community. Likewise, Dashefsky and Shapiro (1974) measured the central role of the Jewish family in maintaining a strong Jewish identity in its children. A more general survey of the role of the family in maintaining ethnicity may be found in Mindel and Habenstein (1976).

10. A persuasive and influential analysis has been that of Hess and Handel (1959).

11. Many of the contributions to the Reiss and Hoffman volume (1979) document differences between families in their capacity to actively initiate and maintain their own adaptive strategies, values, and perspectives in the face of contrary pressures from their surrounding cultures. See in particular the chapters by Kohn, McQueen, and Hetherington.

4. Crisis and the Development of the Family Paradigm

1. A careful analysis will reveal that the concept of "situation-specific" is limited and impressionistic. Who, after all, defines the boundary of the "situation"? When we are talking about families in the laboratory, the problem is not difficult. The situation to us and the family is the laboratory, "this research place where you guys study families." However, consider a more general case. Suppose we define a situation as "a bounded setting

which somehow engages the family" and we add "the boundaries being defined by the family." Families may not define their situations as carefully delimited in time and space. The problem is not solved even if we restrict our attention to problematic situations. For example, families may define the following as problematic situations for themselves: "living in this hick town," "getting through life on welfare checks," or "electing Republicans." If we must use a definition of a family's situation which is general, timeless, and uncircumscribed the notion situation-specific becomes more vague and flabby. We will not attempt here a systematic solution of this theoretical conundrum. Rather, we will intuitively include in our situations only those that are reasonably time-limited and have some spatial referent — that is the situation occurs in a specifiable location or between two or more tangible people or objects.

2. Our introduction of the concept of family paradigm draws heavily, of course, on the notions of Kuhn (1962, 1970, 1977). We recognize that in the fields of the history and philosophy of science this concept has been criticized on a number of accounts. We believe most of the criticism is not germane for its use as a construct for explaining social rather than scientific processes. We will return to a fuller analysis of the concept itself in the Conclusion.

3. A useful summary of more traditional approaches to theorizing about stress and the family may be found in Burr, 1973. A more recent synthesis by Hansen and Johnson (1979) develops, from very different sources, arguments which parallel our own.

4. In this sense, a stressful event can be conceptualized as outside the family. Its "outside" property arises from the fact that its stressful qualities are attributed to it by a common culture rather than by a particular family. If the particular family culture, with its own assumptions and perspectives, precisely duplicates that of the common culture, then the magnitude of the stress — as perceived by the family — will duplicate the scaled values arrived at by a representative sample. In most instances the family will respond as if the event were of greater or lesser magnitude; its idiosyncratic construction of life events — as well as its own broader assumptions on many aspects of life and its circumstances — then becomes more clearly manifest.

5. There is an interesting analogy in Kuhn's analysis of science as a social system. Explicit rules defining how science is to be conducted tend to occur only during periods of emerging crisis when the established theories and assumptions are breaking down.

6. From many perspectives, this phase in the family's response to stress is misnamed. To call it the "emergence of rules" does not fully convey the broad range of adaptive — if not creative — coping strategies which families often develop in this stage. Indeed, we have elaborated on this aspect of the family's first response to stress in a recent paper (see Reiss and Oliveri, 1980). In that paper we have hypothesized very specific connections between a family's typical constructions of its social world (that is, whether a family is high or low in configuration, coordination, and closure) and the specific kinds of coping strategies it develops and sustains during this first phase of response to stress.

7. It is unlikely that, even in advanced states of disorganization, a family becomes aware of its own processes (the roles it assigns its members, its interaction patterns, and its shared affects and fantasies). Indeed, an early task of a family therapist is to recognize these patterns and, depending on the therapist's style, point them out to the family or attempt to change them (or both). During periods of disorganization family members become selectively aware of certain aspects of family process they regard as problematic. Particularly when the family is burdened by explicit constraints or is in a state of rebellion, members will show a very special form of selective awareness: they will be quick to notice behavior that somehow limits them but be unaware of either the feelings in others that produced the behavior or their own role in eliciting it.

8. The work of Hill (1949, 1958) and the syntheses of Burr (1973) and Hansen and Johnson (1979) also deal with the problem of vulnerability. Our analysis departs from theirs in a number of respects.

9. Different aspects of Navaho beliefs about illness, cure, and death may be found in a number of classic references including Reichard, 1950, and Kluckhohn and Leighton, 1958.

10. Although the requirements and practices of traditional Jews, after a death, are quite clear and explicit, interpretations of these practices have tended to vary. The one we have summarized, much too briefly, reflects one theme in current interpretative work. For summaries of a variety of viewpoints see Riemer, 1974, and Katz, 1977.

11. It is important to emphasize that we do not mean to imply that a family develops a crisis construct quickly or succinctly. In that sense, the concept of construct may be misleading. From what we know, a construct may develop over a long period of time, and it may not be fully accessible to an outside observer or to the family itself, particularly if the construct is tinged with shame or guilt. The term construct illustrates an important feature of theory building. As will become apparent, the concept of "crisis construct" is a critical node in our theoretical work for two reasons. First, it describes a crucial set of phenomena in a family which we believe play an important role in both the development and the stabilization of family members' shared conceptions of reality. Thus, "crisis construct" is meant to represent a significant set of observable phenomena of theoretical importance. Second, the concept itself is an important theoretical bridge: it is the fundamental link between stress-induced disorganization in families and the development of stable, routine interaction patterns regulated by their shared paradigm. The selection of the term is something of a semantic compromise. "Construct" suggests in a satisfactory, if not exemplary, way that the family's own interpretation of its predicament is crucial in shaping its long-term resolution of that predicament. In that sense it is meant to embrace what Hill (1958) and others have referred to as the family's "definition" of the event. The term "construct"—as the root of the more active term "construction"—is meant to give particular emphasis to the family's *initiative* in framing and elaborating its interpretations. Simultaneously, the term is meant to point to the relationship between the family's somewhat more immediate response to crisis (however prolonged this may

actually be) and its more permanent reorganization around a highly stable set of conceptions of its place in the world (its paradigm). The sematic compromise, however, becomes apparent when we recognize that the phenomena to which "crisis construct" is meant to refer are far less cognitive than the term implies. Indeed, the interpretive acts we are discussing, in families who are in crisis, are deeply emotional responses organized as much by fantasy and longing as by observations and rational inference. See the Conclusion for more discussion of this point.

12. There are two important qualifications to make in considering the role of outsiders. The first is to emphasize that many families allow non-family members considerable access to their home and dinner table; these families engage outsiders in a broad variety of family activities. It does not require a major crisis—in these families—to *admit* outsiders. Indeed, our conception of environment-sensitive families clearly implies that families of this kind do engage intensively and meaningfully with strangers whose advice, information, attitudes, and experience serve to enlarge the family's own repertoire of knowledge and understanding. However, environment-sensitive families behave in this way because they are guided by a set of assumptions about the world which suggest that open engagements with outsiders will be profitable, helpful, and intriguing. In effect, engagement of outsiders is that part of the family's daily routine which at the same time expresses and reifies its underlying system of constructions of the social world. A second usage of the term "outsiders" follows from the first. When outsiders enter the family during a crisis, their influence is probably not simply cognitive or attitudinal. Outsiders, including therapists, probably do not contribute to a family's conception of its own crisis through simple discussion, verbal persuasion, or the kind of explicit restructuring characteristic of the "cognitive therapies." Clinical and research evidence persuades us that an outsider's influence comes initially and primarily in the character of the relationship he forms with the family. The relationship—at its core a series of affect-laden routines between the outsider and the family—is what constitutes the fresh influence in family affairs. Thus, a family in crisis, trapped in chronically rigid behavior patterns, will be influenced by an outsider who can behave flexibly with the family.

13. For at least the past twenty years, the impact of serious illness of children on families has been of interest to observant clinicians and thoughtful scholars. We are not aware of observations that precisely parallel our own interest in the transforming properties of crisis of this kind. Nonetheless, a variety of studies have influenced our thinking, and some have suggested that transformations of the kind we are discussing here do occur in some families. For example, Darling (1979), in her study of families with children with severe birth defects, describes a typical change in "family career" in response to crisis. In her sample, parents become active—if not radical—proponents of increased services for their children. This outward stance parallels an important inner change. The crisis of dealing with the birth defect gives the family a sense of separation from its own social setting: family members perceive that their social world is no longer adequate in providing for or even understanding their plight.

They experience a shift from being pieces in a larger puzzle to agents acting on, and sometimes against, their surrounding world. They are transformed into missionaries. Similar transformations, though perhaps less dramatic, are also described in Davis's study (1963) of families' response to polio in their children. Davis points out that the family itself is often unaware of the changes; the fundamental shifts in the family's identity and experience of itself come out only incidentally and indirectly. Davis emphasizes that this *semblance* of lack of change may itself serve adaptive functions itself by preserving the family's sense of connection to its own past. The role of interpretation in a family's response to serious illness in a child is described in several studies of families of leukemic children. Chodoff, Friedman, and Hamburg (1964), for example, described the importance of families' understanding of the etiology of leukemia. This was a central part of the families' construction of the crisis they faced, and is quite analogous to the central role played by the Navajo's concept of the supernatural causes of illness, particularly in their healing ceremonies. A comparable search for meaning in crisis has been evocatively described in the study of young widows and widowers by Glick, Weiss, and Parkes (1974). Again, their interest was not in the long-term effects—on the remaining family—of such interpretive processes. Nonetheless, some of their case histories suggest just such an enduring effect.

14. An interesting experience corresponding to this one was obtained by a medical student in our center, Nancy Kolzak, who was doing a research project on married couples coping with the stress of the wife's mastectomy. She found that a path of reconstruction and recovery, very similar to the one we are describing here, often began with the husband carefully viewing and caring for his wife's surgical wound. Indeed, this first exploration and confrontation of the missing breast set the stage for other, open confrontations with the biological realities of mastectomy and cancer.

15. In contrast to all other case reports of families in this volume, the Roberts and Weaver families are composites. In other case reports we have changed a number of details and descriptions to protect the identity of the families. However, with these two "families" we have combined details from several different families in order to fashion a sequential and unfolding picture of a family's transformation through crisis.

5. The Abstraction of the Family Paradigm

1. The fundamental reference for Suzanne Langer's work is her *Mind: An Essay on Human Feeling*, vol. 1 (1967) and vol. 2 (1972). Langer's effort is directed at a reconceptualization of evolution, particularly the evolution of the unique characteristics of human mind and feeling. Importantly, the original sources of her analysis lie in her grasp of the artistic process. Early formulations of these ideas are in *Philosophy in a New Key* (1942) and in *Feeling and Form* (1953). Langer's thinking has influenced our formulations in several ways. At this point we make use of her conception of abstraction. Her concern is how artists abstract from a complex range of experience the essential, epigrammatic, and highly refined forms they develop and present to their artistic audience. Langer has provided an ex-

panded base for interpreting artistic production. She has recognized the limits of analyses that seek specific symbolic import in particular representations in painting or music or literature. Rather she points out that the import of a genuine artistic effort lies in the totality of its form. Moreover, this import derives from a concentrated and intense refinement — entailing selection, emphasis and reemphasis, deletion, distortion, and many other processes — of the artist's own experience. This concept — that the refinement or abstraction of experience is conserved in the totality of form within the product — is helpful to us later in our argument. It draws attention to the elegant and expressive form, the variegated and highly structured patterns of interaction, in family process. Indeed, a beginning family therapist is instructed first to pay close attention to all these formal details in a first interview with the family — where family members sit, who speaks first, how one responds to another. Then he is helped to integrate these disparate details, to appreciate the underlying structure or form which unites what he has observed. Sometimes he is advised to use more cognitive modes in defining such structures. At other times he is advised to use his own emotionally based intuition to grasp the essential forms. Thus, to a seasoned clinician our insistence on the importance of form in family life will come as nothing new. However, we believe that current clinical thinking has overlooked a crucial aspect of family form. That it is both expressive and informative to a clinician geared to understanding and helping families is no longer a mystery. However, that the form serves to *conserve* a refined and abstracted experience from the family's past is not a popular conception. This notion about the conserving function of fundamental forms of family life is one we return to in some detail in the next chapter. It is well at this point to note our debt to Langer's analysis in formulating our own hypotheses.

2. Good form refers to a basic principle of perceptual organization as formulated by Gestalt psychology. It refers to a particular configuration of stimuli that has an inherent conspicuousness and articulation. It impresses the observer and tends to be perceived recurrently and reliably despite distractions. A circle is a good form; so is a triangle or a square. A synoptic account of Gestalt principles of perceptual organization may be found in Boring, 1950. The most fundamental reference in Gestalt psychology is Koffka's *Principles of Gestalt Psychology* (1935), which has provided a number of useful concepts used later in this chapter. In addition, two books by Kohler, another of the founders of the Gestalt school, place the ideas of Gestalt psychology in a broader intellectual context. See his *Gestalt Psychology* (1947) and *The Task of Gestalt Psychology* (1969).

3. It could be argued that the seasons are as much an element of our nascent cosmology as are the brothers. In that case, the additional formulations concerning processes of restoration, are interpolations — connecting brothers and seasons — and not extrapolations after all. This difficulty cannot be systematically resolved and only highlights further the similarity of interpolation and extrapolation.

4. The terms and phrases used to characterize the form assumed by emerging crisis construct were not selected without design. Indeed, they

were meant to indicate those general and formal properties of the crisis constructs which might emerge as paradigmatic after a process of social abstraction has run its course.

5. This should not be dismissed as a speculative or exotic consequence of group process. Messianism in therapy groups and training groups, groups composed of individuals without any family ties to one another, has been described by Bion, 1959, and by Hartman and Gibbard, 1974.

6. Invoking Gestalt principles may seem like an unduly psychologistic strategy for constructing a theory of social process in families. It might be argued that we are, in effect, taking a page from a theory about individual perception and incorporating it into our model of family process. However, the origins and determinants of good form have never been effectively demonstrated. If Kohler's theory of electrical fields in the brain had been substantiated, then good form might be regarded as the property of an individual qua individual and the proper subject of psychology (or neuropsychology). It remains quite reasonable to suggest that good form may have *social* origins, that it may be a product of the growing child's social experiences, experiences which are universal and provide in each human a tendency to organize a perceptual field. Although this unorthodox argument is highly speculative, it does point to how little we know about the role of social experience and group process in the function of elementary, so-called psychological processes such as perception, memory, attention, and thinking.

7. See Koffka, 1935, particularly Chapter 5.

8. It is pertinent here that Chandler (1973) found that children with serious impulse control disorders and records of delinquency achieved low scores on tests of their capacity for referential communication and for changing perspective; in our own research we have found that these children come from families who do not integrate perspectives, have isolated constructs, and may well be operating under a segregated paradigm (Reiss, 1971c).

9. Often this intensely symbolic tie to a healer reflects a displacement of feelings that, in other families, might be directed toward a venerated grandfather or grandmother within the family itself. A psychoanalytic perspective would interpret such an idealizing and dependent tie to a physician or to a person in the family's own past as springing from a similar mechanism. We would not dispute this. We argue here that the difference between directing such feelings toward a member of the family and toward one who is outside is very substantial, in terms of the development of the family paradigm. In other words, similar mechanisms may give rise to idealizing and dependent relationships between the family and some senior figure, but the locus of the individual — within or without the family — is of abiding and enduring importance.

10. See Koffka, 1935, particularly Chapter 8.

6. The Conservation of the Family Paradigm

1. For an account of the Blackwells, see Horn, 1980; for the Rothschilds and Bleichröders, see Landes, 1975.

2. This concept was initially formulated by Bossard and Boll (1950) and elaborated in personal communications and publications by Wolin et al. (1979, 1980).

3. Kantor and Lehr also described mechanisms by which families obtained, mobilized and invested "energy." In their view, energy is a third resource. We believe that this concept of energy was Kantor and Lehr's approach to conceptualizing motivation or drive in family behavior. Our own model accounts for motivational aspects from quite a different perspective; we do not need to invoke the concept of energy. Moreover, Kantor and Lehr's descriptions of family routines for mobilizing and investing energy require a great deal more inference. They are less straightforward and objective than their accounts of routines for the family's use of time and space.

4. Kantor and Lehr discuss a third mechanism; synchronization. We consider this aspect of family routine in a later section.

5. Bermann himself came to a very similar conclusion but, importantly, through very different observations. He did not see that the degradation ceremonials themselves bespoke a freezing of time. Rather, he systematically enumerated all the family's utterances which referred to time and found the vast majority of them were concerned with the present; allusions to the future or the past were contained in only an astonishingly small 3 percent of all interactions. His frequency counts were buttressed by qualitative observations of the fleeting references to the past and future in what was actually said and done by the family.

6. Kantor and Lehr also discuss the linking together, in an overall pattern, of the smaller, more discrete pattern regulators. They call these structures "plans" or "traffic patterns." The Shackelfords show qualities of what Kantor and Lehr would call "parallel movement" but also another pattern they call "eccentric traffic."

7. Orienting Concepts in Family-Environment Organization

1. The family is not alone in using this device of selecting an ambassador to represent its "interests" in the wider special environment. The environment may select its own ambassador to conduct its transactions with the family. This is a useful, although very partial, model of family therapy. To be sure, the therapist clearly represents himself in the therapeutic encounter. It can and should be argued that the effectiveness of family therapy is due, in part, to the therapist's acting as a genuine individual—with his own feelings and intuitions—in his work with the family. Nonetheless, the therapist also acts as the agent or ambassador of several wider communities: the institution in which he works and the family therapy "movement." He can never—nor should he try—free himself from this role, since it is as genuinely a part of him as his more native personality traits and special skills. Nonetheless, a good deal of what transpires in family therapy can be understood from this "diplomatic" perspective in which the therapist is viewed as an ambassador to the family. His status, his power, his healing charisma (see Almond, 1974) are all inherent in his ambassadorial rather than his personal role. To carry this analysis one step

further, it can be argued that some forms of individual psychotherapy are really the meeting of two ambassadors. For example, consider the family who has successfully engineered a scapegoat role for one of its children. The child's misbehavior in the community has been subtly encouraged as a distraction from problems the family cannot bear to acknowledge (marital infidelity, or the fear of it, is a common instance here). If that child is "taken into" psychotherapy as a "delinquent," he serves as his family's covert ambassador to a therapist who is himself, in part, an ambassador of his own discipline and institution.

2. Stierlin, using clinical materials, has delineated these processes in a number of troubled families; see Stierlin, 1974.

3. Some of the pertinent research in group psychotherapy is summarized in Yalom, 1975.

4. For a similar account of slave families who were not dominated by *experienced* coercion see Bond, 1972.

5. While accounts of American utopian life in the nineteenth century abound, the most useful reference I know relating family and communal life is Muncy's monograph; see Muncy, 1973.

6. Suttles's concept of the "defended community" is partially applicable here.

7. As in previous chapters, the work of Berger and Luckmann was influential here; see Berger and Luckmann, 1966.

8. This concept is modified from Silverman, 1970.

9. This traditional view might be particularly true for the family's relationship with its kindred. On the one hand, it is easy to understand how a family might have considerable latitude in the kinds of links it forms with its kindred; thus, there might be room for a family's initiative here. However, in accord with the traditional view, it is very difficult to see how families might have the freedom to select which kindred they wish to join (as they might have in selecting a church or neighborhood). Our interest in the family's ties to its kindred is examined in more detail in the next chapter. Here, it is probably sufficient to note that whereas kin can never or rarely be selected by an established nuclear family (except where new members are legally adopted), kindreds can, in an important sense, be chosen voluntarily. (By kindred we mean here a specified group or set of kin with whom a particular family is somehow engaged.) In other words, nuclear families do have considerable latitude in selecting a kindred. As we have pointed out earlier, a marital couple can—and often does—choose either the wife's or the husband's side but not both. This choice of affiliation can undergo major shifts and slow but steady transformations as the couple grows older. This fundamental affiliation with a particular lineage is a framework for a more specific selection of a kindred. Special subgroups or individuals within the lineage chosen may be selected as particularly important to the nuclear family and will be frequently seen. When this is accomplished the nuclear family joins a particular subunit within a large kinship network. If this subgroup is a dense one—everyone in it is very involved with everyone else—the subgroup can function, in many ways, like a large, cohesive, and bounded group. These processes are examined in greater detail in the next chapter.

10. It is of more than passing interest that the experimental utopias paid great attention to the spatial layout of their communities (see Muncy, 1973). Indeed, the ideological and religious conceptions which undergirded these experiments were often expressed quite concretely and rigidly in specified floor plans for common or separate dwellings for families. The same is true of the carefully regulated Puritan communities in seventeenth-century America (see Demos, 1970, and Flaherty, 1967).

11. To be more precise, they cannot do so under ordinary circumstances. However, as we indicated in Chapter 4, and as we will discuss further in this chapter, the community can exert enormous influence over the family when the latter is in crisis.

12. See also the early history of the kibbutzim. Family identity and history are less feared in many current kibbutzim.

8. Exploring the Cycle Hypothesis

1. To be sure, many families bond their members to the group through remunerative or coercive ties. It is probably safe to argue that ties of this kind are more characteristic for organizations than they are for families. Nonetheless, it is useful to reconsider a point first raised in the previous chapter. The family, the kindred, the community, and the organization are concrete social groups, but they are also analytic perspectives. Thus, it is possible to analyze (see for example the review by Sawhill, 1977) the family as a economic group geared to the management of resources and the creation of a product. This perspective will yield images of remunerative and coercive bonds in families.

2. This statement may have been more strictly true at the time this study was first designed. In recent years there has been a gradual shift — some of it in keeping with scientific data — toward biologic treatments and conceptions of hospitalizable psychiatric disorders (particularly the schizophrenias and serious depressive disorders).

3. Details of this study may be found in Reiss, Costell, and Almond, 1976.

4. See Pollack and Kiev, 1963; Silverman, 1967; and Carson, Harden, and Shows, 1964.

5. See Chapters 4 and 5 for a detailed discussion of mechanisms we have proposed for relating crisis in the family to its susceptibility to outside influence.

6. Details of this study may be found in Reiss et al., 1980.

7. Several studies of individual families and ad hoc groups support this line of reasoning; see, for example, Mishler and Waxler, 1968, and Bales, 1965.

8. A review of much of this work may be found in Lindzey and Byrne, 1968.

9. See, for example, Almond and Esser, 1965, and Hall, 1964.

10. Traditionally, there are two ways to assess a family's network relationships. Anthropologically oriented observers who have an opportunity to live in a community for some time can directly observe the frequency and quality of contact between members of a target family and others in the

community. From a practical point of view this method is impossible with a large sample of target families who live in an urban setting. Our approach delineates the network of other individuals who are subjectively important to the family. This set might exclude individuals with whom the family has regular contact and include those with whom the family has virtually no contact. Nonetheless, the subjectively defined network, we propose, must loom large as a source of influence in the family's conception of itself. Moreover, our approach to defining network relationships in this way has been useful in other network studies such as those by Gordon and Downing (1978) and Tolsdorf (1976).

11. A related measure is network density. Bott and many of those who pursued her findings used this measure, which is computed by dividing the number of linkages by the total number of possible linkages. However, this index is highly vulnerable to network size: the number of possible linkages rises exponentially as size increases. Thus, the actual value of density tends to be smaller for large networks.354362. Details of this study may be found in Oliveri and Reiss, in press.

13. This change had several advantages. First, it made the length system somewhat more attractive. In the older version of the task, a family had to actively work to "see" the length system. They had to be careful to correctly catalogue each card according to length even though the system yielded piles of very unequal size. In these circumstances, the length system — although clearly less elegant than the pattern solution — could be regarded as a genuine solution. In the newer version of the procedure, the length system was much more obvious; subjects were much more quickly tempted by it because it produced just four equal and symmetrical piles. The length system became less of a solution and stood more as evidence that the family had failed to genuinely recognize, through meaningful effort or insight, any system for organizing the cards. The net effect of the change, then, was to elevate the pattern sort as the only true solution. The relative success or failure of the family in achieving the pattern system (and various gradations of success or failure remained a feature of this new procedure) became a simpler, more direct measure of pattern recognition — and hence configuration — by the family. A true problem-solving index could now be more simply derived: the pattern sort score, that is, the degree to which any sorter used the pattern system. The complex and cumbersome problem-solving and change scores of the older procedure could be dropped. The problem-solving score is now identical with the pattern sort score. See Chapter 2 in order to compare this newer, simpler system with the one we have been using so far.

14. Strictly speaking, multivariate analysis of variance would have been as appropriate in many of the previous studies reported in this book as it is here. However, from a practical perspective, its use becomes more important because we have added a third independent variable. This creates the possibility not only for significant three-way interactions, which are difficult to interpret, but for many more two-way interactions than in our previous designs, which had only two independent variables. MANOVA, then, becomes a straightforward way of highlighting effects of particular

strength by taking advantage of the combined use of our three dependent variables whose intercorrelations are greater than zero. These correlations are summarized below (df = 80; an asterisk indicates that $p < .01$; a dagger indicates that $p < .001$):

	Family level		Parental level	
	Size	Degree	Size	Degree
Degree	.40†		.38†	
Shared connection	.31*	.17	.46†	.18

15. Others have directly examined role segregation and network connectedness and failed to replicate Bott's initial observations (see Aldous and Straus, 1966, and Udry and Hall, 1965).

16. These data were obtained in a follow-up study of seventy-three of the eighty-three families in this sample approximately two years after the original network data were obtained. Thus, the family's enumeration of the actual number of kinsmen could not have contaminated in any way their responses concerning kinsmen important to them. We asked them to list all those relatives who had ever lived, those living at the time of our follow-up, and those living within fifty miles. Since the first category contained a number of relatives who had died in childbirth or infancy and the last was partially a product of the family's own initiative, we regarded the second—the number living—as the most pertinent index of the size of the "objective" kinship network. However, analyses using total number of kinsmen—alive or dead—produced approximately the same results.

Conclusion

1. A question of this kind has been raised in response to earlier versions of our model; see Klein and Hill, 1979.

2. A more thorough analysis of these processes may be found in Zinner and Shapiro, 1972.

3. Theorists concerned with the development and internal regulation of groups of unrelated individuals have effectively used the concept of boundary to analyze the relationship of the individual to the larger group. The theoretical synthesis and empirical inquiries of J. A. Reiss, 1980, have been particularly useful to our analysis. See also Gibbard, Hartman, and Mann, 1974, and Slater, 1966.

4. A useful and current summary of the concept of transference may be found in Sandler, Dare, and Holder, 1973.

5. Current psychoanalytic theory does not regard transference as a manifestation of illness. It remains, however, a clinical term because of its immense practical importance in the conduct of therapeutic analyses.

6. Not that transference phenomena disappear at this point; they become less rooted in unalloyed conviction.

References

Ackerknecht, D. H. 1968. *Short History of Psychiatry*. New York: Hafner Publishing Company.

Adams, B. N. 1968. *Kinship in an Urban Setting*. Chicago: Markham.

Aldous, J., and Straus, M. A. 1966. Social Networks and Conjugal Roles: A Test of Bott's Hypothesis." *Social Forces* 44: 576-580.

Almond, R. 1974. *The Healing Community: Dynamics of the Therapeutic Milieu*. New York: Jason Aronson.

Almond, R., and Esser, A. H. 1965. "Tablemate Choices of Psychiatric Patients: A Technique for Measuring Social Contact." *Journal of Nervous and Mental Disease* 141: 68-82.

Almond, R., Keniston, K., and Boltax, S. 1968. "The Value System of a Milieu Therapy Unit." *Archives of General Psychiatry* 19: 545-561.

_____1969. "Patient Value Change in Milieu Therapy." *Archives of General Psychiatry* 20: 339-351.

Ariès, P. 1962. *Centuries of Childhood*. New York: Vintage.

_____1977. "The Family and the City." *Daedalus* 106: 227-235.

Attneave, F. 1959. *Applications of Information Theory to Psychology: A Summary of Basic Concepts, Methods and Results*. New York: Holt.

Bales, R. F. 1965. "The Equilibrium Problem in Small Groups." In Hare, A. P., Borgatta, E. F., and Bales, R. F., eds., *Small Groups*. New York: Alfred A. Knopf.

Baltzell, Edward D. 1958. *Philadelphia Gentlemen: The Making of a National Upper Class*. New York: Free Press.

Bane, M. J. 1976. *Here to Stay*. New York: Basic Books.

Bannister, D., and Mair, J. M. M. 1968. *The Evaluation of Personal Constructs*. New York: Academic Press.

Barber, B. 1961. "Family Status, Local Community Status and Social Stratification: Three Types of Social Ranking." *Pacific Sociological Review* 4: 3-10.

Barenboim, C. 1977. "Developmental Changes in the Interpersonal Cognitive System from Middle Childhood to Adolescence." *Child Development* 48: 1467-1474.

Bauman, R., and Sherzer, J., eds. 1974. *Explorations in the Ethnography of Speaking.* London: Cambridge University Press.

Bavelas, A. 1950. "Communication Patterns in Task Oriented Groups." *Journal Accoustical Society of America* 22: 725-730.

Bennett, L. A. 1978. *Personal Choice in Ethnic Identity Maintenance, Serbs, Croats and Slovenes.* Palo Alto: Ragusan Press.

Berger, P. L., and Luckmann, T. 1966. *The Social Construction of Reality.* New York: Doubleday.

Bermann, E. 1973. *Scapegoat.* Ann Arbor: University of Michigan Press.

Betz, B. J. 1962. "Experiences in Research in Psychotherapy with Schizophrenic Patients." In Strupp, H. H., and Lubrosky, L., eds., *Research in Psychotherapy,* vol. 2. Washington, D.C.: American Psychological Association.

Bilmes, M. 1967. "Shame and Delinquency." *Contemporary Psychoanalysis* 3: 113-133.

Bion, W. 1959. *Experience in Groups.* New York: Basic Books.

Bleuler, E. 1960. *Dementia Praecox or the Group of Schizophrenias,* trans. J. Zinkin. New York: International Universities Press.

Bond, H. M. 1972. *Black American Scholars.* Detroit: Balamp Publishing Co.

Boring, E. G. 1950. *A History of Experimental Psychology.* New York: Appleton, Century, Crofts.

Bossard, J. H. S., and Boll, E. S. 1950. *Ritual in Family Living.* Philadelphia: University of Pennsylvania Press.

Bott, E. 1957. *Family and Social Network.* New York: Free Press.

Broderick, C. B., and Pulliam-Krager, H. 1979. "Family Process and Child Outcomes." In Burr, W. R., Hill, R., Nye, F. I., and Reiss, I. L., eds., *Contemporary Theories about the Family.* Vol. 1, *Research-Based Theories.* New York: Free Press.

Bruner, J. S., Goodnow, J. J. and Austin, G. A. 1956. *A Study of Thinking.* New York: John Wiley.

Brunswick, E. 1955. "The Conceptual Framework of Psychology." *In International Encyclopedia of Unified Science,* vol. 10. Chicago: University of Chicago Press.

Brunswick, E. 1956. *Perception and the Representative Design of Psychological Experiments.* Berkeley: University of California Press.

Burr, W. R. 1973. *Theory Construction and the Sociology of the Family.* New York: John Wiley.

Carson, R. C., Harden, J. A., and Shows, W. 1964. "A-B Distinction and Behavior in Quasi-Therapeutic Situations." *Journal of Consulting Psychology* 28: 426–433.

Cather, W. 1949. *My Antonia.* New York: Houghton Mifflin.

Chandler, M. J. 1973. "Egocentrism and Antisocial Behavior: The Assessment and Training of Social Perspective Taking Skills." *Developmental Psychology* 9: 326–332.

Chodoff, P., Friedman, S. B., and Hamburg, D. A. 1964. "Stress, Defenses and Coping Behavior: Observations in Parents of Children with Malignant Disease." *American Journal of Psychiatry* 120: 743-749.

Chomsky, N. 1957. *Syntactic Structures.* The Hague: Mouton.

Chomsky, N., and Miller, G. A. 1958. "Finite State Languages." *Information and Control* 1: 91-112.

Christie, R., and Geis, F. 1970. *Studies in Machiavellianism.* New York: Academic Press.

Cohen, B. D., Senf, R., and Huston, P. E. 1956. "Perceptual Accuracy in Schizophrenia, Depression and Neurosis and Effects of Amytal." *Journal of Abnormal Social Psychology* 52: 363.

Costell, R., Reiss, D., Berkman, H., and Jones, C. In press. "The Family Meets the Hospital: Predicting the Family's Perception of the Treatment Program from Its Problem-Solving Style." *Archives of General Psychiatry.*

Cromwell, R., Klein, D., and Wieting, S. G. 1975. "Family Power: A Multi-trait, Multimethod Analysis." In Cromwell, R., and Olson, D., eds., *Power in Families.* New York: John Wiley, Halstead Press Division.

Darling, R. B. 1979. *Families against Society.* New York: Sage Publications.

Dashefsky, A., and Shapiro, H. 1974. *Ethnic Identification among American Jews.* Lexington, Mass.: Lexington Books.

Davis, Fred. 1963. *Passage through Crisis: Polio Victims and Their Families.* New York: Bobbs-Merrill.

Demos, J. 1970. *A Little Commonwealth.* New York: Oxford University Press.

Dohrenwend, B. S., Krasnoff, L., Askenasy, A. R., and Dohrenwend, B. P. 1978. "Exemplification of a Method for Scaling Life Events: The PERI Life Events Scale." *Journal of Health and Social Behavior* 19: 205-229.

Duvall, E. M. 1971. *Family Development.* New York: Lippincott.

Etzioni, A. 1961. *A Comparative Analysis of Complex Organizations.* New York: Free Press.

Ferreira, A. J., and Winter, W. D. 1968. "Information Exchange and Silence in Normal and Abnormal Families." *Family Process* 7: 251-276.

Fisher, S., Boyd, I., Walker, D., and Sheer, D. 1959. "Parents of Schizophrenics, Neurotics, and Normals." *Archives of General Psychiatry* 1: 149-166.

Flaherty, D. H. 1967. *Privacy in Colonial New England.* Charlottesville: University Press of Virginia.

Fleck, S., Freedman, D. X., Cornelison, S. R., Lidz, T., and Terry, D. 1965. "The Understanding of Symptomatology through the Study of Family Interaction." In Lidz, T., Fleck, S., and Cornelison, A. R., eds., *Schizophrenia and the Family.* New York: International Universities Press.

Freud, A. 1946. *The Ego and the Mechanisms of Defense.* New York: International Universities Press.

Freud, S. 1955. "Studies of Hysteria." In *The Complete Psychological Works of Sigmund Freud,* ed. J. Starchey. London: Hogarth Press.

Gardner, R. W., Holzman, P. S., Klein, G. W., Linton, H. B., and

Spence, D. P. 1959. "Cognitive Control: A Study of Individual Consistencies in Cognitive Behavior." *Psychological Issues* 1 (4). New York: International Universities Press.

Gardner, R. W., Jackson, D. N., and Messick, S. J. 1960. 'Personality Organization in Cognitive Controls and Intellectual Abilities." *Psychological Issues* 2 (4). New York: International Universities Press.

Garland, H. 1914. *A Son of the Middle Border.* New York: Macmillan.

Gibbard, G. S., Hartman, J. J., and Mann, R. D. 1974. "Analysis of Groups: Contributions to Theory, Research and Practice." San Francisco: Jossey-Bass.

Glick, I. O., Weiss, R. S., and Parkes, C. M. 1974. *The First Year of Bereavement.* New York: John Wiley.

Goldman-Eisler, G. F. 1961. "Hesitation and Information in Speech." In Cherry, C., ed., *Information Theory.* London: Butterworth.

Gordon, M., and Downing, H. 1978. "A Multivariate Test of the Bott Hypothesis in an Urban Irish Setting." *Journal of Marriage and the Family* 40: 585-593.

Gouldner, A. W. 1965. *Wildcat Strike.* New York: Harper.

Hall, E. T. 1964. "Silent Assumptions in Social Communication." In *Disorders of Communication,* vol. 42. New York: Association for Research in Nervous and Mental Diseases.

Hall, R. H. 1968. "Professionalization and Bureaucratization." *American Sociological Review* 33: 92-104.

Halliday, M. A. K. 1973. *Explorations in the Function of Language.* London: Edwards, Arnold.

Hansen, D. A., and Johnson, V. A. 1979. "Rethinking Family Stress Theory: Definitional Aspects." In Burr, W. R., Hill, R., Nye, F. I., and Reiss, I. L., eds., *Contemporary Theories about the Family.* Vol. 1, *Research-Based Theories.* New York: Free Press.

Harbin, H. T. 1978. "Families and Hospitals: Collusion or Cooperation?" *American Journal of Psychiatry* 135: 1496-99.

Hartman, J. J., and Gibbard, S. 1974. "A Note on Fantasy Themes in the Evolution of Group Culture." In Gibbard, G. S., Hartman, J. J., and Mann, R. D., eds., *Analysis of Groups.* San Francisco: Jossey-Bass.

Haley, A. 1976. *Roots.* New York: Doubleday.

Heider, F. 1958. *The Psychology of Interpersonal Relations.* New York: John Wiley.

Heise, G. A., and Miller, G. A. 1951. "Problem Solving by Small Groups Using Various Communication Nets." *Journal of Abnormal Social Psychology* 46: 327-335.

Hess, R. D., and Handel, G. 1959. *Family Worlds.* Chicago: University of Chicago Press.

Hill, L. B. 1955. *Psychotherapeutic Intervention in Schizophrenia.* Chicago: University of Chicago Press.

Hill, R. 1949. *Families under Stress.* New York: Harper.

Hill, R. 1958. "Generic Features of Families under Stress." *Social Casework* 39: 139–150.

Hill, R., and Rodgers, R. H. 1964. "The Developmental Approach." In

Christensen, H. T., eds., *Handbook of Marriage and the Family.* Chicago: Rand McNally.

Holmes, T. H., and Rahe, R. H. 1967. "The Social Readjustment Rating Scale." *Journal of Psychosomatic Research* 11: 213-218.

Hoover, C. F. 1965. "The Embroiled Family: A Blueprint for Schizophrenia." *Family Process* 4: 291-310.

Howell, J. T. 1973. *Hard Living on Clay Street.* New York: Anchor Books.

Horn, M. E. 1980. "Family Ties: The Blackwells, A Study in the Dynamics of Family Life in Nineteenth Century America." Ph.D. dissertation, Tufts University.

Ishwaran, K. 1977. *Family, Kinship and Community.* New York: McGraw-Hill Ryerson Ltd.

Jacob, T. 1975. "Family Interaction in Disturbed and Normal Families: A Methodological and Substantive Review." *Psychological Bulletin* 82: 33-65.

Janowitz, M. 1952. *The Community Press in an Urban Setting. 2d ed.* Chicago: University of Chicago Press.

Kantor, D., and Lehr, W. 1975. *Inside the Family.* San Francisco: Jossey-Bass.

Katz, S. T. 1977. *Jewish Ideas and Concepts.* New York: Shocken Books.

Kaufman, I., Durkin, H., Jr., Frank, T., Heims, L. W., Jones, D. B., Ryter, Z., Stone, E., and Zilbach, J. 1963. "Delineation of Two Diagnostic Groups among Juvenile Delinquents: The Schizophrenic and the Impulse-Ridden Character Disorder." *Journal of the American Academy of Child Psychiatry* 2: 292-318.

Kelly, G. A. 1955. *The Psychology of Personal Constructs,* vols. 1 and 2. New York: Norton.

Kestenberg, J. 1968. "Outside and Inside, Male and Female." *Journal of the American Psychoanalytic Association* 16: 457-470.

Kety, S. S., Rosenthal, D., and Wender, P. H. 1968. "The Types and Prevalence of Mental Illness in the Biological and Adoptive Families of Adopted Schizophrenics." In Rosenthal, D., and Kety, S. S., eds., *The Transmission of Schizophrenia.* Oxford: Pergamon Press.

_____1975. "Mental Illness in the Biological and Adoptive Families of Adopted Individuals Who Have Become Schizophrenic: A Preliminary Report Based on Psychiatric Interviews." In Feive, R. R., Rosenthal, D., Brill, H., eds., *Genetic Research in Psychiatry.* Baltimore: Johns Hopkins University Press.

Klein, D. M., and Hill, R. 1979. "Determinants of Family Problem-Solving Effectiveness." In Burr, W. R., Hill, R., Nye, F. I., and Reiss, I. L., eds., *Contemporary Theories About the Family.* Vol. 1; *Research-Based Theories.* New York: Free Press.

Kluckhohn, C., and Leighton, D. 1958. *The Navajo.* Cambridge: Harvard University Press.

Kluckhohn, F. R. 1960. "Varieties in the Basic Values of Family Systems." In Bell, N. W., and Vogel, E. F., eds., *A Modern Introduction to the Family.* Glencoe, Ill. Free Press.

Koffka, K. 1935. *Principles of Gestalt Psychology.* New York: Harcourt,

Brace and World.

Kohlberg, L. 1964. *Stages in the Development of Moral Thought and Action.* New York: Holt, Rinehart and Winston.

Kohler, W. 1947. *Gestalt Psychology.* New York: Liveright.

———1969. *The Task of Gestalt Psychology.* Princeton, N.J.: Princeton University Press.

Kohn, M. L. 1969. Class and Conformity. Homewood, Ill.: Dorsey Press.

Koran, L. M., Costell, R. 1973. "Early Termination from Group Psychotherapy." *International Journal of Group Psychotherapy* 3: 346-359.

Korn, S. J., Chess, S., and Fernandez, P. 1978. "The Impact of Children's Physical Handicaps on Marital Quality and Family Interaction." In Lerner, R. M., and Spanier, G. B., eds., *Child Influences on Marital and Family Interaction: A Life-Span Perspective.* New York: Academic Press.

Krauss, R. M., and Glucksberg, S. 1969. "The Development of Communication Competence as a Function of Age." *Child Development* 40: 255-266.

Kuhn, T. S. 1962. *The Structure of Scientific Revolutions.* University of Chicago Press.

———1970. *The Structure of Scientific Revolutions.* 2d. ed. Chicago: University of Chicago Press.

———1977. "Second Thoughts on Paradigms." In Suppe, F., ed., *The Structure of Scientific Theories. 2d ed.* Urbana: University of Illinois Press.

Laing, R. D. 1964. *Sanity, Madness and the Family.* Vol. 1, *Families of Schizophrenics.* London: Tavistock.

Landes, D. 1975. "Bleichröders and Rothchilds: The Problem of Continuity in the Family Firm." In Rosenberg, C. E., ed., *The Family in History.* Philadelphia: University of Pennsylvania Press.

Langer, S. K. 1942. *Philosophy in a New Key.* Cambridge, Mass.: Harvard University Press.

———1953. *Feeling and Form.* New York: Charles Scribner's Sons.

———1967. *Mind: An Essay on Human Feeling,* vol. 1. Baltimore: Johns Hopkins University Press.

———1972. *Mind: An Essay on Human Feeling,* vol. 2, Baltimore: Johns Hopkins University Press.

Laslett, B. 1973. "The Family as a Public and Private Institution: An Historical Perspective." *Journal of Marriage and the Family* 35: 480-492.

Leavitt, H. J. 1951. "Some Effects of Certain Communication Patterns upon Group Performance." *Journal of Abnormal Social Psychology* 46: 38-50.

Lefcourt, H. M. 1976. *Locus of Control: Current Trends in Theory and Research.* Hillsdale, N.J.: Lawrence Erlbaum Associates.

Lerner, P. M. 1965. "Resolution of Intrafamilial Role Conflict in Families of Schizophrenic Patients, I. Thought Disturbance." *Journal of Nervous and Mental Disease* 141: 342-351.

Levinson, D., and Gallagher, E. 1964. *Patienthood in the Mental Hospital.* Boston: Houghton Mifflin.

Lidz, T. 1958. "Intrafamilial Environment of the Schizophrenic Patient: VI. The Transmission of Irrationality." *A.M.A. Archives of Psychiatry and Neurology* 79: 305-316.

Lidz, T., Wild, C., Schafer, S., Rosman, B., and Fleck, S. 1963. "Thought Disorders in the Parents of Schizophrenic Patients: A Study Utilizing the Object Sorting Test." *Journal of Psychiatric Research* 1: 193-200.

Lindzey, G., and Byrne, D. 1968. "Measurement of Social Choice and Interpersonal Attractiveness." In Lindzey, G., and Aronson, E., eds., *The Handbook of Social Psychology. 2d ed.* Reading, Mass.: Addison-Wesley.

Merton, R. K. 1949. "Patterns of Influence: A Study of Interpersonal Influence and Communication Behavior in a Local Community." In Lazarsfeld, P. F., and Stanton, F. N., eds., *Communications Research 1948-1949.* New York: Harper and Row.

Miller, G. A. 1967. "Project Grammarama." In *The Psychology of Communication.* New York: Basic Books.

Mindel, C. H., and Habenstein, R. W., eds. 1976. *Ethnic Families in America: Patterns and Variations.* New York: Elsevier.

Minuchin, S., Auerswald, E., King, C. H., and Rabinowitz, C. 1964. "The Study and Treatment of Families that Produce Multiple Acting-Out Boys." *American Journal of Orthopsychiatry* 34: 125-133.

Mishler, E. G., and Waxler, N. E. 1968. *Interaction in Families.* New York: John Wiley.

Moos, R. 1971. *Revision of the Ward Atmosphere Scales: Technical Report.* Palo Alto: Social Ecology Laboratory, Department of Psychiatry, Stanford University.

_____1974. *Evaluating Treatment Environments.* New York: John Wiley.

Moos, R., and Houts, P. 1968. "Assessment of the Social Atmospheres of Psychiatric Wards." *Journal of Abnormal Psychology* 73: 595-604.

Morris, G. O., and Wynne, L. C. 1965. "Schizophrenic Offspring and Parental Styles of Communication: A Predictive Study Utilizing Excerpts of Family Therapy Recordings." *Psychiatry* 28: 19-44.

Muncy, R. L. 1973. *Sex and Marriage in Utopian Communities.* Bloomington: Indiana University Press.

Myers, J., and Bean, L. 1968. *A Decade Later: A Follow-up of Social Class and Mental Illness.* New York: John Wiley.

Nagy, I., and Spark, G. M. 1973. *Invisible Loyalties.* Hagerstown, Md.: Harper and Row.

Oliveri, M. E., and Reiss, D. 1981. "An Approach to Family Classification." Submitted for publication.

_____In press. "The Structure of Families' Ties to their Kin: The Shaping Role of Social Constructions." *Journal of Marriage and the Family.*

Olmstead, M. S. 1954. "Orientation and Role in the Small Group." *American Sociological Review* 19: 741-751.

Olsen, M. E. 1968. *The Process of Social Organization.* New York: Holt, Rinehart and Winston.

Parsons, T. 1965. "The Normal American Family." In Farber, S. M., Mustacchi, P. and Wilson, R. H. L., eds., *Man and Civilization: The Fam-*

ily's Search for Survival. New York: McGraw Hill.

Payne, R. W., Carid, W. L., and Laverty, S. G. 1964. "Overinclusive Thinking and Delusions in Schizophrenic Patients." *Journal of Abnormal Social Psychology* 68: 562-566.

Perrow, C. 1967. "A Framework for the Comparative Analysis of Organizations." *American Sociological Review* 32: 194-208.

Pinneau, S. R., and Newhouse, A. 1964. "Measures of Invariance and Comparability in Factor Analysis for Fixed Variables." *Psychometrika* 29: 271-281.

Pollack, I. W., and Kiev, A. 1963. "Spatial Orientation and Psychotherapy: An Experimental Study of Perception." *Journal of Nervous and Mental Disease* 137: 93-97.

Redfield, R. 1953. *The Primitive World and Its Transformations*. Ithaca, N.Y.: Cornell University Press.

Reichard, G. A. 1950. *Navaho Religion: A Study of Symbolism*. New York: Pantheon.

Reiss, D. 1967a. "Individual Thinking and Family Interaction. I. An Introduction to an Experimental Study of Problem Solving in Families of Normals, Character Disorders and Schizophrenics." *Archives of General Psychiatry* 16: 80-93.

———1967b. "Individual Thinking and Family Interaction. II. A Study of Pattern Recognition and Hypothesis Testing in Families of Normals, Character Disorders and Schizophrenics." *Journal of Psychiatric Research* 5: 193-211.

———1968a. "Individual Thinking and Family Interaction. III. An Experimental Study of Categorization Performance in Families of Normals, Character Disorders and Schizophrenics." *Journal of Nervous and Mental Disease* 146: 384-403.

———1968b. "Family Problem Solving: Two Experiments on the Relationship Between Family Interaction and Individual Thinking in Families of Schizophrenics, Normals and Character Disorders." *Journal of Psychiatric Research* 6 (suppl. 1): 123-134.

———1969. "Individual Thinking and Family Interaction. IV. A Study of Information Exchange in Families of Normals, Those with Character Disorders and Schizophrenia." *Journal of Nervous and Mental Disease* 149: 473-490.

———1970. "Individual Thinking and Family Interaction. V. Proposals for the Contrasting Character of Experiential Sensitivity and Expressive Form in Families." *Journal of Nervous and Mental Disease* 151: 187-202.

———1971a. "Varieties of Consensual Experience I. A Theory for Relating Family Interaction to Individual Thinking." *Family Process* 10: 1-28.

———1971b. "Varieties of Consensual Experience II. Dimensions of a Family's Experience of Its Environment." *Family Process* 10: 28-35.

———1971c. "Varieties of Consensual Experience III. Contrast between Families of Normals, Delinquents and Schizophrenics." *Journal of Nervous and Mental Disease* 152: 73-95.

———1971d. "Intimacy and Problem Solving: An Automated Procedure for Testing a Theory of Consensual Experience in Families." *Archives of General Psychiatry 25:* 442–455.

_____1980. "Pathways to Assessing the Family: Some Choice Points and a Sample Route." In Hofling, C. K., and Lewis, J. M., eds., *The Family: Evaluation and Treatment.* New York: Brunner/Mazel.

Reiss, D., Costell, R., and Almond, R. 1976. "Personal Needs, Values and Technical Preferences in the Psychiatric Hospital: A Replicated Study." *Archives of General Psychiatry* 23: 795-804.

Reiss, D., Costell, R., Berkman, H., and Jones, C. 1980. "How One Family Perceives Another: The Relationship between Social Constructions and Problem Solving Competence." *Family Process.* 19: 239-256.

Reiss, D., Costell, R., Jones, C., and Berkman, H. 1980. "The Family Meets the Hospital: A Laboratory Forecast of the Encounter." *Archives of General Psychiatry* 37: 141-154.

Reiss, D., and Hoffman, H., eds. 1979. *The American Family: Dying or Developing.* New York: Plenum.

Reiss, D., and Oliveri, M. E. 1980. "Family Paradigm and Family Coping: A Proposal for Linking the Family's Intrinsic Adaptive Capacities to Its Responses to Stress." *Family Relations.* 29: 431-444.

Reiss, D., and Salzman, C. 1973. "The Resilience of Family Process: Effect of Secobarbital." *Archives of General Psychiatry* 28: 425-433.

Reiss, D., and Sheriff, W. H., Jr. 1970. "A Computer Automated Procedure for Testing Some Experiences of Family Membership." *Behavioral Science* 15: 431.

Reiss, J. A. 1980. "Participants' perception of themselves, consultants, and the group-as-a-whole in large and small unstructured groups." Ph.D. dissertation, George Washington University.

Riemer, J. 1974. *Jewish Reflections on Death.* New York: Shocken Books.

Roman, M., Bauman, G., Borello, J., and Meltzer, B. 1967. "Interaction Testing in the Measurement of Marital Intelligence." *Journal of Abnormal Psychology* 72: 489-495.

Rosenthal, D., Wender, P. H., and Kety, S. S. 1968. "Schizophrenics' Offspring Reared in Adoptive Homes." In Rosenthal, D., and Kety, S. S., eds., *The Transmission of Schizophrenia.* Oxford: Pergamon Press.

Rosman, B., Wild, C., Ricci, J., Fleck, S., and Lidz, T. 1964. "Thought Disorders in the Parents of Schizophrenic Patients: A Further Study Utilizing the Object Sorting Test." *Journal of Psychiatric Research* 2: 211.

Ryder, R. G. 1966. "Two Replications of Color Matching Factors." *Family Process* 5: 43-48.

Sandler, J., Dare, C., and Holder, A. 1973. *The Patient and the Analyst.* New York: International Universities Press.

Sawhill, Isabel V. 1977. "Economic Perspectives of the Family." *Daedalus* (spring): 115-125.

Schenkein, J., ed. 1978. *Studies in the Organization of Conversational Interaction,* New York: Academic Press.

Schultz, W. 1966. *The Interpersonal Underworld.* Palo Alto, Calif.: Science and Behavior Books.

410   *References*

Scott, R. D., and Ashworth, P. L. 1967. " 'Closure' at the First Schizophrenic Breakdown: A Family Study. *British Journal of Medical Psychology* 40: 103-145.

Searle, J. R. 1969. *Speech Acts.* London: Cambridge University Press.

Searles, H. 1959. "The Effort to Drive the Other Person Crazy—An Element in the Aetiology and Psychotherapy of Schizophrenia." *British Journal of Medical Psychology* 32: 1-18.

Shannon, C. E., and Weaver, W. 1949. *The Mathematical Theory of Communication.* Urbana: University of Illinois Press.

Shorter, Edward 1975. *The Making of the Modern Family.* New York: Basic Books.

Silverman, D. 1970. *The Theory of Organizations.* New York: Basic Books.

Silverman, J. 1967. "Personality and Perceptual Style of Psychotherapists of Schizophrenic Patients." *Journal of Nervous and Mental Disease* 145: 5-17.

Singer, M. T., and Wynne, L. C. 1965. "Thought Disorder and Family Relations of Schizophrenics: III. Methodology Using Projective Techniques." *Archives of General Psychiatry* 12: 187-200.

Slater, P. E. 1966. *Microcosm: Structural, Psychological and Religious Evolution in Groups.* New York: John Wiley.

Snyder, S., Rosenthan, D., and Taylor, I. A. 1961. "Perceptual Closure in Schizophrenia." *Journal of Abnormal Social Psychology* 63: 131.

Stabenau, J. R., Tupin, J., Werner, J., and Rollin, W. A. 1965. "A Comparative Study of Families of Schizophrenics, Delinquents and Normals." *Psychiatry* 28: 45-59.

Steinglass, P. 1978. "The Conceptualization of Marriage from a Systems Theory Perspective." in Peolino, T. J., and McCrady, B. S., eds., *Marriage and Marital Therapy.* New York: Brunner/Mazel.

———1979. "The Home Observation Assessment Method (HOAM): Real-Time Naturalistic Observation of Families in Their Homes." *Family Process* 18: 337-354.

———In press. "The Alcoholic Family at Home: Patterns of Interaction in Dry, Wet and Traditional Stages of Alcoholism." *Archives of General Psychiatry.*

Stierlin, H. 1974. *Separating Parents and Adolescents.* New York: Quadrangle.

Straus, M. A. 1967. "The Influence of Sex of Child and Social Class on Instrumental and Expressive Family Roles in a Laboratory Setting." *Sociology and Social Research* 52: 7-21.

———1968. "Communication, Creativity and Problem-Solving Ability of Middle- and Working-Class Families in Three Societies." *American Journal of Sociology* 73: 417-430.

Strauss, A., Scatzman, L., Bucher, R., et al. 1964. *Psychiatric Ideologies and Institutions.* New York: Free Press.

Streufert, S. and Fromkin, H. L. 1972. "Cognitive Complexity and Social Influence." In Tedeschi, J. T., ed., *The Social Influence Processes.* Chicago: Aldine, Atherton.

Strodtbeck, F. L. 1958. "Family Interaction, Values and Achievement." In McClelland, D. C., Baldwon, A. L., and Bronfenbrenner, U., eds., *Talent and Society*. Princeton, N.J.: D. Van Nostrand Co.

Sudnow, D., ed. 1972. *Studies in Social Interaction*, New York: Free Press.

Suttles, G. D. 1972. *The Social Construction of Communities*. Chicago: University of Chicago Press.

Tolsdorf, C. C. 1976. "Social Networks, Support and Coping: An Exploratory Study." *Family Process* 15: 407-418.

Tonnies, F. 1957. *Community and Society* trans. and ed. C. P. Loomis. East Lansing: Michigan State University.

Turner, R., ed. 1974. *Ethnomethodology*. Harmondsworth: Penguin Books.

Turner, V. 1977. "Variation on a Theme of Liminality." In Moore, S. F., and Myerhodd, B. G., eds., *Secular Ritual*. Amsterdam: Van Gorcum, Assen.

Udry, J. R., and Hall, M. 1965. "Marital Role Segregation and Social Networks in Middle-Aged Couples." *Journal of Marriage and the Family* 27: 392-395.

Vann, Richard T. 1976. "Review of *The Making of the Modern Family* by Edward Shorter." *Journal of Family History* 1: 106-117.

Warren, R. L. 1972. *The Community in America*. 2d ed. Chicago: Rand McNally.

Wender, P. H., Rosenthal, D., and Kety, S. S. 1968. "Psychiatric Assessment of Adoptive Parents of Schizophrenics." In Rosenthal, D., and Kety, S. S., eds., *The Transmission of Schizophrenia*. Oxford: Pergamon Press.

———1974. "Crossfostering: A Research Strategy for Clarifying the Role of Genetic and Experiential Factors in the Etiology of Schizophrenia." *Archives of General Psychiatry* 30: 121-128.

Wender, P. H., Rosenthal, D., Rainer, J. D., Greenhill, L., and Sarlin, M. B. 1977. "Schizophrenics' Adopting Parents." *Archives of General Psychiatry* 34: 777-784.

Whitehorn, J. C., and Betz, B. J. 1960. "Further Studies of the Doctor as a Crucial Variable in the Outcome of Treatment with Schizophrenic Patients." *American Journal of Psychiatry* 117: 215-223.

Wild, C. 1965. "Measuring Disordered Styles of Thinking: Using the Object Sorting Test on Parents of Schizophrenic Patients." *Archives of General Psychiatry* 13: 471-476.

Wild, C., Singer, M. T., Rosman, B., Ricci, J., and Lidz, T. 1965. "Measuring Disordered Styles of Thinking. Using the Object Sorting Test on Parents of Schizophrenic Patients." *Archives of General Psychiatry* 13: 471.

Wilder, L. I. 1937. *On the Banks of Plum Creek*. New York: Harper and Row.

Wilensky, H. L. 1964. "The Professionalization of Everyone?" *American Journal of Sociology* 70: 137-158.

Wolin, S. J., Bennett, L. A. and Noonan, D. L. 1979. "Family Rituals and the Recurrence of Alcoholism over Generations." *American Journal of*

Psychiatry 136: 589–593.

Wolin, S. J., Bennett, L. A., Noonan, D. L., and Teitlebaum, M. A. 1980. "A Factor in the Intergenerational Transmission of Alcoholism." *Journal of Studies on Alcohol* 41: 199-214.

Wynne, L. C., Ryckoff, I. M., Day, J., and Hirsch, S. I. 1958. "Pseudo-Mutuality in the Family Relations of Schizophrenics." *Psychiatry* 21: 205-222.

Wynne, L. C., and Singer, M. T. 1963. "Thought Disorder and Family Relations of Schizophrenics: II. A Classification of Forms of Thinking." *Archives of General Psychiatry* 9: 199-206.

_____1965. "Thought Disorder and Family Relations of Schizophrenics: IV. Results and Implications." *Archives of General Psychiatry* 12: 201-212.

Yalom, I. D. 1966. "A Study of Group Therapy Dropouts." *Archives of General Psychiatry* 14: 393-414.

_____1975. *The Theory and Practice of Group Psychotherapy.* New York: Basic Books.

Zinner, J., and Shapiro, R. 1972. "Projective Identification as a Mode of Perception and Behavior in Families of Adolescents." *International Journal of Psychoanalysis* 53: 523-530.

Index